Schaumburg Township District Library
130 South Roselle Road
Schaumburg, Illinois 60193

Schaumburg Township
District Library
schaumburglibrary.org
Renewals: (847) 923-3158

FIRST OF
THE FEW

5 JUNE - 9 JULY 1940

BRIAN CULL

FONTHILL

Fonthill Media Limited
Fonthill Media LLC
www.fonthillmedia.com
office@fonthillmedia.com

Published in 2013

British Library Cataloguing in Publication Data:
A catalogue record for this book is available from the British Library

ISBN 978-1-78155-116-5

Typeset in 10pt on 13pt Sabon LT
Printed and bound in England

Connect with us
 facebook.com/fonthillmedia   twitter.com/fonthillmedia

CONTENTS

The Shape of Things to Come

As soon as we beat England we shall make an end of you Englishmen once and for all. Able-bodied men and women between the ages of 16 and 45 will be exported as slaves to the Continent. The old and weak will be exterminated. All men remaining in Britain as slaves will be sterilised; a million or two of the young women of the Nordic type will be segregated in a number of stud farms where, with the assistance of picked German sires, during a period of 10 or 12 years, they will produce annually a series of Nordic infants to be brought up in every way as Germans. These infants will form the future population of Britain. They will be partially educated in Germany and only those who fully satisfy the Nazi's requirements will be allowed to return to Britain and take up permanent residence. The rest will be sterilised and sent to join slave gangs in Germany. Thus, in a generation or two, the British will disappear.

Richard Walther Darré, Nazi Reichsminister and Director of the Race and Settlement Office, Berlin, 1940

AUTHOR'S NOTE

This volume covers the story of the RAF fighting in France in June 1940; the author's earlier publication, *Twelve Days in May*, covered the period 10-21 May. This account excludes the epic story of the fighting over Dunkirk during the evacuation, 27 May-4 June, which has been adequately covered elsewhere, but otherwise continues the story of RAF and Luftwaffe operations up to the eve of the 'official' start of Battle of Britain, 10 July.

First of the Few introduces the names of many of the surviving pilots from both sides who were to feature in the forthcoming Battle of Britain. Young men who gained their spurs in French skies or over the Channel.

Volume II and subsequent volumes will continue the epic story that changed the course of world history.

PREAMBLE

France, at the beginning of June 1940, was tottering towards defeat. The German military machine had proved unstoppable and had steamrollered its way across Western Europe. Belgium, Luxembourg, Holland, and soon France would join Norway and Denmark as occupied countries. Poland and Czechoslovakia had earlier fallen to the Germans. The Soviet Union had signed a pact with Germany. Italy was about to throw its weight behind Hitler and declared war on Britain and France on 10 June. Across the sea, the United States remained neutral and seemingly unconcerned. There were sympathetic voices but Britain did not want sympathy, she wanted help, practical help. At this stage of the war words were meaningless. Hitler was at the door. Britain was on her own.[1]

In a last desperate attempt to save France from capitulating and to keep her army fighting, Churchill and de Gaulle proposed that Britain and France become one united nation. In a telephone call from London on June 16 to the French Premier, Paul Reynaud, the message stated:

> The two Governments of the United Kingdom and the French Republic make the declaration of indissoluble union and unyielding resolution in their common defence of justice and freedom against subjection to a system which reduces mankind to a life of robots and slaves. The two Governments declare that France and Great Britain shall no longer be two nations but one Franco-British Union. Every citizen of France will enjoy immediately citizenship of Great Britain; every British subject will become a citizen of France. All the armed forces of Great Britain and France will be placed under the direction of a single War Cabinet.

The full text of the official report for proposed Declaration of Union was published in the press on 18 June:

> At this most fateful moment in the history of the modern world the Governments of the United Kingdom and the French Republic make this declaration of indissoluble union and unyielding resolution in their common defence of justice and freedom, against subjection to a system which reduces mankind to a life of robots and slaves. The two Governments declare that France and Great Britain shall no longer be two nations but one Franco-British Union. The constitution of the Union will provide for joint organs of defence, foreign, financial, and economic policies. Every citizen of France will enjoy immediately citizenship of Great Britain, every British subject will become a citizen of France.
>
> Both countries will share responsibility for the repair of the devastation of war, wherever it occurs in their territories, and the resources of both shall be equally, and as one, applied to that purpose. During the war there shall be a single war Cabinet, and all the forces of Britain and France, whether on land, sea, or in the air, will be placed under its direction. It will govern from wherever it best can. The two Parliaments will be formally associated. The nations of the British Empire are already forming new armies. France will keep her available forces in the field, on the sea, and in the air.
>
> The Union appeals to the United States to fortify the economic resources of the Allies and to bring her powerful material aid to the common cause. The Union will concentrate its whole energy against the power of the enemy no matter where the battle may be. And thus we shall conquer.

The proposal caused uproar, as might well have been expected, in the French Cabinet. Churchill wrote: "Rarely has so generous a proposal encountered such a hostile reception."

Without Cabinet support, French Prime Minister Reynaud resigned and a new government was formed under Marshal Pétain, who immediately negotiated an armistice with Germany. Two days later Churchill told the free world:

> The events which have happened in France in the last fortnight have not come to me with any sense of surprise. Indeed, I indicated a fortnight ago as clearly as I could to the House that the worst possibilities were open, and I made it perfectly clear then that whatever happened in France would make no difference to the resolve of Britain and the British Empire to fight on – if necessary for years, if necessary alone [...]
>
> What General Weygand called the 'Battle of France' is over. I expect that the 'Battle of Britain' is about to begin. Upon this battle depends the survival of the Christian civilisation. Upon it depends our own British way of life and the long-continued history of our institutions and our Empire.

The whole fury and might of the enemy must very soon be turned on us. Hitler knows that he will have to break us on this island or lose the war. If we can stand up to him all Europe may be free and the life of the whole world may move forward into broad and sunlit uplands. If we fail, then the whole world, including the United States, and all that we have known and cared for, will sink into the abyss of a new dark age made more sinister and perhaps more prolonged by the light of a perverted science.

Let us, therefore, do our duty and so bear ourselves that if the British Commonwealth and Empire lasts a thousand years men will still say, 'This was their finest hour.'

France capitulated on 22 June.

CHAPTER I

Dying Embers – The RAF in France, June 1940

Wars are not won by evacuations.

Prime Minister Winston Churchill

By early June the Dunkirk evacuation had succeeded in turning what was deemed to be massive defeat into a Pyrrhic victory of sorts, with some half-million mainly British soldiers safely back in England. During the nine-day evacuation, known as Operation *Dynamo*, the RAF lost 177 aircraft, including 106 fighters. In addition, 235 vessels of the 900 naval and civilian craft sent to help were lost. At least 5,000 soldiers went down with these vessels. But 338,226 British and French soldiers were rescued from Dunkirk.

With the end of the fighting in Northern France and the Low Countries, the victorious Germans immediately turned their attention to the southern front, where the situation was very much as it had been at the start of the war. The Maginot Line still dominated the area and, at the Somme and along the Aisne, some sixty French and one British (the 51st Highland) division were engaged in establishing an in-depth defensive system. The Armée de l'Air could muster some 225 fighters and 125 bombers, while the RAF maintained a small presence south of Paris in the shape of three Hurricane squadrons (67 Wing) and three more equipped with Battle light bombers (76 Wing), tasked with providing cover for British and French forces south of the Somme. A small detachment of PR Spitfires[1] from the Photographic Development Unit at Heston, operating as 212 Squadron, was currently based at Meaux under the command of Flt Lt Louis 'Tug' Wilson. It was to this unit that former Canadian test pilot Flt Lt John Kent AFC found himself attached:

On arriving at Meaux I was welcomed by [Flt Lt] Bob Niven who declared that I was just the chap they wanted and I had better stay. I pointed out that I had no kit of any kind and I would have to go back and get some, which I did, and returned to France the next day. The sorties flown during the incredible period of confusion immediately prior to the French collapse were, for the most part, of relatively short range and were concerned more with tactical reconnaissance than strategic. I made very few flights while I was at Meaux and these were only as far as Givet and Namur, the object of the sorties was to find a large tank army that was rumoured to be somewhere in the area – it was. In fact, the country was so thickly wooded that high level photography was of little value.[2]

The three AASF Hurricane squadrons, 1 (Sqn Ldr D. A. Pemberton) based at Rouen-Boos, 73 (Sqn Ldr J. W. C. More) at Gaye and 501 (Sqn Ldr M. V. Clube) at Anglure, could muster barely twenty-five operational aircraft between them. As for the Battles, 12 Squadron plus detachments from 88 and 103 were based at Échemines. With the fighting over Dunkirk during the past week dominating events, the Hurricane squadrons had experienced a welcomed respite and had received a number of replacement pilots, albeit very green, to fill the gaps of those lost in recent fighting and those who had returned home a rest; thus it was mainly a new crop of inexperienced RAF fighter pilots who were to face the Luftwaffe's aces. More Hurricanes had been also been delivered, bringing the three units up to strength.

The COs of 73 and 501 Squadrons flew to Le Mans to check out the area in readiness for a rumoured withdrawal. Sqn Ldr More's conclusion was that Le Mans would make an excellent target for the Luftwaffe. Nonetheless, 501 Squadron moved to Le Mans the following day.

* * * * *

On the first day of June, a renewed German attack on communications began. In addition to targets at Rouen, attacks on railways were made over a wide area, ranging from Serqueux, Creil, Vitry-le-François, and Nogent-sur-Seine down to the mouth of the Seine. The Rhône Valley attacks were delivered by aircraft which crossed the frontier at Colmar and Mulhouse. Apart from the attack on the harbour at Marseilles most of the bombs were apparently aimed at railway lines and important crossroads. The Lyon-Marseille line was cut at Givors and Livron, and the Lyon-Geneva line at Ambérieu and La Valbonne by He111s and Ju88s.

During a late evening patrol, 73 Squadron's A Flight led, by Plt Off Don Scott, encountered Bf109s from II/JG53 while on a sortie to reconnoitre the Sedan area – Sgt Wilf Millner (TP-K) was promptly shot down over La Malmaison, east of Laon, possibly the victim of Ltn Hans Fleitz of 8 Staffel. His aircraft crashed and burned out at Plesnoy. Plt Off Ian Potts, flying L1565/TP-E, was also shot down east of Laon, probably by Ltn Heinz Kunert also of 8 Staffel. He survived and was taken prisoner. Scott claimed a Bf109 possibly damaged but his own aircraft (TP-D) sustained damage from cannon fire, his probable assailant being Ltn Jakob Stoll of 9 Staffel. Plt Off Bob Rutter also claimed a Messerschmitt damaged. Don Scott recalled:

> I led five kites to Sedan to see if the airfield there was occupied, and we saw nothing on the ground but I heard a shout on the R/T and saw my No. 5 [Sgt Millner] being attacked by a 109. I turned hard on him, and I think I got some strikes, but the other Hurricane was not turning hard enough and I became a sitting duck for another 109. As I broke away and pulled up to cloud base at about 5,000 feet one cannon shell hit the ammunition bay in my port wing and blew a large hole in it. Another hit the starboard wingtip taking most of it off, while a third took off part of the starboard aileron leaving it jammed in the up position. This resulted in the aircraft flying in circles, but as the engine was running well I was reluctant to bale out, and circled up through cloud from 5,000 to around 14,000 feet to take stock of the situation.
>
> The artificial horizon had toppled, and with the very restricted aileron movement I was very lucky to get away with it. I found that I could vary the radius of the turn quite a bit, and was able to proceed erratically in a south-west direction to be sure of being over friendly territory if it came to baling out. When I was confident that I had gone far enough I had one last attempt, standing up in the cockpit to get maximum leverage on the stick and finally forced it in the middle. This left me able to fly straight and to manage very gentle turns. I was unsure of my position but it was now getting dark and I was thankful to find a deserted field – well covered with cows.
>
> Next morning, with the help of some French AA gunners, I cleaned up the wing with a file to get full travel on the ailerons. We transferred all my remaining fuel into the gravity tank for take-off and half-filled the wing tanks with French lorry petrol. I took off and got to Orly, the Paris civil aerodrome, where the French quickly patched up the kite well enough for me to return to Gaye.[3]

Next day, 2 June, Luftwaffe activity in the Rhône Valley continued and the railway south of Lyon suffered. A further attack was launched against Marseille docks and on the oil installations. Aerodromes were among other targets attacked in eastern France. A total of seventeen Battles struck at German communications and airfields at Givet, Mézières and Trier. All returned without loss.

Le Havre was again attacked by German bombers on 3 June, petrol tanks and the iron works suffering, but the major Luftwaffe operation of the day was against targets in and around Paris (Operation *Paula*). Such an attack had been anticipated with an ad hoc defence system instituted by the RAF's AASF comprised just a single Battle of 76 Wing on standing patrol between Rheims and Chalon, flying at 2,000-3,000 feet to warn of approaching enemy aircraft. Any such sighting was to be radioed to RAF Wireless Intelligence cars stationed at Rheims, St Hilaire and Somme-Suippe, whereupon 73 Squadron at Échemines was to bring one flight of Hurricanes to readiness, with a second flight available within thirty minutes. Having maintained this exercise for the first two days of the month, by the third day the telephone communication system had broken down and 73 Squadron, down to six Hurricanes, was in any case unable to provide the fighters. The few Hurricanes available were tasked with providing escorts for French reconnaissance patrols along the Aisne.

Thus, between 13:07 and 13:10, when the French Reporting Centre reported that forces variously estimated at fifty to one hundred bombers were flying westwards from Rethel, nothing could be scrambled to engage them. 1 and 501 Squadrons were also uncontactable, the latter having moved to Rouen-Boos. The odd interception was however made by Hurricanes of 73 and 501 Squadrons, which were at the time escorting French machines between Neufchâtel and Rethel. Pilots reported meeting a large number of Bf109s acting as cover for the bombing force.

The raiding force, including escorting fighters, numbered at least 1,000 aircraft. There were only about 250 French fighters available to meet the German attacks, plus a handful of Hurricanes. The bombers attacked a wide selection of targets, including a dozen or so aerodromes outside Paris, some aircraft factories, the French Air Ministry, and many railways. The Paris-Strasbourg line was cut at Chelles, and the Paris-Soissons, Paris-Dieppe and Paris-Rouen lines were all damaged. Of the seven or so bombers known to have been brought down, the majority fell to AA fire. Casualties amounted to some 250 civilians and military personnel killed, with 650 injured. Oblt Hans von Hahn of 8./JG53 wrote:

> Escort mission to Paris. A lousy outfit of Do17s, which flew like fools. Proper protection was out of the question, for the bombers had spread out all over the sky. My Staffel and I stayed with the larger group. When we reached Meaux the French came at us from all sides with Moranes, Curtisses, Blochs and Hurricanes. We were just able to warn the Do17s before the dance began. Ltn Fleitz had a scrap with a bunch of Moranes, one of which he shot down in flames. Then Ltn [Ernst] Panten and I became involved with six Hurricanes. Ltn Panten had one in front of him, but he turned away and I snapped up the bird. After a burst, during which I yelled: "That's how it's done!" He blew up. Panten then chased another to a French forward airfield. He cracked up on the edge of the landing field and smouldered.

Of the action 501 Squadron reported:

> 08:45 six Hurricanes of A Flight on patrol from Rouen-Boos (codenamed *Thelma*) met 18 Bf109s near Hallencourt, south-west of Abbeville. P/O [John] Sylvester shot down, baled out and tore muscles in his back. P/O Hairs' aircraft (P2867) also hit and force-landed. Two other Hurricanes were hit and rendered u/s.

Plt Off Bob Dafforn added:

> Met 18 Me109s, which dived on six of us out of the sun. Had one on my tail, but evaded him by half-rolling and diving out. No hits.

Plt Off Peter Hairs recalled:

> At the time the squadron was climbing in line-astern when there was a sudden explosion somewhere beneath my seat. As I was not tail-end Charlie I assumed must have been hit by some keen French AA gunner and it was not until later that I was told that a Bf109 had swooped down and fired at me from below. I belly-landed the Hurricane in a field at St Léger-aux-Bois, near Soissons, and a French soldier approached brandishing a rifle. Despite my limited knowledge of the language he obviously realised that I was on his side and did not shoot. Two British soldiers from the 9th Lancers then appeared, crashing through a hedge in their jeep and took me to their unit. After lunch I was driven to the local railway station where I took the train to Paris. Arriving the following day, I discovered the squadron had moved to Le Mans, where I eventually caught up with them.

In addition to the claims of von Hahn and Panten, 9./JG53 also claimed three Hurricanes north of Creil at this time, one each by Ltn Jakob Stoll, Ltn Horst von Weegmann and Uffz Kurt Sauer. However, they may have been French fighters, mistakenly identified.

73 Squadron (Échemines) reported combat near Epernay shortly after 14:00. Plt Off Hugh 'Chubby' Eliot claimed a Bf109, possibly an aircraft of II/JG53 shot down in south-west of Rheims, its pilot believed unhurt. Flt Lt Charles Nicholls and Sgt Alf Scott claimed a Bf110 probable shared, which was possibly an aircraft of 9./ZG26 in which Uffz Ewald Ahrens/Gfr Alfred Fiedler crashed and overturned on landing at Ste-Marie-Chevigny due to combat damage; both were killed, although the Messerschmitt may also have been attacked by two Hawks of GCI/5. 73 Squadron lost Plt Off Ian Hawken, who was shot down and killed in TP-Z, his aircraft crashing into farm buildings near Dormans at 14:20, possibly the victim of 1./JG76.

4 June saw German reconnaissance aircraft probe the French air defences south of Paris, only to find them lamentably weak. Mines were laid outside Cherbourg but the port was not closed. Up until now the civil airline service between London and Paris had been viable, but now all had changed:

> The service to Paris, of vital importance at this time, was kept running as possible. Capt G. R. Buxton piloted the Ensign *Ettrick* (G-ADSX) to Le Bourget. He and his crew were lunching in the restaurant when they were bombed "good and hard". Some 300 bombs were dropped on the airport and

its neighbourhood, 200 people being killed in the little village of Le Blanc-Mesnil over the way, and an unknown number on the airfield itself, on which most of the buildings were partially destroyed. The passengers, who had been waiting by the luggage which was about to be loaded into *Ettrick*, were hurried into a shelter, the last man down, a French porter, being killed as he ran.

Capt Buxton had gone into the cellar of the restaurant, but found it 'a bit fierce' down there, as the building received a direct hit; a water main burst and smoke was being sucked down from the fires above. He came up, walked into a falling bomb and was wounded in the thigh. The Ensign was considerably damaged, although the captain at once climbed into her, tried the controls and thought he could take off; the French authorities, however, would not permit, as the airfield was plastered with time bombs. Eventually *Ettrick* had to be abandoned where she stood.[4]

It was clear that Le Bourget could no longer be used. The terminus was thus shifted farther and farther south, first to Guyancourt, and then to Tours.

Plt Off John Gibson of 501 Squadron had starting trouble with his Hurricane when preparing to take off on a patrol, so followed his section on his own. He encountered two He111s travelling south-west from Rouen at 11,000 feet. He attacked both and believed he had inflicted damage before they entered cloud and escaped.

* * * * *

Prime Minister Churchill gave one his legendary speeches to the House of Commons on 4 June, reporting on the Dunkirk evacuation and ending with his historic declaration (which was appropriate on the eve of the German invasion of France):

Even though large tracts of Europe and many old and famous States have fallen or may fall into the grip of the Gestapo and all the odious apparatus of Nazi rule, we shall not flag or fail. We shall go on to the end, we shall fight in France, we shall fight on the seas and oceans, we shall fight with growing confidence and growing strength in the air, we shall defend our island whatever the cost may be, we shall fight on the beaches and in the streets, we shall fight in the hills; we shall never surrender.

CHAPTER II

RAF HURRICANES IN THE BATTLE OF FRANCE, 5–22 JUNE

Operation Fall Rot (Case Red) – The Second German Offensive

There was no swagger about those boys in wrinkled and stained uniforms. The movies do that sort of thing much more dramatically than it is in real life.
American broadcaster Ed Murrow on meeting aircrew back from France.

The German advance, when it came on 5 June, covered a broad front but the main push occurred (1) south-west of St-Valéry and Abbeville; (2) south from Amiens; (3) south-west from Péronne; (4) south-west from Lafare-Chauny; and (5) south-west from Laon. The capture of Paris was the main priority. Of this day's actions the official British report stated:

On this first day of the new German offensive our air forces could give but little help to the Allied troops engaged. The 51st Division sent to South Component headquarters, now at Boos, to ask for protection against the enemy's bombers, but the Advanced Air Striking Force's three squadrons of fighters, though they were to be made up to strength, were on this day reduced to a total of eighteen serviceable aircraft. They had lost four in battle that morning. Information suggested that the enemy planned a big air attack on targets in and near Rouen itself, which was not only important industrially and as a focal point in road and rail communications, but was also a centre of military and air activity for both the French and the British.

No. 1 Squadron was therefore on early patrol and, together with French fighters, engaged a very large formation of German bombers strongly protected by Messerschmitts. In the bitter fight which ensued some of the enemy were shot down or driven off, but enough got through to bomb Boos airfield and a military camp. And again in the evening, when No. 501 Squadron intercepted a second formation sent to renew the attack, enough got through to bomb the camp and airfield, the main bridge, power station, railway, and the factories of Sotteville. The bald account of these two episodes explains the fact that, while our small fighter forces were exhausting themselves in unequal combat, troops on the ground who suffered the enemy's attacks still complained of inadequate protection.

The close-support bombing undertaken that day by the Advanced Air Striking Force was done in a more easterly sector of the French battlefront, while twenty-four Blenheims of Bomber Command attacked enemy transport immediately behind the new battlefront, with two squadrons of Fighter Command to give cover. By night the enemy concentrations behind the front, his communications in France, and oil targets and marshalling yards in German were attacked by 103 bombers, of whom three failed to return.[1]

* * * * *

Hurricanes of 1 Squadron, joined by Bloch 152s of GCII/10, were sent off at dawn. They engaged a large formation of He111s of I/KG27 from Vechta escorted by Bf110s of I/ZG1. A Flight led by Flt Lt Hilly Brown was attacked by the Bf110s. Brown reported shooting down straggling 'Do17'; Flg Off Peter Matthews claimed a He111, Plt Off Peter Boot a He111 probable and 'Do17' damaged, while Plt Off Dennis Browne fired at two Heinkels but with no apparent result. Canadian Plt Off John Shepherd was shot down and crashed in flames. One Heinkel was seen to force-land in field. A consolidated report revealed:

> The 11 Hurricanes that remained at *Thelma* [codename for Rouen-Boos] took off at 05:50 to patrol a line west of Rouen at 15,000 feet. At 06:00, before reaching patrol height, large formations of enemy bombers were seen at 12,000 feet. Approximately 60 bombers escorted by an equal number of Me110s, above and behind the sun. B Flight made an echelon attack on two formations of He111s. One of these turned on its back and dropped. A Hurricane [Flg Off Harry Hillcoat] forced-landed with bullet through radiator. His machine had caught fire, but the pilot was not prevented from force landing. Sgt [John] Arbuthnot forced-landed with radiator shot away, after gallantly tacking 25 enemy aircraft. Plt Off [Alan] Lindsell forced-landed near Deauville and returned to *Thelma*.

The remaining three Hurricanes of B Flight, flown by Sgt Darky Clowes, Plt Off Benny Goodman and Flt Sgt George Berry, who each claimed a Heinkel shot down, returned to Rouen-Boos to refuel and re-load.

A Flight separated from B when attack commenced. When about to attack bombers, they were themselves attacked by 30 Me110s. A series of dogfights ensued, which ended in Messerschmitts, for no apparent reason, breaking off the engagement. Our pilots then looked for straggling bombers. Flt Lt [Hilly] Brown attacked a Do17 over Amiens and followed it from 20,000 feet down to 5,000 feet. He then broke off the attack after the Dornier's rear gunner ceased firing and each engine had been fired until white smoke and oil came from them. Plt Off [Dennis] Browne fired at two Heinkels. Result not known, but tracer bullets seen to have hit both aircraft. Flg Off [Peter] Matthews climbed into the sun and attacked a single straggling Heinkel at 19,000 feet. Enemy aircraft dived, and Matthews followed down to 14,000 feet. Plt Off [John] Shepherd reported to have crashed in flames.[2]

In addition to the above claims, Plt Off Pat Hancock reported the probable destruction of another Heinkel before his own aircraft (P3590) was hit by return fire:

Without the use of elevators, unable to make sense of the damaged air-speed indicator and with the throttle jammed in emergency boost, I attempted a landing. I had the choice, after going through several phases of panic, of either smashing into a hangar or hitting a Blenheim. After three passes of the airfield, going much too fast, I hit the Blenheim, cutting it in half. I discovered later that – fortunately – it was unoccupied. I tore it apart and burst my petrol tank in the process. Fuel was everywhere, but there was no fire – otherwise I wouldn't have survived.[3]

A Bloch 152 also force-landed at Rouen-Boos following combat with the Bf110s.

I/KG27 lost five (or seven) He111s plus several damaged during this fateful mission, three of which were credited to GCII/10, with 1 Squadron apparently responsible for shooting down at least three aircraft of 3 Staffel, crewed by:

He111 3./KG27 FTR: Ltn Gert Frank, Fw Joachim Schünemann, Uffz Willi Forster and Uffz Alfons Jenau (all POW, but later released)
He111 3./KG27 FTR: Uffz Kurt Meier and Uffz Fritz Wolff (both killed), Oblt Hans-Georg Bätcher (pilot) and Oblt Siegfried Scholz (both POW, but later released)
He111 3./KG27 damaged: Fw Reinhold Boer (pilot), Fw Hans Hegemann, Uffz Rudolf Hengst, unhurt; Uffz Albert Ullmann slightly wounded; aircraft repairable.

Rudi Hengst, air gunner in Fw Boer's aircraft, later wrote:

Today the target will be Rouen, to attack a large British military camp. 04:46 Airborne – and behind us the sun was rising, which appeared today with red-yellow sunbeams. Above the airfield the single aircraft gathered to group formation to cross the border together. Approximately 50km before the front we met our fighter escort, a group of Me110s. Gradually daylight came up and a light haze prevented here and there ground visibility, but the sun would soon provide clear view. In the meantime we climbed to 4,500 m altitude and in approximately 15 minutes we should reach our target.

As far as one could see, everywhere German planes in the air. The sky seemed full of them. A massive attack was planned. Now and then the enemy anti-aircraft defence fired in the air, but did not cause any noticeable damage. As yet no enemy fighters could be seen. The weather was excellent, almost no clouds, flashing sunshine, and underneath us the French scenery. The River Seine could already be seen in the distance. We came closer to our target. Suddenly I noticed aircraft flying behind us were being attacked by French fighter aircraft – Moranes [*sic*]. In the meantime our navigator Hans lay behind his bomb aiming instrument and the flight mechanic was at his machine-gun in the gondola. Our pilot Reinhold Boer did not speak much, but he handled the aircraft very well. I observed the scenery backwards from the wireless operator's position and looked out for enemy aircraft.

By then the Squadron Leader [Hptm Konrad Aschenbrenner] had reached the target and his bombs spun towards the target. We had almost reached the target, only a slight correction to the right for better view. At the same moment when our bombs fell from the aircraft a French Morane [*sic*] attacked us. I called: "Enemy fighter behind us!" The Morane [probably a Hurricane] was flying exactly behind our tail-end and was firing like hell! None of our guns could get at him. I called to Reinhold, our pilot, to step on his left rudder pedal in order to get the Morane in front of my machine-gun. Reinhold grasped the situation immediately and stepped on his left pedal, moving the tail-end of our Heinkel to the right. I now had the Morane in my sight and hammered a full drum of tracer bullets into the fighter. Everything happened lightning fast: the Morane got into a spin with smoke trailing behind her; she spun towards the ground.

As a result of former jams of the machine-gun due to closed cartridge bag, I now left the spring catch of the cartridge bag open. Consequently, the cartridges were catapulted through the cartridge bag with great force, hitting my knee. In the first moment I thought the fighter had hit me. The fire of the fighter was close enough when it hit our aircraft. During the haste of the air to air fighting, one barely recognises the impacts. Only after I had shot down the French fighter I saw the impacts and bullet holes in the aircraft. I saw bullet holes in the plastic hood of the wireless-operator compartment, and much later I found a scratch on the earphone of my flying cap, resulting from a bullet.

Albert Ullmann was wounded in the eye by shrapnel. Our right-hand engine trailed smoke and had to be switched off. All this happened in the space of a few seconds. After the release of our bombs we had to fly a steep turn to the left in order to provide space for the following aircraft. Thereby we drifted too far away from our formation and since we had only one engine we lost speed and altitude, and could not follow the formation of our Squadron. In this situation we were in great danger, flying alone and away from the formation; we were a welcome target for enemy fighters. One of the Me110 of our escort noticed we were in trouble and dived towards our Heinkel; and stayed with us until he had passed the enemy lines. I waved to the pilot of the Me110 to thank him for his escort and help. He tipped his wings a few times and disappeared.

In the meantime we lost altitude and descended to 2,500 m and were just so with half the power. At 11:00 o'clock we landed at Vechta. All comrades including the Squadron Leader came to the airfield to welcome us back. Our comrades believed we had been one of the shot down aircraft. Unfortunately, seven bombers of the I Group had been shot down. Also several of our aircraft had been damaged. The Squadron Leader personally drove our flight mechanic to the hospital.[4]

Although Fw Hengst believed their assailants had been Moranes, it is probable that his Staffel came under attack by 1 Squadron's Hurricanes, and that his claimed victory was one of the five Hurricanes shot down or forced down in this engagement.

Two Bf110s of I/ZG1 also failed to return, although German records suggest that the 1 Staffel aircraft flown by Fw Fritz Dünsing/Uffz Reinhard Ander collided with that crewed by Uffz Josef Rinke/Uffz Heinrich Meyer of 3 Staffel during combat a few miles north of Rouen; the two aircraft were apparently attacking a Bloch 152 and all were killed except Dünsing, who was unhurt. However, these two aircraft may have been the two aircraft identified as 'Do17s' and attacked by Flt Lt Hilly Brown and Plt Off Peter Boot.

At 07:00, Sqn Ldr Hank More led a flight of six Hurricanes from 73 Squadron on patrol in the Rheim area. A reconnaissance Do17 was sighted and attacked by the CO (TP-O), Flt Lt Ian Scouler (P2869/TP-S), Plt Off Alex McGaw (L1826/TP-V) and Sgt Ching Friend (P2796/TP-U). The aircraft, 4N+KL from 3.(F)/22, was last seen gliding down with both engines stopped. It crash-landed and the crew, pilot Fw Walter Rössler, Ltn Wilhelm Telge and Obgfr Josef Heim, set fire to it before going into captivity. During the encounter, an escorting Bf109 of 7./JG53 (possibly Fw Hans Galubinski) got on the tail of Sqn Ldr More's Hurricane but was driven off by Flg Off Cobber Kain, who was attacked by another (possibly Uffz Hermann Neuhoff) and his own aircraft sustained damage.

At 08:00, Battles of 12 Squadron from Sougé attacked in error French tanks near Tricot. An escorting Morane 406 of GCI/6 then attacked two of the Battles in mistake for German aircraft, though both were able to return to base only slightly damaged and without crew casualties. PR pilot Flt Lt Kent, at Meaux, recalled:

Early in June and shortly after landing from a sortie [in P9331] the sirens sounded and the low hum of approaching aircraft could be heard. It turned out to be the first mass raid of the war and some 250 German aircraft took part. Their targets were various factories on the outskirts of Paris but, just for the hell of it, they dropped a number of visiting cards on us at Meaux both on their way to Paris and on their way back. In the middle of all the attendant hullabaloo I managed to get most of the airmen into shelters, but several were unaccounted for, so I set out to find them in case they had been wounded. By this time there was quite a fight going on overhead and jettisoned bombs, spent bullets and cartridges were exploding and spattering around all over the place. It was sickening to be stuck on the ground and unable to do anything about it.

I found most of the men taking shelter in a slit trench, but there were still two or three more adrift so I set out again. At this point one of our aircraft, returning from a sortie, ran slap into the fight and got shot up, the pilot being wounded in the leg. I was just in time to see the Spitfire [believed to have been P9396] come in and land while bombs were bursting all over the airfield. The pilot [possibly Plt Off Peter Barnes] taxied to the hangar and switched off and at the same time another officer, Tim Craxton, ran out. Seeing that the pilot was wounded, he helped him out of the aeroplane, got him into a car and shot off down the road with bombs dropping on either side of them and succeeded in getting the wounded pilot to hospital.

The casualties were not all on one side, however, and just as the Spitfire was crossing the boundary, a Ju88 shot past it, crossed the airfield and belly-landed in the next field. The pilot was the only one of the crew alive and he was very badly hit, having had his knee and pelvis smashed by bullets from a Morane 406 based on nearby Coullomiers.[5]

The next encounter for the RAF fighters occurred at 18:55, when nine Hurricanes of 501 Squadron and Bloch 152s of GC II/10 reported sighting a dozen He111s (in fact, Ju88s of III/LG1), a similar number of Bf110s (probably from I/ZG1), two miles north-east of Buchy. 67 Wing's Operational Report revealed:

Five enemy machines were shot down and one of our pilots lost, in a combat north-east of Rouen at 18:55. Nine of our pilots sighted an enemy force of 12 He111s, 12 Me110s and about 4 Ju88s flying towards the aerodrome and took off to engage them without having received any prior information. Enemy force was not in formation at outset of combat, and scattered, many individual combats resulting.

F/O [Ryan] Cridland, P/O [Dicky] Hulse and P/O [John] Gibson, operating as a section, engaged the He111s about two miles north-east of Buchy. P/O Gibson saw one engine of 'his' Heinkel catch fire, but was unable to follow it down owing to damage to his radiator and petrol tank; this machine was seen to go down in flames by Sgt Proctor, who however, expressed the opinion that it was a Ju88 [Cridland and Hulse each claimed a Heinkel shot down during this engagement.]

F/Sgt [Jammy] Payne took off 10 minutes after the others owing to starting difficulties, and encountered low bombing and ground strafing on the N30 road. Flying in valleys below hills F/Sgt Payne engaged a Me110, experiencing shell bursts to his right. Finding two further Messerschmitts attacking him, F/Sgt Payne executed a vertical right-hand turn, causing them to disappear by [off] his tail. He then continued the attack on his first objective, firing at it until it disappeared into the wood at Maronime, three miles north-west of Rouen. The Messerschmitt was seen to go in to the ground by Sgt [John] Proctor when on his way home.

P/O [Duncan] Hewitt engaged seven Me110s was of Rouen, flying at 500 feet, the enemy being 1,500 feet above him. He fired at one Messerschmitt and definitely saw hits. The Messerschmitt glided off from the other six. P/O Hewitt considered that the Messerschmitt was at least seriously damaged, if not shot down. Sgt Proctor saw a Me110 being chased by P/O Hewitt, who in turn had two of Me110s on his tail. Sgt Proctor engaged one of these, firing a burst at it, but at the same time making sure to keep P/O Hewitt out of his sights. Sgt Proctor closed and fired further shots. He then saw the starboard engine of the Messerschmitt emit grey vapour. The Messerschmitt stood on its tail and dived to the ground from a height of 4,000 feet over Vascoeuil, east of Rouen.

P/O [Anthony] Claydon , pursued by enemy machines, was seen to crash near Dieppe. Pilot was flung a considerable distance away from the machine [P3450].

It seems that two Ju88s fell in this action, both of which were also claimed by or shared with the French pilots. Both German crews were captured, four of whom suffered wounds.

During the day Plt Offs Neville Langham-Hobart and Peter Carter, in 73 Squadron's Magister P6351, became lost while flying from Échemines to Ruaudin and force-landed in a field of stubble, only to find the ground to be boggy. The aircraft became stuck and the two pilots were obliged to continue to Ruaudin by army lorry.

Two more Battles of 12 Squadron were lost, one temporarily, during a night attack on convoys near Hirson and in woods north of St-Michel. 103 Squadron also lost an aircraft that was damaged by AA fire; the pilot belly-landed the Battle at Château-Thierry.

By 6 June, 73 Squadron was down to six serviceable Hurricanes and it fell upon 501 Squadron to provide cover for retreating British troops. At 05:20, five Hurricanes encountered Do17s of 7./KG76 in the Forges-les-Eaux area, south of Abbeville, Plt Off Ken Lee shooting down the Dornier crewed by Ltn Felix Taucar (pilot), Uffz Helmut Mitschke (killed), Uffz Ludwig Menges (wounded) and Uffz Helmut Wagner; the survivors were taken prisoner. 67 Wing's War Diary revealed:

P/O Lee saw 'his' Dornier going down but was unable to follow it as his machine was hit by French anti-aircraft fire, causing a hole in the petrol tank and blowing off his left-hand break-off panel. He definitely reported seeing the Dornier's engine stop, however, and Sgt Proctor afterwards reported seeing the machine in flames in the Forêt-du-Hallet near Neufchâtel.

Meanwhile:

Sgt Proctor launched a three-quarter attack on 'his' Dornier, which turned at 180° and went west. Sgt Proctor saw his ammunition hitting the Dornier and was himself the target of bursts from the Dornier's rear gunner, which, however, soon ceased. Sgt Proctor, after exhausting his ammunition, saw the Dornier dive into the ground within three or four miles of Forges-les-Eaux.

Despite Proctor's account of seeing his victim crash, apparently the badly damaged aircraft managed to reach its base at Bonn-Hangelar, where it crash-landed and was written off. Uffz Johann Dandorfer had been seriously wounded during the combat and two other crew members (Uffz Richard Carl and the pilot Fw Otto Ulbrich) were also wounded.

To help ease the aircraft shortage, 56 and 151 Squadrons from North Weald were ordered to carry out afternoon and evening patrols, refuelling at Manston and then operating from Rouen-Boos before returning to Manston by nightfall (see Chapter III). At the same time, 17 and 242 Squadrons were ordered to prepare for imminent departure to France, to reinforce the AASF units. They were destined for Le Mans and Châteaudun respectively.

The German advance towards the Seine continued relentlessly, forcing the RAF to evacuate Rouen-Boos and Étrépagny for Dreux and Beaumont-le-Roger. The Hurricanes of 73 Squadron were ordered to transfer to Le Mans, while Flt Lt Ian Scoular and Flg Off Kain were advised of their imminent posting to the UK for a rest, but next day, 7 June, Cobber Kain was killed when carrying out low-level aerobatics over Échemines in L1826. On this date, the PR Spitfire detachment from 212 Squadron lost one of its precious aircraft operating from Meaux airfield near Paris, when P9331 took off from on sortie around Liege but a glycol leak forced it to land at Champagne airfield near Rheims. Flt Lt Tug Wilson asked the French to destroy it to avoid its capture by the Germans, but they failed to do so.

Eighteen Blenheims from 2 Group carried out a raid early in the afternoon against German armour and convoys, with little success but also with only minor casualties. Escort was provided by two-dozen Hurricanes but German fighters were not encountered, these being busy combating the French elsewhere. But it was a different story later in the afternoon when nine Battles of 12 Squadron, joined by more from 150 and 103 Squadrons, attempted to attack vehicles in the Poix area, these being engaged by Bf109s of 5./JG3. Two Battles were lost, while two others were damaged.

Battles were claimed by Fw Josef Heinzeller, Uffz Konrad Nelleskamp and Uffz Hermann Freitag, while Oblt Herbert Kijewski claimed his victim as a Spitfire. Escort was provided by Hurricanes of 1 Squadron were joined by those of 43 and 601 Squadrons but since the squadrons were using different R/T frequencies, a lack of co-ordination resulted. Two Messerschmitts were claimed in return by Battle gunners, though no 5 Staffel machine was lost. It seems that 1 Squadron failed to make contact with enemy fighters, although both 43 and 601 Squadrons were heavily engaged with Bf109s of 3./JG3 and 4./JG26 (see Chapter III).

Next day, 8 June, 242 Squadron (Sqn Ldr F. M. Gobiel) with attached pilots from 615 Squadron arrived at Le Mans, together with 17 Squadron (Sqn Ldr R. I. G. MacDougall), to join forces with newly arrived 73 Squadron. However, 242 transferred to Châteaudun the same day. Plt Off Harold 'Birdy' Bird-Wilson of 17 Squadron recalled:

> We landed in the centre of the motor racecourse. We arrived with a new CO, new flight commander [Flt Lt Alf Bayne] and a few new pilots. Some were so green that on take-off from Le Mans, I recall two of the pilots over-shooting the squadron and virtually leading them off as we got airborne! They were so raw on the Hurricane that they just didn't have the experience to throttle back and maintain their formation. We didn't have time to teach these chaps at that particular period so they had to quickly learn the hard way.

One of the new arrivals was Flg Off Count Manfred Czernin[6], of whom Bird-Wilson commented:

> His appearance was a welcome change from the normal run-of-the-mill person. Being slightly older than the majority of us, he had a well-matured outlook on life and was a person who knew his way around and was not afraid to express himself. He had the confidence and self-assurance which we were all looking for. I thought him to be rather debonair and will always remember him using a *Dunhill* cigarette holder for his incessant smoking habits. This habit could have given one the impression of slight nervousness, but on the other hand, at that time it seemed to be the 'Mayfair air' that was impressive.

17 Squadron remained at Le Mans for three days without sighting any enemy aircraft. Of this period at Le Mans, one of 73 Squadron's airmen, Les Armstrong, recalled:

> On the first night after our arrival at Le Mans one of our Hurricanes was expected back from detachment at Échemines. It was very dark when we heard the sound of an approaching aircraft and we were told to switch on vehicle headlights to provide some form of guidance. I was told, also, to signal

to the kite with an Aldis lamp. Nobody could tell me what to signal, so I just pointed the lamp skywards and sent off a few dots and dashes. The aircraft moved off and shortly after bombs were dropped on a railhead close by, so we concluded that it wasn't one of ours after all.

Meanwhile, at about 13:45, seven Hurricanes of 501 Squadron from Dreux provided escort to a dozen Battles of 103 Squadron, operating in the Abbeville area, where they were engaged by Bf109s of I/JG26, which were protecting a swarm of Ju87s bombing a village. Two Hurricanes were promptly shot down by the Messerschmitts with the loss of Flg Off Dicky Hulse (P3542) and Sgt A. A. Lewis (P3347/SD-N), Hulse's aircraft crashing inverted into the woods at Sentelle, south of Poix-de-Picardie. Lewis survived.[7] In return, Flt Lt Cam Malfroy, a New Zealander, claimed two Bf109s and two probables, while fellow New Zealander Plt Off John Gibson claimed another, and Sgt Don McKay a probable. Two Messerschmitts were, in fact, lost. Ltn Walter Reimer of 2 Staffel and Fw Alfred Burkhardt of 3 Staffel were shot down, the former being killed and the latter wounded, taken prisoner, but these may have been victims of GCII/5, or shared with GCII/5. Two Battles were claimed by Ltn Ulenberg and Staffelkapitän Oblt Seifert of 3 Staffel, while Ulenberg and Fw Wilhelm Müller (2) claimed three 'Spitfires', mistaken for Hurricanes.

During mid-afternoon, at about 15:15, a total of 11 Battles of 12 Squadron struck at German columns between Poix and Aumale, but their promised escort of Hurricanes from 1 Squadron failed to materialise due to refuelling problems at Beaumont-le-Roger. Bf109s of Stab I/LG2 engaged the Battles and Hptm Hannes Trübenbach shot down one, with the loss of its crew.

Plt Off Stan Turner, one of the newly arrived Canadians of 242 Squadron recalled:

> One evening (apparently 8 June), just before dusk, my wingman and I went after a Dornier bomber. It was too far ahead to catch, but by the time we turned back, we didn't have enough fuel to reach our base at Châteaudun. We landed in a wheat field and, as we climbed out in the dim light, a bunch of French farm workers sprang out of the hedgerows and came at us, yelling and brandishing scythes and sticks. I was touch-and-go to convince them we were on their side.

On 9 June, Hurricanes of 1 Squadron were in action early in the morning, as recorded in 67 Wing's Daily Operational Summary:

> Eleven aircraft (6 of B Flight, 5 of A Flight) led by Flt Lt [Fritz] Warcup took off at 04:15 for *Maudie* (Dreux). After refuelling, the 11 aircraft took off to patrol between Vernon and Point de l'Arche at 22,000 feet. Plt Off [Harry] Mann sighted what he thought to be a formation of about 27 enemy aircraft

(in three bunches of nine) 10,000 feet below, travelling north towards Rouen up the Seine. He tried to draw the attention of Red Leader of A Flight by waggling the wings, owing to faulty R/T. This signal was acknowledged but leader failed to see enemy aircraft due to Blue Leader being in front. Plt Off Mann dived towards enemy formation for recognition purposes at first, and recognising them to be enemy bombers he climbed towards the sun and then dived to attack a straggler. As attack commenced, the enemy aircraft turned and Mann carried out a slight deflection shot with no immediate apparent result.

After breaking away, the port engine of the enemy aircraft was observed to be emitting black smoke. As Mann turned to prepare for a second attack, he saw 9 or 10 Me110s approaching in a wide circle on his port beam with a view to attacking his tail. Mann immediately turned towards them and at the same time one Me110 came into his sights and he gave him a burst, with no result. After seeing four or five Messerschmitts on his tail, he broke away and returned, landing at Chartres due to shortage of petrol, later rejoining his Squadron at *Robson* (Beaumont-le-Roger). No hits were sustained on our aircraft.

During the morning, 242 Squadron flew from Châteaudun to Marigny and then to Haver from where, in late afternoon, seven Hurricanes carried out a patrol over Rheims, tasked to protect French army units from dive-bombing attacks. When flying at 12,000 feet they were attacked by an estimated fifteen Bf109s from above and out of the sun, Ltn Gehlhaar of 4./JG52 shooting down Plt Off Don MacQueen (P2767). Plt Off Stan Turner called for MacQueen to bale out but the Hurricane crashed near Courtisols at 16:35 with him still on board. Turner followed the Messerschmitt responsible and claimed it shot down; a few minutes later he claimed a second. Possibly another pilot claimed a probable. One of Turner's victims may have been Obfw Willi Maden, also of 4 Staffel, who was killed after reportedly flying into a high-tension cable. 242 returned to Châteaudun that evening.

Sgt Ginger Lacey of 501 Squadron carried out an emergency landing in a swampy area near Sougé following an inconclusive engagement with five Bf109s over Le Havre. He fired four or five times at two different aircraft, but saw only a few strikes on the tail of one and on the wingtip of the other. Within three minutes Lacey found himself alone. As he had not been leading the formation, he had no maps with him. Unsure of his position, the decision was taken from him when his engine faltered and then cut, apparently having been damaged in the skirmish. Urgently scouring the landscape for a suitable place to carry out a force-landing, he soon espied "a huge, flat plain, big enough to land the *Queen Mary* on, if you could have got her airborne", he later remarked. He let the Hurricane sink gracefully to the ground. (See Appendix I)

A second Hurricane was lost when Plt Off David Leary of 17 Squadron force-landed during a patrol over Rouen:

North of Alençon bullets entered my petrol tank although I could see no enemy aircraft. I lost the rest of the squadron. Running short of petrol I tried to land in a field but was machine-gunned from the ground, being hit in starboard mainplane, so climbed again and landed north of Breteuil.

I obtained army transport at Verneuil and was taken in charge as a parachutist, but proved my identity and reported my safety by phone to Le Mans. I was given a meal and a bed at Verneuil hospital. I then proceeded by transport and train and reported to 17 Squadron at Le Mans at 12:30

Also on the move was Flt Lt Kent of 212 Squadron, still at Meaux:

The Germans were advancing more and more rapidly and it was not long before we were ordered to clear out and go south to the airfield at Bricy near Orleans. Two of us remained behind after the main party had gone to finish clearing up and then, on the 9th June, we departed in the sole remaining aircraft – two Tiger Moths! I was seated in mine warming up the engine in the approved manner when the airman at the wing tip rocked the machine, I looked at him and he pointed up. I followed his gesture and there was a formation of German aircraft just approaching the airfield at about 8,000 feet; as I looked I caught the glisten of bombs on their way down. The chocks had by now been pulled away so I opened the throttle wide and took off straight ahead. As I left the ground and started an immediate turn the first bombs were bursting on the edge of the aerodrome – I was quite petrified and kept the little Tiger at tree-top height and headed south closely followed by the second Tiger. For some reason the Germans completely ignored us, but I was expecting one or two of the escort fighters to swoop down on us at any moment. It was a most unpleasant experience and we were very glad to arrive safely at Bricy a little over an hour later.[8]

By now French aerial resistance had virtually ceased, some surviving aircraft withdrawing to French North Africa, although some units remained to assist the RAF. Battles carried out two raids on 10 June, concentrated on German crossings over the Seine, apparently without fighter escort. Although German fighters were occupied elsewhere, two Battles of 103 Squadron were mistakenly shot down by French pilots of GC1/145 flying Caudron 714s. One crew was killed, but the second aircraft carried out a crash-landing and the crew escaped injury.

Hurricanes of 242 and 501 Squadrons carried out an offensive patrol over Le Havre (as noted in Plt Off Willie McKnight's logbook). A formation of Heinkels was espied and pursuit followed, but escorting Bf109s of I/JG76 were encountered by the latter unit. In a swirling dogfight Plt Off John Gibson (SD-B) shot down one, which belly-landed at Yvrech, but was then shot down by another. He baled out unhurt. A second Messerschmitt returned to its base with combat damage. Plt Off Ken Lee was shot down by another. He baled out:

There was a loud bang, a pain in my leg and all of a sudden none of my controls would work anymore. So, when I came out of this cloud, diving pretty swiftly, I decided to jump out. But I was going so fast that the wind just blew me back in again. Fortunately, the Hurricane began to slew from side to side and I half fell and half pushed myself out of the cockpit.

And then there was this huge forest below me and when I got down to about four or five thousand feet, I heard bullets going past. The French of the ground were shooting at me and I could hear them going "Parachutiste! Parachutiste!" So, I took my identity card out of my pocket and said "Je suis Anglais" as loud as I could. I crashed down into the top of a tree and bounced into the lower branches and then landed on the ground. The French were all apologies. A huge unshaven Corsican hugged me and planted a kiss on my cheek.

1 Squadron also lost the services of a Hurricane when Flg Off Peter Matthews crashed at Orléans, similarly escaping injury, probably the result of engine failure.

The official British report for 10-12 June revealed:

While these events were reaching their tragic climax fighters of the Advanced Air Striking Force and of Fighter Command made a great effort to cover the movement of the 51st Division and the projected evacuations from Havre. On the 10th, patrols flown over the 51st Division met no enemy aircraft, but some were fought over Havre where the smoke of burning oil made operations difficult. One vessel, the troop-carrier *Bruges*, was sunk, but thereafter our fighters prevented enemy interference.

On the 11th, patrols of Fighter Command covered the St-Valéry for about seven hours. On three occasions they met and fought the enemy, bringing down a number; and on the 12th they made an even greater effort, patrolling the area for eight hours between five o'clock in the morning and half past nine at night, not realising that St-Valéry had fallen in the morning and that fighting in the area had ceased.

Meanwhile, Battles of the Advanced Air Striking Force and Blenheims of Bomber Command were all employed to attack the enemy in the Seine area. Advancing columns, concentrations, bridges and their approaches were heavily bombed by day in agreement with the French Command, and at night both the Battles and the heavy bombers of Bomber Command attacked widely distributed key points in the enemy's communications, again at the request of the French Command. Among these on the 11th were Laon, La Fère, Soissons, and the Meuse crossings. On the 12th this programme was continued, roads, railways and river crossings again forming the principal targets. By day, bombing attacks were delivered on the enemy's concentrations and columns and on damaged bridges which were being repaired; new bridges which were being built in the Seine area were also repeatedly attacked, some of these operations being covered by fighters of the Advanced Air Striking Force.

The combined remnants of the of the five AASF Hurricanes squadrons (1, 17, 73, 242 and 501) were now mainly involved in flying patrols over Le Havre in protection of ships arriving to assist with a second evacuation – this time moving troops to Cherbourg; and also providing escorts for Battles operating against German troops in the area of the Seine crossings. On 11 June, four Battles were lost, three to AA fire and one to a Bf109 of 4./JG3. Eight of the twelve crewmen were killed and one captured. Two further Battles fell to flak the following day.

At Le Havre, despite heavy bombing throughout the day and into the night, evacuation of troops to Cherbourg went ahead and would continue for another two nights. Poor visibility in the morning hampered Hurricane patrols. Several of the small evacuation boats and larger vessels were sunk during this period, including the French auxiliary patrol vessel *Patrice II* (247grt) off Fécamp; the 2,949 ton steamer *Bruges* was hit by German bombing off Le Havre, and was beached to avoid sinking. Seventy-two men were rescued. French steamers *General Metzinger* (9,345grt), *Niobe* (1,684grt) and *Syrie* (2,460grt) were sunk by German bombers at Le Havre, while Belgian steamers *Albertville* (11,047grt) and *Piriapolis* (7,340grt) were sunk by German bombing off Le Havre; the former was en route to Le Havre from Bordeaux to embark troops. The Norwegian steamer *Ellavore* (3,102grt) was also sunk by bombing at Le Havre. The entire crew was rescued. Nonetheless, during the night of 12/13 June, 11,059 troops were evacuated from Le Havre; 9,000 of them were taken to Cherbourg.

73 Squadron saw some action the same day, 12 June, Flg Off Dicky Drake and Sgt Alf Marshall shooting down a reconnaissance Do17 of 4.(F)/14, in which one of the crew, Uffz Fritz Epp, was wounded. Drake's aircraft was hit by return fire and force-landed. All six operational Hurricanes then flew to Ruaudin during the day, from where they provided escort for Blenheims bombing in the Caen and Angers area. No enemy fighters were encountered but all six Hurricanes failed to return to Ruaudin, much to the consternation of the authorities there. It transpired that four had landed at Nantes, one elsewhere, while Sgt Alf Scott became lost and attempted to land near Commer, where the Hurricane overturned. All bar the one had made their respective ways back to Le Mans by evening time. Next day, 73 Squadron lost another aircraft, and ultimately its pilot, when Plt Off David Anthony was badly injured in a landing accident, succumbing to his injuries the following day.

17 Squadron also enjoyed a successful day, as noted by Plt Off Bird-Wilson:

We were on patrol over Le Havre when we met four He111s which were attacking our troopships. We had a fair amount of success against them. We were giving protection to the Scottish Division which was pulling back towards Rouen. Not only were we being shot at by the German AA gunners and by the French, but also, I suspect by our friendly Scots.

Three Heinkels were claimed shot down. Plt Off David Leary found himself alone with three of the bombers and claimed one destroyed while the other two made off. One of these was then probably shared by Plt Offs William Harper and Plt Off DerekWissler, while Flg Off Count Manfred Czernin (YB-K) became separated in clouds and met another He111, which he claimed shot down. St/KG54 lost three He111s over Le Havre. Bird-Wilson continued:

> While patrolling around the Rouen area the chaps on the ground set fire to the oil tanks there, the smoke going thousands of feet up in to the sky. And right at the very top of the enormous black cloud, which went up many thousands of feet, was a parachutist. We never discovered what happened to him or why he was there [...] we thought it incredible he was so high.

Flt Lt Johnny Kent, now at Bricy, flew at least one more PR sortie:

> Although operating from Bricy, most of us were accommodated in Orleans and the city was filled with refugees all desperately trying to keep ahead of the advancing Germans. Some of the sights were so pathetic that it was impossible to avoid a moist eye – one old lady, I recall particularly, apparently had all her possessions piled into a pram and, swinging from the handle, was a parrot cage with her pet cat inside it. She herself just wandered on as though she was unaware of the crush of people around her, all moving south.
>
> One day French tanks and guns came rumbling through the city and the locals were convinced that they had arrived to make a stand on the Loire and turn the Germans back. The disappointment of the people was painful to see when this force which, by its appearance, had not seen action at all, crossed the Loire and continued on south. The troops themselves looked utterly dejected. During this period anxiety was felt about the bridges over the Seine – had they been destroyed or not? To get some information I was sent out on a flight to cover the river from Paris to Le Havre. The westward run I made at 32,000 feet but it was obvious that not much would be gained from the photographs as much of the area was obscured by the dense clouds of smoke from the many fires burning to the north of the river. In Rouen the flames from the burning oil installations came gulping up through the smoke, deep red in colour and clearly visible even from this height of six miles.
>
> My return run was made at 19,000 feet and I kept a watchful eye open for enemy aircraft but saw none. We had realised for some time that high-level reconnaissance did not really meet the present requirements and that sooner or later we were going to have to resort to low-level. This was not so amusing as we depended entirely on our speed and altitude for defence. With the prospect of this low-level role we re-equipped one of the Spitfires [P9453] with its eight guns and I flew this machine on another reconnaissance of the bridges. There was a considerable amount of cumulus cloud over the area and some cumulonimbus; I did not fancy my chances of getting any photographs at all. Initially I climbed to 15,000 feet, but gradually let down as I approached the river. When

I had reached 10,000 feet I saw, about a mile away, eleven Messerschmitts flying in line astern formation and on a course that would cross my bows. They did not appear to have seen me and I turned and flew almost parallel to them but on a slightly converging course, gained a couple of thousand feet, and continued to watch them. These were the first German aircraft I had seen whilst on a sortie and I was not going to rush into anything.

Without warning four Hurricanes swept from behind one of the towering cumulus straight down on to the leading five Messerschmitts. Instantly everyone seemed to go mad and aeroplanes whirled around in crazy gyrations. Then the rest of the 109s joined in and I latched on to the last one. We went diving down towards the swarm already engaged. I was determined to get as close as possible to make sure of my man and I lost sight of the others, but at about 3,000 feet my 109 pulled out of his dive and started a turn to the right – I was now only about fifty yards behind him and just about to open fire. I think the pilot must have seen me then for the first time as he made a sudden wild half-roll into which I followed him – and immediately regretted it as the ground was much too close. I lost interest in my intended victim and concentrated on getting out of the jam I was in. Luckily the Spitfire is very forgiving and also I was fortunate in being directly over the river. I was able to recover literally between the banks.

As I was rushing downwards, I saw a red flash out of the corner of my eye and as I climbed away I saw a column of smoke coming out of what looked like a bomb crater about 100 yards from the river bank. Of the 109 there was no sign and although I could not claim this as an enemy aircraft destroyed I have always been satisfied that the flash, and the crater were caused by the German machine. I have often wondered why he took such violent evasive action as at that time the German pilots were, for the most part, pretty experienced and I can only conclude that this one got the shock of his life to find a Spitfire on his tail, as there were no squadrons of them in France, and a bright blue one at that. Perhaps he thought that he had met the British ace of aces!

Flg Off Paul Richey of 1 Squadron, who had been wounded and hospitalised on 19 May, arrived at Châteaudun following his discharge from hospital. He wrote:

When I rejoined my re-formed Squadron, I found that Sqn Ldr Pemberton, from Wing, was in command, and that Hilly [Brown] was one of the flight commanders. Sgt Clowes was still there. That evening three mysterious civilians arrived at the château the Squadron was using to collect all the secret documents, which they did after Pemberton had checked them up by telephone with HQ [...] the rumour was that the Squadron was to go to Corsica.

I myself left Châteaudun by air in a mailplane (a DH Rapide) on 13 June. We took off in showery weather, circling the bomb-pitted aerodrome with its destroyed hangars and French aircraft blown on their backs, and then headed north-west for Normandy. Great black storm clouds were rolling across the sky, and I hoped no enemy fighters would pop round them, for we had no armament. Below us, now in rainy shadow, now in mottled sunlight, we could see thousands and thousands of refugees stretched across the green countryside like dirty white ribbons.

Soon we were crossing the Dorset coast; as I looked down of the calm and peaceful English countryside, the smoke curling, not from bombed villages, but from lazy little cottage chimneys, I saw a game of cricket in progress on a village pitch. After the poor war-torn France I had just seen in its death agony, I was seized with a sudden disgust and revulsion at this smug insular contentedness and frivolity that England seemed to be enjoying behind her sea barrier. I thought a few bombs would wake those cricketers up, and that they wouldn't be long in coming, either.

Another wounded member of 1 Squadron to be evacuated at this time was Canadian Plt Off Roland Dibnah, who had been shot down on 24 May. He recorded his memories in graphic fragments:

A feeling that survival was the only thing, and the feeling that you wouldn't probably make it; the shock of being hit and upside down; the false euphoria of blood loss; the shock of hitting the ground; the hissing and crackling of the engine when the aircraft came to rest; not having the strength to get out of the cockpit; a French doctor in britches and muddy boots with a blood-stained smock clamping on an aluminium ball-shaped thing with a mask to cover my nose and mouth, and saying "breeze deep"; the enormous pain and no sedatives in the French hospitals; a feeling of relief at being shot down; finally, a chance to sleep; 39 French officers and myself crying like babies after having our dressings changed in one ward at Bar-le-Duc, all because they were too rushed to bother to soak them off.

The bliss of a cup of hot tea on arrival at the British *Hertford* Hospital in Paris, their very first war wounded; the pleasure of a few lungful's of nitrous oxide, sleep while they changed my dressings and applied a wire boot; the unending kindness and sympathy from the English nurses; my night nurse, Betty, wheeling my bed out onto a balcony so we could enjoy a mild, clear night; listening to the guns coming closer; the rush of three of the nurses to carry me in from the garden during a sudden rain of flak shrapnel; shrapnel fragments on the balcony, putting an end to nightly chats; one night in a British field hospital at Le Mans, seeing a British tank man brought in, burned to a black crisp, and howling; being picked up at the race course in Le Mans by the Squadron Maggie, after getting away from an ambulance convoy at the railyards; the reunion with the Squadron at Châteaudun; the ribald ruderies about my being so stupid as to get myself damaged; the quiet and peaceful flight from Châteaudun to Hendon the next day, as one of two passengers aboard a Flamingo; the pilots wanting to land at Jersey for a cup of tea, but deciding not to, because the starboard engine was acting up.[9]

For 13 June, the official British report stated:

During this final phase our air forces in France had operated under great difficulties. South Component were compelled to abandon in turn three groups of airfields, north of the Seine, south of the Seine, and near Caen. Finally they covered the Cherbourg evacuation from the airfield in Jersey. The Advanced Air Striking Force in the same period was compelled to move in turn to airfields in the areas of Le Mans, Samur and Nantes To continue bombing action by night and fighting by day under such conditions imposed great strain on all concerned.

On June 13th the Royal Air Force made a great effort to assist the hard-pressed French armies. In the east their defence had been broken through at a number of points; the enemy had crossed the Marne and was threatening to turn the Maginot Line. In the west the Seine had been crossed, the French forces defending Paris were falling back, and a widening breach was opening between them and the French Tenth Army on the extreme left. If the German movement here was continued southwards, the airfields in use by the Advanced Air Striking Force would be exposed. Air Marshal Barratt reported this to the Chief of the Air Staff and asked for a directive should his squadrons be compelled to move. He was told to withdraw, if need, towards Nantes or Bordeaux: subsequent action must be dictated by the course of events, 'but so long as the French army is fighting you should endeavour to continue to render support'.

While the inevitable move back was being agreed with the French Air Commander of the Northern Zone – General d'Astier – a heavy day's programme was carried out. Armed reconnaissance of the Seine area began at dawn; thereafter enemy columns were attacked in turn by 10 Battles, 15 and, later, a further 15 Blenheims. Meanwhile, in the Marne area, at the urgent request of the French, 12 Battles attacked a large concentration of enemy troops and armour. Heavy anti-aircraft fire showed the target's importance, a further attack was made by 26 Battles of which six were lost. Fifteen Blenheims of Bomber Command then attacked a third time, four being shot down. The damage done to the enemy on the ground could not be measured but he was stun to violent reaction.

Our bombing attacks were continued during the night; 164 heavy bombers of Bomber Command were employed – 44 in the Seine area, 20 north of Paris, 41 on the Marne and 59 against road, rail communications and woods in which the French reported that the enemy were concentrated. Fighter operations were restricted by bad flying conditions and were chiefly devoted to patrols over the coastal area.

*****

73 Squadron reported the first air raid in vicinity of Le Mans when bombs fell at Parigny, about four miles away. At 15:40 on 13 June, four Hurricanes were ordered off when enemy bombers were again reported approaching. A small formation of He111s was encountered and one was claimed jointly by Plt Off Eliot (L1695/U), Flg Off Drake (3398/Z), Plt Off Langham-Hobart (P2869/S), and Sgt Friend (L2796), and possibly a second over Caen/Le Havre. The flight remained at Caen for the night. It seems that their victim was 1G+DM of 4./KG27, which crashed north of Bolbec. Uffz Willi Krause was seriously wounded and died three days later. A second crewman, Uffz Wilhelm Müller, was also wounded.

Le Mans was now severely affected by bad weather, the Hurricanes being grounded and a proposed Battle escort cancelled.[10] The Battle squadrons paid dearly for this lack of protection. The first flight, off at dawn, returned safely, but the next formation drawn from 150 and 142 Squadrons ran into Bf109s of 8./JG26 and 3./JG3, losing five aircraft. All three 142 Squadron crews survived but four were wounded. Two more Battles were lost, one each of 142 and150 Squadrons during the late afternoon when they ran into Bf109s of I/JG27, and 12 Squadron lost three more during the early evening, also falling to I/JG27. At least three more Battles were lost during the day; all believed victims of the Messerschmitts.

Plt Off Denis Crowley-Milling, one of the 615 Squadron attachees to 242 Squadron, recalled this day for a different reason:

> I woke up to find the whole of the roof of the tent on fire, only to dash out in my pyjamas to be greeted full down the front with a fire extinguisher. The tent burned right down and some of our clothes. We had to beg and borrow and do the best we could, but the Squadron missed a patrol as a result.

While Plt Off Stan Turner remembered:

> One night we had trouble with fifth columnists. A couple slipped past our guards and turned on the yellow lights in the Hurricane cockpits. We couldn't see the glow from the ground, but it was visible from the air. Jerry came over and dropped incendiaries, but fortunately there was no damage.

The official British report for 14 June stated:

> On the 14th bombing attacks were renewed at daybreak against the German penetration across the Seine, but then and throughout the day bad flying weather seriously limited their effect. The most successful was an escorted attack by 24 Blenheims on Merville airfield which our fighters had reported to be 'covered with enemy aircraft'. The night programme this time included

marshalling yards in Germany, parts of the Black Forest in use by the German army and the dropping of drifting mines in the Rhine. Seventy-two heavy bombers were engaged in these night operations of which two were lost against seven in the daylight attacks.

*****

At 15:30, 11 Hurricanes of 17 Squadron met six Bf109s of 3./JG54 over the Seine Estuary and claimed one probably destroyed by Plt Off Jock Ross, and others damaged by Flg Off Czernin, Plt Off Bird-Wilson, Plt Off David Leary and Plt Off David Hanson. It is possible that Ross' victim was Ltn Hans-Eberhard Angeli, who was killed. After the Hurricanes had landed, Bird-Wilson told Plt Off Wissler that he had shot a Messerschmitt 109 off his tail. Wissler had never even seen it. The Hurricanes had been providing escort to Battles of 12 Squadron attacking woods near Evreux, the Battles being attacked by 2./JG3 and losing two aircraft. Four more Battles were lost during the day, 103 Squadron losing two (one to fighters and the other to flak). 142 Squadron lost one, as did 226 Squadron, both to fighters.

Plt Off Wissler noted that everything seemed to be falling apart around them. The station canteen staff had already run for it, leaving all the supplies behind. Wissler, as did others, took off for Dinard with a thousand cigarettes tucked away in the cockpit.

Meanwhile, Hurricanes of 242 Squadron also patrolled the Seine to Paris line at 16:00. An estimated one-dozen Bf109s (probably of 8./JG26) attacked at 9,000 feet. In his logbook Plt Off Willie McKnight wrote "12 Me109s attacked – 12 destroyed [obviously an error] – 2 personally confirmed." Plt Off John Latta also claimed two Bf109s in this action, as noted in his citation:

> [...] his squadron attacked a number of Messerschmitt 109s. This officer destroyed one and, although his own aircraft had been hit in the wings and tail by cannon shells, attacked and destroyed a second enemy aircraft.

One of the Messerschmitts was possibly that flown by Ltn Gustav Sprick, who force-landed slightly wounded, having claimed a Hurricane first. Bf110s of III/ZG26 were also involved in this scrap, Plt Off Noel Stansfeld and Plt Off Alan Eckford (LE-S) each probably claiming one. The 9 Staffel aircraft crewed by Uffz Karl Wissmann and Obgfr Willy Bülow, both of whom were killed, crashed near Marbeuf, while that flown by Ltn Werner Kuhlke and Gfr Paul Eckert was shot down north of Conches-en-Ouche; the crew was captured, having been wounded. The *Zerstörer* crews wildly overclaimed, 7 Staffel claiming three Hurricanes (Ltn Kuno-Adalbert Konopka, Ltn Hans-Arno Seehausen and Obfw Siegfried Haase claiming one apiece); while 9 Staffel claimed four (Oblt Karl Montag, Ltn Kurt Sidow, Uffz Erhard Reinold and Ofw Heinrich Hott also claiming one each). It would seem that only Plt Off Noel Stansfeld, who had become separated and subsequently lost his bearings following combat, failed to return. He attempted a force-landing near Blain, north of Nantes:

Stansfeld selected what appeared to be good landing spot in a field close to a village [Blain]. The place was not as well suited as he had guessed, for he narrowly missed dropping over the bank of a stream as he rolled to stop. From all directions French peasants converged upon him, waving assorted ancient rifles and muskets. They did not believe that he was a British pilot, and he could not clearly explain his presence. It appeared that he was going to be arrested if he was lucky and shot if he was not.

At last one man pushed through the crowd and affected a quick rescue. This person spoke good English; he had once been a cook in England. A brass compass and a *Michelin* road map were produced and the young Canadian was given directions to a French airfield where he might refuel. First of all he had to take off from his improvised landing strip. The French beat down some of the wheat. Stansfeld then stood on his brakes, revved up the engine until he was in danger of nosing over, released the brakes, and took off.

Having secured some gasoline, Stansfeld set course for Rennes, but again lost his way. Below was a railway line on which a train was carrying British troops and equipment. He resolved to land beside the tracks and ask for further directions. This time he was less fortunate. As the Hurricane touched down it ran into a ditch, wiping off the undercarriage. A deafening roar filled the cockpit as an emergency horn went off. Somebody rushed to render assistance. The aircraft was a write-off.

A second Hurricane was late returning to base, LE-B flown by Plt Off Denis Crowley-Milling; he had encountered a Bf109 but lost it in clouds:

The squadron was attacked by a formation of Messerschmitts and, having taken evasive action, Crowley-Milling found himself in apparent possession of an empty sky. Remembering the one thing which had been drummed into him by his flight commander at his OTU, which was never to be on his own; but if he did get split up in combat to join up with the first available aircraft. He diligently searched for a friend and, having espied one, gratefully formated upon him at the same time frantically craning his neck searching for the enemy.

He had no need to look very far – there was an enemy near at hand, the aircraft he was formatting on was one of the 109s! At almost that very moment he realised to his horror what he was about, so did the German pilot and, being ahead, and therefore in the more vulnerable situation, hastily ducked into some conveniently nearby cloud.

Apart from thus losing his adversary, Crowley-Milling had, meanwhile, also lost himself so, after much hopeless searching, put the Hurricane down in a field in order to find someone and ask the way home. As it so happened his aircraft had a faulty starter motor and the ground staff were in the habit of starting it by looping a rope around the propeller and giving it a hearty yank, and so it was doubly important to keep the engine running while he consulted with a nearby farmer. Having been told where he was, Crowley-Milling began taxiing towards the edge of the field preparatory to take-off only to have one wheel thoroughly bogged down. Fortunately there was help to hand, as Crowley-Milling recalled: "A whole gang of farmers, together with their children appeared, and, putting their backs under the wing (not without risk from the spinning propeller) heaved the Hurricane back on to firmer ground and all was well and soon I was safely airborne."[11]

Next morning (15 June), Stansfeld hitched a lift to *Mathew* airfield (Nantes-Château Bougon), to where 242 Squadron had now moved together with the remnants of 1 and 73 Squadrons. While flying a shipping escort patrol over St-Nazaire, Hurricanes of 1 Squadron engaged Heinkels escorted by Bf109s. Sgt Darky Clowes claimed a Bf109 shot down and Flt Lt Hilly Brown of 242 Squadron a second, also claiming a He111. An official report stated:

When leading his flight on patrol, he encountered nine enemy bombers, two of which were destroyed. Later he attacked nine Messerschmitt 109s, destroying one and driving the remainder off. As a result of bullets entering his aircraft he force landed near Caen, and was unable to rejoin his squadron before it withdrew from France.

Hilly Brown added:

I left France on the last boat, having had a spot of airplane trouble in the north and just nicely catching the last transport in each case. None of my kit came out, so I found myself with only an old uniform. It will be quite a while before I am as well equipped again. We have been lucky in not losing many men. The big loss has been in planes and equipment.

From an early morning patrol by eight Hurricanes of 73 Squadron, Sgt Alex McNay (TD-P) failed to return. No flak or enemy aircraft was seen by any of the others, although it transpired that McNay had been bounced, wounded in the shoulder and crash-landed:

Towards the end of the patrol I had the feeling, although I saw nothing, that we were being stalked from the cover of the sun. I therefore fell behind and climbed above the squadron slightly, and zig-zagged to watch our rear. The patrol finished, and we commenced to descend from our altitude of 23,000 feet towards Le Mans, our base. Nothing happened until at 12,000 feet I felt a jerk on my controls. Thinking I was under fire I did a steep turn to the left but saw and felt nothing more. The sky was apparently empty so, completing my turn, I began to chase the remainder of the patrol which was now about a mile or so away.

After about a minute, when I was at 10,000 feet, I saw tracer shooting past, and as I swung away from the burst I felt a sting in my shoulder. Looking up, I saw two single-engined machines coming down on me. I think it was their leader who hit me as they seemed too far away for such close-grouped accurate fire as the burst which had got me. I couldn't see more than two, but knowing myself to be hit, I decided not to linger. I banged my controls as far into the left-hand corner as I could, and with full throttle went down to the treetops and, by luck more than judgement, came out of my dive, heading west.

Satisfied I had shaken off the pursuit, I tried to find where I was but my compass had [been] broken by a bullet which had ricocheted off the inside of my windscreen, and I could not trust my gyro. I continued to fly west by the sun but unable to pick up any landmark, I force-landed in the first available field. I noticed that the machine was apparently undamaged, except for a shot which had broken the runner of the sliding hood, entered the cockpit, and broken the compass; and a clean hole in the hump-back where the shot which hit me had entered.

Some men from a French battery came to my assistance. On learning that I had been wounded, they insisted that I see their MO. When the MO saw my shoulder, he forbade me to try and fly the machine to Le Mans, but I took no notice of what he said until he began to clean my wound. I felt no pain as my shoulder was numb but I began to feel faint – probably just reaction but, as the bullet was in my shoulder and not just a graze as I first thought, I changed my mind. An officer volunteered to phone my squadron so I gave him their location and my name. (See Appendix III)

It seems probable that Sgt McNay had been shot down in error by 501 Squadron's Plt Off John Gibson (SD-V) who reported a combat near Le Mans, and possibly shooting down a Bf109. There appears to have been no Luftwaffe activity in the vicinity.

73 Squadron was now ordered to Saumur airfield, following the withdrawal of a French unit but were redirected to land at Nantes-Château Bougon. The ground personnel meanwhile arrived at Saumur. At Nantes there was total confusion. The remnants of the Hurricane squadrons were given the task of covering the final evacuation of British troops from the ports still in allied hands and were expected to cover Brest, La Pallice and St-Malo, in addition to Cherbourg, Nantes and St-Nazaire. 501 Squadron was about to move once again and among the unflyable aircraft abandoned was P2964.

During this period Hptm Adolf Galland of Stab/JG27 was instructed to carry a flight in an olive-green painted Bf109 to see whether it was less visible than the standard camouflage. On the R/T he picked up the voice of Hptm Wilhelm Balthasar, a Gruppenkommandeur in JG3, whom he knew well, instructing his pilots to watch him shoot down a Hurricane he had sighted below. Galland listened with admiration as Balthasar gave a running commentary as he closed in for the kill – only he realise that he was the target when tracers flew past his wings. Balthasar had mistaken the unusually painted Messerschmitt for a Hurricane, and was taken aback when he heard Galland's familiar voice yelling over the R/T: "That's enough of this bloody nonsense!"

The official British report for 16 June revealed:

Operations had been proceeding concurrently at St-Nazaire and Nantes, where there were greater difficulties to overcome. The former lies at the mouth of the River Loire where there are strong tides and other navigational hazards; the latter is some fifty miles up the river. As pointed out above, the Navy's information was vague and often contradictory. Between 40,000 and 60,000 British and Allied troops were thought to be converging on Nantes, but neither exact numbers nor the times of arrival were known.

In preparation for the lifting of so large a number, Admiral Dunbar-Nasmith ordered the assembly of a considerable concentration of ships, including the destroyers *Havelock*, *Wolverine*, and *Beagle*, the liners *Georgic*, *Franconia*, *Duchess of York*, and *Lancastria*, the Polish ships *Batory* and *Sobieski*, and a number of cargo ships. For the most part these had to lie offshore in Quiberon Bay, twenty miles north-west of the Loire estuary, where there was good anchorage for large ships but no anti-submarine or other defences. It was a risk which had to be taken, for no safer anchorage was available. Movement began on the 16th and over 12,000 troops were embarked that day on the *Georgic*, the *Duchess of York*, and the two Polish ships, and sailed for home. The enemy's bombers attacked the ships in Quiberon Bay, but only the *Franconia* was damaged. The loading of stores went on all night, and additional ships arrived from England – and some from Brest. The destroyers *Highlander* and *Vanoc* also joined the flotilla.

Two sections of 73 Squadron from Nantes patrolled St-Nazaire area at 04:00, but nothing was seen. Another patrol at 16:30 had same result and also ran into severe weather.

*****

The official report for 17 June revealed:

The day that followed, June the 17th, was memorable for the only tragedy that marred the success of these difficult and dangerous operations. At Nantes the sun rose on a scene of great bodies of troops assembling in the port to be taken home, and in and out of the river entrance destroyers and smaller craft were busy ferrying parties to the ships which were waiting for them in the roads. Overhead, fighters of the Royal Air Force patrolled at frequent intervals to keep the sky clear of the enemy's bombers. And more ships arrived to increase the speed of evacuation.

The morning's achievements raised high hopes that again the Navy's task would be completed without loss, but at a quarter to four in the afternoon, when the fighter patrol which had been maintained throughout the day along a thirty-mile stretch of the coast was not over the port, enemy bombers made a heavy attack on the ships assembled in the roadstead and the mouth of the river. While destroyers and all the smaller craft with anti-aircraft weapons defended themselves vigorously, the *Lancastria*, with 5,800 troops – including many of the Royal Air Force – already on board, was heavily hit and set on fire, and within fifteen minutes sank with great loss of life. Nearly 3,000 perished, though why so many lives were lost is something of a mystery. It is true that there were not enough lifebelts on board for the quite exceptional number that had been embarked, and that a film of the ship's oil-fuel spread over the surrounding waters. But the master, who was saved, testified that there was no panic aboard, and the ship sank slowly where small craft were present in considerable numbers. Doubtless many of these were so busy defending themselves from the air attack (which continued for 45 minutes) that they failed to realise the urgent plight of the *Lancastria's* men, yet this does not fully explain why there was so great a loss of life.

*****

Flt Sgt George Berry of 1 Squadron was leading a mixed patrol from 1, 73 and 242 Squadrons at 16:30, when a formation of bombers, believed to have been Heinkels, was sighted. These were, in fact, Ju88s from 5./KG30, and one was seen to score a direct hit on the *Lancastria*. Berry attacked and believed he shot down this aircraft, while two more were jointly claimed by Flg Off Pete Matthews, Plt Offs Peter Boot, Benny Goodman and Bob Rutter; the latter's aircraft was hit by return fire although he was able to land safely. Plt Off Neil Campbell of 242 Squadron wrote:

We covered the evacuation from Nantes and prevented it from becoming another Dunkirk. There were three squadrons at Nantes covering the troopships and with pardonable pride we kept Jerry off. One evening the wily devil sent over five Heinkels. They came over high and approached from different directions. One succeeded in diving through the clouds and bombed one of our ships but that couldn't be helped. They glided down from a height and dived through the clouds. Unfortunately the first bomb got the ship. No. 1 Squadron was on patrol at the time and succeeded in shooting down three of the Huns. One was chased, not shot, into the water. Boy, he must have been scared.

67 Wing's War Diary added:

> Very shortly after the attack, the Hurricanes returned and drew off the enemy. Although favoured by clouds one Ju88 was shot down and two others seriously damaged. It is believed that a further bomber was destroyed by AA fire.

A Lewis gunner aboard the armed trawler *Cambridgeshire* was credited with the latter. At least one Morane of AC5 got airborne with Prem-mâitre Barbe also making a claim. One historian has written:

> A Hurricane flew in with the sun behind it to attack a German plane machine-gunning men in the water [...] Having hit the enemy aircraft, the Hurricane flew off, its pilot believed to have been George Berry. A survivor reported seeing the Luftwaffe plane floating in the water fifty yards from him. The crew stood on the wing as men from the *Lancastria* shouted "Murder the bastards!", but one of the Germans brandished a Luger pistol.[12]

Despite the claims and witness accounts – including the graphic description above – it seems that German losses were just two Ju88s with minor damage, although one crewman was killed and two wounded. Both aircraft were able to return to base:

> Ju88 3./KG30 under 5% damaged by fighter over the Loire River Estuary and safely returned to Merville, piloted by Oblt Sigmund Freiherr von Gravenreuth; three crew wounded, one critically.
> Ju88 5./KG30 flown by Uffz Geffgen 10% damaged by fighter over Loire River Estuary and belly-landed at Louvain-le-Culot.

Oblt Freiherr von Gravenreuth reported hits on a 10,000 ton transporter after which his bomber was attacked by a fighter aircraft, which his radio operator claimed to have shot down (probably Rutter's Hurricane). In the combat, his observer Obfw Ludwig Edmüller was hit in the head and died later from his wounds. Two other aircrew, Fw Franz Erdel and Obgfr Herbert Kraus, were also wounded, while another aircraft, flown by Uffz Geffgen, returned with 70 bullet holes and crash-landed on return. One of the participants, Uffz Peter Stahl also of 5 Staffel, wrote:

> They say France is nearing the end, and that we can soon expect an Armistice. This calls for another celebration, and we have just started when we are ordered to get ready for another operation! It is to be an attack on a large concentration of ships in the Loire estuary. The actual operational orders arrive shortly afterwards; we have to take-off at 15:00hrs.
> This time we are to fly in loose formation, fourteen Ju88s with the Eagle insignia of our Geschwader on their noses. Once again we cross the old

battlefields of the First World War and can also observe the after-effects of the present one. The flight approach seems endlessly long and after a while I fall back behind the formation to save the engines. The risk of being picked on as an especially enticing target seems comparatively small at this phase of the war – I would much rather have a pair of healthy engines as a precondition of getting back home again!

At the target I experience my first contact with fighters – French Moranes – but to begin with they do not attack me. The twisting and turning takes place at the other end of the estuary, and I can clearly see one Ju88 going down with a smoking port engine. There are the ships! A vast fleet of freighters of all sizes lie scattered in the broad river estuary – there is no need for us to fly as far as the port of St-Nazaire. As usual, I fall back a little and have a quiet target approach flight. All at once I hear Moritz's voice on the intercom: "Fighters coming towards us!" "How far are they?" "There is only one, about 500 m away."

There is no time now for the finer points of dive-bombing. With a sharp movement on controls I tip my Ju88 on its head and go down without bothering about the dive brakes. Moritz reports that the Morane is following us. Now for it! The Ju88 gains speed at a tremendous rate and we are soon diving at 600 and then 680kmph. I set my sights on a fat freighter, pull the nose of my Ju88 up a bit, and then let go of the bombs. Now out of here! With continuous control movements I pull the machine in a steep downwards bank that takes us out of the reach of the AA guns. I am still going at a high speed, while Moritz and Jupp keep reporting what the French fighter is up to. It is still following us, but seems unable to catch up.

The way things are this tenacious fellow is bound to catch me when I have to slow down near ground level. There is nothing for it but to start twisting and turning to throw him off his aim. A steep bank upwards temporarily gives me a bit of breathing space, but the Morane is soon back again and tries all kinds of tricks, helped by his higher speed level, to get into a firing position. The moment the French fighter steadies his aircraft, I throw my Ju88 into a steep bank to port or starboard to shake him off, and the game begins again. All at once, as suddenly as the Morane had appeared it turns away. The French pilot had 'broken his teeth' trying to get my Ju88 and now swings back again towards the big turmoil over the target area.

Relieved, we make speedy tracks for home base. The encounter had been rather hairy to say the least! Naturally, due to the air combat there could be no question of observing our bombing results, and so my report on landing at the base was rather thin. However, the total success of our Gruppe is excellent: without losing a single aircraft we have achieved a large number of good hits, some of which can be mutually confirmed by several crews. Uffz Geffgen was also intercepted by a French fighter but was not as fortunate as I; he collected more than 70 hits in his Ju88 but still made it back to base all right. But not only that. Due to shot-up hydraulics he made a first-rate belly landing perforce using his four 250kg underwing bombs as skids – he could not get rid of them because all his electric and mechanical release mechanisms had been shot out of action. Geffgen's landing was something I would not want to imitate. In his situation I would rather have baled out by parachute. I knew all about our bombs being 'safe' against damage by gunfire, but to skid along all four bombs....? Who could tell if the heat caused by friction would not set them off?[13]

Circling the stricken *Lancastria*, Plt Off Pat Hancock brought his Hurricane low over the over the ship, and threw his Mae West down from the cockpit. People below cheered. Then, his fuel running low, Hancock turned and headed back to the airfield at Nantes. There were only 2,477 survivors, at least 800 of whom were picked up by the armed trawler *Cambridgeshire*. The destroyers *Havelock*, *Harvester* and *Highlander* also took part in the rescue action, as did the *Oronsay* and SS *John Holt*. A British steamship, the 400 ton *Teiresias* was also hit by bombs near the entrance canal to St-Nazaire, and sank the next day. One crewman out of the 71-man crew was posted missing.

In total, four waves formed by Ju88 units of Air Corps IV were sent off against these targets. The first wave took off at 11:25 from Merville and consisted of bombers belonging to I/KG30. Following the mission, the last bomber returned at 17:30. The crews reported results from only one attack, on a transport ship, estimated at 1,200 tons that received two SC250 hits and was probably sunk.

The second wave took off from Löwen-Le Culot Airfield around 14:30. It consisted of 14 Ju88s belonging to II/KG30. The last landed later at 19:00. (It seems that Hptm Arved Crüger led the attack.) The following successes were reported: Four SC250 bombs exploded close to a warship estimated at 5,000 tons. The warship was most likely damaged. A troop transport ship estimated at 30,000 tons and fully loaded with troops was attacked in the Loire River Estuary. According to the crewman the silhouette of this ship was similar to a battleship. One SC500 exploded in the middle of the ship and second on the rear part. The ship's stern was blown up and later the ship, according to the eyewitnesses, capsized.

A transport ship estimated at 20,000 tons was hit by one SC500 bomb. It was a direct hit in the middle of the ship. A second bomb detonated close to the ship's hull. Smoke was observed erupting. A merchant vessel of 1,000 tons was hit in the middle with one SC500 bomb. A second bomb detonated close to the ship's hull. Erupting smoke and fire was seen. The ship sat low in the water. A transport ship of 12-15,000 tons developed a list after receiving a direct hit from an SC500 in the bow. The lifeboats were lowered.

One SC500 bomb hit the forward part of a transport ship estimated at 12-15,000 tons. A second SC500 bomb exploded some 5 metres off the ship's bow. The ship began listing and fires were seen breaking out. A steamship estimated at 10,000 tons received four SC250 hits. One of the bombs exploded close to the ship's hull.

The ship was stopped and was on fire. A tanker ship of approximately 5,000 tons received one SC250 hit in the middle. A second bomb exploded 10 metres off the starboard side of the ship. Smoke and fire was seen erupting after the attack and the ship developed a list. Two SC250 bombs exploded close to a medium-sized merchant ship – estimated at about 5,000 tons

The third wave, consisting of some crews belonging to III/LG1, took off around 15:05 from Lille-Vendeville. Only one crew reported a successful attack on a transport ship, estimated at about 10,000 tons, that was left listing.

The last wave was formed by II/LG1 and also took off from Lille-Vendeville at 15:10. The last aircraft returned at 19:36. The crews claimed a large transport ship of about 25,000 tons as damaged, and a smaller 8,000 vessel damaged by two SC500 near-misses. It seems likely that Oblt Stephan Suin de Boutemard of 4./LG1 made the final claim.

* * * * *

Plt Offs Stan Turner and Willie McKnight were now leading most of the 242 Squadron patrols as they were the most experienced pilots. The ground crews left for St-Nazaire to be shipped out so now the pilots had to do everything, including arming and re-fuelling their aircraft. It was a gruelling time with long days and nights spent under the wings of their Hurricanes to ensure that no one would sabotage them. Of this period, Turner recalled:

> One night we went into Nantes, and soon wished we hadn't. As we came out of a bar, we were sniped at – probably by another fifth columnist. We beat it back to the airfield and found the canteen tent abandoned. It was loaded with liquor, so we had a party. Willie McKnight, I remember, refused to drink from a glass. Whenever he needed a drink, he reached for a bottle, smashed the neck, and took it straight.

In addition to fighting, McKnight found time to have a short affair with a young woman who had escaped Paris ahead of the German army and, like thousands, was a refugee on the run to an unknown future. He was reputed to have 'commandeered' a general's staff car on one occasion to help carry out a 'romantic liaison' with the Paris beauty. To his Canadian boyhood friend Mike Pegler he confided in a letter:

> The brass hats pulled out so fast we all had our own private cars. This girl and I, her name was 'M', took a flat in Nantes and had a hell of a time for about two weeks. All the boys kept dropping in every night and we'd all bullshit and listen to the radio and eat then bog off to bed (after the lads had gone). It was sure marvellous and I certainly miss it now – I tried to smuggle the girl back on one of our bombing planes but one of the few big noises left in France caught me and raised merry hell. It was too bad because she was certainly

one first class femme – she had been to university and was a modiste until the Hun started toward Paris when she had to evacuate and then I ran into her. Oh well, I suppose I must have been fated for a bachelor – I can't fall in love anymore like I used to; I get all worked up for about an hour then I just lose interest.[14]

At dawn on June 18, 73 Squadron was placed on readiness at Nantes, two of its pilots – Plt Off Chubby Eliot and Plt Off Alex McGaw having been despatched at 04:15 to fly to Guernsey to deliver messages before continuing to Tangmere, the latter managing to miss Guernsey and landing at Land's End. Sqn Ldr Hank More undertook a dawn recce to try and locate enemy tanks and armoured vehicles, which we rumoured to be approaching Nantes. He went up just north of Le Mans, returning via Tours, but saw nothing of more interest than several agitated female refugee cyclists who rode into a ditch on his approach, thinking he was an enemy machine.

Pilots of 242 Squadron flew a last patrol over Brest and made a couple of sorties inland. Later that day they were ordered to evacuate. The pilots of 17 Squadron, who had moved Dinard, were ordered to get out of France as quickly as possible. Plt Off Bird-Wilson recalled:

That night a crowd of us went to St-Malo and there we relaxed with a naturally moderate amount of drink. We were happy walking along in the docks area but the French got very upset with us. They said, how could we be so happy, when France was capitulating. We replied that we'd been fighting like hell for France ourselves and were now going home. They didn't see the humour of that remark at all and as we had French girls on our arms they didn't like that either.

Plt Off Denis Wissler was among the partying pilots and met an attractive French girl named Irene. Next day turned out to be a day of bad weather and no flying, and after five hours at readiness Wissler took Irene out to dinner again. She offered to wash his dirty clothes! He wrote in his diary: "Oh God! I do wish this war would end." The following day was his day off, but it did not turn out quite as he had expected. He had arranged to see Irene, but in the event did not even have time to say goodbye to her, as Bird-Wilson explained:

When we returned to the aerodrome the French colonel in charge gave our CO 30 minutes to get off, otherwise our Hurricanes would be impounded and destroyed. I've never seen a squadron get into the air so quickly and we flew out to the Channel Islands.

They flew to Jersey from where B Flight was ordered to Guernsey to carry out patrols over Cherbourg until the last troops were clear. They returned to England next day. Bird-Wilson believed one or two girls were given lifts in Hurricanes:

While we were preparing to fly out, some girls came up to us and asked if they could ride back to England in our single-seater Hurricanes. I'm not saying that all the pilots honoured King's Regulations, and I wouldn't be surprised at all if one or two didn't bring a girl back, the pilot sitting on the girl's lap and discarding his parachute.

Plt Off Peter Dawbarn, the newest member of the Squadron, meanwhile recalled:

Just as I was about to get into my Hurricane to fly back, the Flight Commander came up and said, "I'm taking your Hurricane, mine is u/s. You'll have to find your own way back." I thought to myself what am I going to do now? I walked past a hangar and there was a fitter doing something to a Fairey Battle, and I asked him if it would fly. He said yes, but there were no hydraulics, no brakes and no flaps, but the engine was OK, so I said I would take it. He helped me get it out on the airfield, because with no brakes you need someone to push the rear back so you could line up. Anyway, I took off and flew back to England. I hadn't got a map, but I knew it was north, so I flew north. I happened to come right across Exeter airport, so I landed there and missed the far hedge by about three inches, because I didn't have any brakes.

Dawbarn, having explained his sudden and untidy arrival, was given the loan of a Tiger Moth in which to fly back to Debden, and there he rejoined his squadron. Another of the returning 17 Squadron pilots, Sgt Des Fopp, remembered:

We operated out of Le Mans for about three weeks but had little or no success against the enemy as there was a very efficient fifth column being operated by French collaborators who kept the German bombers informed of our movements. Before leaving Le Mans, because of the German advance, we discovered that the army had left a pool of motorbikes, many of which were in running order so the whole squadron turned out in force and we had a hair-raising race around the Le Mans circuit before destroying the bikes. We also found that the NAAFI had evacuated the Grandstand leaving all the stores behind, so we decided that we didn't really need spare clothing or uniforms and filled our kit bags with cigarettes and bottles of spirits, before destroying the remainder of the goods.

We then proceeded on our way to Dinard which is not far from Cherbourg. After one week we again retreated, this time to Jersey and then Guernsey where we only stayed for one night as it was decided that the Channel Islands should be left to the Germans to avoid mass bombing of the civilians. During this evacuation from France it was a case of either find an aircraft to fly or remain and hope to get out by road to St-Nazaire. It was amazing how some people came back. We had three pilots return in a Fairey Battle, which had no flaps and had to be flown with the wheels down. Another two returned in a

Magister and yet another who sat on the lap of his friend in a Hurricane. This meant that the parachute was discarded to make room.

Personally I brought my Hurricane back with a flat tailwheel, no brakes and no ammunition for the guns. On arrival at Tangmere we were sent home for 7 days leave until more aircraft became available. On my arrival home in Bristol I was greeted by my grandmother with the words "Where have you been? You are dirty and untidy. Have you deserted?" But she was grateful for some of the cigarettes in my kit bag!

The 242 Squadron pilots destroyed several Hurricanes (including N2381, P3683 and P3779) that they could not get started, and then smashed the canteen. Turner continued:

All that booze – it was heart-breaking. We armed and fuelled our aircraft and climbed in. We were a wild-looking bunch, unshaven, scruffily dressed, exhausted, and grimed with dirt and smoke. We were also in a pretty Bolshie mood. After weeks of fighting we were all keyed up. Now that the whole shebang was over, there was a tremendous let-down feeling. As we headed for England we felt not so much relief as anger. We wanted to hit something, and there was nothing to hit. The skies were empty – not a German in sight – and the ground below looked deserted too. It was all very sunny and peaceful, and quite unreal. As if the war didn't exist. But we knew the real war had only just begun.

The day France surrendered, French soldiers set up machine-guns along our runway. "All aircraft are grounded," an officer told us. "There's to be no more fighting from French soil." We saw red. A brawl was threatening when I felt a tap on my shoulder. Behind me was a British army officer, who had come out of the blue. "Go ahead and take off," he said. "I'll look after these chaps." He pointed to his platoon which had set up a machine-gun covering the French weapons. The French officer shrugged and left. Time was running out. The Germans were over the Loire River and heading towards us.

Plt Off Crowley-Milling found himself left behind with pilots of 242 Squadron. They managed to make a few Hurricanes serviceable; he recalled

As the aircraft took off for England the squadron's commander was left behind at Nantes airfield, sleeping off a heavy session. The pilots left pinned to his chest a note "We have taken off for Tangmere. When you sober up you had better join us, because the Germans are heading this way."

Sqn Ldr Gobiel must have recovered fairly quickly for he piloted one of the Hurricanes from Nantes that set out for England at 11:00. Without warning he whipped over in a dive, having spotted a Heinkel below but overshot. Stansfeld, following, attacked and believed he shot it down into the sea (see Chapter III). Three more Hurricanes followed 30 minutes later flown by Plt Off Bob Grassick (LE-L), Plt Off Neil Campbell (P2985/LE-N) and Sgt Eric Richardson. Without maps or clear orders about where to land, they ran out of fuel and force-landed in the area of Dunster Beach, between Wachet and Minehead on the Somerset coast. Campbell wrote in a letter to his family:

> Landing on the beach tipped up the nose of my plane, breaking the airscrew. Bob tore his tailwheel and rudder; Sgt Richardson tore off his tail wheel, fairing and rudder, and also went up on his nose. It is really a wizard of a place, quite as nice as anything I have seen. The people very, very nice. They actually pushed my machine up a 200-foot hill that had a one-third rise. The last three feet were perpendicular so my machine literally had to be lifted up.

The remnants of the last Hurricane squadrons – 1, 73 (including Plt Off Peter Carter in P3351/K), and 501 – withdrew via the Channel Islands. Plt Off Pat Hancock of 1 Squadron remembered:

> The local French colonel, in charge of ground defences of the field, seriously suggested we should surrender to him, to be handed over to the Germans when Paris fell. It was appalling. We had gone off the French to such a degree at that stage that our main feeling on leaving France was total gratitude that we'd left the damned place and the perfidious French. We were fighting the Germans, but they were the enemy. The French were a different matter.

A dozen Hurricanes thus flew back to Tangmere, departing Nantes at 11:45. These were followed later by Lt Moses Demozay, 1 Squadron's French liaison officer[15] flying an abandoned Bombay in which he evacuated sixteen ground personnel. Unserviceable Hurricane P3045 was burnt on the evacuation at Nantes.

> The urgent task was to bring home to Britain as many key personnel as possible. It concentrated, for the most part, on bringing back air crews and technicians of the RAF. Every possible aircraft was organised under National Air Communications for the task; each flew back and forth between France and Britain to the limit of its powers. The airmen flew over roads crowded with refugees, over villages and cities smoking with bombardment, sometimes into the thick of combats between our fighters and German bombers. They landed on airfields that were on the verge of panic, struggled to obtain enough fuel for the return journey, and came home crowded from nose to tail with their rescued. They made some strange flights. [16]

501 Squadron was now at Dinard, including Plt Off Peter Hairs:

We had moved on 18 June from Le Mans to Dinard, and one of the Hurricanes had been left behind because they could not start the engine. The CO asked me to go there and fly it back. There were some ground crew left behind, to help me. Gibby [John Gibson] had liberated a French two-seater aircraft, so he flew me over. We got to Le Mans, landed, and he flew off, leaving me behind with the ground crew still working on the Hurricane. They had all the panels and cowlings off the engine, but still they couldn't get it to work.

Then my flight commander, Pat Cox, flew over in his Hurricane, and said, "Look, if you can't get this thing going, we'll both fly back in my Hurricane. You can sit on the seat and I will sit on your lap." He was shorter than I was. Then the men got the engine to fire, hastily put the panels back on, and I was able to get the Hurricane into the air and fly it back. The ground crew had a truck there to drive back to a place of safety. I must admit when I crossed the coast the engine seemed to give a little blip, which was a bit worrying because I am not a swimmer. [17]

At 14:15, ten Hurricanes of 73 Squadron led by Flt Lt Charles Nicholls departed Nantes for England, and were followed by six more at 15:00 led by the Sqn Ldr More – the last Hurricanes to leave France – which provided escort to a Bombay carrying the Squadron's rear party and an Anson with Wg Cdr Cyril Walter, 67 Wing's OC, on board.

A small merchant air fleet was now organised to help evacuate an RAF squadron from an airfield near Lyons. They intended to refuel their aircraft at Bordeaux and Marseilles on the way – by this time Bordeaux had become the most northerly French airfield which they could use. Captain Perry was the first to arrive at Bordeaux in an Ensign airliner:

I spent some time taxying back and forth across the airfield, trying to get some petrol from somebody, getting none and damaging my tailwheel in the process. Suddenly a French officer whom I knew came out of one of the hangars and told me, with a white face, that France had given in.

Of these final days in France, Aircraftman Geoff Turnham, attached to 212 Squadron at Meaux as a driver, recalled:

The Special Survey Flight received orders to evacuate on 16th June but [Wg Cdr Sydney] Cotton decided not to obey. The order was repeated on the 17th. Personnel were instructed to get back to England by whatever means available. Some managed to get into the Blenheim and flew back. The Squadron and its mobile equipment set off in the direction of Poitiers. The roads were very crowded with cars and lorries all trying to make their way south. Cotton circled overhead and along the route watching the men from the Hudson. After a very long day we reached Poitiers where we camped for the night. We had found an abandoned Fairey Battle aircraft [L5360/RH-C of 88 Squadron] on the airfield. It had a damaged wingtip; some of the ground staff made a temporary repair with a piece of fence and some fabric. Cards were drawn for a place on the aircraft and Flight Lieutenant 'Tug' Wilson flew four airmen back to Heston.

The rest of the unit carried on next day to a grass airfield at Fontenay-le-Comte where all the photographic trailers, trucks, tankers, a bowser, a power unit and a van were piled up into a corner of the field and set on fire. Cotton flew four other personnel back to England in the Hudson via Jersey and the rest of us slept in the open. Cotton returned to Bordeaux to pick up more of us stranded there the next day. Morale remained high in spite of the danger. Cotton made another rescue trip with a second pilot to Le Luc to pick up an abandoned Hudson there but found it destroyed on the ground by the Italian Air Force when he got there. At this time some of us decided to make our own way back, sleeping in the open was no fun and we had waited long enough. We took the remaining 15cwt truck and drove to Bordeaux. After a search of the quayside and a little help from the authorities we found a coal boat sailing for England that would take us. Abandoning the truck on the dock we decided to take a chance on this ship, the alternative was being killed, captured by the Germans or interned by the Vichy Authorities. I remember little of the journey home, except being locked in a very large cabin during the day and only allowed on deck when it was dark. We were well fed and warm; I don't know but I think it was a neutral vessel and we had to be kept out of sight from the authorities. Early in July we got back to England, after a long rail journey back to London and then to Heston we were reunited with the unit. Syd Cotton and Flight Lieutenant [R. H.] Niven picked up the rest of the unit from Bordeaux and everyone made it back safely.

During this period, a number of British and French aircraft – many considered unflyable – slowly wound their way across the Channel. The last Blenheim to return from France was flown by Flg Off John Rochfort who arrived at Gatwick. He and his crew had been living rough while HQ BAFF retreated across France. The last remnants of the RAF left in France had finally come under the command of Air Commodore Cole-Hamilton, who returned in the well of the Blenheim. Rochfort's WOp/AG, Robbie Roberts tells how they were confronted by an angry official wearing a top hat on arrival at Gatwick, who then proceeded to tell crew that they had landed right in the middle of a race and had frightened the horses. Rochfort laid him out with just one punch.

A few days later a LeO451 took off at dawn from Nantes Château-Bougon and landed at small airfield near Southampton. It was flown by Lt Yvon Pageot, who reported that at least five other brand new LeO451s had been destroyed on the runway and others sabotaged in the factory to avoid them falling into German hands. Another French aircraft to escape was a Potez 63-11 ex GRI/14 which arrived in England flown by Sous-Lt Neumann, with two other escapees on board. Others followed. Towards the end of the month an abandoned Gladiator force-landed at Lower Beeding near Horsham having been flown from France by Flt Lt Ian Bartlett of 53 Squadron.

Plt Off Willie McKnight of 242 Squadron was one of those admitted to hospital for a rest. He had lost almost two stone in weight during his time in France. He recounted in a letter to his friend Mike Pegler that "I almost looked like an overgrown kid when we arrived back in England." His letter also revealed:

I've been sick in bed for four days now and today is the first day I've been allowed to do anything at all and the MO even put a time limit to writing letters. Everything seemed to go wrong with me all at the same time, stomach, ears, throat, eyes, etc., or in other words I was more of less useless to anyone. The Doc says it was almost two months of no sleep and less food that did it then sort of coming back to a civilized life just floored my system and I was left sucking a hind tit. I should be out in another four or five days though I hope so as the Blitz is just starting again and I've got to keep Turner from hogging all the fun.

We two are the high scorers in the squadron so far, having got twenty-three between us – nine for Stan and fourteen for me [10 plus 4 probables] – as we have a pretty keen competition going on and neither one of us likes to be off duty when the other one is on and we're both afraid we'll miss a chance to get something [...] It's a funny thing this fighting in the air, before you actually start or see any of the Hun you're as nervous and scared as hell but as soon as everything starts you're too busy to be afraid or worried. We've had several fights with Colonel Schumacher's squadron – it's supposed to be in the same class as Richthofen's was in the last do – and I don't mind saying that they're about the finest pilots I've ever met [...] some bloke who must be the personal ace of the Luftwaffe jumped me and succeeded in shooting away nearly all the machine except where I was sitting before I managed to dive into a cloud. Well, anyway after we got home (three out of five) we found out that about eight Jerry squadrons had pooled their resources for the morning and we'd tried to jump about eighty machines. We laugh like hell when we think about it now but it wasn't' so funny then [...] We've only got five of the original twenty-two pilots in the squadron left now and those of us who are left aren't quite the same blokes as before. Its peculiar but war seems to make you older and quieter and change your views a lot in life – you also find out who are the blokes worth knowing and who aren't and I haven't met one yet who wasn't worth knowing.[18]

CHAPTER III

A SEPARATE LITTLE WAR – ITALY ATTACKS FRANCE

On this tenth day of June 1940, the hand that held the dagger has struck it into the back of its neighbour.

US President Franklin Roosevelt

As if France's plight was not sufficiently dire, neighbouring Fascist Italy decided to add to her woe. At 16:00 on 10 June, M. Reynaud was telephoned by the French Ambassador from Rome (M. François-Poncet), informing him that Italy had declared war on France and Great Britain. At 18:00, Italy's dictator, Benito Mussolini, delivered a speech from his balcony in the Palazzo Venezia in Rome (as reported by an American news correspondent):

Soldiers, sailors, and aviators! Black shirts of the revolution and of the [Fascist] legions! Men and women of Italy, of the Empire, and of the kingdom of Albania! Pay heed! An hour appointed by destiny has struck in the heavens of our fatherland [*Very lively cheers.*]

The declaration of war has already been delivered [*cheers, very loud cries of 'War! War!'*] to the ambassadors of Great Britain and France. We go to battle against the plutocratic and reactionary democracies of the west who, at every moment have hindered the advance and have often endangered the very existence of the Italian people.

Recent historical events can be summarized in the following phrases: promises, threats, blackmail, and finally to crown the edifice, the ignoble siege by the fifty-two states of the League of Nations. Our conscience is absolutely tranquil. [*Applause.*] With you the entire world is witness that Fascist Italy has done all that is humanly possible to avoid the torment which is throwing Europe into turmoil; but all was in vain. It would have sufficed to revise the treaties to bring them up to date with the changing needs of the life of nations and not consider them untouchable for eternity; it would have sufficed not to have begun the stupid policy of guarantees, which has shown itself particularly lethal for those who accepted them; it would have sufficed not to reject the proposal [for peace] that the Führer made on 6 October of last year after having finished the campaign in Poland.

But now all of that belongs to the past. If now today we have decided to face the risks and the sacrifices of a war, it is because the honour, the interests, the future impose and iron necessity, since a great people is truly such if it considers sacred its own duties and noes not evade the supreme trials which determine the course of history.

We take up arms to resolve, after having resolved the problem of our land frontier, the problem of our maritime frontiers; we want to break the territorial chains which suffocate us in our own sea; since a people of forty-five million souls is not truly free if it does not have free access to the ocean.

This gigantic struggle is nothing other than a phase in the logical development of our revolution; it is the struggle of peoples that are poor but rich in workers against the exploiters who hold on ferociously to the monopoly off all the riches and all the gold of the earth; it is the struggle of the fertile and young people against the sterile people moving to the sunset; it is the struggle between two centuries and two ideas.

Now that the die are cast and our will has burned our ships at our backs, I solemnly declare that Italy does not intend to drag into the conflict other peoples bordering her on land or on sea. Switzerland, Yugoslavia, Greece, Turkey, Egypt take note of these my words and it depends on them and only on them whether or not they will be rigorously confirmed.

Italians! In a memorable meeting, that which took place in Berlin, I said that according to the laws of Fascist morality, when one has a friend, one marches with him to the end. [*'Duce! Duce! Duce!'*] This we have done with Germany, with its people, with its marvellous armed forces. On this eve of an event of century wide scope, we direct our thought to the majesty of the King and Emperor [*the multitudes break out in great cheers for the House of Savoy*] which as always has understood the soul of the fatherland. And we salute with our voices the Führer, the head of great ally Germany [*The people cheer Hitler at length*]. Proletarian and Fascist Italy stands up a third time, strong, proud, and united as never before. [*The crowd cries with one single voice: 'Yes!'*]

The single order of the day is categorical and obligatory for all. It already spreads and fires hearts from the Alps to the Indian Ocean; Victory! [*The people break out into raucous cheers*]. And we will win, in order finally to give a long period of peace with justice to Italy, to Europe, and to the world.

People of Italy! Rush to arms and show your tenacity, your courage, your valour!

*****

Early on the morning of 11 June, a single BR20 from 8ªSquadriglia (25°Gruppo, based at Ghemme) flew a reconnaissance mission over Toulon, but had to abort after four hours due to bad weather. Another aircraft was sent out at the end of the day to complete the mission. Meanwhile, a lone SM79 from 11ª Squadriglia, 26°Gruppo based in Viterbo, undertook a similar sortie to Bastia and the di Borgo airfield in Corsica. Seaplanes of the *Regia Marina* and the *Regia Aeronautica*, plus some SM79s, flew reconnaissance missions over French North Africa, two aircraft each being sent over Oran, Bizerte, Karouba, Sidi Ahmed and Algiers. There was no French reaction. French aircraft also flew a number of reconnaissance missions, including aircraft of GRI/61 from Voulas-les-Bains, particularly over Italian airfields. Italian bombers from Sicily also attacked Malta.

Under cover of darkness on the night of 11/12 June, the RAF dispatched 36 Whitleys to attack targets in Italy. They refuelled in the Channel Islands before their long flight over France and the Alps to bomb factories in Turin. Twenty-three aircraft were not able to reach Italy because of difficult weather over the Alps. Consequently, nine aircraft bombed Turin but not the designated factories, with most bombs falling on the railway yards. Seventeen people were killed and forty injured. Two other aircraft bombed targets in Genoa. Both cities were fully lit up, as in peacetime, when the bombers arrived. Turin's lights were turned off during the raid but Genoa's were not. A Whitley of 77 Squadron (N1362) crashed in flames near Le Mans, with the loss of the whole crew, as reported:

> Whitleys and Wellingtons were detailed to make the first attack on Italy following the declaration of war by that country. Industries in Turin and Genoa were the targets for this raid, which was made on the night of 11 June. Unfortunately the attack proved abortive. The majority of the 36 Whitleys did not reach Italy because of heavy storms encountered over the Alps, while the twelve Wellingtons, six of which were from 75 Squadron, did not leave the ground at all. They had flown from England to an advanced base in the south of France early in the day, but so anxious were the French to avoid provoking the Italians to retaliation that they drove lorries and carts on to the airfield to prevent the Wellingtons from taking off. The aircraft then returned to England. After several days of recrimination, permission was finally given for the airfield at Salon to be used, but the capitulation of France prevented the development of heavy attacks on Italy for some considerable time.

One of the pilots later made a radio broadcast:

> This was the first time our squadron had done the Italian trip. We'd heard a rumour about a week before that we might be getting the job and everyone was quite thrilled at the idea of the run over the Alps. We were told in the

morning that we were going to Turin and so we started at once drawing our tracks and getting the navigation generally weighed up. My navigator was particularly keen on the show because he's something of a mountaineer and has done a fair bit of climbing in the Alps. The route we were taking worked out at between twelve and thirteen hundred miles there and back. We had to make a bit of a detour to keep clear of Switzerland because we had special instructions to avoid infringing Swiss neutrality.

Briefing was at two o'clock in the afternoon and we took off just as it was getting dark. To start with, the weather was poor and we had to come down to six hundred feet over the English coast to pinpoint ourselves, then we climbed up through what was becoming really nasty weather, and crossed the coast on the other side fairly high. By that time the cloud was what we call ten-tenths – that's to say, it obscured everything, but eventually we got above cloud and then we had the light of the moon which was in its first quarter. Before that it had been very dark indeed.

We were flying blind above cloud until we arrived forty or fifty miles east of Paris and then we ran into clearer weather, the clouds gradually decreased below us until we could see the ground, and when we reached southern France the weather was perfect. It was one of those clear moonlight nights when the stars seem to stand out in the sky and you feel you can put out your hand and grab one. As we flew on towards the Alps, we could make out some of the little mountain villages against a background of snow, the whole scene resembled a picture on a Christmas card.

The aircraft was going wonderfully well and we cleared the highest mountains we went over by three or four thousand feet. You could see the ridges and peaks, well defined, and the moon shining on the snow was half turning the night into day. Flying over this sort of scenery was something completely new to us and pretty awe-inspiring. The nearest we'd got to it was on the Munich raid when we'd seen the Bavarian Alps in the distance. The navigator came up and pointed out Mont Blanc, away on our port side. He was able to identify it from its shape because he'd actually climbed it, and he was telling us how he was beaten by the weather when he got to within six hundred feet of the summit. Immediately we got to the other side of the Alps, with no snow about, it seemed by comparison, intensely dark for a bit. It was like coming out of a lighted room into the black-out. Soon after that we started to glide down, losing height very gradually and arrived slightly west of Turin. Other planes were already over the target because we could see their flares and there was a barrage of anti-aircraft fire in the sky.

Our target was the Fiat works, and the whole time we were looking for them we were still gliding down to our bombing height. Actually we picked the works up in the light of some-body else's flare. They were unmistakable. I've never had such a target before. There seemed to be acres of factory buildings. We almost wept afterwards because we hadn't got any more bombs to give them. Having located our target we flew four or five miles away, turned round and made our run up over it. The wireless operator came along and stood beside me to have a look at the bombing, otherwise he wouldn't have seen anything from his usual position. He's a bit of a wag and when he saw the light flak coming up from the works he said: "Gosh, look at the Roman candles."

We made two attacks and as we came round afterwards to have a look, the fires which we'd started were going strong. There was a big orange-coloured fire burning fiercely inside one block of buildings. Having finished the job, we climbed to get enough height to cross the Alps again. Altogether we were over or round about the town for three-quarters of an hour and whilst we were circling to gain height we saw somebody hit the Royal Arsenal good and proper.

Going home, the Alps didn't look quite the same. The moon had almost set then and the mountains had lost their vivid whiteness. The last two hours of the journey home were, frankly, plain misery. It started with the aircraft suddenly beginning to get iced up. I tried to climb, but she wouldn't take it. Ice was coming off the airscrews and hitting the fuselage. We came down to about seven thousand to thaw out and then we ran into an electrical storm. All this time we were in cloud. It was frightfully bumpy and the aircraft was bucketing about all over the place. At one point the front gunner called me up and said: "Are you quite sure you're flying the right side up, because I think I can see white horses in the sky." That was when we were over the North Sea. When eventually we left the clouds we had to come through snow and sleet and the final bit of the journey we made in a howling gale which reduced our ground speed a lot. Never had we ever taken so long to get inland to our base from the coast, but we got there safely in the end.

Daylight on 12 June witnessed 21 SM79s from 27° and 28°Gruppi based in Sardinia attack Bizerte (Tunisia). Many were veteran crews from the Spanish Civil War, and they destroyed four Loire 70 seaplanes of Esc.E7 and damaged another, while a fuel depot was set afire at Sidi Ahmed. French AA fire claimed seven of the raiders as damaged. Six Ms406 from GCIII/5 were scrambled but arrived too late. However, the Moranes continued providing CAP until the end of the day so that when a lone SM79 arrived to assess the results of the raid it was forced to turn back, though it managed to escape. One Morane crash-landed due to lack of fuel.

Over France, the Italians despatched five reconnaissance missions towards Toulon. The first with a single BR20 from 14ªSquadriglia of 4°Gruppo, which overflew Camps des Maures, Cuers, Hyères and Toulon, before being intercepted by French fighters and having to make an emergency landing near Bergamo. Sufficient information was gathered, however, to prepare next day's bombing attack against Toulon. Four more reconnaissance missions against Toulon were launched but all aborted due to bad weather. Next day eight BR20s of 11° and 43°Gruppi attacked

Toulon but with no great effect since the raid was broken up by heavy AA fire.

At 10:50 on 13 June, CR42s from 23°Gruppo attacked Fayence airfield, a dozen strafing and another 11 providing top cover. They were followed a few minutes later by others from 151°Gruppo, a further 12 CR42s making a strafing attack against Hyères airfield while 15 more provided top cover. French AA was heavy but scored no successes, the Italian pilots claiming twenty aircraft destroyed on the ground and one shot down. The French did lose a Vought 156 from Esc.AB3 returning from a training flight.

At 11:15, a second wave, from 11° and 43°Gruppi, arrived on the scene, nine BR20s attacking Fayence and ten more attacking Hyères. They were, however, a few minutes behind the intended fighter escort and were intercepted by three D.520s of GC III/6 and Bloch 151s from AC3. Four of the bombers jettisoned their bombs on being sighted but were quickly overtaken. MM2105 was promptly shot down and crashed at Agay, about five miles west of St-Raphael in a combined attack by the D.520s. It was alleged that the Italian crewmen, having baled out, were killed on the ground by a mob that included gendarmes. On fact, one crewman was lynched by a frenzied mob and another shot in his parachute, while the pilot had drowned; two others were captured.

The other BR20s attempted to escape individually but MM21503 crashed into the sea off Cap Camarat. This particular aircraft was sighted off the coast of Monaco by the pilot of a 212 Squadron PR Spitfire, Flg Off George Christie, a Canadian who had been despatched to the area at the behest of the RAF to establish the state of play. Unaware that the BR20 had already been attacked and badly damaged, Christie carried out dummy attacks 'by repeatedly diving at it, forced it to land in the sea'. The five occupants of the machine climbed out and swam for the shore, and the aircraft sank almost immediately.

The 212 Squadron detachment had been based at Le Luc airfield since 12 May, and apart from Flg Off Christie included Flg Off Des Sheen, an Australian:

> I flew down to the South of France and Corsica with Sidney Cotton in his Lockheed prior to PR operations over Italy. At Bastai we were met by bayonet-fitted rifles surrounding the aircraft as it was thought we might be Italians (who had yet to enter the war). Operations over Italy started mid-May initially from Le Luc, a French fighter base not far from St-Raphael and then from Ajaccio in Sardinia to give a bit more range.

In describing the PR Spitfires sorties, Sheen commented:

> They were normally flown at full throttle at around 30-32,000 feet, depending upon the tropopause as it was essential not to leave a persistent contrail. The average sortie was about two and-a-half to three hours and the longest I recorded being about 3¼ hours at a maximum height of 34,000 feet. Minor physical problems were the cold, and we found that three loose layers of clothing were

the most effective, and mild attacks of the bends were found at altitudes after a long period but nothing could be done about that. Another small problem in the south of France was that the airfields had long grass and with our fairly long take-offs, grass tended to block the pilot head. The only solution was to fly the sortie without an airspeed indicator and thus burn up the fuel before landing.

We were there [Ajaccio] when Italy entered the war [10 June] and next morning found the airfield completely obstructed. With some difficulty we persuaded the French to clear enough for us to fly back to Le Luc.

After returning to Le Luc the airfield was bombed:

A few days later [15 June] we were ground-attacked by a squadron of CR42s. Our Spitfire fortunately was under cover but our support Hudson was destroyed. I was in a ditch about 20 yards away but saw at least three CR42s shot down by a Dewoitine [piloted by Lt Le Gloan]. The Spitfire was sent home and the remainder of our small party left Toulon on 17 June arriving back in the UK on 12 July via Algiers, Rabat, Casablanca and Gibraltar.

Another BR20 managed to land back at base thanks wholly to the efforts of its pilot. The aircraft commander was dead and three other crewmembers (including the pilot himself) wounded, probably from heavy AA fire. Other bombers landed with lighter damage, one of these from 15ªSquadriglia, probably damaged by a Bloch 151. Italian bomber gunners in return claimed one French fighter shot down, although there was no such loss. Finally, at 11:40, 28 BR20s (7° and 43°Stormi) attacked Toulon. There was no fighter opposition although AA fire was as heavy as during the previous raids.

Elsewhere, 14 SM79s of 30°Stormo and 19 SM79s of 36°Stormo raided Menzel Temine, El Alouina and Kassar Said airfields in Tunisia, escorted by 15 CR42s from 1°Stormo. There were no losses. Meanwhile, nine SM79s of 9°Stormo attempted to locate French shipping off Liguria, but were unsuccessful due to bad weather.

The French attempted to hit back on the night of 13/14 June, albeit with a minimal strike force. The antiquated NC 223.4 *Jules Vernes* from B5 Bombing Flight departed Bordeaux for a 12½-hour mission during which it attacked Rome as well as the Porto-Marghera airfield near Venice. On the latter target a stick of stick of eight bombs was dropped and the crew reported a fuel tank hit and burning, providing 'formidable lighting' of the target. Meanwhile, eight Bloch 210s (4 GB I/23, 4 GB II/11) attacked the Vado Ligure fuel depot (one from II/11 was lost on the return leg, the crew surviving). Visibility was poor and only the commander of the 1st Flight of I/23 attacked the target. The rest of I/23 aborted and the others bombed a railroad north of Savona.

The 3rd French Squadron (cruisers *Foch*, *Algérie*, *Dupleix*, *Colbert* plus destroyer escorts) bombarded Genoa on 14 June, with the French Naval Air Arm in support: AC3 provided fighter cover, AB2 and AB4 with Loire-Nieuports provided anti-surface cover, while AB3 deployed its eight Vought 156s, one of which attacked the Italian submarine *Gondar* without result. In the other direction ten SM79s of 46°Stormo attempted to locate French shipping off Liguria, but was unsuccessful due to unfavourable weather. In the evening, three LeO451s attacked the Turin Fiat factories. The weather was very poor and one crashed on the return leg from engine trouble, the gunner being killed.

In an attempt to suppress French fighter defences on 15 June, the Italians engaged an all-fighter force to avoid the coordination problems encountered with the BR20s earlier. At 13:00, 27 CR42s from 150°Gruppo attacked Cuers airfield, claiming fifteen French planes destroyed on the ground and several others damaged, as well as an ammunition dump. Six Vought 156s from AB3 were in fact destroyed in the attack.

Three sections of Bloch 151s from AC3 were scrambled to meet this raid. The first section engaged 15 CR42s over Le Luc, with no results on either side (though the French pilots were credited with two victories), following which it patrolled over Toulon. The second section was caught while still climbing for altitude. One aircraft was damaged and crash-landed, another was damaged but managed to disengage and joined the first section over Toulon. The third was also damaged but managed to shoot down a Fiat from 365ªSquadriglia, before having to land at Hyères, and flying back to Cuers thirty minutes later. However, the last section was massacred: one was shot down and the pilot killed shortly after take-off, and a second had barely the time to engage in combat when it was forced to crash-land. A third aircraft was shot down and crash-landed, the pilot dying from his wounds. The Italians lost one aircraft in combat and another was forced to land due to engine trouble at Cuers, and was therefore captured by the French.

The other two Gruppi encountered stiffer opposition. At 13:00 the 23°Gruppo raided the Cannet des Maures airfield with 24 CR42, claiming over twenty aircraft destroyed on the ground. Other Fiats of the Gruppo flew top cover and engaged French fighters in a dogfight, losing one and claiming one. Meanwhile 18°Gruppo, flying as distant escort for the raiders, engaged French fighters claiming two victories against two losses. Two patrols of D.520s from GC III/6 took-off from Le Luc to intercept the Italian attack. They intercepted a dozen CR42s from 23°Gruppo, Lt Le Gloan being credited with four of the biplanes before shooting down a BR20 from 172ª Squadron. The Italians lost only lost three CR42s (one from 23°Gruppo and two from 18°Gruppo) with two more from 23°Gruppo heavily damaged.

Meanwhile, the *Regia Aeronautica* launched a series of attacks against Corsican airfields (where no French fighters were based): Calvu was hit by SM79s of 46°Stormo, which were escorted by nine G.50s from 22°Gruppo. Ghisonaccia was attacked by six SM79s from 9°Stormo, losing one to AA fire. Campo dell Oro (near Ajaccio) was also targeted but not hit due to bad weather. From North Africa, GB I/61 attacked Tripoli with six Glenn Martin 167F. One bomb hit the city, killing three and wounding 22. That evening, in very poor weather, four Bloch 210s from GB II/11 attempted to attack the Novi Ligure airfield, only one reaching the target. A second raid, by GB I/23, was similarly unsuccessful due to the weather conditions.

RAF Bomber Command established a small detachment of Wellingtons from 75 Squadron at the French airfield of Salon, near Toulon, so that raids could be more easily carried out against Italian targets. Eight Wellingtons from this force were despatched to Genoa on the night of 15/16 June but only one bombed. The 'Jules Vernes' flew its last mission on this night, also. As it had done two days before, it departed for a 12-hour mission over Livourne – where it remained over the target area for an hour, dropping its bombs one by one until a fuel tank was hit, which provided illumination. Italian AA fire proved ineffective. The aircraft then flew to Rome, where only leaflets were dropped.

16 June saw mainly uneventful patrols and ineffective small-scale bombing raids on various targets. Six SM79s attacked an airfield on Corsica and a dozen Ba.88s raided the island's Bonifacio harbour and airfields. From the other direction, six M.167Fs of GB I/61 attacked Elmas airfield near Cagliari, Sardinia, in the afternoon. One bomb hit a hangar in which there were seven Z.501s, six of which went up in flames. Other aircraft, including some Z.506s were damaged as was an SM79. Six groundcrew and a pilot were killed, and thirty wounded.

17 June was a day of mainly isolated attacks on various targets in Tunisia and on Corsica by the Italians resulting in several losses but most probably to non-combat. After dark French bombers raided various coastal targets on the Italian mainland with little success and no losses. The following day's actions were similar, bad weather continuing to hamper operations. Recce flights were made over the Tunisian coast and harbours, and small-scale bombing raids were carried out by French units during the night. Two failed to return, probably due to the weather. French units renewed operations over the Tunisian coast on 19 June, including Alghero, where two CR32s were damaged). Meanwhile, a total of thirty-seven SM79s carried out attacks on Corsican airfields without much tangible success, since there were few French aircraft resident. Nine Ba.88s of 7°Gruppo continued the attacks in the afternoon, targeting Bonifacio, Ghisonaccia and Portovecchio.

Next day, 20 June, witnessed little action, practically none from the French, but with French and Italian troops clashing in the Alps, both sides flew in reinforcements to assist. The Italians were particularly active on 21 June. At 06:40, six BR20s from 13°Stormo attacked Fort Malgovert near Bourg-Saint-Maurice while a dozen BR20s from 25°Gruppo attacked fortifications on the other side of the town. Over fifty bombs were dropped from 4,500 feet, which missed the forts but hit the city itself. A little later, forty-three BR20s of 7°, 43° and 13°Stormi dropped a total of 170 bombs in Haute Tarentaise. Later, five more from 31°Gruppo paid another visit to the Bourg-Saint-Maurice forts, followed by another eleven from 25° attacking the Plate-Truc forts north-west of the city. Poor weather prevented all but two of the bombers from identifying their target. Several other raids were aborted due to bad weather. Italian bombers also attacked Corsica and others the Marseilles port area. The port itself was not hit, but 122 civilians are killed and others wounded.

Various French fighter units attempted to intercept but such was the confusion that they did not even spot the Italian bombers.

Sporadic Italian raids continued against specific targets, the weather causing problems. The French air force was unable to react due to lack of operational aircraft, although at night a force of 27 M.167Fs carried out attacks on military targets in the Trapani area, but despite a lack of AA and fighter opposition, only minor damage was inflicted though twenty civilians were killed.

Off Karouba, an MS406 from GC III/5 mistakenly attacked two French CAMS 55 seaplanes from 4S1 Squadron, damaging one which eventually belly-landed with two wounded aircrew.

On 23 June, nine M.167Fs (three each from GB II/62, GB I/63 and GB II/63) attacked the port of Zuara, but six abort en route to Gabes due to bad weather. The remaining three claimed a cargo vessel and a fuel depot left burning. The Italians recorded the loss of one 440 grt ship from air attack around that time.

In the afternoon Palermo was bombed by four M.167Fs from GB I/62 and three from GB II/62, killing civilians. Italian fighters claimed one of the raiders shot down. The returning French crews did not report the presence of Italian fighters but one bomber crashed on the return leg with another being damaged on landing at Canrobert. There were losses to the crews. Another attack against Palermo followed, on his occasion by five LeO451s from GB II/11. Only two reached the target and another, short of fuel, tried to land on a beach near Cap Bon but crashed and exploded, killing the crew. A LeO H-470 of E11.2, flying back to its base of Karouba from Toulon, encountered a Z.506 and both large seaplanes engaged in air combat. Gunners traded a few bursts with no visible effect before they disengaged and went their respective ways. This was probably the last air combat of the campaign.

The Armistice was signed at 19:15, becoming effective on 25 June at 00:35.

CHAPTER IV

ANOTHER SEPARATE LITTLE WAR

Germany Invades Swiss Airspace, June 1940[1]

The mass of aircraft was flying around in huge circles at three different height levels. We were in no way prepared to attack such a mass of aircraft ...

Lt Hans Thurnheer, Swiss fighter pilot

German aircraft frequently overflew Swiss territory, sometimes accidentally but often deliberately. There had been several clashes.

While fighting raged elsewhere, during the afternoon of 4 June, a lone Heinkel of KG53 appeared over Swiss/French border in an attempt to provoke a reaction, only this time with a fighter escort of Bf110s from II//ZG1. The Swiss scrambled a number of aircraft, but it was a C-35 reconnaissance machine that initially made contact with the Heinkel, the crew gallantly attempting to carry out an attack. Before long Swiss Bf109s and MS406s arrived in the vicinity and a number of dogfights developed between these and the Bf110s, two of which were claimed damaged by Lt M. Wittwer (J-24) and Lt Robert Heiniger (J-34) flying Ms406s of Fl.Kp.3, while another was claimed damaged jointly by Lt Wachter and Lt Jean-Paul Benoit (J-316) of Fl.Kp.6. One Swiss Messerschmitt, J-329 flown by Oblt Alfred Rufer, returned with bullet strikes in the wings and propeller. Two of the Bf110s were claimed by Oblt Pista Hitz (J-332) of Fl.Kp.9, one of which may have been shared with Lt Rudolf Rickenbacher (J-310), but the latter was shot down in return, the blazing aircraft crashing into the ground near Boécourt. The pilot's body was found, minus his parachute, about 400 yards from the wreck. His victor was believed to have been Uffz Herbert Kutscha of 5 Staffel (his fifth victory).

One Bf110 was lost, from which Uffz Albert Killermann and Uffz Gottfried Wöhl baled out too low and were killed. Their aircraft crashed just over the French border at Fournet-Blancheroche, south of Charquemont at 15:45. The Germans claimed that the Swiss had attacked first over France, but the claim was inconsistent with the location of the Luftwaffe crashes. Diplomatic notes threatened that "the German Reich reserves the right to take any measures necessary for the prevention of attacks of this nature," and warned "In event of any repetition of such incidents,

the Reich will dispense with written communications and resort to other means."
Lt Thurnheer recalled:

> But the worst fight was yet to come – on 8 June. Göring's temper rose, and he
> ordered the Swiss to be challenged by a complete *Zerstörergruppe* of Bf110s
> operating from Freiburg, only 45km from the Swiss border. At 03:30 in the
> morning Fl.Kps 6, 15 and 21 were at a state of readiness. A few minutes
> before noon we were ordered to take off from Thun. Less than 20 minutes
> later we were over the Jura mountains where we soon spotted the Bf110s – 32
> of them! It was a spine-chilling sight.

The Bf110s had already encountered a C-35 (C-125) of Fl.Kp.1 reconnaissance
biplane, which was shot down, crashing near the village of Alle at 11:42, killing
both Lt Emil Gurtler and Lt Rudolf Mauli. Thurnheer added:

> Before we arrived on the scene two 109s of Fl.Kp.10 had engaged the Germans
> and one 109 had been shot down. This mass of aircraft was flying around
> in huge circles at three different height levels. We were in no way prepared
> to attack such a mass of aircraft at that time, and that is why all 12 of us
> each attacked separately. That was a mistake, because the Germans were well
> prepared and when we attacked they immediately tried to encircle us. All we
> could do was try get a 110 in a favourable position for a quick attack – fire,
> then try to escape as fast as possible. There were various methods of getting
> away, such as very tight loop – which the 110 could not follow – or half a loop
> followed by a roll. Anyway it was a rather dangerous situation, as we were
> alone when we attacked. If we had then had the battle experience we later
> accumulated, we would have shot down more than the three we managed
> to get. We had no losses. Hptm Homberger was shot through the lungs, but
> managed to land at Biel. He was also shot in the buttocks, but a good luck
> charm he was carrying in his purse saved him from further harm!

One of the first Bf110s engaged by Fl.Kp.21 was that crewed by Uffz Alois Scholz
and Ogfr Walter Hofmann, that had strayed a few miles into Swiss airspace. Oblt
Victor Streiff, aided by Lts Köpfli and Mühlemann, succeeded in shooting it down,
the aircraft of 4 Staffel impacting near the little village of Wellnau, about one
kilometre east of Triengen, where it burst into flames. Both crewmen were killed,
Hofmann having managed to bale out but his parachute snagged on the tailplane.
Another 4 Staffel machine (2N+DL) fell to the Swiss Bf109s at about the same
time, the victim of Oblt Hans Kuhn of Fl.Kp.15. The stricken machine was nursed
back over the French Jura mountains before it crashed at Sépois-les-Bas, killing Fw
Otto Beiter but his air gunner Obgfr Robert Hink managed to bale out and was
captured unhurt by the French.

A few minutes later, Fw Manfred Dähne's 5 Staffel aircraft (2N+GN), was attacked at 1,500 feet and received hits in the port engine, which promptly failed, forcing Dähne to break off combat and head for Freiburg. Separated from the rest of the Gruppe, the Bf110 was pursued by the two Swiss Messerschmitts flown by Hptm Hans Homberger and Lt Friedrich Egli. The gunner, Obgfr Herbert Klinke, maintained a steady return fire and eventually forced the Swiss fighters to break away after one, that flown by Homberger (J-328), had sustained thirty-four hits with the pilot wounded in the lungs and buttock, although he managed to crash-land safely at Biel-Bözingen. Meanwhile, the damaged Bf110 was engaged by Swiss AA battery (Detachment 80) near Wahlen prior to belly-landing south of Oberkirk church at 12:40. Dähne was unhurt but his gunner was badly concussed and broke two bones in his hand. They were interned until 28 June, when they were repatriated. Their aircraft was returned on 12 September.

A fourth Bf110, an aircraft of 6 Staffel, was damaged in combat with other Swiss Bf109s near Morteau, in which Oblt Gerhard Kadow (Staffelkapitän) was wounded, and his gunner Uffz Fritz Wünnicke killed. Kadow managed to reach Frieberg and was admitted to hospital. His aircraft was deemed irreparable. His Bf110 may have been in combat with Oblt Francis Liardon of Fl.Kp.6, who claimed a Bf110, while Hptm Werner Lindecker and Lt Egli of Fl.Kp.15 jointly claimed a Bf110 damaged. Both Oblt Erwin Hadorn and Lt Thurnheer had problems with their machine-guns and were unable to make claims. Apart from the damaged Bf109D flown by the wounded Hptm Homberger, Oblt Borner of Fl.Kp.21 also returned with a damaged Bf109D, as did Oblt Kuhn, the only casualties recorded apart from the downed C-35. Nonetheless, Swiss Bf109s were claimed by Oblt Rolf Kaldrack of 4 Staffel, while 6 Staffel's Ltn Günther Tonne, Obfw Harras Matthes and Ltn Rolf Hermichen each claimed a victory, one of these presumably the C-35.

Switzerland's airspace received greater respect from its neighbour following this incident.

CHAPTER V

RAF on the Offensive, June 1940

We sat in the sun on the aerodrome for a long time, waiting for our other pilots. We searched the sky for them for what seemed an hour. But no more arrived. So we went to the Mess and we drank to ourselves and to them.

Flt Lt John Simpson 43 Squadron

While units of the Advanced Force attempted to hold the Luftwaffe at bay, Fighter Command continued to provide escorts to 2 Group Blenheims tasked to assist the ground forces.

On 5 June, Lysanders of 26 Squadron operating from Lympne, carried out coastal and inland recces during the day, including N1211 crewed by Plt Off David Fevez and Sgt Bob Cochrane. Unfortunately they were spotted by a Bf109 flown by Hptm Alfred Müller, the Staffelkapitän of 4./JG3, south-west of Abbeville and shot down. The Lysander crashed near Ercourt at 12:10, killing the crew. With the 51st Highland Division holding a line to the west of the Somme, 2 Group sent 24 Blenheims of 107 and 110 Squadrons to raid Albert, attacking supply columns. That night (5/6 June) Wellingtons of 9 Squadron operated over Holland. One was shot down. Two of the crew were killed and four taken prisoner.

Next day, 6 June, Blenheims from 2 Group were again in action, as were escorting Hurricanes, eighteen of which, drawn equally from 17 and 111 Squadrons, escorted a dozen Blenheims from 40 Squadron, which were tasked to bomb targets at Abbeville. Bf109s from JG3 were encountered shortly after 10:00, and, in a series of dogfights that ensued, the Hurricanes were unable to prevent the Messerschmitts reaching the Blenheims, four of which were shot down, and a fifth badly damaged.

The Blenheims had split up into sections to carry out their bombing attacks, as detailed. Three Messerschmitts attacked the rear section, and Blue Section of 17 Squadron came down from 10,000 feet to 2,000 feet to help. The leader, Flt Lt Bill Toyne, made a deflection attack from 250 yards, closing to 50 yards, saw the 109 dive with engine silent, apparently out of control. Sgt George Steward attacked another at

20 yards range, and saw his bullets inflict severe damage, while Plt Off Ken Manger claimed hits on a third. But one Hurricane and pilot were lost. Sgt Sam Holman (P3360) was last seen under attack by Bf109s some 20 miles east of Abbeville. His victor may have been Ltn Hasso von Perthes of 3.(J)/LG2, this unit having arrived in the area in time to do battle. Meanwhile, pilots of 111 Squadron claimed three more Messerschmitts, the action summarised by the Squadron's diarist:

> F/O [Henry] Ferriss Yellow 1 shot down both these aircraft, one of which was attacking Yellow 2 P/O [Basil] Fisher B. Green Section, led by F/O [David] Bruce also accounted for a Me109, which crashed in flames, and F/O Bruce in addition made an attack on the homeward journey on an Hs126, on which he inflicted considerable damage.

The Hs126 may have been a machine of 3.(H)/21 operating from Doullens, north of Amiens, in which the observer Oblt Bruno Dobner was killed. The uninjured pilot was able to return to base with his damaged aircraft and dead passenger. The diarist continued:

> A further Me109 was encountered over the Channel by P/O [Antony] Fisher, who attacked it and prevented a Blenheim from being attacked. The squadron were fired on by a British cruiser 25 miles off Dungeness on returning from patrol. AA fire was described as accurate and fairly heavy. Sgt Brown Green 3 has not returned but he was still flying in formation after the action, and may have forced-landed in friendly territory.

It transpired that Sgt Ron Brown (P2885) had baled out following an attack by a Bf109 as he prepared to engage another. He injured his thigh muscle and was found by a Guards unit that helped him return to England. He may have been the victim of Oblt Herbert Kijewski and Uffz Alfred Heckmann of 5./JG3. Records suggest one Messerschmitt only was totally lost in this action with the two Hurricane units, Ofw Kurt Bühler of 3.(J)/LG2, who was killed south-east of Abbeville.

During the afternoon the Manston Wing patrolled Abbeville-Amiens, providing escort to another Blenheim raid. They rendezvoused with 18 Blenheims at Le Tréport. Their targets were bridges across the Somme at Abbeville, and troops at Abbeville and St-Valéry. Three hits were claimed on bridges and all the Blenheims returned safely, although one force-landed back at base. One of the escorting Hurricanes of 151 Squadron, flown by Flg Off Charles Atkinson, was obliged to force-land near Rouen following an attack by a Messerschmitt, possibly that flown by Fw Josef Bauer of 7./JG53 who claimed a Hurricane west of Aumale at 15:10, and a second two minutes later. Atkinson was unhurt and following repairs to his aircraft, returned later.

As dawn broke on 7 June, three Blenheims of 107 Squadron were despatched from Wattisham to carry out low-level individual recces over the various battlefronts. Two returned safely, one crew having claimed a Bf109 shot down, but the third sustained flak damage, which wounded the pilot although he made a creditable crash-landing about 15 miles south of Dieppe. Later that morning, two more Blenheims – from 82 Squadron – were sent on similar tasks. Although both were attacked by Bf109s only one was badly damaged, and force-landed on return.

At 11:00, ten Hurricanes of 43 Squadron led by Sqn Ldr George Lott and three of 601 Squadron departed from Tangmere to carry out a patrol between Le Tréport and Amiens. 43 Squadron's A Flight commander, Flt Lt John Simpson recalled:

It was a fine, clear summer day. Our squadron was ordered to patrol with nine aircraft on a line between Le Tréport, Abbeville and Amiens. We flew straight from our base on the English coast and made our landfall south of Le Tréport. Along the whole of our patrol line were smoldering villages, columns of black smoke and burning forests. Others had been there before us. As we turned to make for Rouen, where we were to land for lunch, a squadron of Messerschmitt 109 fighters attacked us from out of the sun. In a second we had broken our formation and each one of us engaged an enemy in a dog fight. There were more of them than of us and it was difficult to fire at one without being attacked by two others at the same time. I finished my ammunition, having fired at three of them. But the battle was too hot for me to follow and see if they crashed. I dived to the ground and made my way over the tree tops to Rouen which I found by following the Seine. When I landed I found that six pilots of my squadron had arrived before me. We were two [it was actually four] short.

In this swift but deadly attack, Flg Off John Edmonds (L1931) was the first victim. His Hurricane burst into flames and crashed at Puisenval; he was killed, as was Flg Off Bill Wilkinson a few minutes later, when L1847 crashed at Bailleul Neuville. Sgt Peter Ottewell believed he then shot down the Messerschmitt pilot that had accounted for Wilkinson. With his engine disabled and a bullet wound in the foot, B Flight commander Flt Lt Tom Rowland (L2116) attempted to bale out only to find that his cockpit canopy had been jammed shut by an exploding cannon shell. Faced with no alternative he succeeded in making a skilful crash-landing. Sgt Jim Hallowes (N2585) reported shooting down the Messerschmitt, but was forced to bale out. He was later awarded a DFM for this action, the citation revealing:

Sgt Hallowes was attacking an enemy aircraft over Northern France when he himself was attacked. His engine being disabled, he proceeded to glide back to friendly territory, but was again attacked when about to abandon his aircraft by parachute. He dropped back into his seat, and as the enemy aircraft passed he delivered such an effective burst of fire as to destroy his opponent. He then made a successful parachute landing.

He dislocated his ankle on landing, but was soon assisted by some British troops, who confirmed that a Messerschmitt had crashed nearby. Sqn Ldr Lott landed safely at Rouen and believed that he had damaged another. On landing Sgt Jimmy Buck burst a tyre and therefore placed his aircraft (L1736) unserviceable.

It seems likely that the main combat was with 4./JG26. Uffz Rudolf Iberle flying 'White 13' crashed at Douvrend near Envermeu, south-east of Dieppe and was killed. A second aircraft from this Staffel, flown by Uffz Wilhelm Phillip, also fell near Dieppe, the pilot baling out wounded. He claimed a Hurricane first, while Uffz Hugo Dahmer, also of 4 Staffel, claimed two Hurricanes shot down south of Dieppe, five minutes apart.

It seems that Messerschmitts of III/JG3 may also have been involved: Uffz Josef Stiglmayer of 9 Staffel claimed a 'Spitfire' at 11:45. Ltn Werner Tismar, also of 9 Staffel, a second at 12:18 (his fifth victory), though Ltn Wolf-Karl Wedding of StabIII/JG3, who claimed two Hurricanes in this action, had his claims disallowed. Obfw Georg Schott of 2.(J)/LG2) was also credited with a Hurricane at 12:16.

The three 601 Squadron aircraft, led by Flt Lt Sir Archie Hope landed safely, and were followed by three more from 601 half-an-hour later, led by Flg Off Hugh Riddle. A fourth aircraft, flown by his brother Jack had apparently got lost and landed at Monti, refuelled and continued to Bourge. Meanwhile, at Rouen-Boos the Hurricane survivors awaited news of their missing comrades, but, as Flt Lt Simpson (N2665) recalled:

[Wg Cdr] Dickie Bain, the Station Commander, would not allow us to stay. The aerodrome had been bombed that morning and they were all preparing to move south. So we had to take off again [at 13:00] for an aerodrome thirty miles away [Beaumont-le-Roger]. I had only ten minutes petrol left when we landed in a cut wheat field. While the ten men in the field refuelled our aircraft with only one petrol tanker between them, we climbed on to an American car and were driven at a hellish speed to a village. It seemed to be very peaceful, except for the motor cycles which flashed through on their way to Headquarters. There was a cart, with flowers and fruit and vegetables for sale. We were hot and thirsty. We talked of the combat, but not much of those who were missing. We just felt that they would turn up. We had a miserable lunch of cold sausage meat, brown bread, and quantities of watered down cider. We had no French money and we had to pay the angry madame with an English pound note.

We went back to the farm but the telephone wires had been cut. While the CO went back to the village to telegraph for orders, we stripped to the waist and lay in the sun, in the middle of the wheat field. We were seven, very white and clean, lying in the wheat. In one corner the Frenchmen were making a haystack and in the other corner some Cockney airmen were belting ammunition. We became thirsty again as we lay in the sun, but nothing could be done about it. The Germans had advanced many miles while we were lying there.

A dozen Hurricanes of 111 Squadron departed at midday for a patrol over the Le Tréport–Aumale area, and were back at Hawkinge by 13:30 to refuel. During the patrol small formations of Messerschmitts were observed, and Flt Lt Robin Powell shot down one, the pilot of which was seen to bale out over friendly territory. A Messerschmitt of III/JG3 was lost near Abbeville during the early afternoon from which the pilot baled out unhurt, and was probably that shot down Powell.

Between 13:15-14:50, Hurricanes from 17, 56 and 79 and 151 Squadrons escorted eighteen Blenheims from 21 and 82 Squadrons, which were detailed to attack road transport in the Abbeville area. There was a lack of suitable targets so most of Blenheims released their bombs on the village of Airaines, on the intersection of two important roads, unaware that it was still in French hands. For two days a group of *Sénégalais Tirailleurs*, French colonial soldiers, had gallantly held up the German advance. It is not known what casualties were caused during the RAF attacks, but the survivors were forced to surrender that evening.[1] In spite of attempted attacks by Bf109s, all the Blenheims returned to base. At least one Blenheim pilot had cause to complain about the lack of protection by the Hurricanes:

> They [the Hurricane pilots] were a mixed blessing as they seemed to be incapable of keeping station across the Channel and to be intent on amusing themselves with mock attacks on our formations. We did not appreciate this or the drain on our nervous energy keeping an eye on them and satisfying ourselves that they were not 109s – so much so that I landed at Hawkinge after one raid and had a set-to with them. I left them with the thought that in future we would open up on anyone coming within range in a belligerent manner – which we did, and that put a stop to it.[2]

At 13:30, a number of Do17s were sighted and 17 Squadron pursued them, only for Sqn Ldr George Emms (P3472) to be shot down by crossfire and killed near Bernaville. A second Hurricane (P2905), flown by Suffolk-born Plt Off Dicky Whittaker DFC, who was also engaging a Dornier, was seen by Plt Off Manger being attacked by two Bf109s near Airaines at 3,000 feet. Manger went into the attack and succeeded in driving one off and shooting down the other. Whittaker, however, was not seen again. He had been credited with at least seven victories.

Half an hour later, at 14:00, a number of Bf110s were engaged by 151 Squadron and Plt Off David Blomeley (P3315) claimed one probably destroyed. Meanwhile, 151 Squadron's Australian Plt Off John 'Peter' Pettigrew (P3529) was also shot down by a Bf109, flown by Fw Fritz Albert of 7./JG3, over St-Valéry, west of Abbeville. His Hurricane crashed at Veules-les-Roses, near the road to Manneville-es-Plains. He was sent to a hospital at St- Valéry-en-Caux, slightly wounded, from where, it was rumoured, that he was 'smuggled' back to England. Bf109s were also encountered by 56 Squadron and Sgt George Smythe (P3473) claimed a 'He113' shot down at 14:00. This was possibly an aircraft of 5./JG26 flown by

Obfw Friedrich Lorenz, who was killed when he crashed at Beaumerie-St-Martin, although he may also have been hit by return fire from the Blenheim he was attacking. Meanwhile, 79 Squadron encountered Bf109s of JG3, one being claimed by Flt Lt Jimmy Davies, as he recalled:

> We found ourselves in the thick of six squadrons of Me109s and 110s, when we saw an unusual type of enemy fighter. They were the new Heinkel 113s [*sic*]. Naturally we couldn't resist the appointment. We got one of each type, and three or four of what we call 'probable'. I was attacking a Me110 when I suddenly realised that there were six Heinkel 113s on my tail. I made a very quick turn to get away from them, and then shot down the Heinkel 113 on the extreme left of that particular formation.

Plt Off Don Stones (N2698) claimed one 'unconfirmed', as did Sgt Ron McQueen, while Plt Off Tom Parker and Flt Lt Roberts each claimed a probable, and Sgt Alf Whitby (P2630) reported shooting down an Hs126, some 6 miles west of Abbeville. Stones later wrote:

> I had my very first fight with a Me109, by now highly respected by all who had met them. We had a turning match for few moments and I managed to get behind him, proving the Hurricane's superior turning circles. I gave him a short burst, but when he dived for the ground he was too fast for me.

It seems feasible that 79 Squadron actually accounted for Uffz Max Seidler of 7 Staffel who was shot down south of Abbeville, wounded, while the Staffelkapitän of 8 Staffel, Oblt Karl-Heinz Sandemann, baled out wounded, as did 8 Staffel's Ltn Winfried Schmidt, who was also wounded; he claimed a Hurricane first. Finally, another 8 Staffel machine returned damaged. Ltn Adolf-Waldemar Kinzinger of 3./JG54 also claimed a Hurricane shot down some 20 miles south-west of Abbeville at 15:10.

The evening (17:15-18:35) Blenheim raid comprised aircraft of 15, 40, 107 and 110 Squadrons to attack targets at Le Tréport, with escort provided by 17, 9/32, and 111 Squadrons. 32 Squadron encountered two He111s, one of which was claimed shot down by Flt Lt Mike Crossley (N2401). In the target area 17 Squadron engaged Bf109s, one being claimed damaged by Sgt Glyn Griffiths near Oisement, while 111 Squadron also met Messerschmitts. Flt Lt Dudley Connors (P3548) and Plt Off Jimmy Walker (P2482) dived on two a few miles south-west of Mauberge and claimed both shot down, while Flt Lt Robin Powell (L1823) dived on another and also believed he had destroyed it. After the attack he found himself alone, apart from a formation of seven Messerschmitts that suddenly appeared and promptly endeavoured to engage him. By a series of tight diving turns, followed by hair-raising hedge-hopping, he managed to evade and return home. Ltn Kurt Bildau of 1./JG20 claimed a Hurricane in the Dieppe-Neufchâtel area at about this time, so possibly 111 Squadron had been engaged with Messerschmitts from this unit.

Meanwhile, Flt Lt John Simpson, idling at Beaumont-le-Roger with the survivors of 43 and 601 Squadrons, continued:

Our orders came. We were to patrol the same line [at 17:45], but two miles into enemy territory. We seemed to be very small, only seven [*sic*], taking off. [In fact, five of 43 and three of 601.] We flew in peace for ten minutes after arriving on our line and then the sky was filled with black puffs of smoke, like hundreds of liver spots. We dived and climbed and none of us was hit. When we turned at the eastern end of our patrol line the sky was fantastic. The black puffs of smoke from the anti-aircraft guns had woven weird patterns in the sky.

The guns stopped firing. We knew then that the German fighters were on their way. Coming towards us, in layers of twenty, were what seemed like a hundred of the enemy, looking like bees in the sky. Some were level with us. Some above. Some below. My CO climbed up with us to sixteen thousand feet and there, while we were being circled by all of those hungry fighters, he gave the order to break up and engage. Forty were bombers. They flew south: perhaps to bomb Rouen. I singled out a Messerschmitt 109 and had a very exciting combat with him. He was a good pilot and he hit me several times. We began to do aerobatics and while he was on his back, I got in a burst which set him on fire. He jumped out, but I did not see his parachute open. His machine was almost burned out before it hit the ground. There were scores of fighters about me, but I still had plenty of ammunition. I got on to the tail of another 109 and while I was firing at him two Messerschmitts fired at me from either side. I continued to fire at the 109 which was badly winged. He suddenly stall-turned sharply to the right, went into a spin and crashed straight into one of the other Messerschmitts which was firing at me.

I couldn't resist following them down. It was a wonderful sight. They stuck together in a sort of embrace of flames, until they were a few hundred feet above the ground. Then they parted and crashed, less than twenty yards apart. I turned for home, flying as low as I could. Crossing the Channel seemed to take hours. I was wet through with sweat. I had been fighting at full throttle. The sea looked cool and it made me feel cooler. But I was afraid that I might be caught without ammunition and go into the sea. There were no boats to rescue me. Luck was with me for there was a mist above the sea. I flew in it for twenty minutes before I emerged into the sunlight again. I was lucky. The Germans had lost me. I could see nothing but the sea and the English coast.

My wireless had been disabled so I could not inquire of my friends. At last I flew over land and very soon I was circling the aerodrome. I landed to find that I was the first home. My CO followed, having bagged two himself [but credited with only one]. We sat in the sun on the aerodrome for a long time, waiting for our other pilots. We searched the sky for them for what seemed an hour. But no more arrived. So we went to the Mess and we drank to ourselves and to them.[3]

All four missing Hurricanes had been shot down although all pilots survived, but Sgt Peter Ottewill (L1608), shot down by Bf109, was badly burned. He had just shot down another 109, his second of the day, when another got the better of him; severely burned about the face, he baled out of his Hurricane. He came down behind German lines, and was hidden by a farmer; then, concealed beneath a load of hay on a cart, he was delivered safely to a retreating British unit.[4] Sgt Charlie Ayling (L1737) crash-landed at Rouen Boos, safe. Plt Off Tony Woods-Scawen (L1726) was shot down by Bf109 and baled out, while 601 Squadron's Flg Off Peter Robinson (P3490) was shot down near Abbeville, wounded, and returned by sea. He claimed a Messerschmitt, as did his colleague Flg Off Tom Hubbard (P3484), who returned safely.

Four Hurricanes were claimed by 3./JG3, possibly in this action: Ltn Helmut Tiedmann (his fifth victory), Fw Bernhard Lampskemper, Ltn Eberhard Bock and Ltn Helmut Meckel. Messerschmitts of I/JG76 may also have been engaged with 43 Squadron's Hurricanes, Oblt Joachim Wandel of 2 Staffel being credited with a Hurricane at about this time, south of Dieppe, while 1 Staffel's Ltn Hans Philipp claimed a Spitfire.

Although 43 Squadron had been decimated and were stood down until replacements arrived, it turned out to be not as bad as it might have been.

On the 8th Sgt Buck came back. On the morning of the 10th, Sgt Ayling, who had succeeded in crash-landing at Rouen, evacuated himself from Garnay airfield in a second-hand Hurricane with a punctured port wing, and the same night Tony Woods-Scawen appeared wearing an army shirt and a tin hat, his opened parachute in folds under his arm. Next, from No. 4 Base Hospital at La Bause, came news that Rowland, Hallowes and Ottewill were all there, the last named terribly burned after his non-sealed gravity tank forward of the instrument panel had blown up. But Hallowes [dislocated ankle] would not be long in rejoining, which saved six out of ten pilots to fight another day.[5]

Woods-Scawen related that after he baled out he had hidden in a ditch. After dark he crept out and walked about 20 miles, still hanging on to his parachute. He found a British patrol with whom he was eventually evacuated. When asked why he had lugged his parachute all the way home, he remarked: "Well, I know this one works and I might have to use it again." The official Air Ministry account of his adventures provides more detail:

Plt Off Woods-Scawen was Blue 2 in the section led by Sqn Ldr Lott when numerous Me109s and Me110s were sighted at about 18:30 over Le Tréport. He formed line astern behind his leader and dived after the quarry. The next thing he knew something hit his machine from behind and he headed his aircraft westward. But it became so hot that he was forced to bale out somewhere well to the west of Dieppe.

He trekked 20 miles to Bacqueville, where he fell in with a motorized transport unit who eventually took him to Rouen. The river was crossed by ferry just ahead of the advanced enemy units. The bridge had already been blown up. His recollection of the journey is hazy, as he was continuously being bombed and spent a lot of his time sheltering in cellars. At Le Mans he fell in with 73 Squadron, and travelled by train to Caen and Cherbourg, where he arrived six days after being shot down. He crossed to England the following day and arrived at his home station carrying his Mae West and parachute.

Next day, 8 June, Hurricanes of 32 and II/79 escorted 82 Squadron Blenheims to the Le Tréport-Aumale area. The weather was hot, the sky cloudless and, as there was no urgency behind the mission, 32 Squadron had plenty of time to taxi out and take-off in good order. 79 Squadron followed behind and together they set course for Beachy Head en route for Le Tréport. Orders were to patrol a beat north and south of this harbour for 40 minutes to prevent the Luftwaffe from harrying the evacuation that was taking place.

Half an hour passed. 32 Squadron was flying at a comfortable 10,000 feet with 79 Squadron three miles behind. The pilots were thinking of lunch at Biggin Hill when a large formation of He111s was sighted, 3,000 feet below and apparently unescorted. There were 20 Heinkels of I/KG1 with eight Bf109s of III/JG26 as escort. 32 Squadron waded into the Heinkels led by Flt Lt Mike Crossley (N2461). The bombers flew steadily on in sections of three, line astern. They presented a perfect target. Red, Blue and Yellow Sections moved into position behind Crossley, flying as Red 1, who reported:

> I just spotted one with a section of two and nipped in behind and gave it a clout and it broke out of line and went down to make a crash-landing in a field. I didn't stop to see whether the crew got out. The enemy fighters were so far behind that we got the chance of attacking the bombers before they came up.

Away went Red Section, leaving the Heinkels clear for Yellow Section to attack. Plt Off Jack Daw (N2532) first sent one down in flames, and then another. The initial attack completed, 32 Squadron reformed for a second attack. Crossley picked off another Heinkel and watched it make a far less dignified landing than his first victim. Plt Off Grubby Grice (P3353) went straight for the leader of a Heinkel section instead of an outsider, closed in to point-blank range, pressed the tit – and was shot out of the sky by cross-fire from the other two. He glided 15 miles before crash-landing at 09:25 near a small village some 10 miles from Rouen, behind allied lines and survived unhurt. Two of 79 Squadron's pilots, Flt Lt Jimmy Davies and Plt Off Don Stones (N2698) also engaged a Heinkel about 15 miles south-east of Le Tréport, as the latter noted:

Three of us caught up with some He111s near Le Tréport and managed to detach one from its formation by damaging it in our first attack and then shot it down in flames in our second. We got split up somehow, probably watching the burning wreckage instead of the sky, and I turned for home.

Two of the Heinkels actually crashed, the crew of that flown by Ltn Heinz Wasserberg of 2 Staffel all surviving, though Gfr Oskar Kaluza and Flgr Christian Jetter were both wounded. All were taken prisoner. The other to crash was from 3 Staffel and fell east of Neufchâtel-en-Bray, in which Fw Harry Wunnicke and his crew also survived. Two others returned to base with combat damage and dead and badly wounded crewmembers, Flgr Ernst Huber aboard one, and Uffz Gerhard Lewioda (killed) and Fw Ottmar Jung on the other.

Meanwhile, the other Hurricanes were soon engaged by the Messerschmitts over Neufchâtel-en-Bray, and two of 32 Squadron were promptly shot down. Plt Off Geoffrey Cherrington (N2582) fell at the same time, his aircraft crashing in flames at Fief-Thoubert near St-Saëns. His remains were initially buried alongside the crash site. The third Hurricane came down five minutes later, when Plt Off Ken Kirkcaldie in N2406 crashed near Houville-en-Vexin. He was last seen being chased by three Messerschmitts. The 28-year-old New Zealander from Wellington was also killed.

Five Hurricanes were claimed in this action, one each by Ltn Walter Blume of 7 Staffel (unconfirmed) and Fw Gerhard Grzymalla of 8 Staffel at 09:15, probably Cherrington (the first to go down), followed by Ltn Josef Haiböck (one unconfirmed) and Fw Erwin Busch of 9 Staffel, who claimed two (of which one was unconfirmed), one at 09:30 and the other ten minutes later.

The German pilots did not have it all their own way, however, Plt Off Daw, following his success against the Heinkels, claimed a Bf109 shot down, two more being credited to Sgt Len Pearce (N2533) and Sgt Edward Bayley (N2968). Two Messerschmitts were also claimed by 79 Squadron, one by the CO, Sqn Ldr John Joslin, and the other by Flg Off David Hayson, a South African. 7 Staffel lost two aircraft, Obfw Hermann Dörr crashing near St-Saëns, not far from where Plt Off Cherrington was killed; he was similarly initially buried by his aircraft. Ltn Hans Mietusch, also of 7 Staffel, baled out near Offranville, and was shot in the buttocks by a French farmer on his way down. He survived and was taken prisoner. Two more Messerschmitts returned to base damaged, Uffz Ernst Ripke of 8 Staffel having been wounded.

79 Squadron's Plt Off Don Stones was meanwhile making for the coast when he encountered another Hurricane:

I soon met another 79 Squadron Hurricane on the same course and when he came alongside, I recognised him as my great friend Woody (Plt Off John Wood). We were both out of ammunition and low on fuel. I saw the small aerodrome of Octeville below me and told Woody that I would go down and ask for petrol, if he would fly around and give me cover against any hostile reception, I landed and found the place deserted except for a Frenchman wheeling a bicycle.

Stones learned that Le Havre was to the south, where petrol would probably be available, as it was when they duly arrived, to be confronted by what seemed to be an aerodrome in peacetime mode. He continued:

> On the aerodrome were two squadrons of French fighters drawn up in parade order. We landed and the French Air Force not only refuelled us but gave us petrol and a bottle of champagne each to take home. The commandant politely declined [our invitation to follow us to England] on the grounds that he was still awaiting orders. In vain we argued that by the time he got an order, it would be to surrender. We even tried to suborn a Czech pilot in French Air Force uniform, but with no success.

Having replenished both stomachs and aircraft, Stones and Wood made their way back to Biggin Hill. The dogfight had also taken the 32 Squadron Hurricanes far to the south.

> Looking at his fuel gauge Flt Lt Crossley saw with a shock that he had petrol for barely 20 minutes' flying. A second Hurricane flew alongside his, its pilot frantically gesturing that he, too, was running out of fuel. Lost, unable to reach Biggin Hill or even the nearest RAF station across the Channel, they turned northwards and searched the sinuous course of the Seine. They chose to land at Rouen-Boos, hoping to find the airfield there still in Allied hands. It was deserted. There was petrol aplenty, but stored in bowsers with no means of syphoning out. One by one other Hurricanes straggled in; then a Tiger Moth flown by two strange squadron leaders with news of refuelling facilities at Dreux, some 40 miles away.

Thus, with full tanks the Hurricanes returned to Biggin Hill in time for lunch, leaving three of their number behind – two forever, and one on the loose. Plt Off Grubby Grice, having found the village deserted, returned to his crash-landed aircraft and soon met some British soldiers, from whom he received a chilly reception; they were survivors of an artillery unit who had been bombed and machine-gunned for more days than they could remember without once seeing an RAF machine. They had not received any home mail for over a month. But they soon cheered up when Grice promised to communicate with their families if, and when, he reached Biggin Hill. The soldiers drove him to Rouen. With another RAF officer he drove from aerodrome to aerodrome, and had travelled some 400 miles before arriving at Dreux, where a flyable aircraft was located. The DH Rapide pilot had intended to fly directly across the Channel but was forced to divert to Jersey by black smoke drifting from burning oil tanks. From Jersey they flew back to England and Grice soon returned to 32 Squadron at Biggin Hill.

Taking off at 11:00, together with No 56 Squadron, 151 Squadron was detailed to give support to a bombing attack on Amiens by two squadrons (107 and 110) of Blenheims. No enemy aircraft were encountered in this support operation but anti-aircraft fire was intense. Plt Off David Blomeley's aircraft (P3315) was hit and did not return to base, as Sqn Ldr Teddy Donaldson later related:

P/O Blomeley's aircraft had been hit by anti-aircraft fire south of Amiens and again near Porges where French gunners opened up at him. His Hurricane, now being on fire meant that he had to bale out and during his descent the French again fired at him and his parachute caught fire. Luckily, he was near the ground before his parachute became ineffective and his only injury was a slight sprain to his ankle. He was taken to Nantes, a French Air Force base, but the French evacuated and left him there to his own devices. The base was bombed on June 9 at 06:30 by the Luftwaffe. That day he spent trying to reach Rouen and having successfully evaded a German mechanised column by cutting across fields, he was given a lift in a French car and reached Paris that evening. From Paris he took a train to Cherbourg, but was bombed at Dreux, but he was fortunate to get on board the LMS steamer the *Duke of Argyll* at 03:00 and arrived at Southampton at 10:30 on June 10.

In the afternoon the 56 and 151 Squadrons were again airborne for a repeat operation and Bf109s were encountered. In the skirmishing that ensued only Sqn Ldr Donaldson was successful and claimed two Bf109s probably destroyed, but the Hurricane flown by Plt Off Tom Maxwell sustained damage and the pilot wounded in one leg though he was able to return and land safely. He was possibly the victim of Ltn Schauff of 8./JG26. Sqn Ldr Donaldson later recalled:

151 Squadron returned from France where we had taken a terrible bashing, bombed whenever we landed, and shot at the whole time we were in the air. 151's last base in France was at Rouen Boos near the River Seine, in mid June. I must recall that my pilots had very little regard for the French as fighting men by this time. The French CO of Rouen aerodrome ordered all side arms of the RAF pilots to be collected, and we thought this a nice gesture as we had been using them for target practise shooting at cans, and they were in a filthy state. But then I discovered he had an arrangement with the local German Commander to come in at a certain time and promise that there would be no more trouble with the "bloody Brits". They would not refuel our Hurricanes so we had to syphon petrol out of damaged planes to put into our serviceable ones, and finally I thought that every aircraft had enough to get back to England if we kept low, out of trouble and used the minimum of power and revolutions to keep the aircraft flying. I would have liked to have shot the French Colonel but did not have time to do so. He was horrified when we took off.

Meanwhile, 56 Squadron were bounced by a number of Bf109s, which made a quick pass before climbing away. Without warning, cannon shells smashed into Plt Off Michael Constable-Maxwell's Hurricane, the splinters wounding him in the leg and foot. Anxiously trying the controls, he found that the Hurricane was still flyable and he decided to try to make it back to North Weald.

The Blenheims now re-appeared and Constable-Maxwell closed up with them, hoping they would report his position if he were forced to land in the sea, but their guns swivelled round in his direction so he hurriedly banked away. He soaked his handkerchief in the blood from his leg and again closed in to the bombers, waving it at them. The nearest crew now realised his predicament and allowed him to tuck in close to them. Arriving back at North Weald, he found that the Hurricane was difficult to land:

> Instead of easing back the stick as the speed got down to approach speed, I had to get it further and further forward, because the nose wanted to rise. I landed with the stick almost fully forward. I had only one elevator and only half a tailplane.

Watching his performance from the ground was Sgt George Smythe, who had landed ahead of Constable-Maxwell:

> It was obvious that his aircraft had been badly shot up. One of his tyres burst on landing and he slewed towards the hangars and finished up near our maintenance hangars. We all rushed across from dispersal to help get him out. The maintenance crew from the hangar got there first. By the time I arrived he was out of the cockpit and being helped down the wing. He had been slightly injured in one foot and blood was oozing out of his flying boot, leaving bloody footmarks on the wing. One of the young groundcrew who was helping him down noticed this and said in an awed voice. "Blimey, I fort it was blue." Constable-Maxwell glanced down at his foot and replied somewhat ruefully. "Oh no, my dear fellow, I can assure you it is ordinary red stuff – always has been."[6]

The wounded pilot was whisked off to Epping Hospital for treatment.

Following the frenetics of the previous two days, and in spite of continued patrols, Fighter Command Hurricanes failed to encounter their adversaries over the coastal reaches of France on either 9 or 10 June. On the latter date, sixty-three sorties were flown over the French coast between Le Tréport and Fécamp, including nine Hurricanes of 245 Squadron on a Blenheim escort to Rouen. Apart from some ineffective AA fire the trip was uneventful except for extensive damage caused to Sgt Bill Banks' N2703 when his aircraft hit a flock of birds. Most of the air action was currently taking place over the evacuation of British and French troops from Le Havre, where the AASF squadrons were responsible for their protection (see

Chaper II). At least the break allowed the savaged home-based Hurricane units to lick their wounds and replenish their stock. 43 Squadron in particular was taken out of the line to await replacement aircraft and pilots.

There occurred a resurgence of aerial activity over and off the French coast on 11 June, with Fighter Command flying 147 sorties. Although there were several engagements and claims were made, only one Hurricane was lost. Hurricanes of 32 Squadron were in action at 12:45, meeting several Hs126 observation machines, not the easiest of targets despite their low speed. Two were claimed shot down by Plt Off Jack Daw (P3677) and Plt Off Rupert Smythe (P3481), and possibly a third by another pilot. Indeed, an Hs126 of 1.(H)/14 flown by Fw Gerhard Wendler did go down south-east of Rethel in which the observer Ltn Karl-Heinz Schreiber was seriously wounded, but allegedly shot down by H-75s of GCII/4. The same French unit was also credited with a second Hs126, a machine from 2.(H)/23 in which the observer Ltn Eberhard Peters was wounded. Sgt Eric Jones (N2533/GZ-X) was hit – probably by return fire from one of the Henschels – and was forced to carry out an emergency landing near Montreuil. Unhurt, he climbed out and ran for it (see Appendix II).

111 and 615 Squadrons took-off as escort to Blenheims at 13:30, and then tasked to patrol the Le Havre area, where shipping was under attack. The Blenheims came under attack from Bf109s of 2./JG3, both Hurricane squadrons engaging. Yellow Section of 111 Squadron, led by Sgt Bill Dymond (P2888), were first to engage, Dymond claiming a Messerschmitt that fell in flames. Yellow 3, Flg Off Tom Higgs (P3530), damaged another Messerschmitt but his own aircraft came under attack, and was hit in the port wing. Blue and Green Sections joined the melee, Sqn Ldr Thompson (P3524) reported shooting down a Bf109, and fired at another before emptying his ammunition into a Ju88, whilst Blue 2, Plt Off Jimmy Walker (P3399) chased a Do215 which he claimed shot down in flames. Flg Off David Bruce (P3548) enjoyed even greater success, claiming two Bf109s and a Do215, the latter force-landing in a ploughed field. Two Do17Ms of Stab/KG28 were lost, one crash-landing near Le Havre (apparently Bruce's victim) and the other probably falling into the sea. Both crews survived. A Bf110 was claimed by 615 Squadron's Flg Off Tony Eyre (P2754/O), although this was probably one of the Dorniers. The pilots reported observing two ships sinking off Le Havre. Uffz Lutz Uth of 2./JG3 crashed on the coast between Berneval-le-Grand and Bellville-sur-Mer and was killed, while two more of 2 Staffel's aircraft crash-landed badly damaged following combat north of Le Havre. Neither pilot was hurt.

At 19:00, a dozen Hurricanes of 145 Squadron, accompanied by six of 601 Squadron escorted nine Blenheims to raid Le Havre. This operation was uneventful.

*****

Prime Minister Churchill's presence was again urgently requested by the French, and he promptly flew – with Secretary of State for War Eden, and Generals Ismay and Dill (CIGS) – to Briare airfield near Orléans to where the French government now found itself. With an escort provided by a dozen Spitfires, the two-hour flight aboard the Flamingo (R2764 of 24 Squadron) was achieved without event, but the ensuing meeting was full of venom. With French PM M. Reynaud taking a back seat, the military commander General Weygand declared that every British fighter squadron should immediately be thrown into the battle at this "decisive point." Adding: "It is therefore wrong to keep any squadrons back in England." To which Churchill replied (as recorded by General Ismay):

> This is not the decisive point and this is not the decisive moment. That moment will come when Hitler hurls his Luftwaffe against Great Britain. If we can keep command of the air, and if we can keep the seas open, as we certainly shall keep them open, we will win it all back for you.[7]

The meeting ended with Reynaud's pro-German mistress the Countess Hélène de Portes making an attempt to stab Churchill, with only the timely intervention of his bodyguard Walter Thompson saving the day (12 June). The PM and his party returned to England next day, but on this occasion there was a little excitement, as he later noted:

> Lack of suitable petrol made it impossible for the twelve Spitfires to escort us. We were assured that it would be cloudy all the way. It was urgently necessary to [get] back home. Accordingly we started alone, calling for an escort to meet us, if possible, over the Channel. As we approached the coast the skies cleared and presently became cloudless.
>   Eight thousand feet below us on our right hand was Le Havre, burning. The smoke drifted away to the eastward. No new escort was to be seen. Presently I noticed some consultations going on with the captain, and immediately we dived to a hundred feet or so above the calm sea. What had happened? I learned later that they had seen two German aircraft [He111s] below us firing at the fishing boats. We were lucky their pilots did not look upwards. The new escort met us as we approached the English shore, and the faithful Flamingo alighted safely at Hendon.[8]

According to a companion, Winston later remarked: 'The German pilot was not aware just how close he had been to winning an Iron Cross 1st Class!' Nonetheless, the PM was back in France the following day for one final meeting with his French counterpart, but to no avail.

*****

Although Fighter Command patrols continued across the Channel, no action ensued. However, on 15 June, the unlucky Sgt Bill Banks of 245 Squadron, who had collided with a flock of birds a few days earlier, had his aircraft (N2558) badly damaged by AA shrapnel near Béthune, during another Blenheim escort. Again he was able to return safely. By day on 16 June, squadrons from Fighter Command each flew two sorties either in convoy patrols of squadron strength or as escorts to Blenheims. It was their biggest effort since Dunkirk, but this time they encountered few enemy aircraft. Hurricanes and Spitfires patrolled the area of the evacuation, but the Germans mainly confined their efforts to minelaying. Although this delayed movement, while minesweepers cleared the channels, it had no other effect on operations. This was fortunate, for the shipping used included large troopships, including the *Arandora Star*, the *Strathaird*, and the *Otranto*, which would have been vulnerable to aerial attack.

The only divisive encounter during the day was when a Spitfire shot down a Blenheim in mistake for a Ju88. Plt Off Clive Wylie, a New Zealander from Masterton, flying R3817 of 59 Squadron on a recce, crashed with his crew near Dreux. He, together with Sgt Jimmy Harris and AC1 Tommy Thomas were killed. The identity of the Spitfire pilot responsible for this incident remains unknown.

Next day, 17 June, much flying was curtailed by bad weather and low cloud. One section of 56 Squadron Hurricanes took off from North Weald to undertake a patrol, but soon after becoming airborne the weather closed in. On completion of the patrol, the section leader Flg Off 'Minnie' Ereminsky[9] (P2882) decided to return to base at low level. Visibility was poor even at this altitude and he struck the roof of a house at West Horsley in Surrey.

Wg Cdr Beamish, flying 151 Squadron's DZ-B, again joined 151 Squadron on 18 June, for an escort mission to Blenheims briefed to attack a target south of Cherbourg. Sqn Ldr Teddy Donaldson led the two sections and the Wingco tagged on behind. They rendezvoused with 56 Squadron before picking up the Blenheims at Tangmere. Sqn Ldr Donaldson reported:

> German bombers were intercepted as they attacked shipping. There were three Heinkel 111s operating and in the fight which followed, one of the Heinkels was seen to have its engines on fire, and another disappeared with its undercarriage down and presumably severely damaged. P/O Wright baled out and a destroyer steamed to the spot where he was seen to go down. Sgt Aslin was reported missing from the patrol. The return fire from the enemy aircraft was very severe, it having resulted in two of 151's Hurricanes being shot down.

For his part, Wg Cdr Beamish wrote:

> After escorting bombers we were on patrol near Cherbourg and sighted three He111s slightly above us and with six Me109s above them. There was considerable AA fire in the vicinity. We immediately climbed to head off and attack the Heinkels, closing right in. During my attack I sighted on the fuselage and then on each engine in turn. The gunner was killed and one

engine burst into huge flames. The bomber dived down and hobbled away. The undercarriage was also damaged and it is presumed that the enemy must have been heavily armoured as the range was point blank. Immediately on being attacked the He111s jettisoned the rest of their bombs. The enemy was badly shot up.

Wg Cdr Beamish claimed his victim as 'severely hit', while the two missing pilots were credited with a 'Ju88' destroyed by Sgt Maurice Aslin (P3324), and a Heinkel probable plus another damaged by Plt Off Les Wright (P3313). In fact, the Heinkel of 5./KG51 flown by Fw Herbert Strahl crashed into the sea, with the loss of the pilot and Uffz Siegfried Auerswald, while Fw Alois Dennerl, Uffz Hans Kling and Uffz Wilhelm Zeyer – all wounded – were rescued from the sea by a British destroyer. A second Heinkel from the same Staffel returned damaged, with Uffz Willi Scheeberger badly wounded; he was admitted to hospital in Essen-Mülheim but died of his wounds.

Another tragic case of mistaken identity occurred when eleven Spitfires of 54 Squadron were despatched at 20:33 to recce airfields in the Amiens area, when they were vectored to investigate enemy aircraft reported over Boulogne. Red Section led by Sqn Ldr 'Prof' Leathart (N3160), with Plt Offs Al Deere (P9390) and Johnny Allen (P9389), subsequently encountered three Ju88s, as Deere recalled:

As we levelled out at 4,000 feet, Johnny re-established contact with the enemy aircraft which he identified as three Ju88s flying in loose formation. They were probably in search for shipping targets. We were now closing fast but before we could get within range the enemy spotted us and immediately boke formation, each pilot making for the nearest cloud cover. Before, however, my target could disappear I had him in my sights. The first burst was on target, the De Wilde [tracer] confirming my aim as it burst in yellow splotches along the starboard wing. Almost immediately fire appeared in the engine but before I could repeat the dose the Junkers entered cloud. I followed, peering eagerly into the opaque dampness which now enveloped my aircraft. I had little hope of picking him up in cloud.

Prof and Johnny followed me to land in quick succession. It was obvious from the blackened edges of their wings that they too had fired their guns. Prof's story was similar to mine. Johnny's more conclusive. He had, to use his own words, "set the Junkers alight from stem to stern." Apparently two of the crew members managed to bale out successfully and, as they were but a few miles off the French coast, he thought their chances of being picked up were very good.[10]

However, Allen's own combat report was not quite as revealing:

On looking up, saw an e/a at 20,000 feet. I was at 17,000 feet. I turned to give chase, noticed a second e/a ahead and, when overtaking my objective, saw another 30 still further away. I climbed at full throttle and had no difficulty in overtaking the enemy, which I recognised as a Ju88 when 300 yards away. I got straight on to his tail and gave a short burst of about two seconds. Realising that I was further away than necessary, I close to about 150 yards, firing for about seven seconds. E/a appeared to throttle back and, since I was overtaking the enemy rapidly, I broke away to the left. Enemy fire, which was experienced near the end of my second burst, went above me. The e/a did not lose height during the attack. Both engines of the e/a were hit. The starboard one was badly damaged and black smoke was coming from the port engine. As I broke away, the e/a did likewise and he was not seen again.

There is no record of Ju88 losses or combats, or losses of any other German bomber types in this area, but Blenheim L9266 of 59 Squadron was reported to have fallen to a Spitfire near Fricourt, three miles east of Albert. Flg Off Frank Bird, an Irish volunteer from Co. Cork, managed a crash-landing but he and his crewmen, Sgt Charles Brinn and AC2 Gordon Coles, were killed.

*****

At 06:30 on the morning of 18 June, the first of twelve Blenheims and a similar number of Hurricanes began taking off from Tangmere destined for Egypt. The air convoy was divided into four flights, each of three Blenheims and three Hurricanes. The Hurricane pilots were drawn from 4 Ferry Pilots' Pool at RAF Kemble, as Plt Off Dick Sugden recalled:

The four of us had just got back from Cirencester – Reg Carter, Pat Collins, Arthur Maycock and myself – and over supper were arguing about whether we should visit the local hop. Before we reached any decision, however, someone shouted something about all Hurricane and Blenheim pilots were wanted down by the hangar. We sauntered off, to find a crowd of blokes lounging and smoking, all talking about a buckshee trip to Egypt. It looked as though we might be doing something exciting – most of us were pretty browned off with the usual sort of trip [mainly ferrying Hurricanes to various squadrons].

Anyway, Sqn Ldr Jimmy Wilde soon appeared and we were told that 12 Blenheim pilots and 12 Hurricane pilots were needed to ferry machines to Egypt at a moment's notice. Somewhat to my amazement, I found myself volunteering and being accepted. The other three [Carter, Collins and Maycock] were also chosen and there was a mad rush to our tents to pack a few odds and ends.

All the guns were removed from the Hurricanes and were to be carried by the Blenheims. This was necessary partly because of the difficulties of fitting both long-range underwing fuel tanks and guns, and partly owing to the question of load with the additional fuel aboard. It would have been possible to retain six guns but the fuel pipes to the outboard tanks would have passed very close to these and, if used, there might have been the chance of fire.

The proposed route across France was to start at Cap Frehel and then to Nantes, Bordeaux, Castres and Marignane, and then across the Mediterranean to Tunis, El Djem and on to Mersa Matruh, but at the eleventh hour the crews were advised that a change of route was necessary as a result of information received from Bordeaux. They were now to fly to Perpignan from Bordeaux instead of to Castres, and from there to Sétif (Tunisia) and then to Malta. An hour later the Blenheim leader received a further call, changing the route to Cap Frehel-Marignane-Sétif-Malta.

It was the Air Ministry's intention that in flying to Marignane the aircraft would keep to the route laid down in written orders – i.e. via Nantes and Bordeaux, although the aircraft were not to land at the latter for refuelling purposes. However, the Blenheim leader understood the change to mean that Bordeaux should be cut out altogether, with the aircraft expected to fly directly from Cap Frehel to Maginane, this instruction being subsequently given to his flight commanders. Furthermore, that beyond Marignane the route was to be Tunis to Malta. This course had two major disadvantages: it passed over Monts d'Auvergne, where weather conditions were likely to become more difficult than the route via Nantes and Bordeaux, which led along the coast and thence by the valley of the Gironde; secondly, it would bring the formation nearer to the advancing Germans. Disaster faced the operation: only three Blenheims and six Hurricanes would eventually reach Malta (see Appendix V).

*****

On 19 June, it was the Luftwaffe's turn to be involved in a friendly fire incident. At 12:10, Ju87s of I/StG.1 attacked the fortress at Cherbourg. The Stukas were escorted by Bf109s of II/JG3, which shot down one of their own in error for a Hurricane or Spitfire. Uffz Fritz Mias (Black 8/1464) of 5 Staffel crash-landed and his aircraft was completely burned, although he survived unhurt and returned to his unit next day.

Blenheims of 15, 18 and 82 Squadrons raided German-occupied Rouen-Boos airfield, opening a campaign against airfields that would run almost to the end of the war. ZG26 reported two Bf110s destroyed, one each from 6 and 9 Staffeln, and three more from III Gruppen seriously damaged. The crew of the 6 Staffel machine, Oblt August-Wilhem Bier and Uffz Georg Schutz, were both wounded during the attack.

A further raid on Rouen-Boos was carried out the following morning, 20 June, by Hurricanes from 245 Squadron commanded by New Zealander Sqn Ldr Eric Whitley. Flying with him were fellow-countrymen Flt Lt Noel Mowat from Otago and Plt Off Doug Spence from Christchurch. The attack was made by two sections, led by Whitley and Mowat respectively, a third being left above for protection. There were some 50 German aircraft on the ground – Bf110s, Ju87s and Ju52s – and a considerable number of these were reported damaged and four left on fire. Blenheims of 107 Squadron made a follow-up raid in the afternoon. ZG26 again took the brunt of the attacks, two aircraft from 8 Staffel being written-off, as was one from 1./ZG1; a pilot of this unit, Uffz Erich Michi, was wounded.

At 07:00 on 22 June, Sqn Ldr Joe Kayll (P2871) set off at the head of nine Hurricanes of 615 Squadron to carry out a patrol near Rouen, where a formation of He111s (probably from III/KG1) was encountered, escorted by Bf110s of 7./ZG26. While one flight of Hurricanes went after the Heinkels, with Sqn Ldr Kayll claiming one shot down and another as damaged, and Plt Off Peter Collard (P2768) claiming a probable, the other flight tackled the escort. Flt Lt Jim Sanders (P3487) claimed shot one and one probable, and Flg Off Tony Eyre (P2801) one probable, but lost Plt Off John Lloyd (P2764). He was probably the victim of Ltn Kuno-Adalbert Konopka. No Bf110s appeared to have been lost in this action, but a Heinkel crash-landed at Glisy, near Amiens, and may have been a victim of the Hurricanes. Rather bizarrely, Flg Off Keith Lofts (P2578) reported meeting a Ju52, which he attacked without conclusive results, although the following report appeared in the press:

> According to a report from Zurich, the German General Fritz Löb, who was in command of the German air forces on the Dutch and French coasts, was making a reconnaissance flight when a British fighter shot down the machine in which he was flying, and he was killed.[11]

In the afternoon, 245 Squadron despatched seven Hurricanes of A Flight led by Flt Lt James Thomson to patrol Calais at 10,000 feet. No aircraft were sighted but heavy AA fire was experienced, the extremely unfortunate Sgt Bill Banks being on the receiving end. His aircraft, N2487, was again badly damaged by shrapnel. For the third time in less than two weeks, Banks was obliged to bring back a damaged machine.

There occurred another friendly fire incident on the night of 22/23 June, when the Bf110 crewed by Fw Martin Thier and Fw Adolf Brutsche suffered radio failure when there was zero ground visibility. Thier elected to divert to Paderborn. With his navigation lights illuminated he found himself easy prey for a Bf109 pilot doing a little 'moonlighting' in the air. The over-ambitious pilot from Paderborn was also airborne on his own initiative on a night-fighting sortie, and promptly shot down the Bf110, killing both the crew.

Hurricanes of 245 Squadron and Bf109s from 3.(J)/LG2 skirmished off Calais during the afternoon of 23 June. Plt Off Johnny Southwell (N2486) claimed a Messerschmitt as probably destroyed, while Ltn Erwin Straznicky and Ltn Albert Striberny each claimed a Hurricane. However, there were no losses on either side although an II/LG2 Bf109 was damaged in a crash-landing.

25 June witnessed a clash over Abbeville between nine Spitfires of 65 Squadron and an estimated seven Bf109s, believed from III/JG3. A report that appeared in *Flight* revealed:

> Fighter Command has not confined its energies to defence. Patrols are still sent out over Northern France. Nine Spitfires of one squadron were there and presently they saw seven Me109s at a higher altitude. Both formations began to climb, and a dogfight followed. While this was in progress ten more Messerschmitts of the same type joined in. Our pilots out-manoeuvred them and shot down three, while three others were seriously damaged and are believed to have been destroyed.

Flt Sgt Bill Franklin (N3164) claimed two destroyed, while Flg Off Ken Hart (R6618) was credited with one; two probable were awarded to Plt Off Tommy Smart (K9915), and another to Plt Off Wilf Maitland-Walker (K9909). Two Bf109s force-landed at Valheureux out of fuel, and both sustained damage, but it is unclear if these were involved in combat with 65 Squadron.

Next day, 26 June, 110 Squadron despatched in total a dozen Blenheims – two aircraft each were sent to Gelsenkirchen, Hamburg, Hamm, Münster, Soest and Wedel. The take off times were spread out during the day so everyone went singly. Four Bf109s of 3./JG54 encountered a lone Blenheim near Rotterdam, R3776 flown by Plt Off Cyril Worboys, as recounted by Ltn Hans Schmoller-Haldy:

> A Bristol Blenheim which was attacked in enemy territory by a flight of four 109s should have been easy prey, but it defended with courage and did not give in. The rear-gunner [Sgt Ken Cooper] sent me down with some 20 bullets in my aircraft's body and heavy bleeding from a painful wound in my left leg. I always hoped that the Blenheim, which was apparently severely hit in its port wing, returned safely to England.

However, the Blenheim did not return to its base at Wattisham but fell into the sea with the loss of Plt Off Worboys and his crew. When Bf109s of 4./JG26 attempted to intercept another – possibly Flg Off Hill's R3828 – Ltn Otto-Heinrich Hilleke's aircraft was also hit by return fire from the gunner (Sgt Gray). The German six-victory ace broke his neck attempting to bale out. His friend, Ltn Kurt Ebersberger, provided a tribute:

> We miss his humour and harmonica playing. Often, when we were at Chicore, our second base in Belgium, after dinner in our handsome château, with a bottle of good Burgundy at hand, Hilleke used to play for us. We would discuss the events of the day and air fighting as well as many matters that were not connected with the Service. Anything unpleasant was dismissed with a joke, so that we were always in a happy and confident mood. We were at

ease and out of sight of higher authority. When we felt like it we went out roaming the district. The Gruppe commander flew in the lead with 'Hinnak' (Hilleke's nickname) near him. They were the first to engage the enemy and had a stack of victories. Hinnak was our most successful pilot.

On 27 June, Bf109s of II/JG26 were off at first light to continue escorting bombing raids on Boulogne, Calais and Dunkirk, as Ebersberger recorded:

> Going back and forth we saw below us the widespread fighting in Flanders, burning towns and villages, flames at the mouths of heavy guns which were often a signpost for us when returning with our last drop of petrol [...] we flew almost every day with our bombers as they attacked ports, fuel tanks and ammunition dumps along the coast. The British began to embark their troops and ship them back to their island. It didn't suit the British that we interfered with their withdrawal plan. We were often outnumbered, which didn't bother us in the slightest. Our most enjoyable flights were along the steep coast from Dieppe to Le Havre with British or French warships going to and fro beneath us. On the way back we would fly low over the beaches all the way from Le Touquet and French people peacefully swimming would point at us. How fast we went and what a row we made.

In company with three other squadrons, 79 Squadron took off from Manston at 10:15 to escort a flight of Blenheims on a PR recce over St-Valéry. The outward journey proved uneventful but the formation was attacked by Bf109s of II/JG51 on the return flight. 79 Squadron, flying top cover at 10,000 feet, spotted three Messerschmitts diving out of the sun. Plt Off Tom Parker called out a warning but his R/T was unserviceable and two Hurricanes were shot down in flames by Ltn Hermann Striebel of 5 Staffel and Uffz Rudolf Delfs of 6 Staffel. Sgt Ron McQueen (P3401) was seen to bale out, apparently unhurt, and Hurricanes circled him in the sea for 90 minutes until the Rye lifeboat reached him, but he was found to be dead. The second Hurricane (P3591) had been flown by Flt Lt Jimmy Davies. He was not found. In addition, a Blenheim was claimed by Hptm Horst Tietzen, Staffelkapitän of 5 Staffel.

At about 18:30, Aircraftman Peter Lingard Walker – presumably a frustrated would-be fighter pilot – became airborne in a 17 Squadron Hurricane (P3778) but crashed after being in the air for about five minutes. The Hurricane burst into flames on impact and 24-year-old Walker, from Paignton in Devon, was sadly killed. Of the incident Plt Off Bird-Wilson remembered:

> We were at readiness when I saw the flight commander's Hurricane start up and take off. It headed north on the take-off run then juddered round the airfield at low speed and in a terrible angle of attack. We looked round but all the pilots were accounted for. By this time the Hurricane had staggered to the

west, then it suddenly turned on its back and crashed straight into the ground. We found out later that an airman of the squadron had said to another chap that Hurricanes were easy to fly, which then became a challenge.

Due to lack of information coming out of Holland, six Blenheim fighters of 235 Squadron were despatched during the afternoon to search the Dutch coastline in the vicinity of the Zuider Zee. They did not set off individually but as a formation led by Sqn Ldr Ronnie Clarke. On reaching the Dutch coast, two Bf109s of Stab I/JG54 pounced on the Blenheims from out of cloud, as recalled by Plt Off Ollie Wakefield aboard Flg Off Reg Peacock's N3542:

> The most stunning and frightening moment of my young life when the Bf109s shot out of the glorious sparse cloud in a head-on attack. It was a stupendous sight and last for two or three minutes as we found ourselves breaking formation and milling around with the sky with 109s as our dancing partners![12]

Plt Off Peter Weil's aircraft (N6957) was the first to fall, just off Egmond; there were no survivors; he, Sgt Sid Bartlett and Sgt Alan Kempster all died in the aircraft. The next to go down was P6958 piloted by Plt Off Hugh Pardoe-Williams, which bellied in at Ouderkerk-on-Amstel with its observer Sgt Cliff Thorley already dead. The gunner, Sgt Ed Saunders, was killed while Pardoe-Williams had been badly wounded but was dragged clear of the burning wreck, only to succumb to his injuries two days later. A third Blenheim, N3543 flown by Plt Off Alan Wales, crash-landed on the outskirts of Oegstgeest after his crew baled out, unfortunately too low for their parachutes to open and both Sgt John Needham and Sgt Tom Jordan died from their injuries. The pilot was found dead in the wreckage. Two of the crew of the final Blenheim (L9447) shot down in this tragic action, Plt Off John Cronin, a New Zealander, and his gunner Sgt Phil Lloyd, were killed, the pilot having baled out but was apparently hit by the tailplane, while Lloyd as killed in the attack. Observer Sgt Aubrey Lancaster survived the jump but was taken prisoner.

It seems that the carnage was wrought by just the two pilots, Hptm Hubertus von Bonin, who claimed three Blenheims in fifteen minutes, with the other being claimed by his wingman, Gfr Willi Kopp of 2 Staffel.[13] Thus, only two Blenheims of the six that had set out less than two hours earlier returned to Bircham Newton, those flown by Sqn Ldr Clarke and Flg Off Peacock, whose observer Plt Off Wakefield continued:

> After the attack we decided it would be unwise to return the way we had entered, so we flew south to Amsterdam photographed the harbour with no sign of German naval units, flew along the inner coast of the Zuider Zee and passed Hoorn to Texel where, at 14:30 to the south-west we encountered a He115 seaplane flying at 400 feet. Peacock attacked and only broke off the engagement when all remaining 1,000 rounds were expended.

The fate of the He115 is unrecorded, but Peacock (N3542) was credited with shooting down a Bf109 and sharing in the claimed damage of another.

At 06:58 on 28 June, a single He111 attacked the destroyer HMS *Codrington* about one mile from the Folkestone Light vessel, but caused no damage or casualties. The destroyer had been ordered to pick up a Hurricane pilot seven miles off Boulogne following a skirmish between a patrol of Hurricanes of 151 Squadron and three Bf109s of 3./JG20. Flg Off Ken Newton, an English-born New Zealander, had been seen to bale out of P3322 and fall into the sea, but he was not found. His victor was the Ltn Karl-Heinz Schnell, his third victory. During the day Fw Werner Hübner of 4./JG 51 claimed a Blenheim shot down while in the early afternoon, at 16:10, three Bf109s swept in at sea level and machine-gunned searchlight positions at Dover, passing over the harbour. No radar warning was received due to their low-level approach and the guns did not respond until it was too late. Vice-Admiral, Dover, commented:

These two incidents, unimportant in themselves and their results, were interesting in that they were the first attacks of their kind following the occupation by the enemy of the French coast. The surprising feature was perhaps that such attacks had not occurred sooner and more frequently.

On the morning of 29 June, three Spitfires from 72 Squadron flown by Flt Lt 'Hiram' Smith (P9438), Plt Off Douglas Winter (L1092) and Sgt Malcolm Gray (P9460) out of Acklington on patrol when an unidentified aircraft was seen flying east at 20,000 feet about ten miles north-east of Holy Island. They followed for about 20 minutes while climbing to 25,000 feet. The intruder was identified as a Do17 upon which the Spitfires delivered a line astern attack. The Dornier commenced violent stall turns and after the first two attacks white smoke was seen from both engines. As Sgt Gray attacked, the aircraft stall-turned steeply and he was able to get in three short bursts into the cockpit area. Smith came in again and fired from close range, whereupon the recce machine went into a steep dive into sea and burst into flames before breaking up. Return fire had damaged Smith's engine but he was able to return safely to base. Their victim was in fact a Do215 from Aufkl.ObdL.

2 Group Blenheims were again called to action at 11:00 on 30 June, when twelve from 107 Squadron with an escort of twenty-three Hurricanes (twelve from 111 Squadron and eleven from 615 Squadron) set out to raid Merville. On arrival they met heavy flak and fighter opposition, surviving crew reported being pursued by four Messerschmitts. Three Blenheims were shot down (Ltn Hans Kolbow and Ltn Karl-Heinz Schnell of 3./JG20 claiming one each, as did Ltn Hermann Staiger and Fw Wilhelm Koslowski of 1./JG20); four of the Blenheim crewmen survived to be taken prisoner. A fourth Blenheim was damaged and returned to base where it force-landed. Meanwhile, the Hurricanes engaged the Messerschmitts, Flt Lt James Sanders (P3487) and Plt Off Cecil 'Charlie' Young (P3380) of 615 Squadron each claiming one probably destroyed; the latter was born at Kuala Lumpar in Malaya, where his parent still lived. In a letter home, he wrote:

Approaching Merville at 12,000feet, about 2,000 feet above Blenheim bombers. The section leader gave "Tally Ho! Starboard." We dived down on 3 Me109s. I myself attacked one just as it had begun its attack on the last Blenheim of the formation. I opened fire at 300 yards - at the same moment the Blenheim caught fire. I then closed into about 50 yards. Bits flew off the enemy machine and a large column of smoke issued forth as it went into a vertical dive towards the ground. Ammunition exhausted, I turned towards home and was chased by another 3 Me109s and was forced to land at Martlesham Heath.

One more Messerschmitt was claimed as a probable by Flg Off Herbert Giddings of 111 Squadron.

An hour later, at 12:35, six Blenheims of 110 Squadron set off to attack a refuelling station at Vignacourt, with escort provided by Hurricanes from 151 and 56 Squadrons. On the return flight, six Bf109s attacked the formation at about 14:20, the Hurricanes turning to defend the bombers. In the ensuing series of scraps, 151 Squadron claimed three plus two probables including two by Wg Cdr Victor Beamish, again flying with the North Weald squadrons:

I was on patrol with 56 and 151 Squadrons escorting Blenheims at 15,000 feet. Six Me109s were seen attacking the bombers at 5,000 feet. I dived down with the rest of the squadron and accounted for two Me109s. One disintegrated in the air and the other poured smoke from the fuselage and both wings and crashed into the sea. I attacked from astern and e/a had not time for evasive tactics.

However, the CO, Sqn Ldr Donaldson (P3787) was shot down and baled out into the sea, from where he was rescued. New Zealander Flg Off Buzz Allen claimed a Messerschmitt shot down, while Flt Lt Dick Smith was credited with a probable. It would seem that the Messerschmitts were from I(J)/LG2 led by Ltn Herbert Ihlefeld, who claimed a Blenheim shot down, followed five minutes later by a 'Spitfire'. A second Blenheim was claimed by Obfw Erwin Clausen of 3 Staffel, but it was not allowed. The aircraft of both Ihlefeld and Clausen were badly damaged although each was able to return to base. However, Uffz Herbert Rauhut of 2 Staffel was shot down and killed. By now more Bf109s, from 3./JG20, had joined the battle, Ltn Kolbow, Uffz Theodor Kröll and Fw Friedrich Klotz each claiming a 'Spitfire', though the latter was also shot down, his aircraft (Yellow 7) crashing west of Étaples. He survived.

Meanwhile, two Hurricanes of 56 Squadron had become separated and met five Bf109s over Le Tréport, probably from III/JG3. Sgt Peter Hillwood (P2970) claimed one shot down in flames and another probably destroyed, while Sgt George Smythe (P3473) also reported shooting down one in flames. The combat was with 7 and 9./JG3, the latter unit losing its Staffelkapitän Oblt Heinz Kupka, who was killed when his aircraft crashed near Mons-Boubert. In return, 9 Staffel's Gfr Otto Wessling was credited with his first victory, a Hurricane west of St-Omer. Three pilots of 7 Staffel each claimed a Hurricane but neither Obfw Hans Heitmann, Uffz Eberhard von Boremski nor Gfr Karl Pfeiffer was officially allowed their victories.

Of his enforced dip the sea, Sqn Ldr Donaldson recalled:

Air Vice-Marshal Keith Park, Air Officer Commanding No 11 Group, which directly faced the Luftwaffe across the Channel was utterly dedicated to the winning of the Battle and was not an entirely defensive man. On certain days he sent squadrons over France to fight Germans over their own bases. I think this gave the Germans the impression that the RAF was much stronger than it was.

Eventually, flying home from this, [the Blenheim] squadron was jumped by Messerschmitts low over the sea and a terrific battle started. It was then that a particularly threatening Messerschmitt arrived and went straight for me. We fought for fifteen minutes ending up with head-on attacks on each other. Usually, Messerschmitts did not like this, for a Hurricane could turn more sharply, so it usually made off, which it could do so at 60 mph faster than the Hurricane.

In this case, on about the fourth head-on attack, shells and bullets started to strike my poor aircraft. The first shell knocked my poor oil tank clean out of the leading edge of the wing, so I knew the engine could not run much longer. Then the petrol tank blew up and my clothes caught fire and I became hot but still the bastard continued to shoot. My gloves were burning and my goggles frizzled up but I took neither off – luckily!

I undid my straps and climbed on the wing, for the Hurricane was flying very slowly and I could actually see the burning wing bending upwards. Then I realised with alarm that I was only 800 feet off the sea. I thought this too low for a safe bale out but at this time I fell off and it took me seconds to locate the pull ring, which I must have pulled, for, as I was about to hit the water, my parachute opened. I disappeared to the full extent of the cords and the wind got under the parachute and lifted me like a missile to the surface and started pulling me at about 3 mph towards the French Coast. Boulogne was two miles away, so I got rid of it at once, but then again shells started coming over, even when my head was under water. It certainly hurt my ears.

The Germans had been shooting at pilots in the sea at that time but my Squadron flew over me as long as their fuel lasted. They were not going to let the Germans near me. Later the 'Y' Service which listened to all R/T prattle told me it was Galland who had shot me down. [It was not Galland.]

During the latter days of June, 4./JG26 had been on the move, transferring to Le Touquet. Ltn Ebersberger wrote:

It was an incomparable moment when we were all sitting together on the terrace of our hotel, to see the sun sink into the sea. Hardly had we settled down than we were off inland again; the next day we found ourselves on a big clover field at Bois Jean, south of Montreuil. At Le Touquet we had installed ourselves in big tents captured from the British. A pleasant camp life soon established itself. Our quarters lay a good distance from the airfield. In the evenings after dark the British flew regularly over the aerodrome on their way south to the front. We tried a couple of times to take them by surprise, but never succeeded because of the thick haze.

From Le Touquet and Bois Jean we moved to Morgny, 70km north of Paris. The airfield was the usual sort of place, but with a little contrivance soon became most comfortable. We lived in a château belonging to the Comte de Fabymasnille, a grand place set in a huge estate. Soon after, the French capitulated and we returned to Germany. We would rather have attacked England immediately, but orders are orders.

CHAPTER VI

GERMAN OCCUPATION OF THE CHANNEL ISLANDS

Our beloved Islands in the hands of the enemy, dreading what the future might hold ...

Revd Sidney Beaugie

The decision to demilitarise the Channel Islands was taken by the British Government earlier in June when it became obvious that Jersey, Guernsey and the smaller islands – Alderney, Sark and Herm – could not be defended without huge loss of civilian life. During the next two weeks several thousand children, young people and mothers with babies were evacuated to England and Scotland. There was much unrest among the approximately 90,000 inhabitants of the islands, and understandable fear of the Germans, so that many of the adults also took advantage of the offer to leave the islands. Regular flights by Jersey Airways' six DH86s were suspended on 13 June, thereafter only evacuation flights were permissible. Wives and families of company staff were flown to England, followed by equipment, stores and spare engines, while maintenance personnel, except for a skeleton staff, also departed. Two Ensigns of 24 Squadron arrived to assist and on 18 and 19 June, while the DH86s alone evacuated 320 civilians.

From a cloudy sky appeared one of the oldest types of French monoplanes. It made an unsteady approach. The landing shocked the professional pilots. Its pilot was Frenchman, aged about 50. His hands shook uncontrollably, and his face dripped with the sweat of a great ordeal. He was the adjutant of a French air squadron. His unit had heard that the bulk of the French Air Force was going to Morocco. They decided to give in. The adjutant had not piloted since the Great War, but he took up the ancient monoplane and headed west with the idea of coming down on the water beside the first ship he saw, which he assured himself was bound to be British. The visibility grew worse. He flew helplessly in the clouds. He came lower. The first thing he saw was Jersey airport. The fighter squadron welcomed him and put him aboard one of the evacuation ships.[1]

The Royal Navy provided twenty-two ships and ten barges for this purpose. In total, about 20,000 people set out for England in panic, including many who had made their living in France, now lost, and were therefore in fear for their means of support. It was reported that thousands of dogs and cats were shot on the quayside before the last boat left.

The planned German invasion of the Channel Islands codenamed *Grune Pfeile* (Green Arrow) had also evolved during June. The German High Command was unsure whether or not the islands were defended. Various reconnaissance sorties were flown over the Islands. Meeting little opposition it was decided to proceed with the planned invasion. This would involve Ju87 dive-bombers to soften up the supposed coastal defences followed by landing craft carrying troops armed with light weapons to take the beaches. However before finalizing any arrangements it was decided to send a second armed reconnaissance flight, by He111s of I/KG55, to try and land. If no opposition was met, naval and army units were to follow. Unfortunately, errors of identification by the German aircrews led to the unnecessary deaths of many civilians.

On the evening of 28 June, hundreds of the inhabitants of Guernsey had gathered in Smith Street in St Peter Port, the small port on the east coast, in order to hear an address by the Bailiff on the subject of evacuation. Suddenly the sounds of aircraft were heard and shortly thereafter a bomb whistled down and fell into the harbour. Machine-gun fire barked over the heads of the gathering, which broke up in panicky fear and sought shelter in the houses. Two to three hundred men, women, and children who had been waiting to board the mail boat down on the quay, were taken to safety by port officials between the concrete pillars of the harbour dyke, which was dry because of the ebb tide. An official report stated:

> Just before 7pm three German planes [the Heinkels from Villacoublay] were flying towards Guernsey from the south-east. The island was about to suffer its first air raid. The target was the harbour and bombs landed on the Cambridge Sheds, the Information Bureau and the tomato lorries waiting in the queue to be exported. The lorries had been mistaken by the Germans for troop-carrying vehicles. After delivering another attack on the harbour the planes split up and individually attacked the Fruit Export Sheds, La Vassalerie, St Andrew and the Vazon Area. The all clear sounded at 8pm but the reality of war had hit Guernsey. The death toll was 33 with a further 67 injured. 49 vehicles were burnt out or seriously damaged and bomb craters covered the ground. The Weighbridge was heavily damaged and the clock was stopped at just before seven.

By sheer luck, most of the bombs fell into the harbour and the sea. Flying low, the Heinkels attacked with their guns, boats anchoring in the harbour and a column of lorries standing in front of the port warehouse. Windows and doors of the hotels and shops on the promenade splintered under the hail of bullets. While the aircraft were still circling above them, firemen and ambulances of the St John's Brigade rushed down to the harbour to rescue the wounded, and they themselves came under machine-gun fire.

At the same time almost the identical scene was being enacted in the port city of St Helier in Jersey, where eleven people were killed and many injured in an air attack by three more Heinkels. Proprietor L. P. Sinel of the *Jersey Evening Post* maintained a secret journal of events:

> At about 6:45pm, German planes swept across the south of the Island with machine-guns blazing and dropping bombs. Houses were wrecked at South Hill, stores set on fire in Commercial Buildings and hundreds of panes of glass were shattered in the Weighbridge vicinity, some stained-glass windows of the Town Church being also damaged. Bombs fell on the Fort, the District Office and in the harbour itself, which was primarily the German objective, several small boats and yachts being destroyed. Ten [eleven] people were killed and several were injured, including one in the Guernsey lifeboat when on its way to Jersey

Of this attack on the Islands, the Wehrmacht reported:

> Particularly effective were bombing attacks on troop concentrations [*sic*] and embarkations on the British Channel islands of Jersey and Guernsey, where large fires and heavy explosions were observed in the harbour installations.[2]

Next day German reconnaissance aircraft were over the Islands, causing fear of further attacks, but none came. The following day, 30 June, Hptm Liebe-Piderit – Staffelkapitän of 3.(F)/123 based at Buc – while on a routine reconnaissance flight over the Islands, decided to test the Guernsey defences. Seeing that the airport appeared deserted he landed the Do17 and found it to be undefended. One account of the landing revealed:

> It was 10:30 in the morning when a German aircraft flew low over Guernsey airport, it circled and landed. Clutching a revolver, the pilot walked cautiously into the deserted administration building. The absence of people unnerved him, suddenly a British aircraft roared overhead and he ran out back to his plane, leaving his revolver on a table.

Another account of this event was provided by Sgt Albert Lamy of the Guernsey Police:

> On the Sunday morning [30 June] an RAF launch escorted by three Blenheims came to Guernsey with the intention of picking up some GPO personnel.

The Officer in charge of the launch came to the Police Station and while he was there the air raid siren sounded. I was talking to him at the time and he remarked that the wardens were getting jumpy and mistaking his Blenheim escort. I took him to the window and pointed out a large green-grey aircraft carrying a black cross and I asked him whether he identified his Blenheim. You can well imagine his reply. He went off post-haste.

Hptm Liebe-Piderit, who had flown back to Buc, returned in the early afternoon with three Dorniers of 3.(F)/123. Flgr Roman Gastager, air gunner aboard 4U+FL flown by Ltn Hüber:

Together with two other planes we headed for Guernsey. We had no idea whether the English were still there or whether they had already retreated. We flew straight to the airfield and were relieved to see cows grazing there as that meant there were no mines. We flew at low altitude to disperse the cows and were the first plane to land. We rolled towards the hangars. I jumped out, released the safety catch of my machine-gun and held it in position. The others remained in the aircraft. Luckily the airfield appeared to be deserted and we notified the two planes circling above. The second machine landed and the third provided protection from the air.

No sooner had the second aircraft landed, than three Bristol Blenheim bombers appeared out of nowhere. The alarm was raised and we once again took off. Our watchdog in the sky immediately chased the bombers and was able to shoot two of them down. The third quickly took to its heels and with that our orders had been fulfilled successfully.

The three Blenheims, Coastal Command aircraft of 235 Squadron, were attacked by Ltn Hans Weber's Dornier, whose air gunner Obfw Otto Bauer claimed to have shot down two, while the surviving aircraft fled. Blenheims LA-B flown by Flt Lt Freddie Flood, an Australian, and L9396/LA-T piloted by Plt Off Joe Carr reported an engagement but suffered no damage. The latter believed that the Dornier's gunner had been wounded or killed in the exchange:

Our two Blenheim aircraft were unable to press home their attack owing to the superior speed of the enemy aircraft. The engagement was broken off when all our aircraft's front gun ammunition had been expended.

Police Sgt Lamy recalled:

During this period three large German aircraft landed on the Guernsey airport. That information reached the police station by telephone. At the Police Station there was a letter which had been handed in a few days earlier for my Chief to hand to the Officer Commanding German troops in Guernsey. You can well imagine our feelings on first seeing such an address. However, it was there for delivery and we were told German aircraft were on the aerodrome So, with my Chief and a couple of other police officers, we set out for the airport On the way we were stopped and told that three Blenheims had appeared on the scene and the three German aircraft had taken off and got away.

However, we continued to the airport and saw the marks of their landing wheels across the grass. They had broken into the terminal building and we were then under the impression they had left booby traps with the intention of blowing up the place. We searched and found nothing. It was a peculiar feeling at the airport – a place usually so full of noise and bustle was then as quiet as a grave, with only sufficient wind to rattle the hangar door and these noises did not help our peace of mind. However, we found nothing and returned to the Police Station.

Another account stated:

In the afternoon another German aircraft landed, this time three officers walked across the tarmac. One of them reclaimed the revolver [left earlier by Hptm Liebe-Piderit], whilst another approached a policeman and in perfect English asked him to fetch the island officials. The Nazi occupation of part of the British Isles had begun.

Sgt Lamy continued:

At about 8 o'clock the same evening the sirens again sounded and five large German aircraft circled the Island finally landing on the airport. This time they came to stay. I did not make the journey that evening but Mr Sculpher, my Chief, did with other police officers. As they approached the road leading to the airport they were held up by armed German sentries, who accompanied them the remainder of the distance, riding on the running board. When they reached the terminal building they were immediately told to get out of the motor car and stand up against a pile of sandbags and surrounded by soldiers with machine-guns. The note was then delivered and German troops, by means of commandeered cars, came to the town area. They immediately set up their headquarters at a hotel and asked to see the leading officials of the Island. The following morning there appeared in both local newspapers a Proclamation from the Officer Commanding German troops. Apart from the threat to bomb the town this appeared extremely mild; but it was a true case of the mailed fist inside the velvet glove.

The five Ju52 transport machines arrived at about 20:00 with the first batch of occupation troops. There were problems for the transport pilots at first, because a farmer had driven a herd of cows onto the runway and the pilot of the leading machine had to make several passes to first shoo the leisurely browsing animals away. The soldiers who then landed first had to act as herdsmen to keep the runway clear for the following transports, before they could set up their machine-gun positions and occupy the airfield.

The widely predicted German move came in the form of orders dropped in canvas bags with red streamers attached. White crosses were to be painted on the airport runway, the main square and a car park. Every building was to fly a white flag. "If these signs of a peaceful surrender are not observed [...] heavy bombardment will take place," threatened the Germans. A white sheet was being flown from every house as the Islanders awaited the Germans' arrival. First reports suggest that German behaviour is 'correct' and that the civil population is obeying instructions to offer no resistance.

On 1 July, ten more Ju52s arrived at Guernsey, one of which conveyed Major Albrecht Lanz as Guernsey's Military Commander, and he was accompanied by Hptm Erich Gussek who was to fill a similar role on Jersey. Others brought naval assault troops, a light anti-aircraft unit, and a company from Infantry Regiment 396. A Do17 commanded by Oblt Richard Kern landed at Jersey airport. He summoned the Bailiff for the official surrender. Guernsey's Methodist Revd Sidney Beaugie noted:

On Sunday evening Guernsey was occupied by the German Forces. At 6am on the following day they landed in Jersey. There was no opposition. No one who experienced it will ever forget the feeling of depression with which we awoke... Our beloved Islands in the hands of the enemy, dreading what the future might hold, conscious of our complete isolation, we realised with sinking hearts that life would be totally different, but how different none could guess.

A sentiment undoubtedly expressed by many other islanders. In the report by the Wehrmacht next day, the whole thing sounded far more dramatic:

On 30 June and 1 July respectively the British Channel islands of Jersey and Guernsey were taken in a coup-de-main by the Luftwaffe and subsequently occupied by assault units of the *Kriegsmarine* and *Heer*. In the course of this, a German reconnaissance aircraft shot down [*sic*] two British Bristol Blenheims in an air battle.

The group of Luftwaffe officers that set out for the town in a captured car can hardly be described as an assault unit: with the greatest politeness imaginable they asked the notabilities of the island gathered in the town hall to surrender, which was then accomplished within a matter of minutes. Then the occupation statute was read out loud and its publication in the next edition of the islands newspaper required. The sequence of events took place in the same way on both islands and was synchronised.[3]

By 2 July, radio communications had been set up with the mainland, and the construction of anti-aircraft batteries was begun in Guernsey and Jersey on 4 July. All the existing forts that were initially thought to be a threat were found to be deserted and disused, and the Germans quickly set about putting these to use. The remainder of the early defences were nothing more than earthworks and lightweight structures.

And then, on 6 July, came the first of a number of commando-type forays by British troops, when 2/Lt Hubert Nicolle, a Guernseyman serving with the British army, was dispatched on a fact-finding mission to Guernsey. He was dropped off the south coast by a submarine and rowed ashore in a canoe under cover of night. This was the first of two visits which Nicolle would make to the island. Following the second, he missed his rendezvous and was trapped on the island. After a month and a half in hiding, he gave himself up to the German authorities and was sent to a German prisoner-of-war camp. The residents of the Islands were treated relatively fairly compared to those in other occupied countries.

CHAPTER VII

FLYING SAILORS AT WAR[1]

It was quite a novel experience fighting your way out of this country, weaving and dodging on the enemy side, and then forcing passage back to your own airfield.

Sub-Lt(A) Tom Harrington 801 Squadron

The Fleet Air Arm, which had been fighting its own war over and off the Norwegian coast for several weeks, and had played its part during the Dunkirk and Calais operations, returned to the offensive in mid-June.

On 12 June, Coastal Command Blenheims and Rocs of 801 Squadron, including L3160 flown by Sub-Lt(A) Tom Harrington with N/Air Alf Clayton, dive-bombed E-boats in Boulogne harbour with inconclusive results. Nonetheless, one E-boat was destroyed during the strike and a number of others and barges were near-missed. The reconnaissance flight of 801 Squadron revealed the Germans to be digging in large guns at Cap Griz Nez. Lt Ronnie Hay RM flew one such sortie:

It was pretty hairy – taking low-level pictures, my observer leaning out of the cockpit with a hand-held camera at 500 feet at 240 mph – it was just right for German flak, but we never got hit.

Next day, Harrington and Clayton flew two patrols, the first in Roc L3161, and then in Skua L3135, to protect ships off Calais. That night six Albacores of 826 Squadron repeated the attack on the E-boats in Boulogne harbour, again without apparent success. Of this period, Harrington later commented:

Hectic days indeed, living under canvas [at Detling] in glorious weather and fed like fighting cocks by a local caterer. He really did his stuff for the boys and did not stint us in any way, despite the Admiralty's modest monetary contribution for our victualing.

Our main role was to cut any bridges the army wanted 'done', any enemy installations or barges, which were found from our other role of taking part in a daily reconnaissance of the local French, Belgian and Dutch channel ports, and finally to provide fighter cover for special convoys off the Kent or Essex coasts. We seemed to form a legitimate prey for German and the British defences as well as a worthwhile target for both the Royal Air Force and German air force. It was quite a novel experience fighting your way out of this country, weaving and dodging on the enemy side, and then forcing passage back to your own airfield.

820 (Swordfish) Squadron was temporarily based at Thorney Island when newly qualified Mid(A) Mike Lithgow arrived on posting. On 13 June, the squadron, which had been on readiness armed with torpedoes, was instructed to carry out a reconnaissance of the Le Havre-Cherbourg area, as Lithgow recalled:

> [...] with our bomb racks removed in the hope that the enemy would be deceived into thinking we were Gladiators. It was much consolation to be found masquerading as Gladiators when the opposing aircraft were likely to be Me109s, even though we were allowed six Blenheims as escort. My logbook records the flight of six Swordfish in close formation over Cherbourg as having occupied 4 hours 30 minutes, and as far as I was concerned every minute was pregnant with possibilities.

He continued:

> Two days later [15 June] we were ordered to Jersey. I was sixth aircraft to taxi out behind the CO, and was surprised to see a motorcycle despatch rider hare across the aerodrome at prodigious speed, fling his machine to one side and hand a signal to him. The CO promptly taxied back to dispersal and switched off, followed by the rest of us, in a very curious mood. It transpired that the Germans had just walked and although we were all equipped with W/T, I have often wondered since exactly how close we were to dropping in on an unexpected reception.

Mine-laying occupied the Albacore crews over the next few nights. 825 Squadron, which had returned to Worthy Down, operated detachments from Thorney Island during the three days 16/18 June, carrying out anti-submarine patrols between Poole and Cherbourg, from where the last of the British troops were being evacuated.

While Sub-Lt(A)Tom Harrington and PO(A) Arthur Sluggett flew a convoy patrol in Skua L3003 on 18 June, Lt Edward Savage carried out another of the dangerous photo-recce sorties over Boulogne harbour, dropping down to 4,000 feet to fulfil the task but meeting heavy AA fire from the defences. L2878 was hit and Savage was slightly wounded but he was able to return and land safely, with his observer Lt Harry Hayes unhurt. Undaunted by the risky task, next day,19 June, Lt Moose Martyn of 801 Squadron volunteered to carry out a photo-recce of Boulogne and

Calais, where the Germans were installing long-range guns. Both Martyn and his observer Lt John Collett knew that it would be similar to flying through a shooting gallery, especially at the assigned height of 1,000 feet. They spotted the guns and began taking pictures when 'all hell broke loose'. The Skua (Aircraft P) was shot at repeatedly. The flaps were torn off. There was a huge hole in the port wing. The fuel tank was leaking and an explosion had occurred in the aircraft behind Martyn's head. Collett failed to respond to his call and he realised that his observer was seriously injured. Somehow Martyn managed to gain enough altitude to coast back towards Dover in time to save the life of the badly injured Collett. Meanwhile, Sub-Lt(A) Harrington with N/Air Bill Crone in the turret of Roc L3128 flew a patrol protecting ships in the Boulogne–Ostende area.

Despite the obvious risk of such an operation, 801 Squadron was called upon to carry out a dive-bombing attack on gun positions at Cap Griz Nes on 21 June. Hurricanes provided cover. Sub-Lt(A) Harrington and N/Air Crone were involved, flying Roc L3117, and returned safely, but not so fortunate was the crew of another Roc, both Sub-Lt(A) Tony Day and his gunner N/Air Fred Berry. Their aircraft was hit by AA fire at 14:40 and crashed into the sea. Both were killed. Oblt Adolf Bühl of 1.(J)/LG2 made a claim for a Roc [misidentified as a Hurricane] at about this time, so he may have been involved rather than ground fire. 801 Squadron returned to Donibristle on 24 June.

Later, at 15:25, eight Albacores of 826 Squadron led by Lt-Cdr Frank Hopkins departed Bircham Newton to attack merchant ships at Texel but alternative targets of de Klooy airfield and Wilhelmsoord docks were bombed instead. Bf109s from 3./JG51 and 3./JG76 engaged the raiders and two Albacores were shot down. Lt(A) James Mackenzie-Bell, Sub-Lt(A) Frank Hookins and N/Air Bob Poole were all killed when L7081 fell in flames over Texel, possibly the victim of Uffz Werner Schreiter. The crew of L7089 flown by Sub-Lt(A) William Butterworth initially survived the crash-landing, although the observer Sub-Lt(A) Vic Dyke succumbed to his wounds. Both the pilot, slightly wounded by a bullet in his right thigh, and the TAG N/Air Bob Jackson were taken prisoner. They were believed to have fallen to the fire of Fw Ernst Graf.

A third Albacore was badly damaged – possibly by Gfr Heinrich zur Lage – and on return Sub-Lt(A) P. D. Unwin's L7111/4L was found to have 60 bullet holes and a wounded TAG, N/Air Charlie Homer, who claimed one of the attackers shot down (for which he was awarded a DSM). In fact, one Messerschmitt was shot down – Ltn Erwin Marquard of 3./JG76, who crashed north-west of Texel – and two others were slightly damaged in the action, both aircraft of 3./JG3. N/Air Homer recalled:

When we arrived over the target area, we flew straight into a nest of Me109s. Two out of our six aircraft were shot down, one crew being killed instantly, whilst the other, much to my amazement, somehow survived a severe crash landing. My aircraft was attacked by two Me109s and I received a bullet wound through my stomach. However, I did get my own back by shooting down one of the Me109s. Our aircraft was badly shot up and it was only my observer's prompt action in plugging the holes in the petrol tank with his fingers that enabled us to retain sufficient fuel to get home. The Albacore did not run to such refinements as self-sealing tanks. I have always felt that for his action he should have received some award.

After landing, I was helped out of the aircraft, convinced that, apart from my stomach wound, my legs were paralysed. I was placed on a stretcher and carried to the RAF Sick Berth. Here I learned that my 'paralysis' was caused by the elastic in my underpants being severed by the same shot that damaged my stomach. I was visited by a squadron leader medic together with his corporal orderly. Having examined my wound, the medic turned to his orderly and said, "The first thing we have to do for this young gentleman is to give him a cup of hot, sweet tea." My tiny mind felt that this was quite stupid. I was certain that any fluid I drank would spurt out of the holes in my stomach. The medic dealt with my wounds, wrapped round a great quantity of sticky plaster, assisted me off the plinth, patted me on the shoulder and said, "Off you go, son - you can join your squadron again now." My thoughts of an honourable and comfortable return home were thus extinguished!

Just three days later (24 June), Charlie Homer was again in trouble:

I was a member of a crew carrying out an anti-submarine patrol over the North Sea when the fan (propeller) stopped. My SOS was picked up by Bircham Newton, who told me to 'Wait'. This we would have found a little difficult without an engine to keep us in the air. Luckily, my SOS was also picked up by Chatham and another station. The cross bearings obtained by these two operators were spot on, but it was many hours later that we were located in our dinghy some 17 miles off Grimsby.

Another Albacore of 826 Squadron was lost on the night of 26/27 June, when L7084/4M suffered engine failure on returning from a minelaying sortie. It force-landed in sand dunes at Waxham on the Norfolk coast and was destroyed. Sub-Lt(A) Anthony Tuke and his gunner N/Air Alex Japp were unhurt, while the observer Sub-Lt George Dormand was slightly injured. Active on the night of 29/30 June, were six Swordfish of 812 Squadron from North Coates, laying mines off the Dutch coast. L7633/G3Q flown by Sub-Lt(A) John Davies was shot down by coastal gunfire, the pilot and his observer Sub-Lt(A) Cecil Conn being taken prisoner.

CHAPTER VIII

BATTLE OF BRITAIN PRELIMINARIES, JUNE 1940

How long would they last in battle, they ran from Dunkirk, they deserted France completely for the safety of home, England is there for the taking.

General Hugo Sperrle, June 1940

Although at least a dozen German aircraft had fallen to British aircraft, AA defences and warships during September and October 1939, the first to fall on land – in Scotland – was IH+JA of Stab/KG26 on 28 October. Shot down by Spitfires it force-landed at Humbie near Edinburgh; two of its crew were killed and the other two wounded/injured, and were taken prisoner. The first to crash on English soil was one of four Heinkels shot down on 3 February 1940; three fell into the sea while 1H+FM of 4./KG26 crash-landed near Whitby in Yorkshire; two of the crew were killed and one seriously injured.

The first British civilian to lose his life due to bombing was Scotsman Jim Isbister, who was killed on 16 March, when bombs fell on the Orkneys; six others were injured. The first civilian war casualties in England occurred on 30 April, when AA fire forced down a He111 of 3./KG126 while on a mine-laying sortie off the East Coast. The bomber crashed onto a house in Upper Victoria Road in Clacton-on-Sea in Essex, killing the occupants, Mr and Mrs Frederick Gill. Thus, they became the first civilians, of more than 60,000, to be killed in England during the war.

* * * * *

The German bombing campaign began in June. A concerted attack on the night of 2 June was aimed at RAF Mildenhall, some twenty-three bombs falling nearby, but causing no damage. On the night of 3/4 June, Hampden P1340 of 44 Squadron based at Waddington hit a balloon cable at Harwich; its pilot, Sgt Edwin Spencer, reported:

I struck a balloon cable in the Harwich area. The starboard wing dropped and the aircraft swung violently to port. We dived steeply and I was unable to regain control of the aircraft which was diving at 260 mph. I baled out at 1,000 feet and the parachute opened just before I hit the sea.

The remainder of the crew, Sgt Samuel Connell, Plt Off Reg Roots and Cpl Albert Kendrew, were killed. Spencer owed his life to Petty Officer B. Driver RN who heard his cries for help and who dived into the river and found him clinging to a buoy. The bodies of the others were not recovered.

During the night of 6/7 June, six intrusions into East Anglia were made by German bombers mainly searching for airfields in Norfolk and Cambridgeshire. The third intrusion passed south of Norwich and via Bury St Edmunds, Newmarket and Ely to arrive over RAF Upwood, where Blenheims were night flying. Most of the bombs fell on open land but one airman was killed and two injured. Five bombs fell near Mildenhall. One enemy aircraft which came in over Lowestoft dropped four bombs in the lane to Patrick's Farm, Bedfield, Suffolk. Another fell nearby, at Monk Soham and was exploded by a bomb disposal team two days later, while Beaufort L9797 of 22 Squadron, whose pilot was dazzled by searchlights on returning to North Coates following a night sortie, crashed into a house that was completely demolished and two others were damaged. Three civilians were killed as was the Beaufort's gunner. RAF Thornaby in North Yorkshire was also targeted, just after midnight, when bombs fell on the aerodrome and killed an airman and injured three others. Two Hudsons were destroyed as were two fuel bowsers, and the runway damaged.

The following night, 7/8 June, Heinkels attempted more airfield attacks, but mistook the bombing range west of Honington for the airfield, plastering it with ten HEs. Shortly after dusk a fog belt descended along the coast between Spurn Head and Essex and gradually drifted inland, becoming as much as six miles wide. It was into these conditions that there strayed a He115 mine-layer, 8L+EL of 3./ KüFlGr.906. A searchlight battery was ordered to attempt to illuminate the aircraft as it tried to find a way out towards the south-west. Moments after switching on, the intruder, at only 300 feet, was brilliantly lit and, completely dazzled, the pilot crashed the floatplane at 23:30 in the grounds of The Old Rectory, Eyke, three miles from Woodbridge. For half an hour it burned, only an engine then remaining intact. To the east was a crater twenty feet wide and four feet deep caused, presumably, by a 925kg mine, the parachute of which was resting on some nearby bushes. Although it was suggested that the pilot Oblt z.See Adolf van Hüllen had been dazzled by searchlights, locals believed that he had been deceived by a mist over the land as sea mist and had tried to alight on the 'sea'. The seaplane was destroyed when its mine exploded, killing both van Hüllen and Fw Ludwig Fehr. A third member of the crew Fw Paul Randorf managed to bale out before the aircraft crashed. He was found seriously injured, suspended from a tree by his parachute harness. He died from his injuries next day.

Luftwaffe daylight reconnaissance flights continued, several occurring on 8 June, but poor weather conditions prevented further raids for the next week or so. All during this period Bomber Command was despatching small-scale raids over Germany and occupied France, and Holland and Belgium. A Hampden crew captained by Sqn Ldr Robert Allen of 49 Squadron, en route to Rheims on the night of 12/13 June, encountered a He111 flying almost parallel to their own aircraft with its navigation lights switched on. Allen decided to engage it and manoeuvred the Hampden into position to allow his gunner Sgt Richard Williams to open fire, which he did with devastating effect, as he recalled:

I was standing up and firing right up above my head. All I saw was an immense silhouette and two tongues of flame flowing from each engine. We were then between 3,000 and 4,000 feet. I did not have to use my sights at all, and my tracer bullets were lighting him up all over the place. You could see the light greenish-blue colour which they use on German aircraft as well as the black crosses on the wings. I kept my triggers pressed until all the 100 rounds in each pan had gone, a total of 200 rounds. Just before I'd finished he started to dive over our port side. The tracer still lit him up and queer lights came from him as smoke poured out of him. He disintegrated in the air and that was the last I saw of him as he went down over our port side.[1]

Their victim was a He111 of 2./KGr.126 that crash-landed at Dranouter, north-east of Hazebrouck, shortly after midnight, having suffered damage to both engines. The crew believed they had been attacked by a night fighter.[2] Shortly thereafter a Ju87 was sighted, also with its navigation lights burning. Sqn Ldr Allen announced that he was intending to shoot it down with the Hampden's front guns but gave way to Sgt Williams' desire to have another go. Having reloaded his guns and with the pilot having manoeuvred undetected into position underneath the Ju87, Williams opened fire, aiming for the pilot's cockpit. The aircraft fell away on fire, Sqn Ldr Allen following it down to see it crash, although this is not substantiated in German records.

Early in the morning of 12 June, a He111 of Wekusta 51 flown by Oblt Gerd Nissen, the Staffelkapitän, was plotted, engaged and shot down off Margate following attacks by two Spitfires of 64 Squadron flown by Flt Sgt Ernest Gilbert (N3230) and Sgt Adrian Laws (L3275) of 64 Squadron from Kenley, assisted by two Spitfires of 610 Squadron flown by Flt Lt John Ellis (P9451) and Sgt Stan Arnfield (P9495); Flt Sgt Gilbert was the first to attack:

As Green 1, I was ordered to scramble and climb to 15,000 feet. At 07:43 when at 12,000 feet I noticed another aircraft about 500 feet below me about one mile to port. I dived underneath and established his identity as a He111. I broke away and carried out a No. 1 Attack getting in a short burst of two seconds at 150 yards range. E/a evasive action was to throttle right back to a very slow speed and then turn quickly either port or starboard. Enemy fire appeared to come from blister guns and possibly top gun as well, but it was inaccurate. After this attack e/a dived into clouds at 10,000 feet. I resumed an easterly course and after about three minutes again saw e/a about 6,000 to 4,000 feet below about one mile to port. I carried out further No1. Attack at between 100 and 150 yards, using up the remainder of my ammunition. I observed a large amount of black smoke coming from port engine and e/a finally was lost in cloud at 600 feet about 12 miles east by south of Chatham.

During this attack enemy fire was only observed coming from one position. Fire was not accurate, tracer was observed going well to port side of my aircraft during both attacks and my aircraft was not hit. E/a was camouflaged dark brown and green on top and light blue underneath. I landed at Kenley 08:09. Sgt Laws (Green 2) left Kenley about 10 minutes after me but we were flying independently of each other and he attacked this e/a later.

Sgt Laws added:

Warned that e/a was flying out to sea at zero altitude. I sighted e/a at 08:07 heading east at approximately 600 feet. I flew ahead of the e/a towards sun, losing height and turned for beam attack. I carried out two beam attacks from either side, opening fire at 250 yards. The e/a was travelling very slowly (about 160 mph) as though one engine was damaged. E/a dived to sea level and made gentle turns each way, the tail unit occasionally touching the sea. At that moment two other Spitfires joined in, carrying out attacks from astern and above. I joined in with a similar attack until remainder of my ammunition was expended. E/a then settled on the water and crew was inflating dinghy. I circled for a short period being last to leave the scene.

Flt Lt Ellis reported:

I was leader of Blue Section 610 Squadron which was ordered to take-off at 07:45. There were two aircraft only in the section as Blue 3 had trouble starting and when he did take off he failed to contact us. Immediately we were airborne we were ordered to vector 120° and 'gate'. When in the vicinity of Canterbury we vectored 45° and three minutes later 40°. By this time we were about five miles out to sea off Birchington at 1,500 feet. I then sighted an aircraft flying due east at about 4,000 feet. I put the section into line astern and gave chase. I could see the aircraft was diving steeply for the sea. I recognised it as a Heinkel 111. I ordered the section to carry out a No. 1 Attack but at about 400 yards range I noticed another Spitfire [Sgt Laws of 64 Squadron] below and in front obviously carrying out an attack. I therefore turned away slightly and so started the attack again when the first Spitfire had broken away. I was diving down from above on the e/a and fired a burst of four seconds from 300 yards closing to 50 yards.

My overtaking speed was considerable. I estimated the speed of the e/a to be 200 mph and my speed 250 mph. After No. 2 [Sgt Arnfield] of the section had broken away the Heinkel still appeared to be flying normally so I started another No. 1 Attack from above, opening fire at 200 yards. After a short burst of two seconds at the nose, the e/a crashed into the sea five miles north of Margate. The machine floated well but I saw no sign of life of the crew when circling it, so climbed up to get into R/T touch again and on doing so I was vectored again out into the Channel and saw no more of the Heinkel. There were a number of small boats in the vicinity of the e/a when it crashed.

Three of the crew managed to get out before the aircraft sank but two others – Uffz Franz Bolinski and Uffz Willi Stiegelmeier – were lost. However, one of the survivors – Reg.Rat. Dr Hermann Freudenberg, a weather specialist[3] – drowned before help arrived in the form of the motorised fishing boat *Golden Spray*; skipper Jack Pocock recalled:

We suddenly heard the roar of an aeroplane and saw the Heinkel approaching at a height of only 15 feet from the water. I instinctively ducked. I expected a burst of machine-gunfire, but a moment afterwards saw two British fighters in pursuit. The chase continued for about five miles, when, following a burst of machine-gunfire, the Heinkel dived into the water. We hauled in our nets and dashed at full speed towards it. It took over an hour, and we had almost given up, when two heads appeared and we hauled the men aboard.

One of the crew, 16-year-old Ken Rice dragged the two injured crewmen aboard, including the pilot, who had suffered head injuries and had a machine-gun bullet lodged in his arm.

There was an officer with a badly shot elbow and a mechanic with a gash on his leg and head injuries. I tore off my vest for bandages and we made them mugs of cocoa.

Young Ken ripped his own underwear into strips to use as bandages and, in return, Nissen – who had only a shirt, trousers and socks – gave him his socks suspenders as a gift of gratitude. The other survivor, the portly 16-stone observer Obfw Hans Peckhaus, was also seriously injured.

They kept thanking us for what we had done. Two men were trapped in the wreckage of the plane and another was drowned while swimming about.

On reaching land, both airmen were rushed to a nearby hospital for emergency treatment.

The Harwich balloons claimed another victim on the night of 12/13 June, when Wg Cdr Joseph Watts DSO flying Hampden P4345 of 144 Squadron (from Hemswell), collided with a cable and crashed the other side of the harbour. The guns had opened fire on the approaching bomber, following which it fired the correct recognition flare. The searchlights then attempted to illuminate the balloon barrage but to no avail. The Squadron CO and his crew were all killed when the aircraft crashed in the dock area at Felixstowe, causing a fire in the store at *Marriages* flour mill. One employee at the mill, Mr D. Grayling, died from the injuries he received in the crash.

At first German air operations over Britain were carried out on a small scale, and these began with light probing raids by night, normally in Staffel strength, but sometimes carried out by as few as two aircraft on one target. These harassing attacks were, in the weeks that followed, directed against specific targets such as aircraft factories, dock installations, oil storage tanks, and specialised manufacturing plants. German Radio proudly proclaimed:

Since May 10th enemy and chiefly British aeroplanes have uninterruptingly attacked open German towns. Last night again eight civilians fell victim to these attacks. The Luftwaffe has now begun reprisals against England. The revenge of the German Air Force for England's sly night piracy has begun. German forbearance is exhausted. The time for settlement has come.

Although the damage caused by these nocturnal raids was only slight, their nuisance value was considerable, with a few aircraft often causing sleepless nights over large areas of the country, as well as regularly disrupting production at factories engaged in essential war work. They were, in addition, a valuable way for the bomber crews to learn the art of night navigation but, as a result of their premature use, the radio beams associated with the highly secret *Knickebein* bombing and navigation aid were quickly detected by the British enabling effective counter-measures to be put in hand. *Knickebein* was available to the entire bomber force, its signals being picked up on the 'blind' landing receivers fitted as standard to all German bombers. When used for navigational purposes only one beam was employed, but for radio assisted bombing the system employed two transmitter stations which formed a beam intersection over the prescribed objective, allowing the attack to take place without reference to the ground below.

On his way home shortly after midnight on the night of 17/18 June, Flg Off Alastair Hunter of 604 Squadron sighted a He115 seaplane silhouetted against the sea far beneath his Blenheim. He dived 9,000 feet to attack and after a ten-mile chase up the coast between Dunkirk and Ostend he was able to open fire from astern. After the first burst the German pilot dived his aircraft to sea level and at the same time fired a signal rocket from which dazzling white stars lit up the sky above pursuer and pursued. This made it easier for Hunter to see his quarry and he closed and fired a second burst, whereupon the Heinkel's port engine caught fire. As Hunter broke away, his gunner, Sgt Gordon Thomas, saw the seaplane, 3258 of 3./KüFlGr.106, crash into the sea. There were no reported casualties, so it would appear that the crew was rescued. This was 604 Squadron's first night victory.

The Opening Round of the Battle of Britain...

The largest attack to date was carried out by waves of He111s – 16 of I/KG27, 12 of II/KG27, 12 of III/KG27 and 10 of I/KG4, 11 of II/KG4 and 10 of III/KG4 – on the night of 18/19 June, the Home Office Intelligence Summary revealing the extent of the raids and the damage inflicted during the period 18:00 on 18 June to 06:00 on 19 June:

> Coastal districts from Middlesbrough to Portsmouth were under warning and sirens were sounded in Yorkshire, Lincolnshire, Norfolk, Suffolk, Essex, Huntingdonshire and Kent during the night. London was under yellow warning during the period, and so was the Barrow-in-Furness district on the west coast. Some bombs dropped in the North-Eastern Region, and, a substantial number in the North Midland Region; the chief damage, however, was done at Cambridge, where houses were demolished and nine people were killed, at Southend, where houses and a boys' school were damaged, and to oil installations Canvey Island. Incendiary and high explosive bombs were used. Ten civilian deaths [in total] and 26 people injured have been reported.

KG27 headed for the Midlands while East Anglia bore the brunt of KG4's raids as bombers targeted RAF stations in Suffolk and Norfolk. Warned of the approaching enemy aircraft, Blenheim night fighters of 29 Squadron from RAF Debden were ordered off, while a lone Spitfire of 19 Squadron flown by Flt Sgt Jack Steere was scrambled from RAF Duxford at 23:15. At about the same time more Blenheim night fighters of 23 Squadron were taking-off from RAF Wittering. Heinkel 5J+GA of Stab/KG4 flown by Ltn Erich Simon with Oblt Heinz-Georg Corpus as observer led the way on a pre-attack reconnaissance, and was followed by the main force flying in sections at intervals. The first of these reached Clacton at 23:00, and 15 minutes later another was illuminated by searchlights, at which the crew released their bombs. Three exploded in nearby Holland-on-Sea, damaging houses in King's Cliff Avenue and Medina Road. Another Heinkel jettisoned its bombs over Southend, where one of the thirteen casualties later died. By now the leading section of three Heinkels was approaching Bury St Edmunds, but east of the Suffolk market town they were intercepted by a Blenheim of 29 Squadron flown by Sqn Ldr John McLean. They proved too fast for the Blenheim, one Heinkel opening fire on its pursuer without effect. This, or another, jettisoned its bombs, which fell at Rougham Rectory and near its churchyard.

Another Staffel crossed the coast at Sheringham, near where Sgt Alan Close in a 23 Squadron Blenheim (L1458/S) engaged a Heinkel held in searchlights, only to be shot down by return fire. Close was killed but his gunner LAC Laurence Karasek managed to bale out. The Blenheim crashed in flames at Terrington St Clement. A second Blenheim (YP-L), flown by Flt Lt Myles Duke-Woolley (with Aircraftman Derek Bell as gunner) was soon in the area and engaged the same Heinkel – 5J+DM of Stab II/KG4:

00:45. Observed a ball of fire, which took to be a Blenheim fighter in flames, break away from behind the tail of the E/A. I climbed to engage this E/A and attacked from below the tail after the searchlights were extinguished. I closed to a range of 50 yards and opened fire. E/A returned fire and appeared to throttle back suddenly. My own speed was 130-140 mph and I estimate the E/A slowed to 110 mph. I delivered five attacks with front guns and during these my air gunner fired seven bursts at various ranges. After the last front gun attack my gunner reported that the E/A's port engine was on fire. As my starboard engine was now u/s I broke off the engagement and returned to base, where several bullet holes were found in the wings and fuselage, including cannon strikes in the starboard wing and rear fuselage.

One bullet had lodged in Derek Bell's parachute pack without harming him. The Heinkel finally ditched in shallow water in Blakeney Creek. Coastguards captured the crew, Major Dietrich Fr von Massenbach (the Gruppenkommandeur), Oblt Ulrich Jordan, Obfw Max Leimer and Fw Karl Amberger, who was severely wounded. A subsequent news report revealed:

Two local auxiliary coastguard patrols saw an aircraft in obvious difficulties, off the coast. Flames were issuing from one of its engines, and it crashed in shallow water close to the beach. They gave the alarm and ran to the beach. They intercepted the crew of the aircraft, a Heinkel bomber, as they swam and waded ashore with the help of their rubber dinghy. It seemed at first that the crew, consisting of four men, would show fight. The auxiliary coastguard men thereupon covered the Germans with their firearms. The Germans shouted and surrendered. They were searched and disarmed and detained until the arrival of the military.

By now, other bombers had reached RAF Stradishall, home of Wellingtons, bombs falling around the village of Hargrave, six miles south-west of Bury St Edmunds. The Rectory was hit and the vicar's daughter injured by flying glass. More bombs fell on Lodge Farm, Rede, and in Fersfield Street, Bressingham, without causing further casualties. RAF Marham in Norfolk was attacked by a lone bomber, the bombs missing the airfield and exploding near King's Lynn, while RAF Mildenhall also escaped damage when the intended bombs fell near the village of Culford, four miles north-west of Bury St Edmunds. Bombs also fell near the sugar beet factory – one of the largest in Europe – on the outskirts of the town, slightly injuring two residents of Westfield Cottages in Hollow Road.

In addition to the Blenheims searching for the intruders, which now included aircraft from 604 Squadron, more Spitfires had been scrambled by 19 Squadron. Moments before midnight, a Heinkel released its bombs over Cambridge, where two bombs demolished eight houses in Vicarage Terrace, killing nine persons while another ten were admitted to hospital, three of whom were seriously injured. Among the dead were five children. Bombs also fell at West Fen, Ely, killing one civilian and thirty cattle, and elsewhere in the area. AA guns at RAF Feltwell engaged the raiders but claimed no successes.

Three Heinkels were credited to 29 Squadron's Blenheims, Plt Off John Barnwell (L6636) engaging one illuminated by searchlights over Debden, which reportedly crashed with its starboard engine on fire. However, Barnwell's aircraft was hit by return fire and crashed in the sea off the Stour Estuary. He and his gunner Sgt Ken Long were killed. Plt Off Lionel Kells in L1508 fired at another Heinkel and believed that he had shot this down off Felixstowe. This was possibly a 4 Staffel machine that returned damaged by fighters during a sortie to attack Mildenhall airfield. One of Fw Heinz Schäfer's crew was badly wounded in the stomach and on return was admitted to hospital in Lille. Shortly thereafter, Plt Off Jack Humphreys in L1375 damaged another Heinkel near Debden, but his own aircraft was hit by return fire and crash-landed at Debden. His opponent was possibly Fw Erich Gregor's Stab I machine that belly-landed, badly damaged, on a beach east of Calais on return. Gregor and his crew, Oblt Falk Willis (observer), Fw Karl Brucker and Uffz Josef Jochmann all survived unhurt although their aircraft was written off.

Meanwhile, Flt Lt Sailor Malan in Spitfire K9953 of 74 Squadron encountered a Heinkel, a machine of 4./KG4 in which the Staffelkapitän Hptm Hermann Prochnow was flying. This was probably the aircraft previously engaged by Plt Off Barnwell. Malan pursued it to the coast and finally shot it down to crash into the sea near the Cork Light Vessel moored off Felixstowe. The captain and crew (Obfw Hermann Wojis, Uffz Franz Heyeres and Fw Richard Bunk) were killed and only the Staffelkapitän's body was recovered. Malan's subsequent combat report revealed:

> During an air raid in the locality of Southend, various E/A were observed and held by searchlights for prolonged periods. On request of [74] Squadron I was allowed to take off with one Spitfire. I climbed towards E/A, which was making for the coast and held in searchlight beams at 8,000 feet. I positioned myself astern and opened fire at 200 yards and closed to 50 yards with one burst. Observed bullets entering E/A and had my windscreen covered in oil. Broke off to the left and immediately below as E/A spiralled out of beam.

The reconnaissance Heinkel (5J+GA) was then engaged by Flt Lt Malan and crashed at Springfield Road in Chelmsford, ending up in the Bishop of Chelmsford's garden at 00:30. Oblt Corpus, Obfw Walter Gross and Fw Walter Vick died in the crash, while Ltn Simon had managed to bale out. He was quickly captured. Malan's report continued:

> Climbed to 12,000 feet towards another E/A held by the searchlights on northerly course. Opened fire at 250 yards, taking good care not to overshoot his time. Gave five 2-second bursts and observed bullets entering all over E/A with slight deflection as he was turning to port. E/A emitted heavy smoke and I observed one parachute open very close. E/A went down in spiral dive. Searchlights and I followed him right down until he crashed in flames near Chelmsford.
>
> As I approached target in each case, I flashed succession of dots on downward recognition light before moving into attack. I did not notice AA fire after I had done this. When following second E/A down, I switched on navigation lights for short time to help establish identity. Gave letter of period only once when returning at 3,000 feet from Chelmsford, when one searchlight searched for me. Cine-camera gun in action.

A contemporary account went into a little more detail:

> The plane that crashed at Chelmsford must be claimed as the first plane brought down in the Battle of Britain. It was not the true Battle of Britain, but it certainly was the overture. And the same fighter pilot scored the aircraft brought down at Southend. Shortly after his first success at Chelmsford – it was a Heinkel – he saw another German aircraft, also a Heinkel, held by searchlight beams over the Thames estuary, and attacked it at once, with immediate success.
>
> The Heinkel down at Chelmsford fell in the garden of the Bishop of Chelmsford at Bishopscourt. The crew numbered four. One came down by parachute near Writtle. He knocked at the door of a house and awakened the lady who lived there. Judge of her surprise when, looking through the curtains, she saw a German airman standing on her doorstep. Anyway, he was wounded and glad to be arrested by the local policeman who was called in. The other three were killed in the aircraft.
>
> Meanwhile, the Bishop, who was a keen parashot, had taken his station in the garden, accompanied by his gardener. Dr. Wilson had prudently, in view of the possibility of parachutists, armed himself with a shot-gun. Although he was not actually called upon to use this firearm, a rumour spread soon afterwards that the Bishop had, with unerring aim, brought the bomber down with one discharge of the weapon. He received congratulations from near and far, including a number from other bishops, on his high standard of shooting.
>
> The three Germans were buried in a corner of the borough cemetery at Chelmsford, and the Bishop himself officiated at the service.[4]

The *Manchester Guardian* reported:

> Three German airmen who lost their lives when their bomber was brought
> down in an Essex town during Tuesday night's raid were buried in the town's
> cemetery yesterday. Full military honours were paid by officers and men of the
> RAF and a firing party fired three volleys over the one large grave in which the
> three coffins covered with Nazi flags were interred. The Bishop of Chelmsford
> officiated. The Bishop's wife was one of the mourners. There was a wreath
> from the RAF and another from girl telephonists of the AFS stationed in the
> town inscribed "When duty calls all must obey."

Raiders were reported in the Mildenhall and Honington areas, a salvo exploding
a mile from the latter airfield, and, at 01:20, AA guns at RAF Wattisham opened
fire while searchlights at Honington illuminated one Heinkel, whose gunner fired
down the beams.[5] At about the same time Flg Off John Petre, flying Spitfire L1032
of 19 Squadron, located a bomber near Newmarket. This was 5J+AM of 4./KG4,
which then turned and headed towards RAF Honington. Petre opened fire, seeing
smoke issue from a damaged engine, but had to sheer off hard to one side to avoid
colliding with another aircraft that appeared alongside – a Blenheim – also firing
at the Heinkel. At that moment, searchlights illuminated Petre's Spitfire, allowing
the Heinkel's gunners to return accurate fire. The Spitfire, hit in the fuel tank, burst
into flames. Petre was able to bale out but his face and hands were badly burned.
On landing he was rushed to hospital in Bury St Edmunds. Meanwhile, his burning
Spitfire hit the roof of Thurston House before crashing in its garden.

The Blenheim (K8687/X) was flown by Sqn Ldr Spike O'Brien of 23 Squadron.
He opened fire, seeing smoke gushing from the Heinkel's starboard engine, but had
then lost control and went into a spin. The navigator Plt Off Cuthbert King-Clark
– actually a qualified pilot flying to gain operational experience – baled out but was
killed instantly when hit by a propeller. O'Brien baled out, landing safely, but the
gunner Cpl David Little was killed in the crash. O'Brien reported:

> Opened fire on E/A with our rear turret gun from below and in front as it
> was held by searchlights. The E/A turned to port and dived. I gave him several
> long bursts with the front guns from 50 to 100 yards range and saw clouds
> of smoke from the target's starboard engine and a lesser amount from the
> port engine. I overshot the E/A and passed very close below and in front
> of him. My rear gunner put a burst into the cockpit at close range and the
> E/A disappeared in a diving turn, apparently out of control. I suddenly lost
> control of my own aircraft, which spun violently to the left. Failing to recover
> from the spin I ordered my crew to abandon the aircraft and I followed the
> navigator out of the hatch.

Flt Lt Duke-Woolley later related the story as told to him:

In the gunfight the Heinkel went down, then Spike's Blenheim went out of control in a spin. At that time, popular opinion among pilots was that no pilot had ever got out of a spinning Blenheim alive, because the only way out was through the top sliding hatch and you then fell through one or other of the airscrews! The new boy (King-Clarke) probably didn't know that but nevertheless he froze and Spike had to get him out. He undid his seat belt, unplugged his oxygen and pushed him up out of the top hatch while holding his parachute ripcord. He told me afterwards that he felt sick when the lad fell through the airscrew. Spike then had to get out himself. He grasped the wireless aerial behind the hatch, pulled himself up by it and then turned round so that his feet were on the side of the fuselage. Then he kicked outwards as hard as he could. He felt what he thought was the tip of an airscrew blade tap him on his helmet earpiece but luck was with him that night.

The damaged Heinkel crashed at Fleam Dyke near Six Mile Bottom in Cambridgeshire at 01:15. Oblt Joachim von Armin, Fw Wilhelm Maier and Fw Karl Hauck were captured, but Uffz Paul Görsch was killed. Flt Lt Duke-Woolley added an amusing sequel to the account:

Spike parachuted down safely to the outskirts of a village and went to the nearest pub to ring Wittering and ask for transport to fetch him home. He bought a pint and sat down to await transport and began chatting idly to another chap in uniform who was in the room when he arrived. After a while, thinking that the chap's uniform was a bit unusual, Spike asked him if he was a Pole or a Czech. "Oh no," replied his companion in impeccable English, "I'm a German pilot actually. Just been shot down by one of your chaps." At this point – so the story goes – Spike sprang to his feet and said. "I arrest you in the name of the King. Anyway, where did you learn English?" To which the German [presumably Oblt von Armin] replied, "That's all right. I won't try to get away. In fact, I studied for three years at Cambridge, just down the road. My shout, what's yours?" So that's just what they did: sat and had a drink.

Flg Off George Ball of 19 Squadron, in Spitfire K9807, was vectored to the Newmarket area to investigate another intruder, finding 5J+FP of 6./KG4 illuminated by searchlights. He pursued this, closing in to 50 yards, seeing his fire entering the Heinkel as it flew southwards, jettisoning its bombs on the way. The Heinkel, flown by Ltn Hans-Jürgen Bachaus, eventually ditched off Sacketts Gap, Margate, at 02:15. Bachaus and two members of his crew Uffz Theodor Kühn and Uffz Fritz Böck were rescued; Fw Alfred Reitzig had attempted to bale out but his parachute snagged in the tailplane and he was killed.

One of the last claims on this dramatic night was made by AA gunners at Harwich, who believed they shot down into the sea a departing Heinkel at 01:13. This was probably an aircraft from I Gruppe that returned damaged by AA fire. There were no crew casualties. Their aircraft was deemed 60% damaged but repairable. The last of the raiders was recorded crossing the coast at 02.50, releasing its bombs in the Clacton area. An empty house in Salisbury Road received a direct hit. Claims were submitted for 10 Heinkels but this was reduced to five and two probables. In fact, six were lost including the one that belly-landed near Calais. Two others returned damaged. Three Blenheims were also lost to return fire, as was one Spitfire.

The commander of 5J+AM, Oblt Joachim von Armin, later reflected:

> Until the night of our operation no British night fighter operations were reported. Therefore we did not camouflage our aircraft, flew in at 4,500 metres [15,000 feet], and did not anticipate anything but anti-aircraft gunfire from the ground.

Duxford's station commander Wg Cdr Woody Woodhall witnessed the action in which 5J+AM was shot down – and shot down its first assailant, the Spitfire of 19 Squadron:

> John Petre's Spitfire burst into flames and he had baled out. I was an eye witness to all this because it occurred over the aerodrome. My immediate concern was for John and after giving instructions for civil police to be alerted to round up the enemy, I sent search parties out. I next learned that John had been picked up suffering from nasty burns and taken to the nearest hospital. After giving orders that the prisoners when captured were to be placed in the guardroom if unhurt, in the sick quarters if injured, I set off in my car to see how John was faring in hospital.
>
> Dawn was just breaking when I returned to Duxford and I was informed that the civil police had collected the prisoners and were bringing them to the guardroom. I left strict orders that there was to be no fraternising, and when the prisoners arrived they were to be given a meal and cigarettes and left in cells until collected by the security people. I was told that there were two German NCOs in the cells, but that the pilot, an officer, had been taken over to the Officers Mess.
>
> I found the German pilot taking his ease in the guest room with a cocktail in hand, chatting to Philip Hunter [CO of 264 Squadron] and several of our pilots. Our boys immediately stood up as I came into the room and said "Good morning, sir" but the Hun, an arrogant young Nazi of about 20, remained lounging in his armchair and insolently eyed me up and down, but not for long. I got him to his feet smartly. Needless to say, I had him transferred to the guardroom cell. The boys thought me very hard-hearted and strict. When I told them about John Petre was burnt, I think they understood my anger.[6]

While KG4 was searching for targets in East Anglia, Bomber Command despatched sixty-nine aircraft – thirty-eight Whitleys, twenty-six Wellingtons and five

Hampdens – to attack oil targets at Hamburg, Bremen and in the Ruhr and to railways at many other places. Two Whitleys and one Wellington were lost.

At 20:00 on the evening of 19 June, a patrol of 66 Squadron Spitfires intercepted a Ju88 some 30-40 miles north-east of Gt Yarmouth, which was claimed as destroyed following attacks by Flt Lt Billy Burton (N3048) with Plt Offs Dizzy Allen (N3041) and Leon Collingridge (N3042). Allen reported:

> Blue Section, in which I was No. 2, were ordered to intercept 'bogie' at 19:30 hours. After several vectors being given bandit was sighted 2 or 3 miles ahead. Blue leader gave line astern and proceeded to attack. The first attack was a quarter attack in which I did not fire – not having sufficiently good sight. After breaking off I lost Blue leader and delivered another quarter attack on starboard side, with quite a good sight. I then followed enemy a/c in a stern chase and saw my tracers hit in the fuselage. I was at +6 boost and catching up at 40-50 mph. I tried further deflection shots from slightly to one side and saw my bullets fall into the sea all around the enemy a/c, which had lost height from 12,000 feet to practically sea level in a gentle dive by this time. After the first attack the rear guns were silent, but cannon fire was observed during the first attack. Blue 3 was on my port side and slightly in front during the last stern chase, and when he broke I closed to about 150 yards when my ammunition ran out. Thin white smoke was observed coming from the port engine when I finally broke away.

This aircraft may have been one of several carrying out reconnaissance sorties in advance of planned twin Luftwaffe attacks along the north-east coast, and the West Country.

A lack of Blenheim night fighters based in the Northern counties saw several Spitfire squadrons being requested to fly 'fighter night' sorties during the hours of darkness on the night of 19/20 June, with limited success. County Durham was targeted and West Hartlepool suffered its first air raid with two people killed and seven injured. One of those killed was an air raid warden. Thirty shops were extensively damaged and six houses demolished, with many others damaged. Stockton, Billingham and Norton District also received bombs resulting in two dead and one injured, soldiers who were on duty at the ICI factory in Billingham. An hour before midnight Hull received its first bombs. Little damage was done and there were no casualties.

Plt Off Tim Vigors of 222 Squadron (P9324) was credited with shooting down a He111 near Sunk Island an hour after midnight. Vigors reported:

> I took off at 00:20 to patrol Line B. Later I saw three searchlight beams in the apex of which appeared to be an enemy aircraft. I proceeded to investigate. 10-12 searchlights then concentrated on a He111 at about 10,000 feet. I attacked from below and behind, and was met by very accurate tracer fire from rear

gunner, one bullet at least penetrating my engine cowling. He then dived and I made one attack at right angles and pursuing him, engaged again with full bursts using all my ammunition. No return fire from rear gunner after first attack. He continued to dive steeply into cloud at between 250 and 300 mph.

I tried to find him below base of cloud, which was only at about 1,000 feet but saw no trace then, but subsequently a Heinkel was seen by a gun site crew strike telephone wires and pole and to career across two fields at practically ground level (marks of the airscrew blades being plainly visible across one field) and, still proceeding in an easterly direction, was presumed to have crashed in the water. An HDF station working near afterwards reported that the engines of this aircraft faded out suddenly at a range of about 7,000 yards. The actual time of my combat and the times stated in the reports received from AA and searchlight companies tally very well.

222 Squadron's CO Sqn Ldr Tubby Mermagen claimed another Heinkel damaged near Cottingham some 45 minutes later. Yet another Heinkel was claimed possibly destroyed over Teesmouth by Flt Lt Terry Webster of 41 Squadron. Webster (R6635) took off at 22:59; he wrote:

I was patrolling Sedgefield at 10,000 feet. Very considerable activity from AA guns in Tees area, and bombs were seen to drop north of Middlesborough. Searchlights at Teesmouth then picked up an aircraft and AA guns engaged it. I was about 5 miles north-east of aircraft and climbed after it. I had to use 12lbs boost to catch it. Aircraft caught off Teesmouth. I closed to approximately 150 yards and had no difficulty in getting in gun sight. I fired approximately 800 rounds, closing to 50 yards. Aircraft was losing height throughout the battle and disappeared into low cloud. I broke off the engagement and returned to base.

On landing at 00:12, Webster found one bullet hole in his port mainplane. He claimed the Heinkel as possibly destroyed.

Some twenty minutes after midnight, a German aircraft struck a balloon cable at Middlesborough, the property of No. 928 Balloon Squadron, following which it was reported as having crashed into the of the mouth of the Tees. Guns of the 43rd AA Brigade also claimed a share, as did the Spitfires. A contemporary report stated:

Shortly after midnight the balloon crew heard the sound of bombing. Almost immediately an aircraft was picked up by the searchlights and recognised by the balloon crew as a Ju88 [*sic*]. The aircraft dived to within 1,000 feet of the ground and the balloon crew took shelter. "A few seconds later," said one of the crew, "we heard the bomber turn away, its engines giving out a spluttering note. We came from our shelter and examined the pulley wheel of the balloon.

We found hundreds of feet of cable lying on the ground and knew that the German bomber must have hit our balloon cable." The crew's story was confirmed when messages came from another balloon site and from an AA gun centre stating that the aircraft had been seen falling into the sea.

It seems that the main target/victim of all those involved was a He111 of Stab/KG4 that crash-landed at Kelingholms-Hauen with severe damage following fighter attack, with one crew member lightly wounded. A second Heinkel, of 6./KG4 landed at Lille with the observer, Fw Heinz Schafer, wounded in the stomach following an attack by a night fighter. There was much damage to residential property. An attack the following night killed three policemen in Tynemouth.

German aircraft searched for the missing crew and one of these was picked up on radar approaching Hull and Flg Off John Bell of 616 Squadron was vectored to investigate, and found a He115 claiming it probably destroyed at 23:15. This aircraft, from 1./KüFlGr.106, was tasked to bomb fuel storage tanks at Hull, but jettisoned its bombs when attacked, evaded, and safely returned to base.

However, the following afternoon, another He115, S4+MH of 1./KüFlGr.506 operating from Sylt, was later reported down in the sea west of Smola Island, off the Norwegian coast, the victim of Blenheims J and A of 254 Squadron flown by Flt Lt Hal Randall and Sgt Frank Mottram at 19:37. S4+MH was lost with its crew, Fw Heinrich Bode, Ltn. deR. Hans Bickebach, and Fw Georg Hildebrand.

The first mission carried out against the West Country took place on the same night (19/20 June), when the Bristol Aeroplane Company at Filton, as well as the docks at Avonmouth and Southampton, was targeted by seven He111s of III/KG27 flying from Merville, near the Franco-Belgian border. Although the raiders claimed to have successfully attacked the Filton plant the facts were somewhat different, and Portishead was as near as the German bombers came, ten bombs falling along the shore at about 02:15. One Heinkel returned with flak damage.

With the Heinkels of III/KG27 raiding the Bristol area, RAF Bomber Command had despatched nineteen Hampdens to carry out an attack on the Dortmund-Ems Canal. The raid was considered a success and all aircraft returned safely. Photographs taken later by RAF reconnaissance aircraft showed that the viaducts were badly damaged and that the canal had been rendered unusable, for the water had drained away from it and left barges sitting on the mud. One of those involved in the raid, Sgt Joe Unsworth, recalled:

It was a fine moonlight night and the water shone like silver. We got a direct hit on the side of the aqueduct with a heavy bomb and 20 minutes afterwards we saw water seeping out, so came back highly delighted.

Other crews also claimed hits, some pilots dropping down to 50 feet to ensure accuracy. All found to their happy surprise that the area lacked anti-aircraft defences, allowing repeated and low-level attacks to be made.

Flg Off Jumbo Deansley of 152 Squadron came close to shooting down a BOAC
Ensign during a daylight patrol on 24 June:

> I was a section leader patrolling the Tyne area, which was very sensitive as the
> latest battleship, the *King George V* had been recently launched. The weather
> was cloudy and we were adjacent to the balloon barrage over Newcastle.
> Suddenly a large aircraft appeared quite near which I thought was a flying
> boat. My No. 2, Sgt Barker, correctly identified the aircraft as a BOAC Ensign.
> Later I learned that the Ensign was carrying 605 Squadron ground crew
> following the squadron on their move north after Dunkirk. Little did they
> know that they had a very lucky escape.

The next operation against the Bristol area was undertaken on the night of 24/25
June, when five He111s of I/KG27 were again briefed to attack Filton, which the
Germans claimed to have successfully raided. The facts, however, were somewhat
different, and at 00:17, the first bombs fell in the St Philip's area of Bristol, followed
shortly after by the first bomb that impacted at the corner of Lower Maudlin Street
and Harford Street killing two people. All told, five civilians lost their lives during
this raid, and 32 were injured.

Yet another Heinkel was claimed shot down off Brighton on the night of 25/26
June, on this occasion by a Hurricane of 601 Squadron. Harassing attacks against
targets in the West Country were now being undertaken almost every night, and Sqn
Ldr Max Aitken (P2920) and Flg Off Tom Hubbard took off at 23:00 to conduct
a patrol. There was cloud in patches but a strong moon. By chance a battery of
searchlights picked up a He111 out of a formation of three. Before the bomber
could escape the beam, Sqn Ldr Aitken intercepted:

> I took off and climbed through the clouds. I was excited, for I had waited for
> this chance for the previous three nights; sitting in a chair all night, dressed in
> my flying clothes and Mae West. I had waited from dusk to dawn, but nothing
> whatsoever would come our way. This night they were obviously coming. I
> climbed to my ordered height and remained on my patrol line. After about an
> hour I was told that the enemy were at a certain spot, flying from north-west
> to south-east. Luckily, I was approaching that spot myself.
>
> The searchlights, which had been weaving about beneath light cloud,
> suddenly all converged at a spot. They illuminated the cloud brilliantly,
> and there, silhouetted on the cloud, flying across my port beam, were three
> enemy aircraft. I turned left, and slowed down slightly. One searchlight struck
> through a small gap and showed up the whole of one plane. I recognised the
> plane as a He111. One of the enemy turned left and I lost sight of the other.
>
> I fastened on the last of the three. I got about 100 yards behind and below,
> where I could clearly see his exhaust flames. As we went out of the searchlights
> and crossed the coast, he went into a shallow dive. This upset me for a bit,

for I got rather high, almost directly behind him. I managed to get back and opened my hood to see better. I put my firing button to fire, and pressed it. Bullets poured into him. It was at point-blank range and I could see the tracer disappearing inside, but nothing seemed to happen except that he slowed down considerably. I almost overshot him, but put the propeller into full fine and managed to keep my position.

I fired again, four bursts, and then noticed a glow inside the machine. We had been in a shallow dive and I thought we were getting near the sea, so I fired all the rest of my ammunition into him. The red glow got brighter. He was obviously on fire inside. At 500 feet I broke away to the right and tried to follow, but overshot, so I did not see him strike the water. I climbed and at 1,000 feet pulled off a parachute flare. As the flare fell towards the sea I saw the Heinkel lying on the water. A column of smoke was blowing from his rear section. I circled twice, but there was no movement. No one tried to climb out, so I turned and flew for home.

He111s of I/KG4 were around in the north-east once again on the night of 26/27 June, Spitfires achieving better results than previous with two Heinkels and a Ju88 being claimed, the latter by a 72 Squadron Spitfire at midnight near Blythe, Flg Off Ron Thomson (L1078) being the successful pilot. This may, however, have been misidentified. Its demise was recorded in the diary of Flt Lt Deacon Elliot, thus:

'Happy' Thomson's great success. Shortly after getting airborne [from RAF Acklington] to take up a position on his prescribed patrol line, the air raid warnings sounded and seconds later searchlights illuminated and held onto the 'X' raid. Happy made the interception. And having identified the enemy, backed off a little and blew it to pieces. All this was witnessed by us standing at dispersal. On landing, which in itself must have been difficult, as the whole of his aircraft was covered in oil from the exploding enemy and pieces of the Ju88 lodged in his Spit's air intake duct, Happy, who at the best of times was frightfully modest, simply said, "I think I got him."

His victim was almost certainly Heinkel 5J+BL of 3./KG4 that crashed into the sea off Hull with the loss of Hptm Heinz Schröder, the Staffelkapitän, Ltn Helmut Furcht (pilot), Obfw Martin Hartel and Fw Eugen Seitz. Two bodies from this crew including that of Ltn Furcht were recovered by HMS *Brazen* and believed buried at sea.

Plt Off Donald Smith of 616 Squadron claimed a Heinkel off Withernsea at 00:17, which was probably 5J+EK of 2./KG4, from which Fw Siegfried Gessert, Uffz Karl-Heinz Beck, Uffz Wilhelm Dieter and Gfr Horst Filikowski, were captured. Their aircraft had been coned by searchlights and then riddled by bullets with the cockpit, wings and radiators damaged. Both engines seized and Gessert was forced to carry out a ditching 20 miles east of Tees. The bomber sank almost immediately but the crew was able to scramble into their dingy. After three hours adrift they were picked up by a drifter and landed at Newcastle. Two of the crew had sustained wounds.

A third Heinkel was engaged by Plt Off Roy Morant of 222 Squadron some 35 minutes later over the Humber Mouth area, which had been hit by AA fire, but his aircraft P9420 was hit by return fire and though seriously injured he managed to fly back to base. His opponent was possibly 5J+DH of 1 Staffel which was also attacked near Hull; one crew member (Uffz Oskar Hoffmann) was killed. His CO, Sqn Ldr Mermagen, reported:

> Tally-ho! was given at 00:28 and immediately afterwards the pilot [Morant] complained that he was blinded by our searchlights. This interference continued for some time and apparently caused him to lose his target. It is not yet known if he actually engaged the target on this occasion: he is reported to have stated that he did so. At 00:54, the pilot reported that he had been hit and was returning to base. This time coincides with the report of an E/A being brought down at the mouth of the Humber after engagement by a Spitfire. Patches of oil and recovery of a German parachute from the Humber appear to confirm. The pilot crashed on landing at Q landing ground at Digby and was seriously injured and is not in a fit condition to give any information.

Meanwhile, Heinkels of I/KG26 were active along the Scottish eastern coast, two of these also falling to Spitfires. Flt Lt Ken MacDonald of 603 Squadron shot down Hptm Horst Schwilder's 3 Staffel aircraft at 01:00, about 5 miles south-east of Turnhouse. There were no survivors, with only the body of Ltn Harald Christoph being recovered from the sea. Crewmen Fw Friedrich Bichtemann and Uffz Alfons Mack were also lost. MacDonald later made a radio broadcast:

> Tuesday's was the first night raid over our part of the coast. When the enemy were detected I was told to go up and look for them – that was between midnight and one a.m. I flew around, peering into the gloom – and for some time all I could see was an occasional searchlight beam snooping around the sky. I'd almost begun to think the Hun had managed to get away, when I suddenly spotted, a long way off, flashes on the ground and in the air. So I went over to have a look, and when nearly there, saw a Heinkel sliding across the sky really beautifully lit by our searchlights. Anti-aircraft fire was going off absolutely all round it. It really was a magnificent sight. After all, I had – well, what you might call – a ringside seat.
>
> There was a terrific firework display in progress, and the Heinkel looked to me rather like a puzzled old woman suddenly caught in the spotlight. I'd come up more or less behind and there he was, just ambling along, not quite knowing what to do. As a matter of fact I imagine the pilot was pretty well dazzled with all the lights on him. I got into position right behind and just

below, got my sights on him, and pressed the gun button. A shower of sparks flew out of the enemy, and clouds of smoke, and he wallowed a bit. Then he went down in a slow spiral dive into the darkness. That was the last I saw of him – though I did catch the glare of his incendiary bombs on the ground. He must have jettisoned these as he dropped.

A second 603 Squadron pilot, Flg Off Jack Haig, was airborne during the raid. Low on fuel he requested the flare-path to be switched on, but this was not permitted while the raid was in progress. When the engine failed he was obliged to bale out, coming down safely while his aircraft (N3190) crashed near Harperrigg Reservoir.

An hour later, Flt Lt Sandy Johnstone flying LO-Q (L1004) of 602 Squadron shot down another Heinkel some 10 miles south of Dunbar. In his memoirs, Sandy Johnstone wrote:

Night after night we maintained our state of readiness and around midnight I found myself patrolling at about 10,000 feet on a line between Dalkeith and Musselburgh. There seemed to be a great deal of activity to the east of me but I was forced to focus my attention to the west. I saw three searchlights suddenly burst into action about two miles to the north. Within seconds their powerful beams had converged to form a tripod of light. There, caught like a trapped moth and glistening like a star, sat a silvery-grey aircraft. I couldn't believe my eyes. There had been no word of bogeys or bandits being anywhere near me.

As I closed in on the aircraft, still brilliantly illuminated in the searchlights' glare, I saw the black swastika painted on the large rounded fin and rudder. It was a Heinkel 111. The aircraft was heaving around – the pilot trying to take all positive evasive action to get away from the lights. But the men on the ground were having none of it. They hung on to their Heinkel and gave me ample opportunity to get it lined up in my sights. I squeezed the firing button and the Spitfire shuddered. I was now overtaking the Heinkel so fast that I had to pull away violently to avoid colliding with it. As I fell away in a steep dive I had no time to see whether or not I had inflicted any damage on my quarry.

Being so excited at the chance to make my first kill I had completely forgotten to close my throttle and found myself hurtling downwards through the coal-black sky at a fearful rate. I had no idea what my flying attitude was as most of the instruments on the panel seemed to have gone crazy. I tried to move the rudder pedals. I couldn't find them. Side to side I swept my feet. There was no trace of the two control bars. I tried hard to understand what was happening and was almost sick when the Spitfire tumbled around and fell in an air pocket. In the middle of this fresh buffeting the reason for my discomfort, and my inability to find the rudder pedals, struck me. I was upside down and going into a screaming inverted dive.

Wrenching on the stick and using every trick in the book, and a few more besides, I was able to turn the Spitfire over and point her upwards again. I was shaking now – partly from shock and partly from the efforts to control the aircraft. The Spitfire was behaving normally again.

I was amazed to see that the searchlights still surrounded the Heinkel. Luck was being more than kind to me tonight. As I closed once again, more carefully this time, I was delighted to see a thick stream of smoke pouring from the aircraft's starboard engine. I closed in astern of him and prepared to deliver the coup de grâce. It was almost too easy. My fingers trembled on the firing button but I controlled myself sufficiently until the Heinkel's wingspan filled the orange-coloured image on my reflector sight. I squeezed the firing button and the damage was done.

A mixture of glycol and engine oil swept back towards me from the stricken Heinkel. The thick oil stream burst on my windscreen as I pulled away to port. Eventually the mess cleared and I saw the German was on his way down. Both engines were ablaze and great streams of smoke billowed back behind the Heinkel, which was fast losing height. About a mile or so out to sea he prepared to ditch and I watched the two beams from his landing lights as he switched them on in the final moments. All of a sudden the lights seemed to vanish as the aircraft struck the sea. I circled over the doomed aircraft. Slowly I saw the lights under the surface begin to dim. Soon there was nothing to see.

Flying low over the spot I fired the colours of the day – a two-star Very cartridge. This would mark the spot for any rescue craft which might be making its way towards the scene. My efforts had not been in vain. The crew of the Heinkel were eventually picked up in their rubber dinghy, injured but alive, and sent to Edinburgh Castle for interrogation.

Uffz Hermann Wilm, Gfr Ludwig Riede and Flgr Josef Schwehr were rescued and became POWs, but Gfr Rudolf Wähner was killed; his body was later recovered. This may have been the incident recorded by the skipper of a minesweeper, although he believed it was a victim of AA fire:

At approximately 01:40, I saw an enemy aircraft in the beams of several searchlights over the coast. Anti-aircraft gunfire was exploding all round it. A few minutes later, I saw that the machine was rapidly losing height and tracer bullets could be seen fired in its direction. The 'plane crashed into the sea. I immediately steamed full speed in the direction and sometime later found three survivors clinging to a collapsible boat. I picked these up. One of them, who spoke a little English, said that the first burst of anti-aircraft fire had put both engines of his plane, a twin-engined Heinkel, out of action.

236 Squadron of Coastal Command was requested by Fighter Command to assist in patrolling the night skies with its Blenheims. During a 01:40-02:25 patrol off

the Isle of Wight, English-born Canadian Flt Lt Dick Denison (accompanied by air gunner Plt Off Arthur Price) in L1119 claimed a Heinkel probably destroyed:

> Opened fire at slightly over 400 yards from astern but fire seemed low and to port. E/a turned slightly allowing Blenheim to get astern and I got in second burst from 200 yards. Rear gunner believed silenced. Passed e/a on port side enabling gunner to get in four very short bursts of fire.

"The searchlights," he added, "were very efficient. They never left the target and never illuminated our aircraft," but then the searchlights went off and the Heinkel was lost from sight.

Not all sorties were successful, however, as epitomised by Plt Off Ted Shipman of 41 Squadron:

> Very early in the morning, at about 03:30 [on the night of 27/28 June], I was awakened and ordered off. It was very dark indeed. And I think I must have got into the aircraft and started up almost by instinct, because I certainly did not feel at all awake.

Bombs had been dropped on Middlesbrough at 03:14, damaging fourteen houses in the Grove Hill district. Hutton Hall military camp at Guisborough was also bombed:

> I was sent out to sea off West Hartlepool at about 9,000 feet – the target was said to be some way ahead of me. I must have gone some 70 miles when I lost R/T contact with the controller, a WAAF. As I was getting no joy at all I turned back on a reciprocal heading – there seemed little purpose in going on. When I regained radio contact I was sent again more or less due east, with no better results. Having lost R/T contact once more I came back again, regained contact and was sent out, this time, south-east. The target was said to be 'just in front', but there was nothing to be seen at all. I persevered for quite a while after I had lost R/T contact for the third time, and then I turned back in the direction of home. The chances of an interception were absolutely nil, and I had been airborne for some 50 minutes and my fuel was getting low.
>
> When I managed to get R/T contact again I was told to return to base. Naturally I requested a course to steer home. After a short delay the controller asked me for my position! They were obviously not plotting me and I had no idea where I was. At this I blew my top and my patience was exhausted, having been chasing in and out over the sea. My reply was "How the bloody hell do I know?" I got no further reply or help from the controller that night.

Fortunately, he was able to find his way to Whitby and from there to his base at RAF Leeming. Next morning he was officially reprimanded by the sympathetic Station Commander.

Heinkels were reported intruding south-east of Norwich shortly after midnight on 28/29 June, one of these being sighted by Plt Off Derek Willans and Plt Off Allan Atkinson in Blenheim YP-Z of 23 Squadron:

The aircraft was illuminated by one searchlight, the other searchlights swung onto the target and I identified E/A as a He111. He did a steep turn and flew past us on the starboard side and slightly above. My A/G fired at short burst at about 100 yards. I turned quickly round onto the Heinkel's tail and opened fire from dead astern and slightly above at about 350 yards. This burst of about 7 seconds indicated incendiary bullets striking E/A's fuselage. When I finished my burst I saw tracer bullets fired at me from the E/A. I opened fire again with a 3 second burst and all fire from the E/A's rear gun ceased, and as I passed underneath my A/G opened fire just before the Heinkel passed out of range.

Willans later commented: "aircraft believed to have not reached its home." Another probable was claimed by Plt Off Roy Marples in a 616 Squadron Spitfire off Hornsea. Both Spitfire and Blenheim may have attacked the same aircraft (the combats were timed eight minutes apart) that might have been an aircraft of I/ KG4 that crashed on return to St-Léger when the pilot attempted a one-engine landing, during which the Gruppenkommandeur Major Hans von Ploetz was badly injured.

During the same night, Bomber Command sent a small force of bombers to raid targets in Germany, including Whitleys of 58 Squadron. When a few miles east of Münchengladbach, N1469 flown by Canadian Flg Off Bill Espley, was coned by searchlights, which, at the same time, illuminated a Do17 of I/NJG1 that was closing in. Plt Off R. F. Williams, the Whitley's gunner, reacted the quicker and his burst of fire hit Uffz Hugo Schwarz's aircraft, which crash-landed with all three members of the crew wounded, two seriously. The observer, Fw Ludwig Born, died soon thereafter, but Uffz Schwarz eventually recovered, while Fw Gerhard Palm suffered only minor wounds.

At 16:40 on 30 June, a lone raider, apparently undetected until too late to give a warning, flew over Hull from west to east, made a few sporadic attacks on barrage balloons and then dropped sixteen bombs near the Saltend oil depot. The majority of the bombs fell outside the depot, but pieces of shrapnel from one bomb pierced the side of a tank holding about 2,500 tons of petrol, which caught fire. The flames licked the outside of the tank, bringing the temperature of the petrol inside to a dangerous degree, and burning petrol began to flow to a number of adjacent tanks. Water was sprayed on the adjoining tanks to cool them until the arrival of sufficient stocks of foam arrived to quell the fire. More than 2,000 tons of petrol in the affected tank was saved, apart from the vast quantities in peril in adjacent holders.

Five George Medals were subsequently awarded for bravery during this incident. They went to George Howe, manager of Shell-Mex and BP for gallantry and leadership in fighting fire at the oil depot; George Sewell, engineer of Shell-Mex and BP for working continuously on a tank roof while gas inside was burning; William Sigsworth, manager, Anglo-American Oil for displaying courage and resource, when he assisted Mr Howe; Jack Owen, fireman of Kingston-upon-Hull Fire Brigade for volunteering to operate a hose on top of an almost red-hot tank; and Leading Fireman Clifford Turner for displaying outstanding courage in extinguishing fire.

*****

At the end of the month Göring issued a general order regarding the air war against Great Britain. In it he stated:

The Luftwaffe War Command in the fight against England makes it necessary to co-ordinate as closely as possible, with respect to time and targets, the attacks of Luftflotten 2, 3 and 5. Distribution of the duties to the Luftflotten will, therefore, in general be tied to firm targets and firm dates of attack so that not only can the most effective results on important targets be achieved but the well-developed defence forces of the enemy can be split and be faced with the maximum forms of attack.

After the original disposition of the forces has been carried out in its new operational areas, that is after making sure of adequate anti-aircraft and fighter defence, adequate provisioning and an absolutely trouble-free chain of command, then a planned offensive against selected targets can be put in motion to fit in with the overall requirements of the commanders-in-chief of the Luftwaffe.

To save us time as well as ensuring that the forces concerned are ready:-

(A) The war against England is to be restricted to destructive attacks against industry and air force targets which have weak defensive forces. These attacks under suitable weather conditions, which should allow for surprise, can be carried out individually or in groups by day. The most thorough study of the target and its surrounding area from the map and the parts of the target concerned, that is the vital parts of the target, is a pre-requisite for success. It is also stressed that every effort should be made to avoid unnecessary loss of life amongst the civil population.

(B) By means of reconnaissance and the engagement of units of smaller size it should be possible to draw out smaller enemy formations and by this means to ascertain the strength and grouping of the enemy defences. The engagement of the Luftwaffe after the initial attacks have been carried out and after all forces are completely battleworthy has for its objectives:

By attacking the enemy air force, its ground organisations, and its own industry to provide the necessary conditions for a satisfactory overall war against enemy imports, provisions and defence economy, and at the same time provide necessary protection for those territories occupied by ourselves.

By attacking importing harbours and their installations, importing transports and warships to destroy the English system of replenishment. Both tasks must be carried out separately, but must be carried out in co-ordination one with another.

As long as the enemy air force is not defeated the prime requirement for the air force on every possible opportunity by day or by night, in the air or on the ground, without consideration of other tasks.

* * * * *

The RAF's Bomber Command showed the desperation of the situation when it issued counter-invasion instructions to its groups:

> Now the enemy occupies the western seaboard of Europe, the threat of invasion is very real. If it comes it will be by air and sea preceded by attacks on communications, airfields and naval bases. 2 Group is to be reinforced, at a time to be decided later, by aircraft operating from these stations:
> RAF Bassingbourn – 24 Audax and up to 18 Ansons
> RAF Cottesmore – 24 Audax and up to 18 Ansons
> RAF Upwood – 16 Blenheims and up to 18 Ansons
> RAF Wyton – 15 Blenheims
> In the event of a landing the Commander's authority is to have control of 50% of the available effort of the affiliated stations. This call takes authority over all other tasks.
> All aircraft not under army control are to attack enemy convoys at sea. If a landing is effected the main body of the convoys at sea may be attacked at places where the landing has been made, depending on the situation at the time. Enemy forces caught at sea, and craft containing landing parties, are to be primary targets irrespective of enemy warships in the vicinity. If a landing has been effected and it is decided to attack beaches, enemy craft laying off the beaches and stores on them are to be primary targets.

AOC 2 Group added his own instructions to his squadrons:

> You must bear in mind that your forces may have to play a most important part in repelling an invasion of this country, and you should be prepared at short notice to divert your squadrons to the attack of the invading enemy force at points of departure and subsequently at sea, and points of landing in this country. To meet the threat of invasion twelve aircraft are to stand by (at each station) every morning at 20 minutes' notice from twilight to sunrise.

A plan to use every available aircraft in a last-ditch effort to repel a threatened German invasion was also devised, known as *Operation Banquet*. An Air Ministry meeting outlined a series of ambitious plans to make use of various aircraft in the event of an invasion, thus the AOC-in-C Training Command was ordered to plan to make the maximum practical number of aircraft available for operations. The overall plan was divided into a number of separate operations that could be enacted independently. Sub-groups of the plan, as envisaged, were: Training (Battle, Audax, Harvard, Hind etc), Transport (Harrow), 2 Group (Blenheim, Battle), Technical (Wallace) and 6 and 7 Groups (Whitley, Anson, Hereford)

Aircraft allocated under *Banquet* would, in many cases, lack bombsights, armour for the protection of the crew, defensive guns and self-sealing fuel tanks. While these were to be fitted where possible, RAF instructions were very clear that no aircraft was to be considered unfit for want of such niceties. Anything that could fly and drop bombs would suffice. The air crew would be the experienced instructors as well as those students that had reached 'a reasonably satisfactory standard of training'.

The most ominous – and potentially suicidal – of the plans was *Banquet Light* which would see the formation of striking forces composed of Tiger Moth biplanes and other light aircraft of the EFTS. De Havilland put forward plans for converting the Tiger Moth into a bomber by equipping it with eight under-fuselage racks beneath the rear cockpit, each able to carry a 20lb bomb. As an alternative, the bomb-racks could be installed four on each side beneath the lower wings, this obviated trimming difficulties. The racks had been designed for the military version of the Dragons supplied toIraq eight years previously. Modification of the relatively small number, sixteen, of Magister trainers were also attempted, but this proved troublesome, therefore *Banquet Light* would use Tiger Moths.

Another proposed use for the Tiger was the 'Paraslasher'; fitted with a scythe-like blade intended to cut parachutists' canopies as they descended to earth. Flight tests proved the idea, but it was not officially adopted. There was also the 'Human Crop-Sprayer' version, which had a tank fitted in the front cockpit with powder dispensers located under the wings. The tank would be filled with an extremely poisonous insecticide and probably violating the terms of the Geneva Convention. It was intended that low flying aircraft would dust the German troops as they waded ashore.

The *Banquet Light* strike force was to be employed in an army co-operation role, which would likely mean being sent to bomb concentrations of airborne troops or soldiers landing on the beaches. They were to be based at advanced landing grounds around the country including Grangemouth, Inverness, Macmerry, York, Firbeck, Hooton, Hatfield, Snailwell, Bury St Edmunds, Sawbridgeworth, Gatwick, Odiham, Tilshead, and Weston Zoyland. The intention was that the two-seater Tiger Moth bombers should be flown solo into an attack at low altitude until the enemy was identified and then climb to 800 feet and dive to 500 feet to release the bombs.

Most of the pilots for *Banquet Light* would be students who had not yet graduated. The scheme required that trainee pilots were introduced to bombing at an early stage in their instruction – just in case they needed to go into action immediately. Instructors were told to take every opportunity to carry out practice bombing. However, with no dummy bombs available, training exercises were carried out with the aircraft flown from the front cockpit by instructors and house bricks were thrown over the side from the rear cockpit. It was discovered that the bricks fell faster than a diving Tiger Moth and instructions were given to throw the bricks forcibly away from the aircraft. About 350 aircraft were available. This was not an insignificant force, but the Moths and their inexperienced pilots would have been very vulnerable to enemy aircraft and the plan was widely regarded as virtually suicidal.

Other proposals included Lysanders fitted with twin 20 mm belly-cannon, and another fitted with a four-gun turret in the tail. Both modifications were made and the respective aircraft flew. There already existed a few cannon-armed Hurricanes and Spitfires, although these had proved problematical due to continuous gun stoppages. Undoubtedly, Harvard advanced trainers would have been made available, suitably equipped. By mid-summer, some twenty-four Masters had been converted to fighters by having the second seat removed along with some of the excessive cockpit glazing, and three .303 Brownings installed in each wing. Practically everything that could fly would have been thrown into the battle. Consideration was also given to adapting civilian aircraft for *Banquet Civil*. However, the plan was not thought worthwhile and the idea was dropped.[7]

During the latter part of May, a number of Station Defence Flights were strengthened with the arrival of redundant Gladiators. Manston operated G Flight with K6970, K7928 and K8033; Andover received N5702; Gosport received K6149, K7898 and K7995; RAE Farnborough received K5200; and Prestwick formed a Fighter Flight with N5912 and N5514.

Decoy airfields (known as K-sites) sprang up where cows had previously grazed, and often dummy aircraft, made of wood and fabric, appeared overnight. Even similarly-constructed hangars and other buildings would soon adorn the 'airfield'. Many hundreds of dummy 'aircraft' were produced, representing Spitfires, Hurricanes, Blenheims and Wellingtons amongst other types. Elsewhere similar sites were prepared to bamboozle German night bombers, being fields equipped with gooseneck flares, known as Q-sites, to mimic operational airfields.

Across southern and eastern England many feared a parachutist and glider invasion, with airfields being possible targets. Defences of airfields left much to be desired, with inadequate arming for troops who were to be the first line of defence. At RAF Honington for example, Gunner Harry Cull and his comrades of 429th Searchlight Battery, 9/Middlesex, were issued one rifle and five bullets between six men, the other five of the party being ordered to cut staves from the nearby woods with which to not only defend themselves but also to use to attack the heavy-armed would-be invaders. Harry Cull fondly remembered: "After a couple of bottles of beer we were ready to take on all-comers!"

Those in the know, however, were quietly confident that the one great advantage the RAF had over the Luftwaffe was its embryonic radar system, particularly as

1. A Bf110 heavy fighter of I/ZG76.

2. A Bf110 prepares to take-off. Slow and ungainly, the Bf110 was outclassed by the Hurricane and Spitfire.

3. Hurricane L2001 JU-B of 111 Squadron being prepared for another patrol.

4. Hurricane L2052 SD-B of 501 Squadron.

5. The rear-gunner's view within the Bf110 heavy fighter, also known as the *Zerstörer*.

Right: 6. Bf109s of JG51. Notice the narrow undercarriage that was prone to fatal landings for inexperienced pilots.

Below: 7. Inside the nose section of a He111 bomber. Although the all-glass cockpit offered excellent visibility, it was highly vulnerable to head-on attacks by RAF fighters.

8. Plt Off Willie McKnight, top Canadian ace of 242 Squadron.

9. Plt Off Al Deere of 54 Squadron survived a head-on collision with a Bf109 flown by Obfw Johann Illner of 4./JG51.

10. Pilots of 501 Squadron in May: Flt Lt Cam Malfroy, Plt Off Dicky Hulse, Sgt Ginger Lacy (in helmet), Flg Off Derrick Pickup and Flg Off Michael Smith (killed in May).

Far left: 11. Flt Lt John Kent served with 212 Squadron.

Left: 12. Flt Sgt Bill Franklin of 610 Squadron, one of the top-scoring pilots of the period.

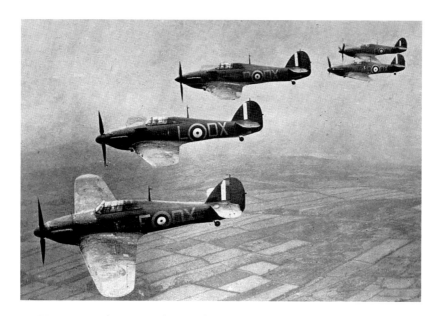

13. Hurricanes of 245 Squadron in formation over Southern England.

14. No return: the final moments of a Hurricane captured by a Luftwaffe gun camera.

15. The burnt-out ruins of a Hurricane fighter.

16. Ltn Hans Schmoller-Haldy of 3(J)JG54.

17. Plt Off Roland Dibnah of 1 Squadron. A Canadian, he flew a Hurricane during the battle.

18. Deadly duo: a Hurricane and Spitfire in formation.

Above: 19. He111 5J+AM shot down at Fleam Dyke, Six Mile Bottom, in Cambridgeshire, the victim of Sqn Leader Spike O'Brien of 23 Squadron and Flg Off John Petre of 19 Squadron. Both the Blenheim and Spitfire were shot down in this combat.

Right: 20. Sqn Ldr 'Spike' O'Brien of 23 Squadron whose Blenheim was shot down with the loss of his two crewmen.

Below: 21. He111 5J+DM shot down by Flt Lt Myles Duke-Woolley of 23 Squadron that ditched into the sea off Cley-next-the-Sea on the Norfolk coast.

Above: 22. Bf109 of Stab/JG53 being refuelled on Guernsey Airfield following the German occupation.

Below: 23. A Bf109 having its guns serviced.

Above: 24. Sqn Ldr
Teddy Donaldson of
151 Squadron with
North Weald Station
Commander Wg Cdr
Victor Beamish.

Right: 25. Flg Off
Jack Hamar of 151
Squadron was credited
with six victories
before his death in
July.

26. Pilots of 32 Squadron relax in the sun awaiting the next scramble and all had seen action over the Channel. Seen here are Plt Off Rupert Smythe, Plt Off Keith Gillman, Plt Off Peter Gardner, Flt Lt Peter Brothers, Plt Off Grubby Grice and Plt Off Alan Eckford.

27. Hurricane P3522/GZ-I of 32 Squadron about to take-off.

28. A damaged Bf109 of 6./JG26 on its way for repairs following a crash landing.

29. Air Sea Rescue He59 D-ASUO of Seenotkdo.1 was forced to alight on the sea by Plt Off John Allen of 54 Squadron on 9 July. It was towed ashore.

30. Bf109s of 2./JG3 being prepared for another escort mission over England.

31. Ltn Hasso von Perthes with his Bf109 from 3./LG2.

Above: 32. The remains of a Hurricane. Note that its machine guns had been used in anger prior to its total destruction.

Right: 33. The tail section of a downed He111 that was peppered with .303 ammunition. Such bullets were inefficient to armoured bombers and cannon-armed fighters became a priority.

34. Bf109s hunt for Spitfires and Hurricanes as they approach the white cliffs of Dover.

Clockwise from top:

5. Plt Off Vivian Rosewarne of 38 Squadron (see Appendix IX).

6. Plt Off John Mansel-Lewis courageously pancaked his Hurricane on the sea in an attempt to rescue the crew of a ditched Blenheim (see page 229). He later fought in the Battle of Britain.

7. The remains of Ltn Striberny's Bf109 are excavated from the Kent countryside on 8 July.

8. Ltn Johann Böhm of 4./JG51 was shot down over Kent on 8 July. Both pilot and aircraft survived relatively unscathed.

9. Ltn Albert Striberny of 3.(J)/LG2.

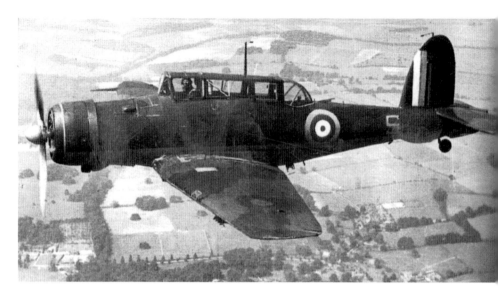

Above: 40. A camouflaged Skua of 801 Squadron.

Left: 41. Sub-Lt(A) Guy Brokensha of 803 Squadron clashed with French Hawk-75s of GCII/5 over Mersel-Kébir. He received a DSC for operations over Norway.

Below: 42. Hawk-75 of GCII/5 flown by Sgt-chef Jean Gisclon was involved in the fighting the Skuas of 803 Squadron.

its operators gained experience; in fact, the first successful use of radar by ground control to guide an interceptor had occurred on 12 May, when a He111 from 2./LG1 was intercepted near Vlissingen by Blenheim P4834 of A&AEE from Martlesham Heath, crewed by Flt Lt Chris Smith and Aircraftman A. Newton. The bomber was damaged and its gunner, Gfr Walter Jenderny, wounded.

Although Britain had acquired an example of the German *Enigma* coding machine, its use and value during the coming summer months was limited, and had little bearing on the forthcoming battle. AOC Fighter Command, Air Chief Marshal Dowding, appreciated the difficulty of his task:

> After the evacuation from Dunkerque [Dunkirk] the pressure on the Fighter Command became less intense, but it by no means disappeared. Hard fighting took place along the coast from Calais to Le Havre to cover the successive evacuations from that coast. Then the centre of gravity shifted to Cherbourg and its neighbourhood, and the Battle of Britain followed on without any appreciable opportunity to rest and reform the units which had borne the brunt of the fighting.
>
> The fall of Belgium and France had increased the danger to the South and West of England, and had necessitated a considerable modification of the original arrangements when bombing attacks could start only from German soil.
>
> As has been explained above, few squadrons were fresh and intact when the Battle began. No sufficient respite has been granted since the conclusion of the Dunkerque fighting to rest the squadrons which had not left the Fighter Command and to rebuild those which had undergone the ordeal of fighting from aerodromes in northern France. These last had been driven from aerodrome to aerodrome, able only to aim at self-preservation from almost continuous attack by bombers and fighters; they were desperately weary and had lost the greater part of their equipment, since aircraft which were unserviceable only from slight defects had to be abandoned.

CHAPTER IX

THE BATTLE FOR THE CHANNEL BEGINS ...

My Luftwaffe is invincible. And now we turn to England. How long will this one last – two, three weeks?

Hermann Göring in June 1940

RAF Fighter Command Order of Battle, 1 July 1940

11 Group (HQ Uxbridge)

Sector	Sqn	Aircraft	Based At	Commanding Officer
Biggin Hill	32	Hurricane	Biggin Hill	Sqn Ldr J. Worrall
	79	Hurricane	Biggin Hill	Sqn Ldr J. D. C. Joslin
	245	Hurricane	Hawkinge	Sqn Ldr E. W. Whitley
	600	Blenheim	Manston	Sqn Ldr D. de B. Clark
	610	Spitfire	Gravesend	Sqn Ldr A. T. Smith
North Weald	25	Blenheim	Martlesham	Sqn Ldr K. A. K. McEwan
	56	Hurricane	North Weald	Sqn Ldr G. A. L. Manton
	85	Hurricane	Martlesham	Sqn Ldr P. W. Townsend
	151	Hurricane	North Weald	Sqn Ldr E. M. Donaldson DSO
Kenley	64	Spitfire	Kenley	Sqn Ldr N. C. Odbert
	111	Hurricane	Croydon	Sqn Ldr J. M. Thompson
	501	Hurricane	Croydon	Sqn Ldr H. A. V. Hogan
	615	Hurricane	Kenley	Sqn Ldr J. R. Kayll DSO DFC
Hornchurch	54	Spitfire	Rochford	Sqn Ldr J. A. Leathart DSO
	65	Spitfire	Hornchurch	Sqn Ldr D. Cooke
	74	Spitfire	Hornchurch	Sqn Ldr F. L. White
Tangmere	43	Hurricane	Tangmere	Sqn Ldr C. G. Lott
	145	Hurricane	Tangmere	Sqn Ldr J. R. A. Peel

	601	Hurricane	Tangmere	Sqn Ldr the Hon. Max Aitken
	FIU	Blenheim	Tangmere	Wg Cdr G. P. Chamberlain
Debden	17	Hurricane	Debden	Sqn Ldr R. I. G. McDougall
Northolt	1	Hurricane	Northolt	Sqn Ldr D. A. Pemberton
	257	Hurricane	Hendon	Sqn Ldr D. W. Bayne
	604	Blenheim	Northolt	Sqn Ldr M. F. Anderson
	609	Spitfire	Middle Wallop	Sqn Ldr H. S. Darley
Filton	92	Spitfire	Pembury	Sqn Ldr P. J. Sanders
	213	Hurricane	Exeter	Sqn Ldr H. D. McGregor
	234	Spitfire	St Eval	Sqn Ldr R. E. Barnett
Middle Wallop	236	Blenheim	Middle Wallop	Sqn Ldr P. R. Drew
	238	Hurricane	Middle Wallop	Sqn Ldr C. E. G. Baines

(Filton and Middle Wallop became part of 10 Group on 21 July)

12 Group (HQ Nottingham)

Sector	Sqn	Aircraft	Based at	Commanding Officer
Duxford	19	Spitfire	Fowlmere	Sqn Ldr P. C. Pinkham
	264	Defiant	Duxford	Sqn Ldr P. A. Hunter DSO
Coltishall	66	Spitfire	Coltishall	Sqn Ldr R. H. A. Leigh
	242	Hurricane	Coltishall	Sqn Ldr D. R. S. Bader
Kirton-in-Lindsey	222	Spitfire	Kirton	Sqn Ldr H. W. Mermagen
Digby	29	Blenheim	Digby	Flt Lt J. S. Adams
	46	Hurricane	Digby	Flt Lt A. D. Murray
	611	Spitfire	Digby	Sqn Ldr J. E. McComb
Wittering	23	Blenheim	Collyweston	Sqn Ldr L. C. Bicknell
	229	Hurricane	Wittering	Sqn Ldr H. J. Maguire
	266	Spitfire	Wittering	Sqn Ldr J. W. A. Hunnard

13 Group (HQ Newcastle)

Sector	Sqn	Aircraft	Based At	Commanding Officer
Church Fenton	73	Hurricane	Church Fenton	Sqn Ldr J. W. C. More
	87	Hurricane	Church Feton	Sqn Ldr J. S. Dewar DSO DFC
	249	Hurricane	Leconfield	Sqn Ldr J. Grandy
	616	Spitfire	Church Fenton	Sqn Ldr M. Robinson
Catterick	41	Spitfire	Catterick	Sqn Ldr H. West
	219	Blenheim	Catterick	Sqn Ldr J. H. Little
Usworth	72	Spitfire	Acklington	Sqn Ldr R. B. Lees
	152	Spitfire	Acklington	Sqn Ldr P. K. Devitt
	607	Hurricane	Usworth	Sqn Ldr J. A. Vick
Turnhouse	141	Defiant	Turnhouse	Sqn Ldr W. A. Richardson
	253	Hurricane	Turnhouse	Sqn Ldr H. M. Starr
	602	Spitfire	Drem	Sqn Ldr G. C. Pinkerton
	603	Spitfire	Turnhouse	Sqn Ldr E. H. Stevens

	605	Hurricane	Drem	Sqn Ldr W. M. Churchill
				DSO DFC
Dyce	263	Hurricane	Grangemouth	Sqn Ldr H. Eeles
Wick	3	Hurricane	Wick	Sqn Ldr S. F. Godden
	504	Hurricane	Castletown	Sqn Ldr J. Sample DFC

* * * * *

At Prime Minister Churchill's insistence, the Air Ministry now asked the Admiralty for the loan of fifty FAA fighter pilots to partially make good losses suffered in France and over Dunkirk. Fighter Command reported its pilot losses as 284 killed, missing or prisoners of war, plus sixty-three wounded or injured during May and June including those who became casualties due to flying accidents. The Admiralty responded by placing 804 (Sea Gladiators) and newly formed 808 Squadrons under Fighter Command control, although the former remained at Hatston for local defence while the latter, formed on 1 July, was under training at Worthy Down with a few Skuas and a dozen Fulmars that were just being introduced into service.

Cecil James at the Air Historical Branch of the Air Ministry later wrote:

The measures that were taken to increase pilot output during June and July chiefly concerned Flying Training Command. But the earliest important accession of strength, and the more welcome because it came so shortly after the heavy losses in France, was the result of an agreement with the Admiralty for the loan of Fleet Air Arm pilots. The matter was first discussed in the War Cabinet as the Dunkirk evacuation drew to a close; and the Prime Minister instructed the Air and Naval staffs to see whether any naval pilots could be transferred to Fighter Command. He had in mind an allocation of fifty pilots by the end of June.

On 6 June the Admiralty issued instructions for the release of 45 pilots (including seven [*sic*] RAFVR pilots who had been serving with the Fleet Air Arm), half of them trained, half semi-trained. The Air Ministry, however, asked for half the output of the two flying training schools serving the Fleet Air Arm to be allotted to the RAF, beginning with thirty pilots by the end of June. The Admiralty could not agree on the grounds that the casualties amongst their pilots in April and May had been nearly four times as large as postulated and that, in addition, the war with Italy meant more work for the Fleet Air Arm than had been visualised earlier. Thirty more pilots – making sixty-eight naval pilots in all – were loaned during June; but ten were recalled early in July for service in the Mediterranean; and later in the month the First Lord informed the Secretary of State for Air that no further attachments would be possible. The loans, however, were timely and, considering the Admiralty's difficulties, substantial.

As it transpired, neither 804 or 808 Squadrons were required for operational duties per se, the FAA's major contribution being the twenty-seven fighter pilots seconded to RAF squadrons during the coming weeks: Sub-Lt(A) A. G. Blake joined 19 Squadron (Spitfires); Sub-Lt(A) G. G. R. Bulmer to 32 Squadron (Hurricanes); Sub-Lts(A) J. H. C. Sykes, F. Dawson-Paul and G. B. Pudney to 64 Squadron (Spitfires); Sub-Lt(A)s D. A. Hutchison and T/Sub-Lt I. J. Wallace to 74 Squadron (Spitfires); Mid(A) M. A. Birrell to 79 Squadron (Hurricanes); Sub-Lts(A) D. H. Richards, R. W. M. Walsh, T. V. Worrall and Mid(A) P. R. J. Gilbert to 111 Squadron (Hurricanes); Sub-Lts(A) I. H. Kestin and F. A. Smith to 145 Squadron (Hurricanes); Sub-Lt(A) H. W. Beggs and Mid(A) O. M. Wightman to 151 Squadron (Hurricanes); Sub-Lts(A) H. G. K. Bramah, D. M. Jeram and W. J. M. Moss to 213 Squadron (Hurricanes); Sub-Lt(A) J. C. Carpenter to 229 Squadron (Hurricanes); Sub-Lt(A)s R. J. Cork, R. E. Gardner and Mid(A) P. J. Patterson to 242 Squadron (Hurricanes); Mid(A) R. F. Bryant to 245 Squadron (Hurricanes); Sub-Lt(A) H. laF. Greenshields to 266 Squadron (Spitfires); and Mid(A) P. L. Lennard to 501 Squadron (Hurricanes). In addition, Sub-Lt(A) David Marks had been killed while flying a Hurricane of 7 OTU in preparation for his transfer to an RAF squadron. It should be noted that most of these pilots were not considered operational and were sent to RAF OTUs initially for conversion training and a rapid course in fighter tactics. Some did not reach squadrons until late August/early September. Others lasted only a few days and were sent away for further training.

Eight RAFVR fighter pilots who had been seconded to the FAA and were currently undergoing a refresher fighter course at Donibristle with 769(T) Squadron were released to return to Fighter Command; these being Sgt D. Ashton to 32 Squadron; Sgt D. Ayres to 600 Squadron; Sgt H. W. Ayre to 266 Squadron; Sgt O. R. Bowerman to 222 Squadron; Sgt E. N. Kelsey to 611 Squadron; Sgt R. O'Donnell to 19 Squadron; Sgt J. Pickering to 64 Squadron; Sgt W. Timms to 43 Squadron. Two who had deliberately failed the FAA course – Sgt F. N. Robertson and New Zealander Sgt J. W. Hyde – were already flying Spitfires with 66 Squadron. Another former RN pilot, Plt Off A. R. H. Barton (who had been trained to fly Swordfish) arrived to posting to 32 Squadron following a brief conversion course.

A number of FAA pilots and observers were also seconded to Bomber and Coastal Commands during this period.

Monday, 1 July

During the hours of darkness a He115 (M2+CL of 3./KüF1Gr.106) crashed into the sea at 02:15, some thirty miles off Whitby, due to engine failure during a mine-laying sortie. The crew of three was rescued from their dinghy after twenty-eight hours at sea and landed at Grimsby. The aircraft was lost. One of the German ASR craft sent out to search for the downed aircrew was He59 D-ASAM from Seenotflugkdo.3, but this was forced to alight on the sea eight miles east of Sunderland after being badly damaged by Spitfires from 72 Squadron at 06:12, as reported by Flt Lt Ted Graham:

On receiving order from control to intercept bandit eight miles east of Sunderland, I took Blue Section off. On the way control informed me that the bandit was close in shore at height unknown. Approximately eight miles east of Sunderland I spotted a twin-engined biplane with floats, coloured white and with large Red Cross on upper surface of upper plane, flying at 500 feet in south-east direction. I circled floatplane two or three times close in [...] on my last circuit I got a good view of the black swastika with red background on the fin and rudder. I ordered No. 1 Attack and went in, overtaking very rapidly from above and behind. Fire was opened about 200 yards range and continued until about 30 yards. My incendiary bullets appeared to hit E/A and I saw faint greyish smoke coming from fuselage. Immediately the water below E/A was covered with splashes and this I took to be petrol. As I broke away to port, E/A turned slowly starboard and lost height slowly. I then saw No. 2 and No. 3 deliver their attacks, E/A settling on the water during No. 3's attack. No return fire was encountered though E/A appeared to have both upper and lower gun emplacements.

The crew of four including one severely wounded airman, Uffz Struckmann, were picked up in their dinghy by HMS *Black Swan's* sea boat. The aircraft was beached and examined for armament. The observer, Ltn Hans-Joachim Fehske, recalled:

Our *Gruppenkommandeur* ordered us to fly to the area in question and to look for this aircraft. The sea is large, a plane small, the speed of the current very high because of the strong turn of the tide off the east coast. My pilot had not been trained in instrument flying and that was why we had to wait until first light for take-off. Consequently, another loss of time was unavoidable. According to our dead reckonings, we arrived at the correct latitude shortly before 06:00 hrs. There we changed course and headed towards the British east coast. My intention was to orientate myself by finding a clear landmark. By doing this I would be able to correct my position and improve the chances of a successful search.

During our approach, we were flying in low stratus/haze. Immediately after changing course direction west, the fog lifted. The visibility was excellent and we were flying between the coast and a convoy headed south. One can understand that the RAF did not like that. Consequently, there were two British fighters behind us a few minutes later and very quickly we were shot down. Our plane was painted white with big red crosses. According to international agreements, we carried no armament on our search and rescue plane. One engine and the light metal floats had been hit. The radio equipment failed and our Bordwart [medical orderly] received two gunshot wounds (the bullets had passed right through). The floats failed to keep the plane afloat so we took to our dinghy and tried to row towards England. A short time after, we were fished out of the sea by the escort vessel *Black Swan* and were taken prisoners of war.[1]

Gfr Erich Philipp, the other member of the crew, joined his companions 'in the bag'. This was the first British violation of a white-painted, Red Cross-marked aircraft that was on a genuine search and rescue mission. The aircraft's markings were clearly visible and seen by the RAF pilots concerned, who also commented on the fact that no return fire or armament was discernible.

At 09:30, nine Hurricanes of 145 Squadron and nine of 43 Squadron departed Tangmere to provide escort for three Blenheims of 15 Squadron tasked to carry out photo recce of the French coastline from St-Valéry-en-Caux to Abbeville. On reaching St-Valéry the coastline was completely hidden by cloud, so the Blenheims returned to Hawkinge and the Hurricanes to Manston.

Two Spitfires of 616 Squadron (flown by Flt Lt Bob Miller and Plt Off Don Smith) intercepted a Do17 some ten miles south of Leconfield at 10:20 and claimed it damaged. It would seem that their shooting was better than they anticipated. Their target was probably a reconnaissance Do215 from 3./Aufkl.ObdL flown by Obfw Artur Kresse, which FTR with the loss of the crew. Approaching Plymouth shortly after midday, convoy JUMBO came under attack by Ju87s from III/StG.51. Three Hurricanes from 213 Squadron were scrambled to provide protection but arrived too late.

Three Blenheims from 15 Squadron again carried out PR sorties in the vicinity of St-Valéry to Abbeville between 14:00 and 16:00, again escorted by Hurricanes of 43 and 145 Squadrons and all returned safely. The heavy cloud had dispersed and the mission was carried out successfully. There was no interference from enemy fighters.

During the afternoon a new chapter opened in the tale of German air attacks on Great Britain, in that the Luftwaffe made a daylight raid. Wick was on the receiving end of a bombing raid at 16:20, fourteen people being killed and sixteen others injured. The casualties were mostly women and children. Four of the children were killed while playing in the streets. The bombs, which seem to have been two in number, demolished a row of houses.

The day witnessed several isolated raids against ports on the North-East coast and AA guns were in action on the Humber, Mersey and Bramley. At 17:45, three Spitfires from 616 Squadron (Yellow Section: Flt Lt Miller with Flg Off John Bell and Plt Off John Brewster) shot down He111 5J+EL from 3./KG4 flown by Obfw Hermann Draisbach, an aircraft that had been involved in a single aircraft raid on Hull (two others having aborted due to lack of cloud cover). Plt Off Brewster's aircraft was slightly dented by piece of debris from the crippled aircraft:

> I followed Number 2 [Bell] into the attack. On going into the attack, I noticed that the port engine was on fire and a little smoke appeared from the starboard engine. Fire was opened at about 220 yards and tracer bullets were seen to go into the fuselage and wings. A lot of debris fell off from the enemy aircraft approximately halfway up the fuselage on the top port side. Range was now about 100 yards. Oil then appeared on my windscreen and when closing to

about 50 yards, enemy aircraft was completely enveloped in a circular cloud of black smoke. My windscreen was now completely covered in oil and it was impossible to distinguish enemy aircraft in the smoke. I broke right because I was very near the enemy aircraft and it seemed better to break right than left where Number 2 had broken. I then turned east at about 1,000 feet and saw enemy aircraft below me diving down to the sea on fire. I manoeuvred to attack again and on turning dead astern of the enemy aircraft in a diving turn, I lost sight of it due to the oil on my windscreen. I had dived to 2,000 feet and then turned to starboard and circled for enemy aircraft but failed to locate it. I then returned to base and landed.

Brewster continued:

Tracer ammunition was most useful and enabled me to see where my bullets were hitting enemy aircraft. No enemy fire was encountered. On landing, I found that there were three dents in my wing caused by flying debris from enemy aircraft. Also, the leading edge of my mainplane, especially the port, spinner, wireless aerial mast, tailplane leading edge and fin were covered with a film of oil in addition to the windscreen through which it was impossible to see for landing, necessitating looking over the side.

The Heinkel crashed into the sea some thirty miles east of Spurn Head. The crew was rescued and Ltn z.See Friedrich Koch, the observer, told his interrogators:

After a delay of two hours due to a fault found during the pre-take-off check, the Heinkel set off for a high-level attack on the chemical works at Middlesbrough, with the secondary target, the oil tanks at Hull. On arrival at the Yorkshire coast there was not enough cloud cover for an attack on Middlesbrough so Hull became the target. Unaware that the British were using radar directed fighter control, and getting occasional glimpses of British fighters, we dithered between the two target areas until the pilot's oxygen was down to 20 minutes in his emergency supply, which he was having to use because of a fault in the main oxygen system.

Time was running out, so the oil tanks at Hull were selected as the target. AA gunfire was being troublesome and during the final run-in, a shell fragment entered the cockpit and damaged the instrument panel. After releasing the load of 50kg bombs, which straddled the oil-tanks, the Heinkel headed for home. As soon as we were out of the AA fire zone the Spitfires pounced. First the instrument panel was shot to pieces, then one engine put out of action, next the landing gear became unlatched and fell down, the flaps came off after the second engine was put out of action, all that was left for the pilot to do was to use his skill to make the best possible crash-landing.[2]

The crash, when it came, was made worse by the lowered landing gear. The aircraft toppled over and started to sink rapidly – the rubber dinghy was eventually freed and inflated, the crew scrambled in. Ltn Koch, suffering from a knock on the head, the pilot was unhurt, the wireless operator Fw Alfred Weber had been shot through the eye, head, arm and chest and the mechanic Obfw Rudolf Ernst had bullet wounds in his buttocks and leg. A Sunderland flying boat spotted the flares and called up HMS *Black Swan*. After ditching their pistols and co-ordinating their stories ready for the interrogations to come, the Germans were rescued. They were taken on board, the injured receiving medical attention, the uninjured being separated and interrogated, and then all were given a meal. During the night Koch lay on a stretcher in a gangway guarded by a sailor with a fixed bayonet. About 10:00 the next day, the German airmen were transferred to another vessel that put them ashore at Harwich about noon.

Later, between 18:52 and 19:55, a section of patrolling Spitfires from 64 Squadron led by Flg Off Don Taylor joined three Hurricanes from Flt Lt Roy Dutton's Red Section from 145 Squadron in shooting down another snooping Do215 of 3./Aufkl. ObdL some forty-five miles off Beachy Head. Oblt Werner Rotherberg and his crew were lost. Flt Lt Dutton's Combat Report revealed:

I was leader of Red Section. At 18:51, I was ordered off to patrol base at 25,000 feet. At 19:05 whilst at 22,000 feet south of Littlehampton I noticed a smoke trail east of me ... and almost immediately sighted a Do17. I ordered my section into line astern, pulled the plug and gave chase. The Do17 lost height in a series of sweeps and turns, first losing height slowly and latterly very steeply. My average indicated speed was over 300 mph and I found the overtaking speed very slow. It took me over 5 minutes chasing before I came within 400 yards range. I received fire from the top rear gunner from about 700-800 yards and at about 600 yards was hit by one bullet in my starboard wing root. Soon after this, as I found that I was still unable to overtake with any great speed and as the coast of France was getting close, I opened fire in a series of cbursts, some of which I saw hit the enemy aircraft. Following one of these bursts, smoke issued out of both engines. I continued firing and silenced all the return fire. With my remaining ammunition I slowed the enemy aircraft noticeably and broke away to allow my No. 2 and No. 3 to engage. My No. 3 however put a finish to it, and the enemy aircraft crashed into the sea, breaking up completely.

I wish to add that a Spitfire made an attack after my break away but had nothing to do with the finish of the Do17.

Despite Dutton's suggestion that the Spitfire made little impression, two Spitfires of 64 Squadron made a claim, including Sub-Lt(A) Frank Dawson-Paul:

As Blue 2, I was ordered to scramble with Blue Section at 18:50 and to patrol base at 20,000 feet. I first sighted a streak of white smoke, which I identified

as condensing exhaust gases coming from what I thought was the e/a. This
streak was about 14 miles ahead and to the starboard of me. I was about two
miles behind Blue 1 [Flg Off Don Taylor], as my engine was not giving full
power. Crossing the coast I passed one section of Hurricanes and as I drew
nearer to the e/a I saw another section of Hurricanes in line astern preparing
to attack. Blue 1 was also positioning himself for an attack.

I concurred that the e/a must have sighted the Hurricanes and Blue 1 and
it started to take avoiding action, and lost height in deep spirals. I followed it
down, drawing closer to it and after the Hurricanes and Blue 1 had delivered
their attack, I overhauled it and opened fire at approximately 150 yards and
closed up to about 50 yards, giving three bursts. I saw some of my bullets
enter the rear position of the e/a. I broke away to port, gained height and
delivered another attack from the rear. This time the e/a turned to port and I
broke to starboard and was just positioning myself for another attack when
I saw the e/a strike the water and sink ahead of me. My aircraft was hit four
times in the starboard main plane and twice underneath the rudder. I returned
to Kenley at 19:55.

At just about the time Dawson-Paul was landing back at Kenley, off the Scottish
coast two Spitfires of 602 Squadron sighted a Ju88 heading for Dunbar. After a
chase during which the intruder dodged from cloud to cloud, Flg Off Paul Webb
was able to fire a short burst, leading him to believe that he had damaged one of its
engines before it escaped in the mist. One source[3] suggests that this was an aircraft
of I/KG51 that came down in northern France with its instruments and compass
damaged, and one engine out.

A Sunderland of 10 RAAF piloted by Flt Lt W. N. Gibson RAAF achieved a
success when *U-26* was sunk by anti-submarine bombs after it had been damaged
by HMS *Gladiolus* off Ushant. The U-boat had just sunk SS *Zarian* (her eighth
victim) before being depth-charged. Forty-one German survivors including Kapt
Heinz Scherringer were rescued by HMS *Rochester*.

Operational Accidents: Two RAF fighters were lost due to accidents, a Hurricane
from 3 Squadron was badly damaged at Wick, and Spitfire R6640 of 5 OTU crashed
during a training flight. Shortly after midnight, Blenheim L1376 of 29 Squadron
flown by Plt Off Peter Sisman on a night fighter patrol, crashed in Lincolnshire when
the pilot was dazzled by searchlights. He and his navigator Sgt Andrew Reed were
killed. Across the Channel, a Ju88 of 3.(F)/121 crashed and burned out attempting
forced-landing near Livry-Gargan during a practice flight to photograph bombing
results for LG1, cause unknown. Uffz Wilhelm Kraus, Uffz Max Seeber, and Obgfr
Rudolf Ehrich were all killed, and another crewman injured.

Night Operations: Thirty Hampdens, twenty-four Wellingtons and thirteen Whitleys
carried out night attacks on targets at Kiel, Hamburg, Osnabrück and Duisburg, a

Hampden of 83 Squadron and a Whitley from 58 Squadron FTR, both victims of flak. There was only one survivor from the two aircraft. Flg Off Guy Gibson of 83 Squadron dropped the first 2,000lb bomb of the war, which exploded in the town of Kiel having overshot its intended target. Of the raid, one Sgt observer recalled:

Information had come through that the *Scharnhorst* was in a floating dock at Kiel, for repairs, and we were to bomb it. We all had a feeling of general jubilation. We were glad to have the job. When the time came, with the good wishes of those who had to stay behind, our squadron got into the air very quickly. I gave my captain the first course to steer, and soon we were on our way, climbing through heavy, wet cloud. The temperature dropped considerably and was actually below freezing point, but apart from that it looked as though the weather was going to be good to us.

We crossed over without incident until we reached the enemy coast, when searchlights fingered the sky without finding us. By this time it was a very clear night and we could see water reflections sixty miles away. Visibility was excellent. We flew on over enemy territory, meeting occasional AA fire and search-lights but we ignored them and picked up the part of the eastern coast line we were looking for, and with our maps pinpointed our exact position. Then we flew on to our target – the floating dock and the *Scharnhorst*.

Everything was very quiet. The estuary was plainly marked, and as we approached we spotted the German balloon barrage, but still no ground defences were in action. It was now dead midnight. Just at that moment we saw the AA batteries open up on another of our aircraft that was making its attack. We located the position of the defences and decided how we would go in. We were flying fairly high. When we were in position, I gave the captain the word "Now, sir", and he replied with "Over she goes" and dived to attack. I directed my line of sight on the floating dock, which stood out sharply in the estuary, and gave necessary correction to the captain. Searchlights caught us up in the dive, but we went under the beam. Then I had to put the captain into an almost vertical dive as we came on the target. The *Scharnhorst* couldn't be missed; she stood out so plainly.

By this time a curtain of fierce AA fire was floating around us. The defences seemed to be giving everything they had got, and I could clearly see tracers of the pom-pom on the deck of the *Scharnhorst* at work. Besides that, the shore batteries and other ships in the harbour were doing their best to blow us out of the sky. We took several heavy jars from exploding shells. The lower part of the starboard tail plane was blown away, the main spar was hit, we got a two-foot hole through the tailplane, which broke a rib, and narrowly missed our rudder post and we had another hole a foot wide through the fuselage. The rear gunner said he expected to be launched into space any minute, because he felt sure the turret had been shot away. He gets the worst of the jolts back there and, on pulling out of a dive he swung through a much wider arc. But still everything held together, thanks to the splendid material and fine workmanship that went to the making of our aircraft.

We came down very low to make sure, and when we were dead in line I released a stick of bombs. At that moment, I could only see the ship gun turrets, masts and control tower. A vast sheet of reddish yellow flame came from the deck, and what seemed to be the heart of the *Scharnhorst*, right from the edge of the dock across her. The flashes lit the whole estuary, and while we banked to go over the town it seemed as though I was looking up at other ships anchored in the estuary.

We had finished bombing and went off, pursued by AA fire, and then circled for height over the quiet waters of the harbour. While we were doing this, we could see fires breaking out on the dockside, and our own comrades going in, one after the other to do their stuff. We saw their bombs exploding dead in the target area. The fires got bigger, and there were a lot of explosions that seemed to come from the middle of the fires until they merged into one vast inferno. One explosion outdid all the others and it was probably either an ammunition dump or oil tanks. When we began to climb we realised the damage that had been done to us, and so, on reaching height, I gave the captain a course for home. But while we were still over the estuary at only about 1,000 feet, a German AA ship opened fire. I turned my front gun and pumped about two hundred rounds at him and he ceased fire

We flew on down the enemy coast. The rear gunner was chattering all the time something about the fires. We didn't get what he meant at first, but when we were over the coast we turned the aircraft so that we could have a look and we actually pinpointed the position, from which we could see it – I don't mean see the glow in the sky, but the actual fire. This distance was eighty-five miles. Then we sent a signal to base, giving our position and telling them that the aircraft was damaged so that they would know where to search for us if anything untoward did happen. That was the last message we were able to send as we flew into a storm which earthed the aerial and the radio went up in smoke. Still, damaged as we were, after crossing three hundred and fifty miles of sea, we struck our point only three miles off our bearing, and came quietly home and made a smooth landing. We were bubbling over with excitement at such a successful night's hunting – a bit tired but pretty certain that the *Scharnhorst* will be unserviceable for many months to come.

A few German raiders were over England and an estimated sixty bombs were dropped mainly in the Bristol area, which injured a dozen people and caused damage to the main railway line (see Appendix VII).

Fighter Command Claims & Casualties, 1 July

3 Spitfires/72 Squadron – 8 miles east of Hartlepool 06:12

P9457	Flt Lt E. Graham		
K9959	Flg Off E. J. Wilcox	He59	Seenotkdo.3
K9935	Flt Sgt H. Steere		

2 Spitfires/616 Squadron – 10 miles south of Leconfield 10:20

Red 1	Flt Lt R. R. Miller	Do17 damaged	3./Auflk.ObdL
Red 2	Plt Off R. A. Smith	(Do215 FTR)	

3 Spitfires/616 Squadron – 30 miles south-east of Spurn Head 17:45

Yellow 1	Flt Lt R. R. Miller		
Yellow 2	Flg Off J. S. Bell	He111	I/KG4
Yellow 3	Plt Off J. Brewster		

3 Spitfires/64 Squadron – 45 miles south of Beachy Head 18:52-19:55

L1055	Flg Off D. M. Taylor	Do215	3./Aufkl.ObdL
L1035	Sub-Lt(A) F. Dawson-Paul RNVR		shared with 145 Sqn

3 Hurricanes/145 Squadron – 45 miles south of Beachy Head 18:52-19:55

P3521	Flt Lt R. G. Dutton		
P2770	Plt Off R. D. Yule	Do215	3./Aufkl.ObdL
N2496	Plt Off L. A. Sears		shared with 64 Sqn

2 Spitfires/602 Squadron – 3 miles east of Dunbar 19:50

N3119	Flg Off P. C. Webb	Ju88 damaged
		possibly I/KG51, crashed

Luftwaffe Operational Bomber & Reconnaissance Casualties, 1 July
3./Aufkl.ObdL

Do215 FTR: Obfw Artur Kresse (pilot), Ltn Karl Vockel, Fw Wilhelm Wagner, Obgfr Johann Braun all killed; the bodies of Vockel and Wagner were washed ashore; victim of 616 Squadron.

Do215 FTR: Oblt Werner Rothenberg (pilot), Ltn Günther Kikat, Uffz Siegfried Oster, Uffz Hans Wanzenberg all killed; victim of 64/145 Squadrons.

3./KG4

He111 5J+EL FTR: Obfw Hermann Draisbach (pilot), Ltn z.See Friedrich Koch (injured), Fw Alfred Weber (wounded), Obfw Rudolf Ernst (wounded) rescued by RN and POW; victim of 616 Squadron.

I/KG51

Ju88 crashed Melun-Villaroche (60-70% damaged). Crew unhurt; possibly victim of 602 Sqn.

3./KüFlGr.106
He115 M2+CL FTR: Obfw Rudolph Worms (pilot), Ltn z.See Gottfried Schroeder, Uffz Siegfried Soest rescued from sea and POW; engine failure during minelaying sortie.

Seenotflugkdo.3
D-ASAM FTR: Uffz Ernst-Otto Neilsen (pilot), Ltn Hans-Joachim Fehske, Ogfr Erich Philipp, Uffz Struckmann (severely wounded) rescued by RN and POW; victim of 72 Squadron.

RAF Bomber Command Operational Losses, Night 1/2 July
83 Squadron
Hampden P1171 FTR: Plt Off D. Redmayne (pilot), Sgt C. Lee, Sgt O. S. Gander and Sgt G. E. Little (all killed); victim of flak.

58 Squadron
Whitley N1461 FTR: Plt Off C. J. T. Jones (pilot), Flg Off L. H. McFarlane, Sgt D. Lishman, Sgt H. E. A. Craven (all killed); Sgt J. P. Caldwell POW; victim of flak.

Tuesday, 2 July

It was not until 2 July that Hitler issued the first orders to prepare for an invasion; a fortnight later these were followed by a directive stating that:

> As England, in spite of the hopelessness of her military position, has so far shown herself unwilling to come to any compromise, I have therefore decided to prepare for, and if necessary, carry out an invasion of England. I therefore issue the following orders: 1) The British Air Force must be eliminated to such an extent that it will be incapable of putting up any substantial opposition to the invading troops ...

Out at sea a Sunderland of 204 Squadron reported that the *Arandora Star* had been sunk 100 miles off Bora Head, and that naval vessels were picking up survivors. Having left Liverpool unescorted the day before, the *Arandora Star* was bound for St John's, Newfoundland and Canadian internment camps with nearly 1,200 German and Italian internees, including eighty-six prisoners of war, being transported from Britain. There were also 374 British men, comprising both military guards and the ship's crew. The Italians numbered 712 men of all ages, most of whom had been residing in Britain when Italy declared war on 10 June. The ship was bearing no Red Cross sign, which could have shown that she was carrying prisoners, and especially civilians.

At 06:58, off the northwest coast of Ireland, she was struck by a torpedo from the *U-47*, commanded by U-Boat ace Günther Prien. All power was lost at once, and thirty-five minutes after the torpedo impact, *Arandora Star* sank. More than eight hundred lives were lost including 470 Italians and 243 Germans. The Canadian destroyer HMCS *St. Laurent* arrived to pick up the survivors. There were 586 survivors out of 1,216 detainees.

A HSL searching for the missing Whitley crew picked up three Germans in a dinghy – Obfw Rudolf Worms, Ltn Gottfried Schroeder, and Uffz Siegfried – whose He115 had ditched due to engine trouble some 28 hours earlier.

During the morning a recce Do215 from 4./Aufkl.ObdL, G2+EH flown by Fw Helmuth Apitz, was intercepted about 100 miles east of Withensea and shot down by a section of Spitfires from 611 Squadron led by Flt Lt Jack Leather, although it was claimed only as a probable since it was not seen to crash. Leather reported:

E/a fired a recognition cartridge just before attack. Rear-gunner opened fire with tracer, which went high over my port wing. After the second burst of my first attack I experienced no further fire from the rear gun. My first attack got e/a's port engine; there was a flash and black smoke. I broke off and renewed the attack at 17,000 feet after Red 2 and Red 3 had attacked. Thick black smoke was observed from both engines of e/a. It was gliding down fairly steeply and losing speed.

Red 2, Plt Off James Sutton, added:

I attacked after Red 1 had given his first attack. I was receiving some fire (tracer) without effect from e/a rear gunner, who I believed was out of action. I broke away and followed Red 1 into his second attack. After his attack I saw black smoke coming from e/a's port engine, then white smoke from both engines. I then emptied my guns into e/a as he was losing height and, as I had no more ammunition, I circled round until e/a had disappeared out of sight below me.

Plt Off Lund (Red 3) also managed to get in an attack:

I attacked after Red 1 and Red 2 had delivered first attack. I saw a flash from e/a's port engine and Red 1's first attack. It was followed by thick black smoke and white smoke from both engines. I broke away and saw e/a diving fairly steeply to sea.

A relatively quiet morning was followed by a small-scale attack on Newcastle at 17:36. Despite unfavourable weather three Ju88s of 7./KG4 led by Oblt Hajo Herrmann attempted a daring daylight raid the Vickers-Armstrong factory plant at Elswick. Two crews reported bombing accurately, though one of Herrmann's bombs hit the *Spiller's* flour mill:

The final seconds ticked by. Then – down! The last scraps of cloud flittered past me. There was the Tyne, there was the target [...] and there were the same plump, odious monsters again – the balloons. Then the flak tracers whizzed past us and disappeared into the clouds. I took hold of my crate. "Come on, observer, finger out! Drop the bloody things! Now, now– it doesn't matter if you hit the near end or the far end!" He had a long fuse and stayed calm. His eye was glued to the eye-piece. He didn't have the slightest idea what was going on to the left, the right, or all around the area.

At last, the bombs were dropped. I hauled the aircraft mercilessly into a climbing turn [...] Thank God for the clouds! I was enveloped in them. The heavy anti-aircraft fired a few rounds of deterrent flak. As if from nowhere, black wads of cotton wool appeared suddenly [...] Then, full throttle, I pulled away, homeward bound.

Uffz Wilhelm Knobling's 5J+BR sustained shrapnel damage from the AA fire, including to one engine. However, he succeeded in nursing the aircraft across the Channel and carried out a force-landing near Iheringsfehn in the Frisians. All four of the crew suffered serious injuries and the aircraft was written off. The bombs fell in Newcastle and Jarrow, on the southern bank of the Tyne Estuary, total casualties being thirteen dead and 123 injured. It seems that two of the fatalities occurred in Newcastle, the vast majority occurring in Jarrow when Ltn Weinrich's bombs apparently fell wide of the intended target (oil tanks). The Vickers-Armstrong factory, the main target, was not hit.

A Do17 was claimed shot down by AA guns on the Tyne but no other loss was reported. This was possibly an aircraft of Stab KG2 that returned damaged from a sortie and crashed on landing. A barrage balloon located at Scotswood Bridge in Newcastle was reportedly shot down in flames by the bomber. Of this period, Plt Off Eric Marrs of 152 Squadron, stationed at nearby RAF Acklington, wrote to his father:

I was very interested to hear that Hawkhurst had been bombed and machine-gunned and I'm very glad that worse casualties were not sustained. You mention that no British fighters were around, but they were probably all above the cloud. In these cloudy conditions it is almost impossible to catch lone raiders. They nip out and in again and don't give one any time to get near them. We are having the same difficulty up here in catching them. One dropped four bombs on Newcastle the other day. There were 15 fighters up at the time but he got away. He could have flown back to Germany in cloud if he had wanted to for that day the cloud went from about 6,000 feet to 20,000 feet in several layers, which merged into each other in places.

We have been having some work to do these nights, but up to now only two have been shot down in our sector. One by anti-aircraft fire and the other by the squadron. On Friday night we had a proper go at them. There was however, a general over-excitement of the ground defences, and searchlights and guns were not up to much. Most of our own fighters were fired on and some had a bad time. The guns did, however, get their one enemy aircraft that night. They also received a large and powerful raspberry for firing on us. I was not actually on duty that night, but was aerodrome control pilot and was out on the flare-path all the time,

The next three nights they did not visit us again. On the fourth night my flight was on again and I went up this time. The guns and searchlights were, however, too shy this time and they never even picked up a friendly aeroplane, much less an enemy one. We searched and patrolled and did what we could, but unless the searchlights illuminate aircraft for us we are not much use. The next day we had a big conference with searchlight officers from all the sectors round and cleared up many points and questions. That night the other squadron was on, the searchlights were a 100 per cent better and they fixed on a Hun, which was promptly shot down. We now feel that with good co-operation between searchlights and fighters we can do fairly well. That happened last night. Tonight we are on again, but it is the other flight's turn.

Already damaged in an earlier attack, the SS *Aeneas* (Convoy OA177G) was steaming at seven knots some twenty miles south-east of Start Point at 16:30 when Stukas arrived. Her master, Captain David Evans, reported:

We were bound from London to Glasgow with a general cargo of 5,000 tons. We were armed with a 4.7-inch, a 12-pdr and a Lewis gun. The number of the crew, including myself was 109 and we also had aboard the Vice-Commodore of the convoy, Captain Robert, three naval ratings and one Lewis gunner. The attack came from right overhead. The plane seemed to stall at about 3,000 feet and dived almost vertically, and from photographs shown to me I think I can almost certainly identify the machine as a Junkers 87. The first bomb dropped ahead of the port side and made a hole about 6-inches diameter amidships, but it dropped back into the sea. The explosion shook the vessel considerably and set her on fire. The second bomb fell abaft the funnel. She took a list of about 25 degrees to starboard. He dropped another bomb about 100 yards away on the starboard beam.

A further attack followed, resulting only in a near miss but the damage had already been done.

I could see that now they were definitely intending to get us so I immediately put all confidential books in a weighted bag and threw it overboard. There were several wounded on deck; I gave the order for the boats to be got ready and we put the wounded in the starboard boats. While getting the port boats ready the plane made another attack but the bombs missed us. I was not at all worried about the ship capsizing although she kept going over, but the

Vice-Commodore said we must abandon ship. The steam pipe had burst and, although I realised we could not do anything, I did not like leaving the vessel. They were all in the boats and kept calling for me to leave, but I said I was going to have another try to find the missing men. I again went all over the ship, listening mainly for groans, but I could hear nothing at all and left satisfied that there could not possibly be anyone left alive. I then left the ship. Our escort, the *Witherington*, convoyed the ships a little while before coming back for us, and as the small boat we were in was damaged by the last attack, he picked us up first. After getting aboard the *Witherington* we saw a man on the *Aeneas* waving his arms. It turned out to be the steward. The *Witherington* sent over a boat to bring him back. The crew had another look round the *Aeneas* but could find no one else. We returned to Plymouth that night. I did not see my ship sink.

Three died in the attack and eighteen were reported missing. The SS *Baron Ruthven* (3,178 tons) was also damaged by bombing but safely reached port.

Eleven Blenheims of 82 Squadron were tasked to attack Dortmund-Ems Canal in daylight. There was a lack of suitable cloud cover and all bar one returned early. The remaining aircraft (P6895) flown by Sqn Ldr H. F. Chester and crew FTR. Two Blenheims were claimed by pilots of 2./JG51, Oblt Leo Eggers at 11:44 and Fw Jakob Schmitt at 11:55.

Operational Accidents: Three Hurricanes reported lost due to accidents were N2342 of 32 Squadron, N2712 of 85 Squadron and P2988 of 263 Squadron. The pilots survived. Across the Channel Uffz Rudolf Dally 3./JG21 was killed in a crash north-west of Soesterberg

Night operations: Fourteen Hampdens, twenty-four Wellingtons, sixteen Whitleys and six Blenheims from Bomber Command raided targets at Evre, Hingene, Hamm, Hamburg, Osnabrück, Soerst, Scherte, Koln, Dortmund and Rotterdam, while six Hampdens dropped mines in German waters. All returned safely.

Six Swordfish of 825 Squadron from Detling attempted to bomb barges on the River Maas. They met fierce AA opposition. L2829 was shot down over Schipol and the TAG, L/Air Harry Burt was killed. His pilot, Sub-Lt(A) John Kiddell survived to be taken prisoner. L7646 also failed to return, with the loss of Sub-Lt(A) Barry Grigson and Sub-Lt(A) Fred Lees. Their bodies were recovered from the sea and buried at Rozenburg. A third Swordfish, 5M, suffered engine failure on the return flight and forced-landed on Harrock Island without injury to the crew. Five Albacores of 826 Squadron were also out to bomb targets along the Maas River just above Rotterdam. Owing to low cloud reaching up to 5,000 feet and poor visibility, only two aircraft reached the objective. All Albacores were grounded next day awaiting modified engines. One pilot wrote:

The squadron was divided into two waves, the first wave taking off 20 minutes before the second wave. It was a cloudy, dark night when we set out, but over the sea the weather cleared and we climbed to our operational height. As my observer told me we ought to be just about there, the first searchlights began showing and one or two balls of fire were shot up, which lit up the whole sky above the clouds. More and more searchlights came on but, naturally, could not pierce the clouds. We then went into line astern and I thought I would go down through the cloud and see if I could see the barges. However, when I got through the cloud to about 2,000 feet all was pitch black below, but I thought I saw a reflection of a light on some water so I realized I was over the river. Marking the spot by a group of searchlights, I climbed again, intending to do a decent bombing attack. Just as I came out of the cloud again, the Hun opened fire and stuff came up all round. I cursed myself for not letting the bombs go when I'd been down there first time. However, all went well and down we went and away went the bombs. My observer reported a large flash but otherwise could see no result due to the darkness. Personally I was too busy trying to shake off the searchlights.

Breathing a sigh of relief, we headed home only to find when we got there England was covered in a very low ground fog, making it all look like the Thames Estuary at low tide with mud banks showing. My observer first of all thought we were over Harwich and told me to look out for balloons. Then he thought we were over Deal, where there were more balloons. I was so intent looking for balloons in the dark that when suddenly there was a terrific jar through the aircraft and I thought we had hit a cable. It was time to get out. However, glancing at my altimeter I saw it reading zero and realized we had only hit the sea and bounced off it. So I'm glad we didn't have to jump, as it would have been only a six feet fall and we would have looked rather stupid! Margate pier was sighted and at last we knew where we were. We were the fourth and last aircraft to get back to the aerodrome. The other members the squadron had come down all over the place, one upside down in the Thames mud, the crew of which smelled horrible for a long time afterwards. Another came down in a wood; a third knocked up a farmer, having landed in his field. A fourth crew also landed infield and got held up by Royal Marines, who took some convincing that they were really British. The last crew to ring in, very late, was a young crew who had also landed in a field. Upon knocking at a nearby house the door was answered by two very pretty girls – and they took a very long time to report their whereabouts. We lost two crews over the target area.

Six Swordfish from 812 Squadron departed from North Coates briefed to attack same target, but only one was successful. All returned safely.

Fighter Command Claims, 2 July
3 Spitfires/611 Squadron – 100 miles east of Withernsea 09:15

K9970	Flt Lt W. J. Leather		
K988	Plt Off J. R. G. Sutton	Do215 probable	4./Aufkl.ObdL
N9351	Plt Off J. W. Lund		FTR

2 Group (Blenheim) Casualties, 2 July
Blenheim P6895 FTR: Sqn Ldr H. F. Chester, Sgt H. Histon, Sgt R. J. McAllister all killed; victim of 2./JG21

Luftwaffe Fighter Claims & Casualties, 2 July
2./JG21

Oblt Leo Eggers	Blenheim 11:44 north-west of Hom
Fw Jakob Schmitt	Blenheim 11:55 20 m south of Den Helder

Luftwaffe Operational Bomber & Reconnaissance Casualties, 2 July
4./Aufkl.ObdL

Do215 (0040) G2+EH FTR: Fw Helmuth Apitz (pilot), Obfw Heinz Fredrich, Uffz Walter Neige, Gfr Herbert Habel all killed; victim of 611 Squadron.

7./KG4

Ju88 (5066) 5J+BR crashed on return: Uffz Wilhelm Knobling (pilot), Uffz Gerhard Lewandowski, Uffz Hans Krahn, and Gfr Karl Rauchfuss all badly injured; victim of AA fire (Newcastle).

St/KG2

Do17 – returned damaged and crashed at base (w/o); apparently damaged by AA (Tyne).

FAA Casualties, Night 2/3 July
825 Squadron

Swordfish L2829 FTR: Sub-Lt(A) J. B. Kiddell (POW); L/Air H. W. V. Burt (killed); victim of flak

Swordfish L7646 FTR: Sub-Lt(A) B. P. Grigson, Sub-Lt(A) F. L. Lees (both killed); victim of flak

Wednesday, 3 July

The day proved to be very successful for RAF fighters and costly for KG77, which lost six Do17s plus one damaged, while another went down from 3./KG3. Three Ju88s of 8./KG30 also fell, as did a Bf109 of I/JG54. The only damage suffered by Fighter Command was to three Spitfires and one Hurricane with minor damage from return fire.

08:40-09:18: Green Section of 616 Squadron led by Flg Off George Moberley encountered a Do17 from I/KG3 at 4,500 feet. All three Spitfires attacked twice and the aircraft crashed into the sea with the loss of Oblt Schrapowski and his crew. Plt Off Hugh Dundas and Sgt Fred Burnard fired short bursts at a second Dornier but it escaped into cloud with, it was believed, one engine out of action and possibly the rear gunner killed. Dundas later wrote:

> Green Section was scrambled and sent off at full speed out to sea, crossing the coast north of Spurn Point. George Moberley was leading; Sergeant Burnard and I followed him. There was a layer of broken cloud at about five thousand feet and we were ordered to keep below it. We thundered along at full throttle, bumping violently in the turbulent air just below the cloud. George gave the tally-ho and altered course sharply. Then I saw it – the pencil shape of a Dornier 17 twin-engined bomber just below the cloud, stalking a convoy. As George went into the attack the Dornier pulled up into cloud. I climbed hard and in a few seconds burst through into the bright blue above. Almost immediately the Dornier also popped through close by and I was able to get in a short attack before it again disappeared into cloud. There followed an exciting chase as the German pilot tried frantically to elude us. But nowhere was the cloud solid, he was bound to come out into gaps and by good fortune we maintained contact with him, worrying at his heels like spaniels hunting in cover. He fought back gallantly – desperately would perhaps be a more appropriate word – and for a time his rear-gunner returned our fire, though it was an unequal exchange, which must have been utterly terrifying for him. His tracer bullets streamed past and I received a hit on the outer part of my port wing. But the advantage was all in our favour. The rear-gunner was silenced and the dying Dornier descended in its shroud of black smoke, to crash into the sea a few miles east of the convoy. A second Dornier was sighted, scurrying away among the clouds Sergeant Burnard and I managed to get in one attack each before our ammunition was all gone, but though we damaged it we did not see it crash.
>
> Back at Leconfield I experienced for the first time the exhilaration of landing and taxiing in after a successful engagement with the enemy. Those who waited on the ground could always tell when a Spitfire's machine guns had been fired. Normally the eight gun ports on the leading edge of the wing were covered by little patches of canvas. But when the guns were fired these patches were, of course, shot away, leaving the ports open, and the plane made a distinctive whistling noise on the glide. This clear signal that you had been in action could be made more pronounced by a bit of sideslipping, which, though sternly discouraged by the authorities, was hard to resist on such occasions. And so, when they recognized this signal of action, the ground crews, who identified themselves enthusiastically with the pilots whose planes they serviced, would run out in high excitement to hear the news.

They regarded a victory for their plane as a victory for themselves – and justly so, for our reliance on their skills was absolute. I felt twelve feet tall after that combat, which in retrospect certainly does not seem anything to be particularly proud of. At last I had broken my duck. I could only claim one-third of one enemy aircraft destroyed and one-half of another damaged – but that was better than nothing at all.[4]

In order to maintain the pressure on the defences, the Luftwaffe had been ordered to carry out daylight precision pinpoint attacks against specific important targets, usually associated with the local docks or aircraft industry. These surprise attacks were to be carried out by aircraft, either singly or in small groups, only with the aid of suitable cloud cover. The first such mission undertaken against a target in the Bristol area was that attempted on the Portishead Docks by three Ju88s of II/KG51 during the afternoon.

At 13:10 three Hurricanes from 145 Squadron's Blue Section led by Flt Lt Adrian Boyd claimed a He111 probably destroyed off St Catherine's Point. All three aircraft carried out No. 1 Attack, observing pieces falling from port wing and engine before the aircraft was lost in cloud. This was possibly a Do17 from 7./KG77 that returned with one crew member wounded.

Green Section led by Flg Off Brian Carbury with Plt Off Ras Berry and Plt Off Stapme Stapleton from 603 Squadron shot down a Ju88 of 8./KG30 at 14:05, about six miles south of Dyce. Three members of Fw Heidinger's crew of 4D+IS were seen in their dinghy but all three were lost. Only Uffz Rupert Hehringleher was picked up by trawler. Stapleton's report revealed:

Green 1 attacked, then I attacked slightly on the starboard quarter as e/a was turning to starboard. I only had time for one short burst, after which e/a entered cloud bank. I lost my section so I proceeded to patrol 20 miles east of Montrose where there was no cloud.

A section of Spitfires from 54 Squadron claimed a Do215 probably destroyed north-west of Deal at 15:15. Their victim may have been a Do17 of 9./KG77 that FTR from nuisance raid on Dover. Oblt Hermann Kapsch and his crew were rescued but all wounded.

Another Ju88 from 8./KG30 was lost at 16:07, the second victim of 603 Squadron whose pilots Sqn Ldr George Denholm/Plt Off Dudley Stewart-Clarke/Sgt Ivor Arber claimed it as a He111. Fw Wilzer and his crew were reported missing after their aircraft crashed in the sea some 25 miles north-east of Peterhead.

Flt Lt John Ellis was leading a flight of 610 Squadron on convoy patrol when, at 16:20, a Do17 was sighted, as he later reported:

I was leading Blue Section with Red Section in line astern on a patrol between Margate and Dungeness. Both sections had been patrolling for about 1 hour

5 minutes when we were ordered to intercept a bandit over Hawkinge below cloud. I saw the bandit, a Do17, approaching from the north at right angles to our course.

Sgt Ron Hamlyn fired the final burst and as he broke away saw a splash in the sea. The Do17 was probably the aircraft flown by Fw Richard Saft who was reported missing with his crew while on a nuisance raid to Dover.

At about the same time (16:20) a Do17 from 1./KG77 that had been engaged in a nuisance raid on the Harwich/Ipswich area was shot down off Felixstowe by a section from 56 Squadron; Oblt Kurt Steiner and his crew were lost. Bombs had fallen in and around Lowestoft, killing four, seriously wounding five and injuring twenty others. One person was killed in Ipswich and seventeen injured. Meanwhile, Flt Lt Tom Dalton-Morgan and Plt Off David Gorrie of 43 Squadron engaged a Do17 off Beachy Head at 16:30 and claimed it damaged. This was possibly an aircraft from 8./KG77 that had been involved in a nuisance raid on Aldershot. Fw Werner Patrzich and his crew were reported missing.

Flt Lt Bill Warner's Green Section of 610 Squadron took-off at 16:50 to relieve Red and Blue Sections on convoy patrol. A 'Do215' was sighted and pursued across the Channel by Flg Off Peter Litchfield. On reaching Cap Griz Nes he silenced the rear gunner and caused the aircraft to 'wobble'. Its nose went up and it stalled at 100 feet after his third burst. Plt Off Fred Gardiner, who was following him, had the port wing of his aircraft holed by AA fire. This was possibly Fw Ludwig Eichhorn's Do17 from 4./KG77 that crashed near Vraucourt in which all the crew were killed.

Do17s attacked Manston in a minor raid at about 17:00, and mines were also laid in the Thames Estuary. Plt Off Peter Gardner together with Sgts Bill Higgins and Ted Bayley of 32 Squadron engaged 3Z+GS of 8./KG77 and shot it down south of Kenley, where it careered through hop vines at Baybrooks, Horsmonden near Marden. H. R. Pratt Boorman, proprietor of the *Kent Messenger*, wrote:

> A Jerry plane was brought down in a hop garden in Collier Street. Tractors are noisy things and a farmer driving one did not hear the dogfight in the sky above him, nor the plane crash. The first he knew was when the pilot came over to him and saluted. He pulled up, and was told in perfect English what had happened, and how the pilot had scrambled out of the wrecked plane. The farmer looked him up and down and said, "I suppose you had better come along to my house." He took him home, his wife gave him a cup of tea, and there the pilot waited till the police came.

Oblt Hans-Georg Gallion (observer) and Uffz Richard Brandes (pilot) were both injured; Obgfr Erich Hofmann and Uffz Waldemar Theilig were both killed.

Bombs also fell on Kenley, as noted by Plt Off Cecil 'Charlie' Young of 615 Squadron in a letter to his parents in Malaya:

Well, I expect you all know about the situation at home nowadays. At the moment we're working terribly hard, 24 hours a day, 7 days a week more or less. The chief thing as far as we're concerned is lack of sleep. They've started bombing over here now, yesterday we were bombed. 8 bombs were dropped but only two hit the aerodrome doing no damage at all. Needless to say the two aeroplanes responsible didn't get back. We're expecting the real 'Blitzkrieg' as far as this country is concerned to begin any day now, we're all ready for them so all I say is good luck to them.

At 18:30, south of Middle Wallop, Sqn Ldr Baines led three Hurricanes of 238 Squadron to pursue a Ju88 from 1.(F)/123. Flt Lt John Kennedy engaged and both machines were damaged in the exchange though both were able to return to their respective bases. Ltn Watchel was among the recce aircraft's crew. Kennedy's machine sustained damage to the radiator while another bullet penetrated near the pilot's seat.

603 Squadron got its third 8./KG30 Ju88 4D+NS of the day when Red Section – Flg Off Ian Ritchie/Plt Off George Gilroy/Sgt Jim Caister (aged 34) – shot down Ltn Heinrich-Alexander Bieroth's aircraft in flames 2 miles south-east of Inverberwie at 19:10. All four crew were lost including Hptm von Schulze-Lansdorf.

Hudsons from 206 Squadron attacked targets at Ijmuiden and Texel in daylight. All returned safely. P5143/VX-M flown by Plt Off Tommy Burne,[5] having bombed a factory six miles north of Ijmuiden, was attacked by two Bf109s of 2./JG54 from Amsterdam/Schipol. Rear gunner LAC Norman Deighton returned fire (600 rounds) and saw pieces off tail, then flames before it rolled over and spun down in flames. The unidentified German pilot baled out and aircraft crashed in Assendelft (Holland).

Thirty-five Blenheims of 2 Group raided targets in daylight at Kiel, the Ruhr, and airfields at Evere, Béthune and Abbeville, and barges in the River Lek near Rotterdam. All returned safely. Five Skuas of 801 Squadron, escorted by three Blenheims from 18 Group, departed Hatston to attack concentrations of German boats and oil tanks at Bergen. All returned safely without sighting the boats.

During this day of sporadic raids, AA guns were in action at Bramley, Newport, Bristol, Holton Heath, Dover and Harwich. Bombs fell in Suffolk and Essex. No fatalities were reported. Cardiff was bombed. At least thirteen bombs fell in the Bridgetown area, where two horses were injured and two rabbits killed.

Operational Accidents: 74 Squadron lost a pilot and aircraft when Sgt John White's Spitfire (K9928) was struck by lightning and crashed near Margate at about 17:00. A He111 crashed into a barracks on take-off from Neuruppin. Among the casualties was Oblt Hermann Erbprinz zy Solmslich, a pilot of 6./ZG26; a Bf109 of 6./JG52 crashed at Herrenberg with the death of Fw Heinrich Hoffmann.

Night operations: Thirty Hampdens and Wellingtons attacked various targets while others laid mines. One of the latter, a Hampden P4352 of 44 Squadron FTR, was believed to have been shot down by a Bf109 from I/JG76. Plt Off Desmond

Todd and his crew were killed.

Fighter Command Claims & Casualties, 3 July

3 Spitfires/616 Squadron – 10 miles off Withernsea 08:40-09:18

Blue 1	Flg Off G. E. Moberley		
Blue 2	Plt Off H. S. L. Dundas	Do17	I/KG3
Blue 3	Flt Sgt F. P. Burnard		
Blue 2	Plt Off H. S. L. Dundas	Do17 damaged	
Blue 3	Flt Sgt F. P. Burnard		

3 Hurricanes/145 Squadron – off St Catherine's Point (IoW) 13:10

P3381	Flt Lt A. H. Boyd	
N2545	Flg Off P. L. Parrott	He111 probable
P3517	Plt Off L. D. M. Scott	

3 Spitfires/603 Squadron – 6 miles south-east of Aberdeen 14:05

R6835	Flg Off B. J. G. Carbury (NZ)		
L1046	Plt Off R. Berry	Ju88	8./KG30
L1024	Plt Off B. G. Stapleton (SA)		

6 Spitfires/54 Squadron – 5 miles north of Deal 15:15

R6708	Flt Lt B. H. Way		
R6709	Plt Off C. F. Gray (NZ)	Do215 probable	9./KG77
N3173	Sgt J. K. Norwell	(Do17)	

6 Spitfires/610 Squadron – off Folkestone 16:20

L1009	Flt Lt E. B. B. Smith		
N3284	Flg Off P. G. Lamb		
R6694	Sgt R. F. Hamlyn	Do17	2./KG77
P9451	Flt Lt J. Ellis		
P9496	Sgt P. Else		
L1076	Sgt N. H. D. Ramsey		

3 Spitfires/603 Squadron – 25 miles north-east of Peterhead 16:07

Red 1	Sqn Ldr G. L. Denholm		
Red 2	Plt Off D. Stewart-Clarke	He111 (Ju88)	8./KG30
Red 3	Sgt I. K. Arber		

All three Spitfires hit by return fire, none seriously

3 Hurricanes/43 Squadron – off Beachy Head 16:30

N3784	Flt Lt T. D. F. Dalton-Morgan	Do17 damaged	7./KG77
N3466	Plt Off D. G. Gorrie		

3 Hurricanes/56 Squadron – west of Felixstowe 16:20
P3547   Flt Lt J. H. Coghlan
P3587   Flg Off R. E. P. Brooker   Do215 probable (Do17 FTR) I/KG77

9 Hurricanes/32 Squadron – south of Kenley 17:05
N2671   Plt Off P. M. Gardner
N2670   Sgt W. B. Higgins   Do17   8./KG77
N2463   Sgt E. A. Bayley

1 Spitfire/610 Squadron – near Marquise 17:25
P9452   Plt Off P. Litchfield   Do215 probable (Do17 4./KG77)

3 Hurricanes/238 Squadron – near Middle Wallop 18:30
P3700   Flt Lt J. C. Kennedy   Ju88 damaged   1.(F)/123
P3700 damaged by return fire.

3 Spitfires/603 Squadron – off Inverberwie 19:10
Red 1   Flg Off I. S. Ritchie
Red 2   Plt Off G. K. Gilroy   Ju88   8./KG30
Red 3   Sgt J. R. Caister

Coastal Command Claims, 3 July
1 Hudson/206 Squadron –
P5143   Plt Off T. R. Burne   Bf109   2./JG54
Shot down by rear gunner LAC Norman Deighton (awarded DFM)

Luftwaffe Fighter Claims & Casualties, 3 July
I/JG76
Unidentified pilot shot down 'Whitley' – Hampden 44 Sqn FTR

2./JG54
Bf109 FTR: Unidentifield pilot – shot down by return fire from Hudson of 206 Sqn (baled out)

Luftwaffe Operational Bomber & Reconnaissance Casualties, 3 July
3./KG3
Do17 FTR: Oblt Wolfgang Schrapowski (Staffelkaptän), Fw Otto Kretzschmar, Fw Rudolf Pohl, Fw Georg Heberle (all killed); victim of 616 Squadron.

8./KG30
Ju88 4D+IS FTR: Fw Otto Heidinger (pilot), Uffz Friedrich Rabe, Uffz Paul Wieczoreck (all killed); Uffz Rupert Hehringlehner rescued by trawler, unhurt

(POW); Rabe's body later recovered from the sea and buried at Dyce; victim of 603 Squadron (Carbury/ Berry/Stapleton)

Ju88 4D+NS FTR: Ltn Heinrich-Alexander Bieroth (pilot), Hptm Werner von Schulze-Langsdorf, Fw Willi Engelskirchen, Uffz Bernhard Brüggen (all killed); Bieroth's body later recovered from the sea and buried at Dyce; victim of 603 Squadron (Ritchie/Gilroy/ Caister).

Ju88 4D+?? FTR: Fw Robert Wilzer (pilot), Fw Hans-Ewald Stichler, Uffz Josef Sobola, Gfr Helmut Frähsdorf. victim of 603 Squadron (Denholm/Stewart-Clarke/ Arber)

1./KG77
Do17 FTR: Oblt Kurt Steiner, Obfw Kurt Birks, Uffz Johannes Flugel, Gfr Kurt Dietel (all killed); victim of 56 Squadron.

2./KG77
Do17 FTR: Fw Richard Saft, Oblt Fritz Kretzscmar, Fw Gerhard Joppich, Obfw Alfred Penzel (all killed); probably victim of 610 Squadron.

4./KG77
Do17 FTR: Fw Ludwig Eichhorn, Uffz Gerhard Hartmann, Uffz Heinz Boost, Uffz Georg Hollerauer (all killed); probably victim of 610 Squadron.

7./KG77
Do17 damaged: Uffz Oskar Gerber (observer) slightly wounded; possibly victim of 145 Squadron.

8./KG77
Do17 FTR: Fw Werner Patrzich, Uffz Wilhelm Kuske, Uffz Rudolf Pfeiffer, Gfr Walter Mair (all killed); possibly victim of 43 Squadron.

Do17 3Z+GS (2642) FTR: Uffz Richard Brandes wounded, POW; Oblt Hans-Georg Gallion wounded, POW; Obgfr Erich Hofmann killed, Uffz Waldemar Theilig killed; victim of 32 Squadron.

9./KG77
Do17 FTR: Oblt Hermann Kapsch, Uffz Karl Schwarzbach, Uffz Ernst Goldhorn, Gfr Kurt Thiemicke (all wounded); possibly victim of 54 Squadron – or badly damaged by AA during raid over Maidenhead; believed to have crashed on return.

RAF Bomber Command Operational Casualties, night 3/4 July
44 Squadron
Hampden P4352 FTR: Plt Off D. A. Todd (pilot), Flt Lt W. S. Bull, Sgt E. T. Appleton, Sgt A. Baird (all killed); the body of Flt Lt Bull drifted ashore near Klegod, Denmark. Believed shot down by I/JG76

Thursday, 4 July[6]

Following the attack on the French Fleet at Mers-el-Kébir the previous day (see Chapter X) Prime Minister Churchill rallied the Commons:

> I call upon all subjects of His Majesty, and upon our Allies, and well-wishers – and they are not a few – all over the world, on both sides of the Atlantic, to give us the utmost aid. In the fullest harmony with our Dominions, we are moving through a period of extreme danger and of splendid hope, when every virtue of our race will be tested, and all that we have and are will be freely staked. This is no time for doubt or weakness. It is the supreme hour to which we have been called.
>
> The action we have already taken should be, in itself, sufficient to dispose once and for all of the lies and rumours which have been so industriously spread by German propaganda and through Fifth Column activities that we have the slightest intention of entering into negotiations in any form and through any channel with the German and Italian governments. We shall, on the contrary, prosecute the war with the utmost vigour by all the means that are open to us until the righteous purposes for which we entered upon it have been fulfilled.

4 July witnessed the opening of the German assault on Channel convoys. The attacks on the convoys would it was hoped, draw out the British fighters from their bases. This way the Luftwaffe could analyse the strength of the RAF and determine the speed and the efficiency with which the RAF could deploy its squadrons. A battlegroup consisting of KG2's Do17s, and Ju87s from II/StG 1, IV(Stuka)./LG 1 supported by Erpr.Gr.210 (Bf110s) and Bf109s of I and III/JG51 were concentrated into a shipping strike force under the Geschwaderkommodore of KG2, Oberst Johannes Fink, who was given the title *Kanalkampfführer* of the Channel Battle.

Thirty-three Ju87s of II/StG51 took off at 08:00 to attack shipping in Portland. The crews reported sinking an 'old warship' of 8-10,000 tons with six bombs, a 10,000 ton freighter and a 5,000 ton freighter. They in fact sank a tug and damaged three large freighters. The anti-aircraft vessel HMS *Foylebank* was also bombed, and sank at 08:15, with the loss of sixty lives. The VC was awarded posthumously to Act/Seaman Jack Mantle, gunner on board the ship, who continued to man his gun despite fatal wounds. The cost to II/StG51 was just one Ju87 shot down with the loss of Ltn Schwarze and his gunner, although a second Stuka landed at Cherbourg with damage.

Stukas were active off the Channel coast again during the afternoon. Convoy *OA178* consisting of fourteen merchant ships outward bound from London was attacked off Portland at about 13:00 by two Gruppen of Ju87s from StG51. The Stukas, in waves of six, continued their attacks for more than an hour, sinking four of the freighters - the Dutch steamers *Britsum* (5,255 tons) and *Deucalion* (1,796 tons), the Estonian *Kolga* (3,526 tons) and the British *Dallas City* (4,952 tons). Due to bomb damage, the *Dallas City* went out of control and collided with the British steamer *Flimstone* before sinking. In the meantime, her crew was taken aboard the destroyer HMS *Shikari*, which also came under attack but escaped damage. At least six other freighters sustained damage during the series of attacks. No fighters were sent to protect the stricken convoy and the Navy wanted to know why the RAF had not responded.

The Naval view was that standing patrols should be flown over the convoys; but this would have been an extravagant use of our precious fighters. The Royal Air Force therefore preferred to extend cover to the convoys from various Sector Headquarters off whose area of responsibility a convoy might be passing. This, however, tended to result in the arrival of the fighters after the enemy bombers had done their worst and withdrawn.

A section of three Spitfires of 54 Squadron had scrambled at 12:30 to investigate a plot off Manston but were intercepted by Bf109s from 2.(J)/LG1. Two Spitfires were damaged but were able to return to base. Obfw Hermann Staege claimed one Spitfire and Ltn Friedrich Geisshardt a second, although his was not confirmed.

Another attack on the convoy followed at 14:00, the first by the Dorniers of KG2, comprising eighteen aircraft of II Gruppe escorted by some thirty Bf109s from II/JG51. The raid was countered by Hurricanes of 79 Squadron. Four KG2 crewmen were wounded and two Do17s damaged in the running battle that developed, while a 2,000 ton cargo ship was claimed probably sunk. Obfw Hans-Walter Wolff of 6./KG2 reported:

This is it – we are flying the first sortie against England! Escorted by fighters we are to attack a convoy steaming off Dover close to the British coast. We are airborne at 14:30 after 4 and 5 Staffeln. We crossed the Channel at an altitude of 2,000 metres – the sky is partially covered which will hinder our bomb run and escape. We fly several passes but lose the formation when entering and flying through a cloud bank. I attach myself to the first Kette. Suddenly three Hurricanes hove into view, diving down on us. The clatter of our guns is matched only by the crashing and banging of their shells as they slam into our cockpit and fuselage. I draw my neck into my shoulders and duck instinctively and close up tighter to the lead machine of our formation. The attack goes on relentlessly. Our *Beobachter* [observer] Oblt Dörwaldt and *Bordfunker* [radio operator] Uffz Krehl are wounded. They bleed heavily from gunshot wounds to the head and thigh. Our starboard engine is hit and oil pressure rapidly falls away. Luckily for us our escort then arrives on the scene, so there are no further attacks on us from the British fighters.

I manage to nurse our shot-up Do17 back to the nearest airfield and attempt a landing – it is St-Omer. The tail wheel has been shot away and it impossible to feather the starboard engine. Once safely down we count over one hundred bullet strikes on the airframe, including four the size of a fist that must have been caused by tracers. The rudder controls have been shot away, the radio operator's position has taken four shells and the cockpit is awash with blood ['*eine Blutlache*']. Although we had fired off red flares as we over-flew the field there was no-one there to meet us as we rolled to a stand at the end of the runway. When help eventually arrived I was in a blind rage, cursing and swearing at anyone in my way. I have never been so livid. Our two badly injured crewmen were taken to hospital and we went with them. In the end Krehl's wounds proved to be skin grazes. Later that evening a truck came for us. According to reports filed by our fighters two ships had been sunk and three enemy fighters shot down by our Me109s [...]⁷

Two Do17s of 6./KG2 each returned with two wounded crewmen aboard, the other having observer Ltn Wolf-Dietrich Riedinger and Fw Alois Bohrer wounded. The pilot and air gunner Gfr Helmut Reiter were unhurt. Bombs fell on the Kentish town of Lenham, as noted by the *Kent Messenger*:

> In a house nearby, an old lady of 80 was found sitting by herself downstairs with her gasmask on, a saucepan on her head, sobbing for all she was worth.

The Hurricane pilots of 79 Squadron reported being engaged by Bf109s and Sgt Henry Cartwright DFM was shot down and killed when his aircraft crashed near St Margaret's Bay. Plt Off Don Stones' aircraft was damaged in the encounter. It seems probable that Sgt Cartwright was the pilot who damaged the two 6 Staffel Do17s before his own demise. Two Hurricanes were claimed by Ltn Hermann Striebel and Hptm Horst Tietzen at 13:43 and 13:45, respectively.

During the night E-boats would strike and sink another ship of the convoy and damaged two more. When he learned of the convoy's misfortune, Prime Minister Churchill subsequently sent an 'Action This Day' memo to the Vice-Chief of the Naval Staff:

> Could you let me know on one sheet of paper what arrangements you are making about the Channel convoys now that the Germans are all along the French coast? The attacks on the convoys yesterday, both from the air and by E-boats, were very serious, and I should like to be assured this morning that the situation is in hand and that the Air Force is contributing effectively.

The PM was advised that the situation was not under control and that the RAF was not contributing effectively.

During the afternoon, a raid was carried out on the Bristol Aeroplane Company by a lone He111 of III/KG54, and although slight damage was caused to the roof of the Rodney Works the bomber was shot down by Spitfires of 92 Squadron on its return flight. Yellow Section operating from Pembrey intercepted B3+DM (2480) over Weston-super-Mare. Severely damaged, it crashed at 15:15 at Longmoor Farm near Gillingham in Dorset, killing the pilot Ltn Hans-Heinrich Delfs and two of his crew (Uffz Gerhard Bischoff and Uffz Hermann Krack) with only the air gunner Uffz Heinz Karwelat surviving with a foot wound, to become a POW. Plt Off Sammy Saunders and Sgt Ron Fokes landed alongside wreck and assisted in rescue work. Saunders had also fired at a second Heinkel which he believed crashed into the sea.

At 19:00, Hurricanes from 32 Squadron and Bf109s of 2.(J)/LG2 clashed over Dungeness. Two Hurricanes were shot down, Plt Off Grubby Grice force-landing near Manston, and Plt Off Ken Gillman force-landing at Hawkinge. Neither pilot was hurt. Ltn Fredreich Geisshardt claimed one, over Dungeness. In return, Plt Off Rupert Smythe claimed one Bf109 shot down into the sea, and a second probably destroyed. Uffz Gustav Schiller FTR.

Coastal Command Ansons of 48 and 612 Sqns carried out anti-submarine escort duties – two possibly sighted and attacks made with results. A British submarine was attacked in error, on this occasion by Hudson N7298 of 224 Squadron operating out of Leuchars. Plt Off B. K. Hurley and his crew, during an evening sortie, sighted the submarine and challenged with a light for three minutes while diving to attack. There was no response, so Hurley opened fire with his front guns and opened the bomb doors in readiness. Just in time, the submarine gave the correct signals and disaster was averted.

Two Hudsons of 206 Squadron on search for the Hampden crew missing from night raid were shot down 80km north-north-west of Texel at 0907 by Bf109s from 3./JG51 flown by Ltn Rudolf Busch and Uffz Heinz zur Lage. There were no survivors from the crews of P5162 or N7368.

Twenty Blenheims carried out daylight attacks on various targets at Hamm and Soerst, Hanover and Emmerich, airfields at Evere and Schipol, shipping west of Den Helder. One FTR – L8866 of 18 Squadron falling to Uffz Günther Behse of 2./JG76 at 12:10, with the loss of the crew. The aircraft crashed west of Rotterdam.

Operational Accidents: Two RAF fighters were lost during training flights, Spitfire N3294 of 222 Squadron crashed near Withernsea killing Sgt Emrys Lewis, a 24-year-old from Anglesey, while Sgt Jensen flying Hurricane L1936 of 601 Squadron survived when his aircraft force-landed near Lewes following a glycol leak. The Luftwaffe lost a Bf109 of 7./JG3 in which Uffz Christoph Schumann killed in a crash at St-Saëns.

Night Operations: A total of sixty-seven Wellingtons, Hampdens and Whitleys struck at various targets in Germany. Hampden P4361 of 144 Squadron was shot down by flak near Kiel and the crew killed.

Fighter Command Claims & Casualties, 4 July
Spitfires/54 Squadron – near Manston 12:30+

No claims

| P9387 | Plt Off J. L. Kemp aircraft damaged by Bf109 | 2.(J)/LG1 |
| N3160 | Flg Off D. A. P. McMullen aircraft damaged by Bf109 | 2.(J)/LG1 |

9 Hurricanes/79 Squadron – over St Margaret's Bay 14:05-14:40

No claims but two Do17s damaged, so possibly by Sgt H. Cartwright (FTR).

P2619 Sgt H. Cartwight DFM shot down by Bf109 (killed)   (5./JG51)
Plt Off D. W. A. Stones aircraft damaged by Bf109   (5./JG51)

3 Spitfires/92 Squadron – Weston-super-Mare 15:25

P9433	Plt Off H. D. Edwards		
R5624	Plt Off C. H. Saunders	He111P	III/KG54
R5597	Sgt R. H. Fokes		
R5624	Plt Off C. H. Saunders	He111 probable	

9 Hurricanes/32 Squadron – Straits of Dover 18:35-19:30

P3522	Plt Off R. F. Smythe	Bf109, Bf109 probable	2./LG2
N2569	Plt Off D. H. Grice shot down, force-landed near Manston, unhurt.		
N2724	Plt Off K. R. Gillman shot down, force-landed Hawkinge, unhurt.		

Coastal Command Casualties, 4 July
206 Squadron

Hudson P5162/VX-V FTR: Plt Off S. J. Lester, Plt Off J. E. MacKinnon, Sgt K. S. Bushell, Sgt K. E. Lewis (all killed); victim of 3./JG51

Hudson N7368/VX-? FTR: Plt Off S. R. Henderson, Sgt G. H. Goldsmith, Sgt G. C. Sumner, LAC J. L. Williamson (all killed); victim of 3./JG51

2 Group (Blenheim) Casualties, 4 July
18 Squadron

Blenheim L8886 FTR: Flt Lt I. C. B. Worthington-Wilmer, Sgt J. G. Stanley, Sgt G. E. Maydon (all killed); victim of 2./JG76

RAF Bomber Command Operational Casualties, night 4/5 July
144 Squadron

Hampden P4361 FTR Kiel: Flg Off E. B. Lancaster, Plt Off J. H. Gilling, Sgt P. F. Bailey, Sgt I. A. I. J. Nicol (all killed); victim of flak.

Luftwaffe Fighter Claims & Casualties, 4 July
3./JG51

| Ltn Rudolf Busch (2) | Hudson 206 Sqn (09:07) |
| Uffz Heinz zur Lage (2) | Hudson 206 Sqn (09:07) |

5./JG51

Ltn Hermann Striebel (2)	Hurricane (14:43)
Hptm Horst Tietzen (4)	Hurricane (14:45)

2.(J)/LG1

Obfw Hermann Staege (3)	Spitfire (15:18)
Ltn Friedrich Geisshardt (2)	Spitfire – not confirmed (15:30),
	Hurricane (20:00)

Bf109 FTR: Uffz Gustav Schiller shot down by Hurricane 19:55 (killed); victim of 32 Sqn.

2./JG76

Uffz Günther Behse (1) Blenheim 18 Sqn

III/JG27

Bf109 damaged landing at Therville following combat (25%); pilot unhurt.

Luftwaffe Bomber & Reconnaissance Operational Casualties, 4 July

7./StG51

Ju87B FTR: Ltn Wilhelm Schwarze/Uffz Julius Dörflinger missing; victim of HMS *Foyle Bank*.
Ju87B landed Cherbourg, 50% damaged by AA fire.

6./KG2

Do17 damaged & emergency landing at St-Omer: Obfw Hans-Walter Wolff, Oblt Friedrich Dörwaldt (wounded); Uffz Helmut Krehl (wounded); victim of 79 Sqn.
Do17 returned with two crewmen wounded; Ltn Wolf-Dietrich Riedinger and Fw Alois Böhrer wounded; unidentified pilot and air gunner Gfr Helmut Reiter unhurt; victim of 79 Sqn.

III/KG54

He111P B3+DM FTR: Ltn Hans-Heinrich Delfs, Uffz Gerhard Bischoff, Uffz Hermann Krack killed, Uffz Heinz Karwelat, wounded, POW; victim of 92 Sqn.

Friday, 5 July

Another quiet day. At 06:15, an 8./KG1 He111 was shot down by Blue Section of 65 Squadron and it ditched in sea off Folkestone. One of the crew was killed and two badly wounded, both of whom drowned. The pilot, Obfw Hermann Frischmuth and one other were rescued.

Red Section/92 Squadron chased a Heinkel down the coast in the afternoon. On the way back Plt Off Tony Bartley's engine failed and he force-landed in a bog.

'There is some doubt whether it will be possible to save the Spitfire [P9454] as it is sinking in the mud,' noted the squadron diarist. Later three Spitfires of 611 Squadron scrambled and Flt Lt Doug Watkins claimed a Ju88 damaged east of Spurn Head. A Ju88 from II/LG1 crashed at Limoges following combat and was destroyed, probably the victim of Watkins.

Later that evening Sub-Lt(A) Frank Dawson-Paul of 64 Squadron encountered Bf109s for the first time:

For the first time the Hun appeared in large numbers and in broad daylight. We (three of us) were directed over the Channel to meet a reported 50 plus of aircraft. We climbed rapidly to 20,000 feet, and then I saw them in the bright blue of the sky – three solitary white trails coming out of a high layer of cloud, and growing steadily longer. They were some 4,000 feet above us. We gave our Spitfires everything they had and climbed up towards them. Instead of attacking us they climbed rapidly and went into a defensive circle, making no attempt to attack. We reached them at last at 32,000 feet, our Spitfires on the point of stall and with no manoeuvrability at all. Still they did not attempt to attack us, although they had manoeuvrability and about twelve times our number. We separated and I flew inside their circle, in the opposite direction to them, and waited until one flew into my sights. I fired and the recoil immediately stalled me and I started to spin. I got out in about 2,000 feet, and looking about me found there wasn't an aircraft in the sky; in 30 seconds some 40 aircraft had completely disappeared and I had the sky to myself.

I think after the excitement and the exertion at that height I was a bit dozy, anyway I was rudely awakened by long, flickering streams of tracer which seemed uncommonly near my head. Then he shot by in a steep dive, a lean black little blighter – my first 109. I dived as hard as I could make my Spitfire at any moment expecting a wing to break off, and still the 109 drew away. Suddenly, near the French coast, he started to level off and, quite satisfied apparently that he was safe, headed over the town of Calais. I got my sight on him, pressed, saw flickering tendrils reach out from my wings to his tail, saw a large piece come adrift and slip by me. Smoke started to trail, then crumpled, and I seemed to do a complete somersault. Flak had opened up at me, despite their own machine. I shot off home as fast as I could, having gained my first probable.

Dawson-Paul's opponents were from 4./JG51, Ltn Erich Hohagen having claimed a Spitfire north of Hythe – probably having seen Dawson-Paul's aircraft in a spin – before Obfw Johann Illner shot down Dawson-Paul's companion, Plt Off Milne, who crashed near Rouen and was killed. None of the Messerschmitts was lost or reported damaged, so the crashing aircraft he had seen was probably that of Milne. Dawson-Paul's aircraft returned with damage, but whether caused by Hohagen or AA fire is not known.

A Blenheim of 59 Squadron flown by Flg Off G. T. Palmer was attacked off Dungeness by a Bf109 flown by Fw Willi Gasthaus of 4./JG51 but managed to escape, although claimed destroyed. Meanwhile, fifteen Blenheims of 2 Group were despatched on varied small-scale sorties throughout the afternoon, mainly to targets in north-west Germany. Two FTR including the CO of 101 Squadron, shot down by a Bf109 of 6./JG52, while an aircraft of 114 Squadron fell to a Messerschmitt of 5./JG26.

On the Norwegian front yet another RN submarine was attacked in error. Six Swordfish of 823 Squadron and nine Skuas of 801 Squadron departed Hatston to attack a damaged merchant ship reported by a Hudson of 269 Squadron off the Norwegian coast. No contact was made, but returning Swordfish attacked submarine *Telrarch* mistaking her for a German U-boat. Although five torpedoes were launched not strikes were made.

Operational Accidents: 18-year-old Plt Off Brian Firminger of 238 Squadron, in Hurricane P3703, crashed into Pennings Hill near Tidworth in bad weather at 09:50 and was killed. A Blenheim of 23 Squadron crashed during an exercise near Digby (w/o); crew unhurt.

Night Operations: Bomber Command sent forty-seven bombers – Wellingtons, Whitleys and Hampdens – to various targets. Only one was lost, a Wellington of 99 Squadron being shot down by flak over Kiel. During the night there was scattered German bombing along the East Coast. Seventy casualties were reported including eleven dead.

Fighter Command Claims & Casualties, 5 July
9 Spitfires/65 Squadron – off Folkestone 05:35-07:10

R6615	Flg Off G. V. Proudman		
R6618	Plt Off K. G. Hart	He111	8./KG1
N3164	Sgt J. K. Kilner		

3 Spitfires/611 Squadron – 60-80 miles off Spurn Head

P9351	Flg Off D. H. Watkins	Ju88 damaged	II/LG1 FTR

3 Spitfires/64 Squadron – near Rouen 19:57-21:20

P9450	Sub-Lt(A) F. Dawson-Paul RNVR Bf109 probable	4./JG51
P9449	Plt Off D. K. Milne FTR shot down by Bf109 of 4./JG51	
P9450	Sub-Lt(A) F. Dawson-Paul RNVR Cat.2 damaged by Bf109 of 4./JG51	

2 Group (Blenheim) Casualties, 5 July
101 Squadron
Blenheim N6140 FTR: Wg Cdr J. H. Hargroves, Sgt E. E. Smith, Sgt R. M. Livermore (all killed); victim of I/JG52

114 Squadron
Blenheim R3804 FTR: Plt Off A. Stewart, Sgt G. Rimmer, Sgt R. J. S. Ellicott (all killed); victim of II/JG26

Bomber Command Casualties, Night 5/6 July
99 Squadron
Wellington R3170 FTR: Plt Off R. A. G. Willis, Plt Off Perkins, Sgt K. A. R. MacArthur, Sgt C. J. Scanlon (all POW); Sgt G. F. Sexton killed; victim of flak.

Luftwaffe Fighter Claims & Casualties, 5 July
4./JG51
  Ltn Erich Hohagen (1)   Spitfire north of Hythe
  Obfw Johann Illner (1)   Spitfire west of Le Touquet (21:52)
  Fw Willi Gasthaus (2)   Blenheim south of Dungeness

5./JG26
  Oblt Hubertus von Holtey (1)   Blenheim (114 Sqn) south-west of Münster (14:15)

6./JG52
  Fw Otto Junge (2)   Blenheim (101 Sqn) west of Amrun, over North Sea.

2,/JG51
  Bf109 landed 30% damaged; possibly victim of 64 Sqn.

Luftwaffe Bomber & Reconnaissance Operational Casualties, 5 July
8./KG1
He111 V4+GS FTR: Uffz Rudolf Marcklovitz, Gfr Franz Burger, Gfr Franz Martinek killed; Obfw Hermann Frischmuth (pilot), Uffz Gotleib Wagner rescued; the bodies of Burger and Martinek came ashore at Shakespeare Beach a week later, another unidentified German airman being washed ashore there six days thereafter; victim of 65 Sqn.

II/LG1
Ju88 crashed Limoges (100%); no casualties; probably victim of 611 Sqn.

Saturday, 6 July

This proved to be a relatively quiet day, with little aerial activity. At 05:20, the first of ten bombs fell near Dover, the stick crossing Coombe Farm towards Buckland Rectory. No casualties were reported. Later, a single He111 attacked Aldershot's Guillemont Barracks, inflicting seven fatalities. Among those scrambled in search of the intruder was Sqn Ldr Arthur Clouston, a New Zealand-born test pilot at the RAE Farnborough. He took-off without authority in the RAE's Spitfire K9852:

> A Heinkel flew in at 2,000 feet in a clear sky and dropped bombs in the direction of Aldershot. I had just returned from a test flight, and was standing on the tarmac near the watch office. The fact that the bomber should have the audacity to fly over 100 miles inland on such a clear day made me hopping mad. I ran to the [unarmed] Spitfire that I had just landed, and started up as the Heinkel passed back over my head.
>
> I climbed up after him in a matter of seconds. He had turned towards the Continent, but I was gaining on him rapidly, and was only a few thousand yards away when he gained the cover of a thin layer of cloud. I jumped above, dived below, then climbed up above again. The cloud was so thin I was sure he could not hide in it for long.
>
> The Spitfire was unarmed, so I had decided, once I had given chase, that I would fly slowly up behind him and chew into his tail with my propeller, hoping to do enough damage to force him down. I would then make a forced-landing or use my parachute. Perhaps I was fortunate that I did not get the chance of putting it to the test. Although I kept looking above and below the cloud layer until I reached the Channel, I could find no trace of my Heinkel again. I returned to base. My Commanding Officer was furious and grounded me. I pleaded for our guns to be loaded, but without success.

100 miles off the coast of Aberdeen, at 13:00, another reconnaissance machine fell to the Spitfires of 603 Squadron, their fourth such victory in the last four days. Although claimed at a Do215, their victim was in fact Bf110 K9+AH of Aufkl. ObdL, in which Ltn Otto Brix and his crew were killed. During the early afternoon He111s of 4/KG1 were intercepted by a flight of Spitfires from 74 Squadron shortly before 15:30. Oblt Walter Harbeck's aircraft was shot down 10 miles west of Dover, and a second was claimed probably destroyed.

Nineteen 2 Group Blenheims were detailed to carry out daylight attacks on airfields in France and against invasion barges at Zwolle (Holland), but only three bombed owing to lack of cloud cover and one FTR. The 18 Squadron aircraft was intercepted and shot down west of Rotterdam by a Bf109 of 2./JG54. Coastal Command Blenheims of 254 Squadron operated off the Norwegian coast, escorting a Royal Navy task force. Bf110s of 3./ZG76 and Bf109s of 7./JG77 then appeared and shot down two Blenheims; the pilot of P3590 was killed but his crew were rescued by HMS *Fortune*, while the crew of L8842 were picked up by HMS *Cossack*, although one died from his injuries. A PDU Spitfire flown by Flt Lt Tug Wilson, operating with Coastal Command, secured pictures of Hardanger Fjord from 34,000 feet.

Operational Accidents: Sub Lt(A) Dicky Cork of 242 Squadron crashed near Coltishall in Hurricane P3813 (w/o), unhurt; Flt Lt Bob Deacon-Elliott 72 Squadron fainted from lack of oxygen recovered but overstrained Spitfire P9444 (w/o). Across the Channel Uffz Hermann Marquardt of 1./JG3 crashed at Grandvilliers and was killed; Do17 5K+HS of 8./KG3 was destroyed on the ground by a premature bomb explosion; Ar196 of 1./BoGr.196 crashed in Sola Sea (Ltn Stelter and crewman rescued).

Night Operations: Overnight sixty-two people were killed in raids on Goldalming, Aldershot, Haslemere, Farnborough and Plymouth. Bomber Command sent twenty-two Wellingtons to Emden, Bremen and Hamburg, but severe icing was experienced and only six reached the target. One FTR. Ten Whitleys went to Kiel and eleven Hampdens carried out mine-laying duties. One Whitley also FTR.

<u>Fighter Command Claims, 6 July</u>
3 Spitfires/603 Squadron – 100 miles east-north-east of Aberdeen 12:29-13:36
Red 1	Plt Off G. K. Gilroy		
Red 2	Plt Off D. Stewart-Clarke	Do215 (Bf110)	Aufkl.ObdL
Red 3	Sgt J. K. Caister		

3 Spitfires/74 Squadron – 10 miles west of Dover 14:58-15:43
P9398	Flt Lt W. E. G. Measures	He111	4./KG1
P9379	Plt Off Hon D. H. T. Dowding	He111 probable	

<u>Coastal Command Casualties, 6 July</u>
254 Squadron
Blenheim L8842 FTR: Sgt A. W. Tubbs, Sgt R. A. MacVeigh (wounded), Sgt A. C. Johnston – ditched and rescued by HMS *Cossack* (MacVeigh died of wounds); victim of 3./ZG76.
Blenheim N3640 FTR: Plt Off V. J. Pattison (killed), Sgt R. D. Maclaren (burned), Sgt A. P. Savage – ditched and NCOs rescued by HMS *Fortune;* victim of 7./JG77

<u>2 Group (Blenheims) Casualties, 6 July</u>
18 Squadron
Blenheim R3662 FTR: Plt Off B. A. Davidson, Sgt J. Gilmour, Sgt R. J. Fisk (all POW); victim of 2./JG54

<u>Bomber Command Casualties, night 6/7 July</u>
37 Squadron
Wellington R3236 FTR: Flg Off D. W. Lindsay, Plt Off R. A. A. Ball, Sgt A. Atkinson, Sgt J. H. Waterfall DFM, Sgt A. Glen (all killed)

102 Squadron
Whitley N1523 FTR: Plt Off J. M. Lewis, Plt Off D. F. M. MacKarness, Sgt J. Fisk, Sgt L. Askham, Sgt S. Fieldhouse (all POW)

<u>Luftwaffe Fighter Claims, 6 July</u>
   2./JG54
   Fw Alfred Schunk   Blenheim (18 Sqn) west of Rotterdam

   3./ZG76
   Uffz Erich Zickler   Blenheim (254 Sqn) off Norwegian coast

   7./JG77
   Oblt Wilhelm Moritz   Blenheim (254 Sqn) off Norwegian coast

<u>Luftwaffe Bomber & Reconnaissance Casualties, 6 July</u>
4./KG1
He111 FTR: Oblt Walter Harbeck (pilot), Ltn Christian Hacker, Uffz Paul Noack, Uffz Herbert Sack, Uffz Hermann Weichlt (all killed); victim of 74 Sqn.

Aufkl.ObdL
Bf110 K9+AH (3164) FTR: Ltn Otto Brix, Ltn Ewald Kösters, Uffz Hans Beganau (all killed); victim of 603 Sqn.

Sunday, 7 July

Sqn Ldr John Peel was leading Yellow Section of 145 Squadron on a convoy patrol near the Isle of Wight when a Do17 was sighted 5 miles away, travelling north-west at 20,000 feet. Leaving Flg Off Michael Rowley to cover the ships, Sqn Ldr Peel and Plt Off John Wakeham gave chase and eventually shot down the reconnaissance aircraft some 20 miles south-west of the Needles at 05:30. Fw Walter Plotzitzka and his crew of 4U+KK of 2.(F)/123 were lost.

At 09:15, Spitfires of Blue Section/234 Squadron based at St Eval were on patrol north-east of Falmouth when AA guns opened fire at them. One aircraft dived down to almost ground level to avoid the gunfire, which followed him all the way down although it was not hit. A message of protest was sent to 10 Group HQ. The following day, Green Section of 234 Squadron was again fired on by the same guns, some of the rounds 'uncomfortably close'. A further protest was sent to HQ 10 Group. It transpired that the culprits were armed merchant vessels or RN warships located offshore, rather than shore-based batteries, not that this revelation was of much comfort to the pilots concerned.

Another reconnaissance Do17P, this from 3.(F)/121, was encountered by a section of Hurricanes of 43 Squadron off Brighton at 09:47, but escaped in a damaged condition. Return fire hit the aircraft flown by Plt Off John Cruttenden, who force-landed. The Dornier crash-landed near Rouen on return and was badly damaged.

2.(F)/123 lost a second aircraft and crew at 10:26, when Sqn Ldr Max Aitken and Flg Off Billy Clyde of 601 Squadron, patrolling some 15 miles off Cherbourg encountered the reconnaissance machine on its way to photograph Bournemouth and Lyme Regis. 4F+UK was swiftly shot down into the sea.

A He111 from 4./KG55 was damaged by three Spitfires of 54 Squadron at 13:15, during a mission to bomb Portland. One of the crew was wounded. The Spitfires were then attacked by Bf109s of from 7./JG51 and all three damaged. Two crash-landed with slightly wounded pilots. The third pilot was also slightly wounded. The German pilots claimed four victories. The minesweeper *Mercury* was damaged by bombing at Portland, with four of its crew killed and three wounded.

Three Spitfires of 234 Squadron were scrambled at about 17:00, Plt Off Ken Dewhurst intercepting a Ju88 near Plymouth some 10 minutes later, but it escaped major damage. However, at the other end of the country, three Spitfires of 602 Squadron achieved greater success when they encountered a Ju88 of 1./KG30 some 30 miles east-north-east of St Abbs Head, Flt Lt Finlay Boyd and Flg Off Charles MacLean shooting it down into the sea. Ltn Fritz Meinhold and his crew were lost.

Main activity centred on a convoy approaching Dover from the Channel, an estimated 45 Do17s from KG2 carrying out a heavy raid at about 20:30 during the evening. One ship was sunk and a further three damaged. Spitfires from 64 and 65 Squadrons were joined by Hurricanes of 79 Squadron reported being bounced by Bf109s of II/JG51, which promptly shot down three of their Spitfires with the loss of all three pilots, Flg Off George Proudman, whose aircraft crashed in flames into Hougham Woods, while Plt Off Norman Brisbane and Sgt Pat Hayes both crashed into the sea. The three missing Spitfires fell to pilots of 5 Staffel (two claims) and 6 Staffel (three claims) for no losses, although Flg Sgt Bill Franklin claimed two of the Messerschmitts, and Flt Lt Gerry Saunders one. Another press report gave a more detailed account of the engagement:

> One Spitfire pilot [Franklin] shot down two Messerschmitt 109s over the English Channel last night and made attacks on three more before retreating unscathed to his base, states an Air Ministry bulletin. He first attacked a formation of five enemy fighters and after two bursts shot one down into the sea. Later he attacked and completely broke up a further formation of enemy fighters. The first three broke away. The pilot followed one of the others almost down to sea level. After three short bursts this Messerschmitt fell on its side and crashed into the sea. A fellow pilot of the same squadron [Saunders] saw a third Messerschmitt leave its formation and dive towards the sea. He followed, firing bursts. He saw it hit the sea. Another squadron [64] chased a Messerserschmitt right over the French coast, scoring repeated hits and sent the twin-engined fighter [in fact a Do17] plunging into the sea. Shortly before this the last machine had shot down a Hurricane [*sic*].

A Hurricane had indeed been shot down, but was sadly the victim of friendly fire, resulting in the death of the CO of 79 Squadron, Canadian-born Sqn Ldr John Joslin. He had taken off at 20:50 with two others to patrol the convoy off Folkestone when he was bounced from above and astern and shot down. His companions, Plt Offs Don Stones DFC and Tom Parker, turned to face the attackers and saw, to their horror, that the 'enemy' were Spitfires, probably from 65 Squadron. Joslin was seen to bale out at 20,000 feet but did not pull the ripcord, possibly due to wounds. His Hurricane (P2756) crashed in flames at Chilverton Elms near Folkestone. Stones later wrote:

> He was tough, enthusiastic and every inch a leader. He inspired us with the hope that we would no longer be a rudderless ship and morale rose as he led us into the new battles with increasing numbers of Me109s escorting their bombers over our convoys.

Reginald Foster, a reporter from the *Daily Herald*, who had witnessed the action and believed Joslin to have been a German pilot, described his demise thus:

> They were quite low, and we realised unpleasantly, this was the kill. There was a burst of machine-gun fire and a sugar-like glow appeared in the body of the Messerschmitt. The glow spread to a flame and the machine rocketed to earth in a shroud of smoke and flame. The whole terrible drama lasted less than a minute.

The returning pilots of 64 Squadron claimed two Bf110s shot down, but in fact they had pursued Dorniers of KG2 not Messerschmitts, two of which were damaged, one crash-landing near Boulogne with wounded crew.

During the day seven HE bombs fell on Whitley Road, Eastbourne, where nine houses were destroyed and sixty damaged. Two residents were killed and twenty-two injured. More bombs fell at Penhale, Falmouth and Plymouth, and East Nudham, while Dover was raided twice. Total casualties were eighty-one killed and thirty-three injured.

A total of twenty-four Blenheims from 2 Group were detailed to reconnoitre and attack airfields and invasion barges in France and Belgium. Poor weather resulted in only three being able to drop their bombs while the others aborted with the exception of two that FTR – Sgt Hutton's 82 Squadron machine fell to Fw Wilhelm Müller of 3./JG26 at 12:50, while Plt Off Bamber's aircraft from 15 Squadron was shot down by Fw Georg Kiening of 6./JG54 at 17:55 and crashed near Bruges. Bamber managed to avoid crashing on the village of Dudzele and ditched his aircraft in the nearby canal, where the crew drowned. 53 Squadron Blenheim L8789 returning from an attack on a canal near Amsterdam was unable to find Detling in bad weather and landed on disused airfield at Ramsgate. The aircraft was damaged when it hit several anti-invasion obstructions.

Coastal Command Hudsons were active during the day, two from 220 Squadron attacking three small minesweepers northwest of Terschelling while, further north, two from 233 Squadron operating from Leuchers went after shipping off Obrestad. Another from this unit narrowly escaped the attentions of a Bf110 while attacking six motor vessels off Karmo. Spitfire PRle (N3117) of 212 Squadron fitted with two F.24 cameras pointing outwards for low-level ops flew to Boulogne where the pilot took some excellent photos from 300 feet.

A Sunderland from 10(RAAF) Squadron assisted in the rescue of survivors from a torpedoed Swedish vessel by providing cover, and another sighted a sinking Portuguese tanker and stood-by while rescue was affected. Further north, eight Skuas of 801 Squadron departed Hatston to attack oil tanks at Bergen. No damage was done to intended targets and no aircraft were lost.

Operational Accidents: Plt Off L. D. M. Scott of 145 Squadron crashed Hurricane N2497 in attempting to take-off in coarse pitch, the aircraft being considerably damaged. Plt Off D. N. Forde also of 145 Squadron taxied P3545 into P2924, which was stationary, causing damage to both aircraft.

Night Operations: Eighteen Hampdens and a dozen each of Wellingtons and Whitleys carried out raids, the Hampdens attacking Frankfurt, Soest, Duisburg and Dortmund-Ems, where an aircraft from 61 Squadron was shot down. Sgt Ken Wood, was the Wop/AG on P4390 flown by Flt Lt E. C. S. Fewtrell:

We were briefed to drop a mine in the aqueduct on the Dortmund-Ems canal, supposedly from 50 feet but in fact, just skimming the water. We followed the canal for miles and reached the target without incident. However, with bomb doors open and the drop point coming up, we were suddenly met with 4x20 mm anti-aircraft batteries: and they didn't miss. Eadie dropped the mine and at that moment our port engine was hit fair and square. 'Fanny' [Flt Lt Fewtrell] managed to pull up to a dangerous bale-out height and we evacuated without delay. Unfortunately, Eadie didn't manage to get through the escape hatch in the nose and sadly perished when the plane crashed a couple of miles away. The rest of us travelled around unable to move far because Fanny hurt his back when he baled out and inevitably we were picked up by the local police at the crash site [...][8]

Meanwhile, the Wellingtons raided the docks at Wilhelmshaven and the marshalling yards at Osnabrük and Gremberg, while the Whitleys attacked Kiel and Hamm. All these aircraft returned safely. However, a Hampden from 83 Squadron had crashed three miles north-east of Clacton soon after take-off, killing three members of the crew with the fourth later dying from his injuries.

Coastal Command Blenheims were also active during the hours of darkness, six from 53 Squadron attacking shipping at Brest, while two from 59 Squadron attacked the M/V *Condorcet* near Brest.

Individual raiders were over the Yorkshire coast during the night, bombs falling at Leightin Cap, Whitley Bay and Monkseaton. Total casualties were six people injured. All the German bombers returned safely (see Appendix VIII).

Fighter Command Claims & Casualties, 7 July

3 Hurricanes/145 Squadron – 20 miles south of The Needles (IoW) 05:20

P3400	Sqn Ldr J. R. A. Peel	Do17P	2.(F)/123
P2957	Plt Off E. J. C. Wakeham		

6 Hurricanes/43 Squadron – off Brighton 09:47

L1824	Plt Off G. C. Brunner		
L1849	Plt Off J. Cruttenden	Do17P damaged	3.(F)/121
N2665	Sgt J. A. Buck		
L1849	Plt Off J. Cruttenden force-landed (Cat 3)		

6 Hurricanes/601 Squadron – 15 miles off Cherbourg 09:55-10:55

P2920	Sqn Ldr J. W. M. Aitken	Do17P	2.(F)/123
P3393	Flg Off W. P. Clyde		

3 Spitfires/54 Squadron – off Dover 13:05-13:22

P9389	Flg Off D. A. P. McMullen		
R6711	Plt Off A. R. McL. Campbell	He111	4./KG55
P9390	Plt Off E. J. Coleman		

P9389   Flg Off D. A. P. McMullen aircraft damaged by Bf109, slightly wounded – landed Manston (Cat.2)

R6711   Plt Off A. R. McL. Campbell slightly wounded; aircraft damaged by Bf109 and force-landed Deal (w/o)

P9390   Plt Off E. J. Coleman slightly wounded by Bf109; aircraft force-landed near Deal (w/o)

3 Spitfires/234 Squadron – Plymouth 17:10

P9320	Plt Off K. S. Dewhurst	Ju88 damaged

3 Spitfires/602 Squadron – 30 miles east-north-east of St Abbs Head 17:31-18:40

N3228	Flt Lt R. F. Boyd		
L1040	Flg Off C. H. MacLean	Ju88	1./KG30

6 Spitfires/65 Squadron – Straits of Dover 20:19-21:38

N3164	Flt Sgt W. H. Franklin	2 Bf109
P9436	Flt Lt G. A. W. Saunders	Bf109
R6651	Flg Off G. V. Proudman FTR – shot down by Bf109 (KiA)	
R6609	Plt Off N. J. Brisbane FTR – shot down by Bf109 (KiA)	
N3129	Sgt P. S. Hayes FTR – shot down by Bf109 (KiA)	

Spitfires/64 Squadron – Straits of Dover 20:30-21:48

| L1055 | Sub-Lt(A) F. Dawson-Paul RNVR | Bf110 (Do17Z) | II/KG2 |
| P9421 | Flg Off A. J. O. Jeffery | Bf110 (Do17Z) | II/KG2 |

10 Hurricanes/79 Squadron – off Folkestone 20:50-21:48

P2756   Sqn Ldr J. D. C. Joslin FTR – crashed in flames near Folkestone (killed) shot down by Spitfires of 65 Sqn in error.

2 Group (Blenheim) Casualties, 7 July

15 Squadron

R3896 FTR: Plt Off H. C. M. Bamber, Sgt J. Holdsworth, Sgt G. Reid (all killed); victim of 6./JG54

82 Squadron

P4843 FTR: Sgt F. Hutton, Sgt C. W. Pickering, Sgt J. A. Rogers (all killed); victim of 3./JG26

Bomber Command Casualties, night 7/8 July

61 Squadron

Hampden P4390 FTR: Flt Lt E. C. S. Fewtrell, Sgt E. V. Gawith, Sgt K. B. Wood (all POW); Plt Off J. Eadie (killed); victim of flak

83 Squadron

Hampden L4066 crashed on outward journey – Plt Off O. H. Launders, Sgt C. R. Hallet, Sgt B. Kinton (all killed); Sgt L. Howard died from injuries.

Luftwaffe Fighter Claims & Casualties, 7 July

3./JG26

| Fw Wilhelm Müller | Blenheim near Dusseldorf (12:50) 82 Squadron. |

5./JG51

| Ltn Hermann Segatz | Spitfire SW of Dover (21:20) |
| Ltn Hermann Striebel | Spitfire south of Hastings (21:32) |

6./JG51

Ltn Herbert Huppertz	Spitfire NW Dungeness (21:38)
Obfw Fritz Beeck (1)	Spitfire east of Dungeness (21:40)
Uffz Eduard Hemmerling	Spitfire NW Folkestone

7./JG51

| Oblt Walter Oesau | Spitfire 3 m south of Dover (14:05) |
| Ltn Harald Jung | Spitfire 3 m south of Dover (14:07) |

| Obfw Arthur Dau | Spitfire 4 m south of Dover |
| Uffz Robert Fuchs | Spitfire 4 m south of Dover |

6./JG54

| Fw Georg Kiening | Blenheim (17:55) 15 Squadron. |

Luftwaffe Bomber & Reconnaissance Casualties, 7 July

3.(F)/121
Do17P damaged by fighters; crashed near Rouen (60%); victim of 43 Sqn.

2.(F)/123
Do17P 4U+KK FTR: Fw Walter Plotzitzka killed, Fw Rudolf Scherzinger and Uffz Richard Storch both missing. The pilot's body was later washed ashore in France and is buried at Bourdon; victim of 145 Sqn.
Do17P 4U+FK FTR: Ltn Hans-Joachim Nest, Ltn Bernhard Vedder, and Uffz Friedrich-Wilhelm Elicker all missing; Vedder's body was later washed ashore in Belgium and is buried at Lommel; victim of 601 Sqn.

II/KG2
Do17Z crash-landed at Boulogne (80%) Oblt Seidel wounded; victim of 64 Sqn.

III/KG2
Do17Z damaged (10%); victim of 64 Sqn.

4./KG4
He111 damaged: Fw Hans Jaffke (flight engineer) wounded; victim of 54 Sqn.

1./KG30
Ju88 FTR: Ltn Fritz Meinhold (pilot), Ltn Heinz-Günther Wallenstein, Fw Walter Ölschläger, Flgr Fritz Schwarz killed; victim of 602 Sqn.

Monday, 8 July

At 09:20, a Do17 of 4.(F)/121 from Villacoublay flew over the Bristol area, where it photographed Filton and Whitchurch. According to Flt Lt Myles Duke-Woolley, Sqn Ldr Spike O'Brien, his former CO, was at Pembrey on a controllers' course. However, on sighting the intruder, he jumped into one of 92 Squadron's Spitfires, sans helmet and parachute, to take up pursuit:

> One morning, when strolling along the tarmac of the airfield, he was surprised to see a Do17 overhead at 2,000 feet. Alongside the perimeter track was a

Spitfire. 'Spike' leapt in, started up, and took off in pursuit. No helmet, no parachute. He caught the Dornier and shot it down [sic].[9]

In fact, a section of 92 Squadron Spitfires led by Flt Lt Bob Tuck was on patrol and apparently intercepted the same aircraft, some 15 miles south-east of Bristol. Tuck and Plt Off Holland saw their fire striking its wings and fuselage but it escaped in cloud, Tuck commenting later:

If those had been 20-millimetre shells that clobbered it, instead of just .303 bullets, we'd have had a kill [...] Why the hell don't they give us cannons?

A Heinkel of StabSt/KG1 was not so fortunate when intercepted off the coast of Felixstowe shortly before 11:00. Attacked by both a single Hurricane of 85 Squadron and then three Spitfires from 74 Squadron, it struggled to reach the French coast before finally ditching off Boulogne with the loss of Oblt Hans-Martin Paulsen and his crew.

Further up the East coast, two Spitfires of 41 Squadron flown by Flg Off Tony Lovell and Sgt Jack Allison intercepted a Ju88 of 9./KG4 near Scarborough at 11:30. Allison reported:

I was following Flg Off Lovell and received his call to attack an e/a, which he had confirmed to be a Ju88. Flg Off Lovell attacked and I saw a large piece of what appeared to be a portion of the tail fall off. I then proceeded with my attack – I gave two bursts and fired 221 rounds – when the e/a went amongst the clouds. I then saw Flg Off Lovell following it again and got into position but lost him in the clouds. Three Hurricanes were circling round at the time.

The intruder, returning from a sortie to Sunderland, although damaged managed to evade the Spitfires only to run into three Hurricanes of 249 Squadron's B Flight's Green Section, led by Flg Off Denis Parnall, off Flamborough Head. Flying at 17,000 feet, the Ju88 was immediately engaged. Parnall recorded:

I observed a Ju88 proceeding south at same height. I formed section into line astern and was about to commence No. 1 Attack when Spitfire observed attacking. The Spitfire fired for about three seconds then broke away. With slight smoke issuing from port engine, no evasive tactics taken by Ju88. Then commenced No. 1 Attack and Ju88 immediately started evasive tactics of stall turns and slow flying. I fired a nine-seconds burst, commencing 350 yards, breaking away at 40 yards. Return fire not observed.

Plt Off John Beazley (Green 2) followed his leader into the attack:

I attacked enemy after No. 1 had broken away. After a two-second burst enemy stall-turned to right and I had to go into fine pitch to pull up and follow him round. Enemy entered cloud but I caught him coming out the other side and got in a burst before he again turned sharply to the left, diving slightly. I again opened fire as he straightened out. I observed white streaks coming past the starboard wing. I ceased firing as he dived into cloud again. There was a strong smell of burning metal as I went into the cloud. Enemy not seen again.

Flying No. 3 was Sgt Alistair Main, who reported:

I gave a short burst before No. 2 broke away. Following e/a through cloud I came out to find myself on his tail, gave a burst of three four seconds. By this time both engines appeared to be on fire. I then broke away and regained section.

The bomber (5J+AT) crashed in flames at Aldbrough near Darlington, killing the pilot, Staffelkapitän Hptm Kurt Rohloff, although his crew managed to bale out. One landed at Aldbrough close to the Cardwell farm, where one of the workers saw the German airman land and hurried to the farmhouse to warn the farmer's wife, Mrs Eveline Cardwell. She tried, unsuccessfully, to telephone her husband at the Local Defence Volunteer office, and then sent the farm worker to fetch the police. When the limping German approached the farmhouse, she unwaveringly walked to the airman and gestured him to raise his hands and then relieved him of his pistol. The police arrived shortly afterwards and took him into custody. Mrs Cardwell was later awarded the MBE for her bravery and initiative.

At 14:00, Flt Lt Bill Warner led Blue Section of 610 Squadron on a convoy patrol off Dover when nine Do17s approached. Sgt Peter Else silenced the rear gunner of one and also saw Plt Off Arthur Raven's aircraft shot down in flames into the sea. The pilot was seen to leave the aircraft and start to swim. Sadly, he drowned. Red and Green Sections were also on patrol and encountered seven Dorniers and a dozen Bf109s from II/JG51. Attacks were carried out on the bombers but without result. Plt Off Joe Pegge, after breaking away, encountered three 109s. He attacked one and saw it dive for the sea, emitting black smoke and over the vertical.

32 Squadron put up a patrol at 15:04 and eventually encountered Bf109s west of Dungeness. In the ensuring skirmish, a Messerschmitt was claimed probably destroyed and a Hurricane was damaged. 79 Squadron lost two more pilots during the day. Nine Hurricanes had been ordered off at about 15:15 for a convoy patrol, meeting very cloudy and overcast conditions. After an hour they were ordered to return to Hawkinge to refuel but a surprise fighter attack from above and astern despatched Plt Off John Wood and Flg Off Tubby Mitchell. Wood was able to get out of his blazing aircraft and parachute into the sea, but was terribly

burned and already dead when a boat reached him. Mitchell's Hurricane went into the ground at Temple Ewell, where a crater burned for well over an hour and no positive identification could be made until armourers had checked the numbers stamped on the twisted machine-guns. It was believed that Spitfires were again responsible but 7./JG51 claimed two Spitfires at about this time and location.

Nine Spitfires of 65 Squadron were scrambled at about 15:30, also meeting Bf109s and losing their CO, Sqn Ldr Desmond Cooke, who was shot down off Dover. In return a Messerschmitt was claimed destroyed by Flt Sgt Bill Franklin (his eleventh victory including four shared), and a second as probably destroyed. 74 Squadron achieved success during a patrol at 15:46, Ltn Johann Böhm of 4./JG51 in White 4 (1162) was shot down by Sgt Tony Mould, whereupon he force-landed at Bladbean Hill, Eltham; Mould reported:

> I was Red leader of A Flight of 74 Squadron, with No. 2 of Blue Section also in company. The four of us were on interception patrol over Dover when I sighted four Me109s flying in line astern on my starboard beam. I gave the order 'Line Astern' and turned to starboard, climbing under the tail of the rear Me109. I gave him a short 30-degree deflection shot and he immediately half-rolled and dived to ground level, followed by Red 2. In trying to locate him I blacked myself out but then saw another Me109 also flying at low level, so I dived on him from 3,000 feet. He immediately dived to ground and used evasive tactics by flying along the valleys behind Dover and Folkestone, which only allowed me to fire short deflection bursts at him. After two of these bursts smoke or vapour came from the radiator beneath his port wing and other bursts appeared to enter the fuselage. He eventually landed wheels up as I fired another burst at him near Elham. The pilot was apparently uninjured and I circled round him until he was taken prisoner.

Böhm was found to be carrying a diary, which listed several pilots of his Staffel and included details of the aircraft assigned to them.

The Messerschmitt forays over the Channel continued into the early evening, nine Spitfires of 54 Squadron meeting aircraft from I/LG2 at about 20:00, claiming two shot down, with Flt Lt Basil 'Wonky' Way involved in both combats:

> I was leading three sections of the Squadron with orders to patrol Dover at 3,000 feet. Whilst orbiting over the coast, I was informed by R/T that there were three Me109s at 12,000 feet in the vicinity. I was at 5,000 feet and proceeded to climb. I saw two aircraft behind Green Section – I warned them that they might be enemy and former [*sic*] turned towards cloud. I continued to climb and immediately aircraft began to execute climbing spiral turns. I got right behind them (identified as Me109s) they were in vic formation and I attacked rear one, giving it a three-second burst from astern at 200 yards. I don't think that enemy aircraft could have seen me until the moment of the

attack. Glycol began to pour from its radiator with a certain amount of black smoke. I left this enemy aircraft and turned to attack the second. The second enemy aircraft dived straight down and I managed to get a long burst at 250 yards. Enemy aircraft continued to dive, skirting edge of cloud, 9,000 feet over the coast. It came below and at 5,000 feet, pilot baled out. I judged his position as 5 miles inland, north-west of Deal; parachute opened.

Way's victim was Ltn Albert Striberny of 3 Staffel, who recalled his experience:

Having reached an altitude of 4,500 m over the Channel we found ourselves in sunshine but saw that there were a lot of cumulus clouds over the English coast and Dover [...] At about 1,700 m, the clouds ended and together we flew over Dover [...] I quickly noticed the Do17 near us but then, much higher, saw the sun shining on many aircraft – Spitfires! Our situation was bad – low speed due to climbing through the cloud and so many aircraft coming down on us with the advantage of speed. I think now of the clear silhouette of our three aircraft against the white clouds.

In spite of our efforts to try and gain more speed, in no time they were on us and the battle was short. Whilst I was behind a Spitfire, another was behind me. I hear the sound as if one throws peas against a metal sheet and my cabin was full of dark smoke. I felt splashes of fuel on my face so I switched off the electrical system, dived back into the cloud and threw off the cabin roof. The smoke disappeared and I could breathe freely and noticed that the wings there came white streams of glycol. Whilst diving, I tried several times to start the engine, switching on the electrical system, but in vain. When I came out of cloud, I decided to bale out and undid the clasp of my seat belt and was about to climb onto the seat and jump when I thought of the high speed of the aircraft and I was afraid to be thrown against the tailplane so I pulled back the stick and slow the aircraft down. This took a matter of seconds; I did a half roll and fell out.[10]

Striberny landed safely and was soon in custody. His aircraft (2964) crashed near Sandwich.

Elsewhere, away from the main battle area, three Hurricanes of 238 Squadron were detailed for a convoy patrol east of the Isle of Wight. At about 18:15, two shadowing Do17s were sighted and one was shot down into the sea near to the Needles. During a sudden bombing raid on Falmouth (possibly by the same aircraft) the French sloop *Suippe* had been damaged. There was no crew on board at the time and when the raid was over a party went aboard and beached the sloop at St Just's Pool.

Another reconnaissance aircraft fell to the guns of 602 Squadron's Spitfires at 19:35. The He111 of 1.(F)/120 was engaged off St Abbs Head by Green Section while on a recce of the Firth of Forth. Following an attack by Flg Off Paul Webb it escaped with its port engine alight. Before it crashed into the sea, its bombs were jettisoned, one of which killed a cow peacefully grazing in a field near the coast. Fw Rudolf Zöphel and his crew were lost.

At noon Do17s of II/KG3 commenced taking off from Laon, but as those from 4 Staffel were slowly climbing away from the airfield, their path was crossed by several Blenheims on their way to attack the airfield, where 5 Staffel was waiting to take off. Suddenly, Uffz Blasche, pilot of 5K+CN spotted three specks near Laon cathedral. His fears materialised when these grew alarmingly and headed towards the airfield. Defencelessly caught in the open, the only thing the aircrew could do was to run for cover. With bomb doors open three Blenheims buzzed the field with blazing machine-guns and dropping bombs before flying away at low level. Only two of the Dorniers were slightly damaged and were able to join the rest with only two hours delay.[11]

Operational Accidents: A Defiant of 141 Squadron was involved in ground collision with another Defiant at Turnhouse – crew slightly injured. Other prominent accidents included Botha L6205 on air test from Blackburn's at Brough crashed near Ellerker, Yorkshire, killing civilian test pilot Douglas Brencknell, a former Jersey Airways pilot. Also killed on this date was 30-year-old Canadian-born Third Officer Elsie Davison, a female volunteer of the ATA, who lost her life in the crash of Master N7539 at RAF Upavon, together with her instructor Flt Sgt Edgar L'Estrange. A Bf109 of 5./JG54 crashed Waalhaven killing Fw Albert Manske; and a Bf109 of 3./ErprGr.210 crashed south-east of Cologne, Fw Josef Welter killed.

Night Operations: Twenty-eight Wellingtons attacked various industrial targets in northern Germany, while a dozen Whitleys bombed Kiel, and a dozen Hampdens were engaged on mine-laying. During the Whitley raid on Kiel a bomb struck the heavy cruiser *Lützow* but failed to explode. All returned safely. German bombers were over during the night, inflicting fifty-one casualties, eight of whom were killed.

Fighter Command Claims & Casualties, 8 July

3 Spitfires/92 Squadron – 15 miles south-east Bristol 0830-0945

P9434	Flt Lt R. R. S. Tuck		
P9371	Flg Off R. H. Holland	Do17 damaged	4.(F)/121

1 Spitfire/92 Squadron – Bristol area 09:20

N3249	Sqn Ldr J. S. O'Brien	Do17 damaged as above

1 Hurricane/85 Squadron – 10 miles south-east of Felixstowe 09:45-10:50

L1915	Flt Sgt G. Allard	He111	Stab/KG1 shared with 3/74 Sqn

3 Spitfires/74 Squadron – Pegwell Bay 10:47-11:05

P9398	Flt Lt W. E. G. Measures		
P9379	Plt Off Hon D. H. T. Dowding	He111	Stab/KG1

L1001   Sgt W. M. Skinner   shared with 1/85 Sqn

2 Spitfires/41 Squadron – south-east of Scarborough 11:30
P9429   Flg Off A. D. J. Lovell   Ju88   9./KG4
N3113   Sgt J. A. Allison   shared with 3/249 Sqn

3 Hurricanes/249 Squadron – south-east of Scarborough 11:30
P3615   Flg Off D. G. Parnall
P3055   Plt Off H. J. S. Beazley   Ju88   9./KG4
P2995   Sgt A. D. W. Main   shared with 2/41 Sqn

3 Spitfires/610 Squadron – off Dover 13:45-16:39
R6806   Plt Off A. L. B. Raven
P9496   Sgt P. Else   Do17 damaged
R6806   Plt Off A. L. B. Raven FTR – shot down by return fire from Do17;
ditched but drowned

3 Spitfires/74 Squadron – Elham-Dover 16:00+
P9446   Sgt E. A. Mould   Bf109   4./JG51
P9465   Plt Off P. C. F. Stevenson   Bf109 probable
P9465   Plt Off P. C. F. Stevenson - damaged by Bf109 and crash-landed Manston
(Cat.2)

2 Hurricanes/32 Squadron – west of Dungeness 15:04-16:22
N2459   Plt Off D. H. Grice   Bf109 probable
N2460   Flg Off R. F. Smythe – damaged by Bf109; unhurt (Cat.1)

9 Spitfires/65 Squadron – off Dover 15:29-16:49
N3164   Flt Sgt W. H. Franklin   Bf109   II/JG51
N3161   Sqn Ldr H. C. Sawyer   Bf109 probable
K9907   Sqn Ldr D. Cooke FTR (killed) shot down by Bf109

9 Hurricanes/79 Squadron – off Deal 15:15-16:05
N2984   Plt Off J. E. R. Wood FTR – shot down by Bf109 7/JG51 (baled out into
                                       sea, burned, died)
P3461   Flg Off E. W. Mitchell FTR – shot down by Bf109 7/JG51 (killed)
6 Spitfires/610 Squadron – Straits of Dover 14:59-17:30
L1044   Plt Off C. O. J. Pegge   Bf109   II/JG51

3 Spitfires/234 Squadron – 20 miles south of Lands' End 18:15
P9366   Flt Lt P. C. Hughes (Aus)
N3280   Plt Off K. A. Lawrence (NZ)   Ju88   Stab/LG1
N3279   Sgt G. T. Bailey

9 Spitfires/54 Squadron – off South Foreland 19:30-20:40

R6708	Flt Lt B. H. Way	Bf109	LG2
R6708	Flt Lt B. H. Way	Bf109	III/JG51
R6705	Plt Off J. W. Garton		

3 Spitfires/602 Squadron – 70 miles east-south-east of St Abbs Head 19:35

N3119	Flg Off P. C. Webb	He111 probable	1.(F)/120 FTR

Luftwaffe Fighter Claims & Casualties, 8 July

3./LG2

Bf109 FTR: Ltn Albert Striberny POW; victim of 54 Sqn.

4/JG51

Oblt Josef Fozo (2) Spitfire (16:45) north of Dover
Bf109 (White 4/1162) FTR: Ltn Johann Böhm POW; victim of 74 Sqn.
Bf109 damaged (15%) in combat with Spitfire – Fw Willi Gasthaus

7./JG51

Ltn Hermann Staiger (3) Spitfire (16:35) NW Cap Gris Nez
Ltn Kurt Bildau (2) Spitfire (16:35) NW of Cap Gris Nez
Bf109 FTR: Uffz Konrad Schneiderberger killed; victim of 65 Sqn.
Bf109 – force-landed France (12%), pilot wounded; victim of 610 Sqn.

9./JG51

Oblt Arnold Lignitz (5) Hurricane (16:35) NW Cap Gris Nez
Bf109 FTR: pilot killed; victim of 54 Sqn.

4./JG54

Obfw Maximilian Stotz (9) Blenheim (14:10) south of Rotterdam

8./NJG1

Fw Hermann Förster (6) Whitley (02:50) 20km north of Heligoland

Luftwaffe Bomber & Reconnaissance Casualties, 8 July

1.(F)/120

He111 FTR: Fw Rudolf Zöphel, Ltn Werner Bank, Uffz Erich Kuhn, Fw Kurt Goldau and Uffz Erich Rentschler all lost; victim of 602 Squadron. The body of Rudolf Zöphel was later washed ashore on the island of Amrum and is buried in Westerland along with Werner Bank. Erich Kuhn came ashore at Spiekeroog and is buried at Wangerooge.

StabSt/KG1
He111 FTR: Oblt Hans-Martin Paulsen (pilot), Fw Fritz Leinert, Uffz Paul Hertel, Gfr Ludwig Hotz (all drowned when aircraft ditched off Boulogne following combat); victim of 85/74 Sqns.

StSt/LG1
Ju88 FTR: Oblt Waldemar Meyer (pilot), Fw Friedrich Schramme, Gfr Felix Schrauber, Uffz Fritz Schwetlick killed; victim of 234 Sqn.

9./KG4
Ju88 5J+AT FTR: Hptm Kurt Rohloff (Staffelkapitän) killed; Uffz Georg Abel, Uffz Artur Kühnapfel, Uffz Heinz Öchler, baled out, POWs; victim of 41/249 Sqn Sqns.

Bomber Command Casualties, night 8/9 July
10 Squadron
Whitley N1496 FTR: Flt Lt D. A. Ffrench-Mullen, Plt Off W. A. K. Carr, Sgt P. R. Donaldson, AC1 A. G. W. Miller, Sgt J. P. Atkinson (all POW); victim of 8./NJG1

Tuesday, 9 July

A lone Dornier of 4./KG3 on a reconnaissance mission was intercepted off the Kent coast at 05:45 by a patrol of Hurricanes of 257 Squadron. A deadly cat and mouse game developed and the German outran two of its adversaries. The third, piloted by Sgt Ron Forward, managed to follow, firing every time an opportunity presented. After a while the Hurricane ran out of ammunition and fuel and had to leave its prey to return home. The Dornier was badly damaged, however, and all the crew wounded, the gunner having been killed. The pilot gamely endeavoured to reach his base at Deune but lost his way in the neighbourhood of Antwerp. Short on fuel, he decided to belly land the crippled aircraft and chose a meadow, where he made an almost perfect landing, sliding to a halt after chopping off a tree with his right wing. They were north of Antwerp in a place called Stabroek. A local doctor administered aid until German forces arrived.

Another lone Do17 suddenly appeared over Penrhos airfield near Pwlheli in mid-Wales and carried out a bombing attack and strafed parked aircraft. Two Henleys (L3290 and L3359) of 1AACU were destroyed. Three blocks of officers' quarters were also destroyed and a hangar damaged. Two RAF officers were killed, Flg Off Brian Page and Canadian Plt Off Geoffrey Goldsmith-Jones. The British steamer *San Felipe* (5919grt) was damaged by German bombing at Roath Docks, Cardiff. The sloop *Foxglove*, proceeding to Portsmouth, was bombed at 11:30 and badly damaged off the Nab. One of her AA gunners died of his wounds. She was able to proceed under tow by naval trawler to Portsmouth.

Following a quiet morning, several engagements occurred during the afternoon.

At 13:36, A Flight of 151 Squadron, with Wg Cdr Victor Beamish in the No. 2 position, was airborne from North Weald climbing hard through scattered cloud on an easterly course. The pilots suddenly found themselves confronted by a huge mass of around one hundred fighters and bombers stepped up from 12,000 to 20,000 feet. Quickly recognising the lower formations of He111s and Ju88s, the six Hurricane pilots split into two sections, one diving on the bombers and the other turning to face an estimated sixty Bf109s and 110s of the escort, which rapidly engaged the Hurricanes. The Wingco's section singled out a Bf110, which was jointly claimed destroyed, but the Bf109s bounced the other section, shooting down two. Flt Lt Harry Ironside received a shell in the cockpit which inflicted a bad wound to his face, but he managed to bring his aircraft home safely. His No. 2, FAA pilot Midshipman(A) Owen Wightman baled out into the sea, having claimed a Bf109 first, and was fortuitously picked up by a trawler. Evidently unaware of the small number of British fighters engaging their escort, the German bomber pilots split into six formations, of which only one actually found the convoy. Bombing was scattered and no ships were sunk, although both the British steamer *Kenneth Hawksfield* (1,546grt) and the smaller *Pol Grange* (804grt) were damaged by German bombing.

Although none of the other sections sent up were able to intercept the bombers, Red Section of 43 Squadron, up from Tangmere, sighted six Bf110s. The Messerschmitts turned and attacked head-on, Sqn Ldr George Lott's aircraft being hit in the armour-plated windscreen by a cannon shell:

> Jousting like a couple of knights of old, we rushed at each other head-on. At 300 yards I pressed the firing button and at that very instant there was a terrific bang. I felt a blow in my face and right eye. Too late, I remembered that I had left my goggles up. A smell of escaping coolant filled the cockpit as I keeled over and, corkscrewing hard, dived for cloud cover.
>
> Although I was inwardly raging, I was still thinking clearly, and arranged to enter the cloud on a northerly heading which would take me to the nearest land. I put my hand to my left eye. All I could see was a white opaqueness. I was blind in my right eye ... so I prepared for a quick bale out ... I heaved myself over the side and without waiting streamed my parachute ... I landed on my back in the middle of a road which turned out to be the main road to Fontwell. Two men ran to me from a van which had stopped nearby. Blood soaked and gasping from breath, I must have looked in a bad way. They asked me if I was alright. I just nodded. I couldn't speak.[12]

Two of the Bf110s, aircraft of 8./ZG26, were claimed shot down, one by Plt Off Frank Carey. One Messerschmitt FTR and the other badly damaged; on returning to base the pilot discovered that his gunner had baled out into the sea, and was lost. A section of Hurricanes from 79 Squadron had also been scrambled, the pilots claiming a Bf109 and a probable for no loss.

At 14:20, two patrolling Spitfires of 610 Squadron intercepted a Dornier off Cap Griz Nes, which they believed was a reconnaissance Do215. However, the aircraft was a Do17 of StSt/KG76, which was claimed shot down. Despite much damages it managed to reach base, where it force-landed, with two wounded crewmen on board.

Dissatisfied with their efforts against the Thames convoy, the Germans mounted a second heavy raid, the seventy-strong formation setting course north-westerly to pass the North Foreland at about 15:50. In the meantime, three Spitfire squadrons had arrived at Manston, and nine aircraft of 65 Squadron were scrambled, as noted by the Squadron diarist:

> Three Sections were ordered off to intercept raiders off the North Foreland. One aircraft failed to start and another returned with engine trouble. The remaining seven pilots climbed to 10,000 feet and almost at once sighted about seventy enemy aircraft heading for the Thames Estuary. The enemy were in vies of five, seven and nine stepped up from 8,000 to 14,000 feet, three vies abreast and in line astern. There was a layer of bombers well protected above and at the sides by 109s and 110s.
>
> [Flt Lt Gerry] Saunders, who was leading, climbed to 18,000 feet and found himself slightly above five 109s; he dived on one of them and opened fire with slight deflection at 400 yards. After a further short burst the enemy aircraft pulled up sharply into a half roll; a final burst from 100 yards and the enemy fell away and something appeared to break off from the tail. [Plt Off Stan] Grant damaged another enemy aircraft but was unable to confirm it as he was attacked by two others. [Flg Off Bill] Walker (Red 1) sighted enemy aircraft over Margate and fired at one, but had to break off as his Section was being attacked by 109s. He attacked a 109 from below at about 200 yards and this aircraft went into a turning dive with smoke pouring from the fuselage. F/Sgt [Norman] Phillips (Red 2) fired at several enemy aircraft and eventually got in a 5-second burst at a 109 and saw it go into a vertical dive five miles north-east of Ramsgate; a 109 was subsequently found to have crashed near where the combat took place. All our aircraft returned safely.

Although three Bf109s were claimed, only one Bf109 was lost, that flown by Ltn Hermann Striebel of 5./JG51.

Further up the East Coast, two He111s from I/KG53 penetrated inland over Norfolk and bombs fell on Norwich. The most serious aspect of this raid was the high casualty list – due to the incident coinciding with the time at which *Colman's* employees were leaving work for the day, and the fact that no air-raid warning had been given. Twenty-six were killed, including five *Colman's* employees with many more injured. Hurricanes from 17 Squadron pursued a 3 Staffel Heinkel out to sea and shot it down at 16:50, killing Oblt Willi Kollmer and his crew.[13]

Another Ju88 was claimed by 602 Squadron during the early evening, Flt Lt

Dunlop Urie's section catching a pair from KG30 engaged in mine-laying east of Fife Ness at 17:50. Urie reported that his victim went straight into the sea some twenty miles off May Island, while Flg Off Don Jack claimed the other as damaged.

A second Luftwaffe white-painted civilian-registered Red Cross-marked aircraft was forced down by 54 Squadron Spitfires, Plt Off Johnny Allen being credited with forcing D-ASUO of Seenotflugkdo.1 to land on the Goodwin Sands at 20:30. It was later towed ashore by the Walmer lifeboat and beached at Deal. The Heinkel had departed on a mission from Boulogne to search for a missing Messerschmitt pilot (Ltn Striebel of 5./JG51 shot down earlier by Spitfires of 65 Squadron). Into the bag to join their colleagues went Uffz Helmut Bartmann (pilot), Uffz Erich Schiele, Uffz Walter Anders, and Fw Günther Maywald.

While Plt Off Allen was dealing from the He59, his colleagues were fighting a losing battle with the escorting Bf109s of 4./JG51. Both Plt Offs Jack Garton and Tony Evershed were shot down and killed, causing Plt Off Al Deere to later comment:

> I knew that at least one of our chaps had been shot down; I had heard Yellow 2 [Garton] screaming for help over the R/T. He said he was on fire and needed assistance as there were four Huns on his tail. He sounded hysterical, poor blighter. There wasn't anything I could do about it.

Deere had problems of his own. Having damaged a Bf109 he then collided with another, flown by Obfw Johann Illner:

> I soon found another target. At about 3,000 yards directly ahead of me, and on the same level, a Hun was just completing a turn preparatory to re-entering the fray. He saw me almost immediately and rolled out of his turn towards me so that a head-on attack became inevitable. Using both hands on the control column to steady the aircraft, and thus keep my aim steady, I peered through the reflector sight at the rapidly closing enemy aircraft. We opened fire together, and immediately a hail of lead thudded into my Spitfire.
>
> One moment the Messerschmitt was a clearly defined shape, its wingspan nicely enclosed within the circle of my reflector sight, and the next it was on top of me, a tarrying blur which blotted out the sky ahead. Then we hit. The force of the impact pitched me violently forward on to my shoulders. At the same moment the control column was snatched abruptly from my gripping fingers by a momentary but powerful reversal of elevator load. In a flash it was over; there was clear sky ahead of me, and I was still alive. But smoke and flame were pouring from the engine, which began to vibrate.[14]

Deere force-landed at Manston while Illner returned safely with just 10% damage to his wing, although Deere assumed that the Messerschmitt would have crashed and claimed it as destroyed accordingly.

With much of the action occurring in the Channel off Dover, squadrons along the south coast awaited the call to action. However, by late afternoon the weather had deteriorated and the readiness section of 609 Squadron, operating from the satellite airfield at Warmwell, did not expect to see any of the action, but at about 18:30, they were scrambled and ordered to patrol Weymouth. Having uneventfully circled for forty-five minutes, they requested permission to land, as Plt Off David Crook later wrote: [15]

We were told, however, to continue our patrol and turned out again over Weymouth at about 7,000 feet. A moment later, looking out towards the left, I saw an aircraft dive into a layer of cloud about two miles away and then reappear. I immediately called up Peter [Flg Off Drummond-Hay] on the R/T, and he swung us into line astern, and turned left towards the enemy. A moment later I saw one or two more Huns appear, and recognized them as Junkers 87 dive-bombers. I immediately turned on my reflector sights, put my gun button on to 'fire' and settled down to enjoy a little slaughter of a few Ju87s, as they are rather helpless machines.

I was flying last on the line, and we were now travelling at high speed and rapidly approaching the enemy, when I happened to look round behind. To my intense surprise and dismay, I saw at least nine Messerschmitt 110s about 2,000 feet above us. They were just starting to dive on us when I saw them, and as they were diving they were overtaking us rapidly.

This completely altered the situation. We were now hopelessly outnumbered, and in a very dangerous position, and altogether I began to see that if we were not jolly quick we should all be dead in a few seconds. I immediately called up Peter and Michael and shouted desperately, "Look out behind, Messerschmitts behind" – all the time looking over my shoulder at the leading enemy fighter, who was now almost in range. But though I kept shouting, both Peter and Michael [Plt Off Appleby] continued straight on at the bombers ahead, and they were now almost in range and about to open fire.

I have never felt so desperate or so helpless in my life, as when, in spite of my warnings, these two flew steadily on, apparently quite oblivious of the fact that they were going to be struck down from the rear in a few seconds. At that moment the leading Messerschmitt opened fire at me and I saw his shells and tracer bullets going past just above my head. They were jolly close too. I immediately did a very violent turn to the left and dived through a layer of cloud just below. I emerged from the cloud going at very high speed – probably over 400 mph, and saw a Ju87 just ahead of me. I opened (my first real shot of the war), and he seemed to fly right through my tracer bullets, but when I turned round to follow him, he disappeared. I then climbed up into the cloud again to try to rejoin others. I saw a Me110 some distance above me, and I pulled up into a steep climb and fired at him but without result. Turned away immediately, and I lost him.

At that moment I saw dimly a machine moving in the cloud my left and flying parallel to me. I stalked him through cloud, and when he emerged into a patch of clear sky I saw it was a Ju87. I was in an ideal position to attack and opened fire and put remainder of my ammunition – about 2,000 rounds – into him at very close range. Even in the heat of the moment I well remember my amazement at the shattering effect of my fire. Pieces flew off his fuselage and cockpit covering, a stream of smoke appeared from the engine, and a moment later a great sheet flame licked out from the engine cowling and he dived down vertically. The flames enveloped the whole machine and he went straight down, apparently quite slowly, for about five thousand feet, till he was just a shapeless burning mass of wreckage. Absolutely fascinated by the sight, I followed him down saw him hit the sea with a great burst of white foam. He disappeared immediately, and apart from a green patch in the water there was no sign that anything had happened. The crew made no attempt to get out, and they were obviously killed by my burst of fire.

Plt Off Crook's victim was none other than the Gruppenkommandeur of StG77, Hptm Friedrich-Karl Frhr von Dalwigk zu Lichtenfels, who was killed with his gunner Fw Karl Götz. Crook continued:

I had often wondered what would be my feelings when killing somebody like this, and especially when seeing them go down flames. I was rather surprised to reflect afterwards that my feeling had been one of considerable elation – and a sort of bewildered surprise because it had all been so easy.

I turned back for the coast, and started to call up Peter and Michael on the R/T. But there was no response, and as far Peter was concerned, I was already calling to the void. A moment later I saw another Spitfire flying home on a very erratic course, obviously keeping a very good look behind. I joined up with it, and recognized Michael, and together we bolted for the English coast like a couple of startled rabbits. I made a perfectly bloody landing on the aerodrome and overshot so badly that I nearly turned the Spitfire on her nose in my efforts to pull up before hitting the hedge.

Plt Off Appleby reported firing at various Bf110s and Ju87s but made no definite claims, and said that he had seen a "great flurry of machines in the sky about a mile away" that he assumed he been the demise of Flg Off Drummond-Hay, who FTR. Two Spitfires were claimed destroyed by the Bf110 pilots of 13./LG1, including one by Oblt Joachim Gleinke. However, he was forced to ditch while over the Channel, presumably having been hit by one of the Spitfires in return. Obfw Kobert noticed Gleinke's aircraft steadily losing height, and attempts to establish radio contact failed. Kobert escorted his CO down to sea level and witnessed the Messerschmitt carry out a successful ditching. After a few seconds Gleinke and his gunner, Uffz Hoyer, were seen to appear in their yellow life jackets, whereupon Kobert took a fix and flew back to Cherbourg, while others circled overhead. A He59 immediately set out and once Kobert had refuelled he followed and escorted the ASR aircraft. Although darkness was setting in, the two men were soon sighted, rescued and on their way back to Cherbourg.

While the air battle raged, ships of Convoy CW.2 were being singled out for attack by the Ju87s, a number sustaining damage, while the Latvian steamer *Talvadis* (534grt) was sunk by bombing three miles from Prawle Point. One crewman was lost. The British steamer *Empire Daffodil* (398grt) was damaged 13 miles south-south-west of Portland, the Dutch steamer *Jola* (269grt) three miles south-west of Start Point, and the Greek steamer *Aegeon* (5,285grt) was damaged by German bombing at Weymouth.

PR pilot Flg Off Alistair Taylor departed Heston at 16:41 in Spitfire R6598 of the PRU (formerly PDU) bound for northern Germany and Holland, refuelling at Coltishall en route. He returned at 21:05, having taken photographs of Bremen, Delmenhorst, Leeuwarden and Wilhelmshaven, one of the longest PR sorties to date.

On the Norway front, Blenheims of 21 and 57 Squadrons led by Wg Cdr Leslie Bennett carried out a raid on Sola aerodrome at Stavanger that proved to be one of a series of disastrous attacks made by unescorted or inadequately escorted Blenheims during this desperate period. Operating from Lossiemouth, the dozen Blenheims set out at 08:00, and located the aerodrome where they found aircraft lined up, attacking mainly Do215s and destroying one; two others were badly damaged, but the cost was horrendous. As they set course for home they were set upon by Bf109s from II/JG77 and a section of Bf110s of I/ZG76. Seven Blenheims failed to return. One of the surviving pilots, Plt Off John Rodger of 21 Squadron, told the following story:[16]

I arrived over target in company with other flights of aircraft. Owing to intense anti-aircraft fire over target, my flight became detached from the leading flight, and I did not see it again. Each of the three aircraft in my flight dropped its bombs. There was no opportunity to observe the result owing to having to take avoiding action. I saw that the port aircraft of my flight had most of its rudder blown away, presumably by anti-aircraft fire. On leaving the target, the flight was still intact. Saw also three Blenheim fighter aircraft of another squadron ahead, flying west. Endeavoured to join up with them for mutual protection, but before this could be done enemy aircraft in large numbers were attacking, about 30 in number, mostly Messerschmitt 109s, joined later by three or more Messerschmitt 110s. The flight ahead took such violent avoiding action that my flight could not keep with them.

While repelling formation attacks of enemy aircraft, the rear gunner of the port aircraft was killed, and the aircraft was subsequently shot down in flames. The aircraft on the starboard side was shot down in flames soon after the signal "engines on fire." My aircraft again tried to join up with the flight ahead, but the starboard engine and oil tank were hit by cannon fire, the engine seized and died, and the airscrew and reduction gear dropped off. The attack by enemy aircraft tasted for over 30 minutes after leaving the target, including two attacks by two Messerschmitt 110s while in the clouds well out over the sea and after the starboard engine seized up. I continued on the course for home, and, owing to lack of petrol, was considering landing beside some minesweepers when the coast line became visible. Made forced landing at coastal aerodrome, when the undercarriage jammed in the 'up' position. All the hydraulic system had been put out of action during the fight with the enemy. The air observer, during the action with enemy fighters, shot down one Messerschmitt, and possibly damaged several others. The rear gunner damaged one Messerschmitt. His gun was put out of action by explosive bullet from which he received slight damage to one eye.

Another survivor, Observer Sgt James Dunnet of 57 Squadron recalled:

I remember vividly limping back over the North Sea on one engine and hoping that we would not have to ditch. As we were gradually losing height, I gave the pilot a course for Dyce (Aberdeen). Coming into land some fool in an Anson started to take off right in front of us. My pilot yanked down the emergency nine boost lever and hauled back on the stick. There was no way he could control the tremendous torque from the one engine, and the Blenheim just rolled over. It was a strange experience for me. Just before we hit the ground, my pilot shouted "Goodbye" and crossed his arms over his face. Sitting beside him, I watched the ground rush up and the, now well known, slow motion effect materialised. I watched the nose of the plane hit the ground and the Mk. 9 bombsight crumble towards me. I thought, "This is how I'm going to die". I had no fear. It was a total disassociation of personality, complete detachment. Then I was conscious of being racked from side to side, tremendous noise, stones, dirt, all sorts of rubble flying about, then nothing but the realisation that I was still alive. All the crew survived.[17]

The Bf109 pilots of II/JG77 claimed eight of the Blenheims and lost one of their pilots to the Blenheim gunners, while the Bf110s claimed a further six but two were not allowed.

The destroyer *Diana* that had departed Scapa Flow the previous evening to rendezvous with a Finnish steamer, failed to locate the ship. On heading back to base, the destroyer was ordered to search for a Blenheim (or Blenheims) in the sea but this search was also unsuccessful.

A Sunderland (N6133 of 201 Squadron) and a Hudson (N7377 of 233 Squadron) were also shot down later in the day, presumably searching for the missing crews, both falling to Bf110s of 3./ZG76.

Incredibly, the two Blenheim squadrons were ordered to repeat the attack the following day, but fortunately they were recalled when the weather deteriorated.

Operational Losses: A Hurricane of 43 Squadron crashed and two Spitfires of 19 Squadron were damaged in a gound collision. An Hs126 of 1.(H)/11 and a Ju88 of II/ KG51 were lost in separate accidents, while, during the night, Do17 2N+CH of I/NJG1 was abandoned by its crew (Fw Adolf Iburg and Uffz Heinrich Hagmeier) at 00:30.

Night Operations: Bad weather forced the abandonment of planned Bomber Command raids although Wellingtons and Hampdens were out. There were no losses. An estimated thirty German aircraft were over the UK but negligible damage resulted. All aircraft returned safely.

Fighter Command Claims & Casualties, 9 July

3 Hurricanes/257 Squadron – off Kent coast 05:45

P3641	Sgt R. V. Forward	Do17 damaged	II/KG3

crashed Belgium

Hurricanes/43 Squadron – 10 miles south-west of St Catherine's Point (IoW) 12:10+

P3464	Sqn Ldr C. G. Lott		
P3786	Plt Off F. R. Carey	2 Bf110	8./ZG26
N2621	Sgt J. P. Mills		
P3464	Sqn Ldr C. G. Lott hit by return fire, wounded, baled out (lost eye)		

Spitfires/610 Squadron – off Cap Griz Nes 14:20+

R6976	Sqn Ldr A. T. Smith	Do215	StSt/KG76
R6630	Sgt C. A. Parsons	(Do17)	

Hurricanes/79 Squadron – off Dover 15:36+

Blue 1	Plt Off W. H. Millington	Bf109
Blue 2	Plt Off D. W. A. Stones	Bf109 probable
Blue 3	Mid(A) M. A. Birrell RNVR	Bf109 damaged

Spitfires/65 Squadron – off Ramsgate 15:35+

P9436	Flt Lt G. A. W. Saunders	Bf109
K9905	Flt Sgt N. T. Phillips	Bf109
K9909	Flg Off W. H. Maitland-Walker	Bf109, Bf110 damaged
K9915	Plt Off S. B. Grant	Bf109 probable

Hurricanes/151 Squadron – off Margate 16:10+

P3307	Flg Off R. M. Milne	Bf109	
P3806	Mid(A) O. M. Wightman RNVR	Bf109	
P3304	Wg Cdr F. V. Beamish		
P3273	Flg Off A. D. Forster	Bf110	8./ZG26
P3316	Plt Off J. R. Hamer		

P3806   Mid(A) O. M. Wightman RNVR shot down by Bf109, baled out, rescued by trawler.

P3309   Flt Lt H. H. A. Ironside – damaged in combat, wounded in face, returned safely (Cat.1)

Hurricanes/17 Squadron – off Orfordness 16:50

P3673	Plt Off K. Manger		
Red 3	Plt Off G. R. Bennette	He111	3./KG53
N2526	Sgt G. Griffiths		

Spitfires/602 Squadron – 20 miles off May Island 17:50

| P9461 | Flt Lt J. R. Urie | Ju88 |
| K9910 | Flg Off D. M. Jack | Ju88 damaged |

6 Spitfires/54 Squadron – south of Deal 20:10+

P9367	Plt Off J. L. Allen	He59	Seenotkdo.1
N3183	Plt Off A. C. Deere	Bf109, Bf109 damaged	
N3097	Sgt N. A. Lawrence	Bf109, Bf109 probable	
R6705	Plt Off J. W. Garton FTR – shot down by Bf109 (killed)		
L1093	Plt Off A. Evershed FTR – shot down by Bf109 (killed)		
N3183	Plt Off A. C. Deere collided with Bf109, force-landed Manston		

3 Spitfires/609 Squadron – off Portland 21:30+

P9322	Plt Off D. M. Crook	Ju87	StabI/StG77
R6637	Flg Off P. Drummond-Hay	Ju87 probable	
N3023	Plt Off M. J. Appleby	)	
R6637	Flg Off P. Drummond-Hay FTR		

2 Group (Blenheim) Casualties, 9 July

21 Squadron

R3732   FTR: Wg Cdr L. C. Bennett (NZ), Sgt A. T. Summers, Sgt C. J. Burt (all killed); Wg Cdr Bennett's body washed ashore near Longstrupp 26/9/40.

R3822   FTR: Plt Off J. Heath-Brown, Sgt W. A. Hamlyn, Sgt E. Williams (all killed)

R3876   FTR: Sgt J. B. M. Brown, Sgt C. D. Stevens, Sgt J. Morton (all killed)

N3619   FTR: Plt Off W. Macley, Sgt R. W. Rawson, Sgt J. B. Dorrington (all killed)

L8872   FTR: Flt Lt J. D. W. Murray (NZ), Sgt T. W. Hartley, Sgt G. E. Duck (all killed)

R3915   badly damaged and crash-landed on return; Plt Off J. K. Rodger, Sgt Spillard (both injured)

57 Squadron
  R3750   FTR: Plt Off R. A. Hopkinson, Sgt J. G. Andrew, Sgt G. A. Miles (all killed)
  R3847   FTR: Sgt F. G. Mills, Sgt S. J. Newcombe, Sgt T. J. Jervis (all killed)
  R3608   forced-landed Wick; Flt Lt Hird and crew unhurt.

201 Squadron (Search and Rescue mission)
  Sunderland N6133 FTR: Flt Lt J. D. Middleton, Plt Off D. M. Harry, Plt Off J. Seeds, Sgt L. E. Worthington, LAC M. J. E. Jarvis, LAC J. H. Lane, LAC R. H. F. Hammond, LAC J. F. Hindle, AC1 J. B. Belderson, AC1 P. Clark missing; shot down by Bf110 of 3./ZG76
233 Squadron (Search mission)
  Hudson N7377 FTR: Plt Off L. J. E. Ewing, Plt Off R. M. Buchanan, Sgt D. C. Sinclair, Sgt R. G. Ireland missing; shot down by 3 Bf110s of 3./ZG76

Luftwaffe Fighter Claims & Casualties, 9 July
Stab I(J)/LG2
  Oblt Herbert Ihlefeld (4)   Spitfire (17:04) Thames Estuary

1./JG2
  Oblt Anton Mader (1)   Spitfire (20:30) south of Portland
  Uffz Willi Reins (1)   Spitfire (20:30) south of Portland

4./JG51
  Fw Hans John (2)   Spitfire (21:40) east of Dover
  Ltn Erich Hohagen (2)   Spitfire (21:45) NE Dover
  Obfw Johann Illner (2)   Spitfire east of Dover (by collision)
  Uffz Alfred Lenz (1)   Spitfire Dover
  Bf109 damaged (10%) in collision with Spitfire of 54 Sqn – Obfw Johann Illner unhurt .

5./JG51
  Uffz Wolfgang Stocker (1)   Spitfire (16:55) NE Margate
  Hptm Horst Tietzen (5)   Spitfire (17:00) NE Margate
  Bf109 FTR: Ltn Hermann Striebel killed; victim of 65 Sqn.

6./JG51
  Uffz Eduard Hemmerling (2)   Blenheim (07:55) Cap Gris Nez

8./ZG26
  Bf110 FTR: Fw Hans Langbein, Obgfr Walter Franzke both killed; victim of 43 Sqn.

Bf110 returned 50% damaged; AG baled out, missing; victim of 43 Squadron.

13./LG1

Oblt Joachim Glienke/Uffz Karl Hoyer	Spitfire (20:30) SW Portland
Fw Hans Datz/Uffz Georg Lämmel (?)	Spitfire (20:30) SW Portland

Bf110 FTR: Oblt Joachim Gleinke, Uffz Karl Hoyer (wounded) rescued by He59; victim of 609 Sqn.

II/JG77

Ltn Horst Carganico (3)	2 Blenheims (off Stavanger)
Oblt Heinz Deuschle (2)	Blenheim (off Stavanger)
Oblt Berthold Jung (2)	2 Blenheims (off Stavanger)
Fw Robert Menge (7)	Blenheim (off Stavanger)
Fw Werner Petermann (3)	Blenheim (off Stavanger)
Gfr Rudolf Schmidt (1)	Blenheim (off Stavenger)

Bf109 FTR: Uffz Gerhard Weber (5./JG77) shot down by Blenheim (killed)

2./ZG76

Uffz Heinz Freisa	4 Blenheims (2 not awarded)
Fw Leo Schumacher	2 Blenheims

3./ZG76

Olbt Gordon Gollob	Sunderland
Oblt Gordon Gollob	
Oblt Gerhard Böhmel	Hudson
Obfw Herbert Schob	

Luftwaffe Bomber & Reconnaissance Casualties, 9 July
StabI/StG77

Ju87 FTR: Hptm Friedrich-Karl Frhr von Dalwigk zu Lichtenfels (Grpkdr) & Fw Karl Götz missing; victim of 609 Sqn.

4./KG3

He111 crashed Belgium; two wounded (Uffz Fritz Kostropetsch, Gfr Johannes Schneider, believe died); victim of 257 Sqn.

3./KG53

He111 FTR: Oblt Willi Kollmer, Oblt Eduard Fritz, Uffz Franz Huber, Uffz Ernst Neuburger, Gfr Walter Stiller; victim of 17 Sqn.

StSt/KG76

Do17 force-landed 40% damaged; two crew wounded (Fw Hans Lemke, Fw Werner Sankowski); victim of 610 Sqn.

Seenotkdo.1
He59 D-ASUO forced-down: Uffz Helmut Bartmann, Uffz Walter Anders, Uffz
Erich Schiele, Fw Günther Maywald (all POW); victim of 54 Sqn.

Aufkl.ObdL
Do215 destroyed, one Do215 60% damaged, one Do215 40% damaged on ground
by Blenheims.

And so ended a costly day for the RAF. On the morrow – 10 July – the Battle of
Britain would (officially) commence.

* * * * *

Meanwhile, Britain was embroiled in battle with elements of the 'sitting on the
fence' French Naval Fleet. Five days before the fall of France, French Admiral
Darlan sent coded orders to the captains of warships based in French African ports
to not surrender their ships intact to the Germans. Four days later, he repeated
this order with specific instructions to make preparations to scuttle their ships if
it seemed likely that they would be captured. However, Darlan had not informed
the British of this instruction and, on 27 June, the British government took the
decision that the French ships could not be allowed to fall into the hands of the
Germans and that it would be the responsibility of the Royal Navy to ensure that
this would not happen. Thus, on 28 June, Force H was created under the command
of Vice-Admiral James Somerville. The flagship for Force H was to be HMS *Hood*,
while battleships *Resolution* and *Valiant* and the carrier *Ark Royal*, plus eleven
destroyers, were to make up this force, with Gibraltar as its base.

CHAPTER X

OPERATIONS AGAINST
THE FRENCH, PART 1

Operation Catapult: Mers-el-Kébir, 3-4 July 1940

This Melancholy Act.

Prime Minister Churchill

Ark Royal's air component comprised twenty-four Skuas drawn equally from 800 (Lt Richard Smeeton) and 803 Squadrons (Lt John 'Bill' Bruen), and thirty Swordfish, with 810 Squadron (Capt Alan Newson RM) having 12 aircraft and 818 (Lt-Cdr Sydney-Turner) and 820 Squadrons (Lt-Cdr Guy Hodgkinson) each with nine.

803 Squadron's crews and their aircraft were:

Green Flight
L2927/A7A	Lt J. M. Bruen/Lt D. J. Godden
L2997/A7B	Sub-Lt(A) G. W. Brokensha DSC/L/Air F. Costan
L2915/A7C	PO(A) T. F. Riddler/N/Air H. T. Chatterley

Blue Flight
L2953/A7F	Lt I. Easton/Sub-Lt(A) A. H. S. Gore-Langton
L2961/A7F	Mid(A) A. S. Griffith/L/Air F. P. Dooley
L2996/A7H	Mid(A) A. T. Easton/N/Air J. A. Irwin

Yellow Flight
L2909/A7K	Lt C. W. Peever/PO(A) S. Andrews
L3017/A7L	PO(A) A. W. Theobold/ N/Air F. J. L. de Frias
L2891/A7M	PO(A) H. A. Glover/N/Air J. A. Burkey

Red Flight

L2897/A7P	Lt D. C. E. F. Gibson/Sub-Lt(A) M. P. Gordon-Smith
L2974/ALQ	PO(A) J. A. Gardner DSM/N/Air H. Pickering
L2956/A7R	PO(A) G. W. Peacock/L/Air B. P. Dearnley

The *Ark* (Captain Cedric Holland) had arrived at Gibraltar on 23 June, to make good her defects (she had been at sea for 87 of the last 100 days) and for her crew to have a rest. Three days later, 26 June, she and *Hood* were off again with orders to intercept the 35,000 ton French battleship *Richelieu* off the West African coast and to persuade her to join the British fleet at Gibraltar. The battleship was, however, intercepted by the cruiser *Dorsetshire*, declined the offer and returned to Dakar. While *Ark* was off Casablanca, Captain Holland had been instructed to fly to the French base, presumably in the rear seat of a Swordfish, in an effort to persuade the French in Morocco to remain on the side of the British. His return was witnessed by, among many others, Mid(A) Mike Lithgow of 820 Squadron:

> ... a Swordfish with 'boots' appeared – that is a Swordfish fitted with floats instead of the more usual undercarriage – with the Captain on board as a passenger. Standing on the flight deck, I imagined that the pilot would land in the sea alongside, but to my surprise the arrester wires were unrigged and the Swordfish started to make a normal deck-landing approach. I wonder whether the pilot had not forgotten what the underneath of his aeroplane looked like. However, it made a perfect landing and our Captain climbed out. How nice, I thought, to be of such importance that one's presence is worth damaging a perfectly good aeroplane! But the crane swung over, picked up the Swordfish, engine still running, and deposited it in the sea. Whereupon it took off again, apparently none the worse for its unusual adventure.[1]

Captain Holland's only success was to be followed back to the carrier by a number of French training aircraft whose occupants did wish to continue the fight. One of these brought an RAF pilot who had ditched his Hurricane in the sea off Tunisia while making for Egypt;[2] another conveyed his colleague to the carrier. Other escaping French airmen headed for Gibraltar, where most arrived safely, although one aircraft that had stayed over the Spanish border was shot down by AA fire and the crew killed.[3]

On 1 July, Somerville received his first order as the commander of Force H "to secure the transfer, surrender or destruction" of the French warships in North Africa. Thus, Operation *Catapult* came into being. Many senior officers in Force H were wary of using force against a navy that had until recently been fighting on their side. They had expressed their reservations to Somerville who, impressed by their arguments and stance, forwarded this information to the Admiralty. He received a curt reply that the government expected the French ships to be destroyed and that was their "firm intention".

Before dawn on 3 July, Force H arrived off Mers-el-Kébir, *Ark Royal* flying off two Swordfish at 04:58 to carry out an anti-submarine patrol, followed at 05:30 by six more Swordfish which were to patrol independently with the object of reporting any Italian or French warships that might be at sea. Three Skuas were sent off with orders to engage any aircraft that might threaten the Fleet. On board the Ark, Mid(A) Stephen Griffith of 803 Squadron maintained a journal for the period:

> The ship went to action stations at 08:45 as we were now off Oran. Reconnaissance aircraft are up and fighter patrols from my squadron flew off at 09:30. The first batch of fighters [from 800 Squadron] took at about 06:00.

The aerial activity coincided with the departure of a motorboat from HMS *Foxhound* carrying the man-for-all-occasions Captain Holland,[4] who was to act as intermediary with Admiral Marcel-Bruno Gensoul, Naval C-in-C Oran, who was given four choices in the British ultimatum:

> It is impossible for us, your comrades up to now, to allow your fine ships to fall into the power of the German enemy. We are determined to fight on until the end, and if we win, as we think we shall, we shall never forget that France was our Allie, that our interests are the same as hers, and that our common enemy is Germany. Should we conquer we solemnly declare that we shall restore the greatness and territory of France. For this purpose we must make sure that the best ships of the French Navy are not used against us by the common foe. In these circumstances, His Majesty's Government have instructed me to demand that the French Fleet now at Mers-el-Kébir and Oran shall act in accordance with one of the following alternatives:
>
> (a) Sail with us and continue the fight until victory against the Germans.
>
> (b) Sail with reduced crews under our control to a British port. The reduced crews would be repatriated at the earliest moment.
>
> If either of these courses is adopted by you we will restore your ships to France at the conclusion of the war or pay full compensation if they are damaged meanwhile.
>
> (c) Alternatively if you feel bound to stipulate that your ships should not be used against the Germans unless they break the Armistice then sail them with us with reduced crews to some French port in the West Indies – Martinique for instance – where they can be demilitarised to our satisfaction, or perhaps be entrusted to the United States and remain safe until the end of the war, the crews being repatriated.
>
> If you refuse these fair offers, I must with profound regret, require you to sink your ships within 6 hours.
>
> Finally, failing the above, I have the orders from His Majesty's Government to use whatever force may be necessary to prevent your ships from falling into German hands.

Holland was informed that the French would not start any action but force would be met with force if the Royal Navy started to attack the French fleet. Admiral Gensoul remained in contact with Admiral Darlan during this stand-off. However, it transpired that he only told Darlan of one of the British ultimatums – that the fleet would be destroyed within six hours – the other choices were never relayed to him. In response to this message, Darlan ordered all other French naval ships in the Mediterranean to steam to Mers-el-Kébir to assist Gensoul. The Admiralty picked up this message and relayed it to Somerville – that he could shortly expect far more French warships in the area around Oran. This effectively forced Somerville's hand.

The prestigious French Navy base was not without its own fighter defence, albeit immobilized, based at the satellite airfield at Saint-Denis Du-Sig were Hawk 75As of GCI/5 and GCII/5, while at Relizane were GCII/3 and GCIII/3 equipped with D.520s. Admiral Gensoul telephoned Colonel Rougevin-Baville, Oran air base commander, to enquire about their availability and was assured that some of the fighter force could be made ready within a few hours, but the bomber units based at La Senia would require at least 24 hours; the bombers' tyres had been deflated and batteries removed to avoid independently-minded pilots 'defecting' to Gibraltar, which some had already done. Rougevin-Baville then contacted the commanders of GCI/5 and GCII/5 at Saint-Denis to bring their aircraft to a state of combat readiness and, by 14:15, a patrol of three Hawks was available. The two D.520s units at Relizane, GCII/3 and GCIII/3 were similarly contacted. One of the Czech pilots who had been flying D.520s with the Armeé de l'Air was Lt Jan Cĕrmàk, who had escaped in a D.520 from Perpignan; he later wrote:

After landing at Maison Blanche and rejoining the French air command with French pilots, we were briefed for the first sorties against the English ships at Oran. I was so astonished I refused to fly. I was the put in jail. The Zouave, French colonial troops, smuggled me out at night after three days and I escaped, spending a month wandering about by foot, by train and by camel caravan with the Arabs. Eventually I reached Casablanca. To my astonishment the Gestapo were there, too! I was in the depths of despair. I was interrogated repeatedly by the French Secret Service who told me I would perish in England. With great difficulty I was finally able to board a mysterious Portuguese ship bound for Lisbon. With the help of the British Embassy there, I was flown to England in a DC-3.

The Hawk units possessed a number of experienced veterans from the fighting in France. These pilots in particular would see action against the FAA in the coming days. Both types of French fighter were superior in performance to the Skuas aboard *Ark Royal*.[5]

Meanwhile, as Captain Holland and his party made its way back to report to Admiral Somerville in *Foxhound's* motorboat, matters were made tenser when two

Swordfish from 820 Squadron – A4K flown by Lt Bob Everett and A4M (L7643) piloted by Sub-Lt Alan Owensmith – took off from the *Ark* at 15:25 to mine the inner harbour of Oran. A4K dived over the breakwater, turned towards the entrance and dropped its mine from a height of 150 feet inside the narrow entrance and in the centre of the channel. A4M followed suit, dropping its mine in the same general area, thus making it seemingly impossible for any large vessel to leave the harbour. Lt Everett then flew along the breakwater towards the inner docks in order to count the assemblage of warships at anchor among the many transports, auxiliaries and small craft. A total of seventeen destroyers was noted and also a large hospital ship. Mid(A) Griffith's perception of the unfolding drama was recorded thus:

> Battle Fleet has delivered an ultimatum, expiring at 14:00, to the French battleships at anchor and is roughly 'Join us, scuttle yourselves or be sunk!' At 10:50, the Commander broadcast that reconnaissance aircraft have reported the French ships to be raising steam and it is hoped that they may be coming with us. Capt Cedric Holland is in the destroyer *Foxhound* and is negotiating with the French Admiral [Gensoul]. The Battle Cruiser squadron is under the command of Admiral Somerville and we are cruising steadily up and down before Oran awaiting events. The entrance to the harbour has been mined from Swordfish. Blue Section [which included himself as Blue 3] took off on fighter patrol at 14:00 and we patrolled at the stupid height of 15,000 feet, where we obviously could not see any French aircraft beneath us. We landed at 18:00 to learn that the battle cruisers had opened fire on the packed French ships at 17:50, with awful result. Even the shore batteries were blown up.

The British ships were in open water and could manoeuvre into a perfect firing position; the French could not do this as they were in the confined space of a harbour. Skuas from 800 Squadron flew CAP while in case of a French counter-strike. The first ship to be sunk was the 22,000 ton battleship *Bretagne*. A shell exploded her ammunition and within seconds the she capsized. 977 men were lost. The *Dunkerque* (26,500 tons) was also hit and damage to her boiler room took away her power so that she had to drop anchor in harbour. The *Provence* (also 22,000 tons) was also hit and was beached by her captain to prevent the ship from sinking with subsequent loss of life. The destroyer *Mogador* was hit with the loss of thirty-seven men. After a thirteen-minute bombardment, Somerville ordered an end to the firing. For Mid(A) Mike Lithgow of 820 Squadron it was his first real taste of action:

> My aircraft was one of those detailed to spot for the bombardment, which was an awe-inspiring and unforgettable sight. I had never before seen a group of battleships open fire a concentrated fire with primary armament. The accuracy, from the first salvo, seemed uncanny. The six large warships alongside the mole were hit immediately, and it was hardly necessary for us

to make any corrections. The newest and finest battleship, the *Strasbourg*, managed however to escape damage.[6]

When the bombardment started, Gensoul had requested immediate fighter support and in less than 15 minutes nine Hawks were in the air above Mers-el-Kébir, as were sections of D.520s. Two of the spotting Swordfish from 820 Squadron were engaged by a section of fighters, identified as Dewoitines, although both Lt(A) Gordon Humphries (L2787/A4B) and Lt Hughie Hunter RN (L2840) were able to evade when attacked, Humphries' aircraft sustaining minor damage to its port lower mainplane. The Swordfish had in fact been engaged by two patrols of Hawks from GCII/5 led by Cne Arnaud and Cne Gérard Portalis, who believed the biplanes to be Gladiators. Arnaud opened fire at one and claimed several hits before it reached the safety of the British guns. Cne Portalis and Sous-Lt Paul Boudier also attacked Swordfish but without result. Of his part in the action Portalis wrote:

> Immediately after taking off from Saint-Denis-du-Sig, I saw many explosions inside the harbour of Oran and some flak explosions at the height of 2,000 m over the port. At 18:10, I arrived over the harbour, the situation was the following: three ships burning inside the harbour, one of them was the *Dunkerque*. The British fleet, ten miles in north-north-westerly direction was covered by a thick smoke curtain. Twenty miles in the northern direction a British carrier was cruising under escort of three destroyers. There were no British planes over the harbour. I brought my formation between the British fleet and the French fleet, ten miles away I discovered some small British two-seaters, probably Gloster Gladiators [*sic*]. We attacked immediately; three combats started.
>
> Capitaine Arnaud attacked one of the two-seaters that escaped nose-diving and twisting towards the carrier. Arnaud hit it many times and left it only over the carrier at the height of 500 m. I and Sous-Lieutenant Boudier attacked first a two-seater then a section of three biplanes. All the British aircraft escaped at height of 500 m over the carrier. We followed them, firing. During the pursuit Boudier was attacked by a patrol of British single-seaters. He disengaged and joined me. During the combat, one of the single-seaters – against which we didn't even fire a shot – fell in an uncontrolled spin and crashed into the sea. We climbed to 2,000 metres going 15 to 20 miles straight out. At 18:30, no more British planes were seen.

The 'British single-seaters' were in fact a section of 803 Squadron Skuas led Lt Bill Bruen (with Lt Jasper Godden in L2927/A7A):

> We took off at 18:25, with orders to escort 6 Swordfish [810 Squadron] proceeding to carry out high dive-bombing attack on French battleships; then to return and carry out a fighter patrol over the ship. About five minutes after

taking off, five French Curtiss 75As were observed, attacking spotting aircraft on starboard quarter of *Ark Royal*. The Section broke up to attack these, and after a short engagement, the French fighters returned to Oran. During the engagement the aircraft flown by Petty Officer Airman Riddler [L2915/A7C] was observed to spin into the sea. The remaining two Skuas continued to escort the Swordfish.

Sous-Lt Boudier reported being attacked by a Skua, following which he pulled his aircraft in tight turns at less than 250 feet. He believed that the Skua fell out of control, entered into a spin and crashed into the sea. Both 24-year-old Cornishman PO(A) Tom Riddler and his TAG, N/Air 'Chats' Chatterley (aged 20) were lost.

With just Sub-Lt(A) Guy Brokensha (flying L2997/A7B with L/Air Frank Coston) remaining to accompany him, Lt Bruen continued the escort six Swordfish from 810 Squadron that had departed *Ark* at 18:20 and were initially tasked to complete the destruction of any surviving warships in the harbour. However, in the confusion – and disguised by the extensive smoke – the battleship *Strasbourg* and the ancient seaplane carrier *Commandant Teste*, plus five destroyers, had managed to sneak away and somehow avoided the mines at the harbour entrance. Their escape was reported by a spotting Swordfish but this was thought to be an error, but the error was made by Admiral Somerville in not accepting the validity of the sighting, as he later admitted:

> Fire on the French ships ceased at 18:04. My appreciation of the situation at this time was that resistance from the French ships had ceased and that, by ceasing fire, I should give them an opportunity to abandon their ships and thus avoid further loss of life. Since the French knew the entrance to the harbour had been mined, I felt quite positive that no attempt would be made by them to put to sea. Force H proceeded to the westward with a view to taking up a position from which further bombardment of the French ships could be carried out if necessary, without causing casualties to men proceeding ashore in boats and without exposing the ships of Force H unduly to the fire of the forts.

The Swordfish were diverted to attack *Strasbourg*. In the meantime (18:50), three more sections of Hawks from GCII/5 were scrambling; Cne Hubert-Marie Monraisse leading Sous-Lt Marcel Hébrard and Adjt Paul de Montgolfier; with Lt René Trémolet leading Sgt-chef André Legrand and Sgt-chef Edouard Salés; the third section did not engage. Lt Bruen continued:

> At about 19:10 while at 12,000 feet, nine French fighters (Curtiss 75As and Morane 406s – *sic*) were observed above and astern of the Swordfish. A section which appeared to be about to attack them was engaged and a dogfight ensued with all the fighters, during which Sub-Lt (A) Brokensha obtained some hits on a Curtiss 75 which broke off the engagement. I was able to get

a long burst on a Morane [*sic*], which was on Sub-Lt Brokensha's tail. This aircraft was also steadily engaged by L/Air Coston. Several hits were observed and the machine broke off the combat and dived away. Several other aircraft were engaged by both Skuas. Three guns on each Skua jammed during this fight. At about 19:30 three Curtisses appeared, and a dogfight ensued with no apparent results on either side. Shortly after this the Swordfish started their attack, and the *Strasbourg* put up a barrage in front of us.

Cne Monraisse, leading Sioux Escadrille, described the action:

Arriving over the British fleet I saw six Gladiators [*sic*] in two patrols of three. They were protected by three Skuas. I closed into them and – without being previously attacked by us – they assaulted one of our Patrouilles. The right Patrouille of Lieutenant Trémolet was attacked frontally by two Skuas. The plane of Trémolet was seriously damaged (hits in the engine and tanks) and he had to disengage and land back immediately. Sergeant-chef Legrand attacked the Skua but was shot at by the second Skua. Adjutant De Montgolfier shot the enemy off the tail of Legrand but his plane was already damaged by many hits. Sergeant-chef Legrand shot down the first Skua after a turning combat [this was obviously Riddler's aircraft spinning into the sea]. Sergeant-chef Salés mixed with the third Skua but didn't even try to shoot it down, instead he waved his wings and didn't open fire. The Skua inverted its course and joined the second Skua in formation heading for the carrier.

Another of the French pilots, Sgt-chef Jean Gisclon, recalled:

... when we came into Saint-Denis-du-Sig, Lieutenant Trémolet was already there. He was pointing out to the mechanics the twelve bullet impacts in the fuselage of his Curtiss – "If Legrand hadn't shouted a warning, my career would have come to an end today", he said with a smile. His patrol been jumped by six [*sic*] Skuas. Legrand had shot down the enemy fighter that had caught Trémolet but had then had a narrow escape himself for which he could thank the armour plate in his machine...

While this engagement was taking place, Cne Monraisse and Sous-Lt René Hébrard had caught up with the Swordfish, but "as these did not show any hostile intentions", they did not open fire on them. Monraisse's aircraft was then attacked by Lt Bruen though not hit. His report continued:

[We] flew around the Gladiators without attacking but Capitaine Monraisse was attacked frontally by two Skuas without suffering damage. [We] disengaged without returning fire and directed for the coast. All the planes were back after 20:00.

The Swordfish meanwhile, at 19:45, closed in on the *Strasbourg*, protected by intense AA fire, and released their bombs – each aircraft carried four SAPs and eight 20lb bombs – albeit without success although one or two probable hits were claimed, including one by Lt(A) Lawrence 'Tan' Tivy from Jamaica. Two of the attacking aircraft were hit by AA and ditched in the sea on their way back to the carrier but both crews were rescued by HMS *Wrestler*. A Skua from 803 Squadron flown by PO(A) Harry Glover was despatched to shadow the French warships but eventually he forced-landed L2817/A7M in the sea through lack of petrol, Glover and his TAG N/Air Burkey being picked up by a destroyer. Meanwhile, Lt Bruen and Sub-Lt Brokensha were making their way back to the *Ark*:

> We returned towards the carrier. On the way back we met a Berguet Bizerte flying boat and carried out attacks on it. During my second attack [with only one gun working] she dropped some bombs on a destroyer. Sub-Lt Brokensha put one engine out of action and observed streams of petrol come out of the tank. We returned to the carrier and landed on just after sunset.

The Bizerte (No. 22/E2-1) of Esc E.2 commanded by Lt.deV Duval and flown by Premier-maitre Michel had taken off from Arzew to establish the situation at Mers-el-Kébir but had the bad luck to be sighted by the Skuas. It was badly damaged and alighted on the sea near Oran leaking fuel and with one crewman, Quartier-mâitre Dubost, wounded. Later, when it returned to Arzew, a total of forty or more bullet holes were counted in the wings and fuselage – and presumably in the damaged engine. A second Bizerte (No. 521/E2-3) commanded by Lt.deV. Viellard was following close behind the first and carried out a bombing attack on the destroyer *Wrestler*, but was badly damaged by AA shrapnel during the attempt and was also forced to carry out an emergency landing.

At the start of the bombardment of Mers-el-Kébir, moored to bouys in the harbour, were four Loire 130 seaplanes of Esc HS2 – two from *Dunkerque* (No. 69/HS2-1 and No. 70/HS2-3) and two from *Strasbourg* (No. 60/HS2-4 and No. 50/HS2-5) – and all four took off when the attack began. HS2-5 was badly damaged by AA fire but managed to reach Arzew by nightfall, as did HS2-1, which initially alighted in the sea to shake off a 'Skua' although this was probably Hawk. HS2-4 (Mâitre André Troadec/Ens.deV Pujade) contrived to signal the movements of the British fleet but was also allegedly attacked by a 'Skua' and then by a French fighter, but succeeded in reaching Mostaganem, while the fourth, HS2-3 piloted by Lt.deV Pierre Evin, shadowed the British Fleet, reported being attacked but also safely reached Arzew. However, none of the Skua pilots airborne reported contact with any floatplanes. Escadrille HS1 at Arzew had also launched three sections of Loire 130s at the start of the battle and one of these, HS1-2 flown by Ens.deV Gisbert attempted to bomb a British cruiser with its two small bombs; an attack was also made by Ens.deV Jolivet in HS1-8, while HS1-9 flown by Ens.deV Lambert was damaged by shrapnel when he attempted to bomb some destroyers. All three managed to return to base.

At 20:55, one last attempt to strike at the *Strasbourg* was made by six torpedo-armed Swordfish from 810 Squadron, led by Capt Alan Newson (with the 820 Squadron's CO Lt-Cdr Guy Hodgkinson as his observer). The attack took place at 20 minutes past sunset. It was well planned and well executed, the aircraft approaching from the land so that the target would be silhouetted against the afterglow. They came on the ship in two columns of three, 20 feet above the water and separated from each other by intervals of only 300 yards. Only two aircraft were fired on by machine-guns from the destroyers. One torpedo was seen to explode under the stern of the ship and there was some evidence of a hit amidships but darkness and funnel smoke made definite observation all but impossible. No casualties were sustained and none of the six aircraft damaged.[7] Cne Portalis of GCII/5 was still over the French ships when the attack started but failed to notice the Swordfish in the darkness. His only comment was: '... the *Strasbourg* turned to the right as if was avoiding a torpedo ...'. Which, of course, is what she was doing, but despite the determined attempts of 810 Squadron, the French warships succeeded in escaping from Mers-el-Kébir and safely reached Toulon at 08:10 the following morning.

At 04:30 on the morning of 4 July, two Italian Z506B floatplanes of 31°Stormo departed from Elmas (Sardinia) and flew over Oran in an effort to determine events. They sighted several ships but otherwise the flights were uneventful.

Force H was by now back at Gibraltar. This was a day of reflection. For the British, what to do next? For the Vichy French, how to gain revenge? Meanwhile, in the Mediterranean off the Algerian coast, the British continued their act of aggression when the RN submarine HMS *Pandora* torpedoed the French sloop *Rigault de Genouilly*.[8] This was swiftly followed by an attack on the *Pandora* by a patrolling LeO451 from GBII/25. The bombs missed but the French had shown their hand – they were prepared to strike back.

This was rammed home by a surprise attack on Gibraltar after dark, by three LeO H-257bis seaplanes from Escadrille B1 bombing individually at intervals. Two others turned back before making landfall. The first to arrive, B1-6, released four bombs from 10,000 feet on the fully illuminated town. B1-11 arrived at 00:32 and bombed from 4,500 feet but by now the lights had been extinguished. Some 45 minutes later, B1-2 dropped its bombs on the again illuminated town, but damage sustained was insignificant. Between 03:15 and 03:30, five Martin 167Fs from Escadrille 3B departed Mediouna to repeat the attack but one crashed on take-off, killing its crew. Two others failed to locate the target in darkness, and only two completed the mission.

At dawn on 5 July, a reconnaissance Po63/11 from GRI/52 flew over the Rock, as noted by 803 Squadron's Mid(A) Griffith in his diary:

Air raid warnings were sounded at 06:15, and the *Hood* and *Ark Royal* opened fire against a reconnaissance aircraft of unknown nationality.

At about 10:30, three patrolling Hawks from GCI/5 led by Cne de la Martin encountered a reconnaissance Sunderland (P9621) from 228 Squadron some six miles off Oran. During an exchange of fire the Sunderland sustained damage but its gunners claimed one if not two of its attackers shot down. None was hit however and all returned safely to Saint-Denis. The damaged flying boat reached the safety of Gibraltar.

Off the North African coast the cruiser *Dorsetshire* was sighted by a Late 302 seaplane (E4-1) out from Dakar, the crew calling in two submarines in the area but, although torpedoes were fired by the *Heros* and the *Glorieux,* neither gained a hit. Air reconnaissance of Mers-el-Kébir had not confirmed conclusively the disablement of the battleship *Dunkerque,* leaving Admiral Somerville with little choice but to carry out another attack on the harbour. The operation was given the codename *Lever.* Griffith noted:

> *Ark Royal* sailed again at about 20:00, with the *Hood* and *Valiant* and we set course once more for Oran to ensure that the French battleship *Dunkerque,* which had run aground, will not be refloated.

Ironically, Free French leader General Charles de Gaulle had not been taken into the confidence of the British, and later wrote:

> On July 4th the radio and the newspapers announced that on the previous day the British Mediterranean Fleet had attacked the French Squadron at anchor at Mers-el-Kébir. At the same time we were informed that the British had occupied by surprise the French warships which had taken refuge in British ports and had taken ashore and interned – not without some bloodshed – their officers and crews. Finally, on the 10th, the news was made public of the torpedoing, by British aircraft, of the battleship *Richelieu,* at anchor in Dakar Roads. In London the official communiqués and the newspapers tended to represent this series of aggressions as a sort of naval victory. In the British Government and Admiralty – this was clear the fear caused by the danger they were in, the stale reek of an old naval rivalry, and the resentments accumulated since the beginning of the Battle of France and brought to the point of paroxysm with the armistice concluded by Vichy, had exploded in one of those dark bursts by which the repressed instinct of this people sometimes smashes all barriers.
>
> It had never, though, been likely that the French Fleet would of itself open hostilities against the British. Ever since my arrival in London I had stressed this both to the British Government and to the Admiralty. Besides, it was certain that Darlan, quite apart from all the obvious patriotic motives, would not of his own accord go and surrender to the Germans his own wealth – the Navy – as long as it was under his control. At bottom, if Darlan and his

advisers renounced the chance of playing the magnificent part offered them by events and becoming the last resort of France at a time when, in contrast to the army, the Fleet was intact, it was because they thought they were certain of keeping their ships. Lord Lloyd, the British Minister for Colonies, and Admiral Sir Dudley Pound, the First Sea Lord, when they came to Bordeaux on June 18th, had obtained from Darlan his word of honour that our ships would not be handed over. Pétain and Baudouin, for their part, had given formal undertakings. Lastly – contrary to what the British and American agencies had at first suggested – the terms of the armistice included no direct provision entitling the Germans to lay hands on the French Fleet.

On the other hand, it must be recognised that, faced by the capitulation of the Bordeaux authorities and the prospect of future flinchings on their part, England might well fear that the enemy would one day manage to gain control of our fleet. In that case Great Britain would have been mortally menaced. In spite of the pain and anger into which I and my companions were plunged by the tragedy of Mers-el-Kébir, by the behaviour of the British and by the way they gloried in it, I considered that the saving of France ranked above everything, even above the fate of her ships, and that our duty was still to go on with the fight.

I expressed myself frankly about this on July 8th, in a broadcast. The British Government, on the advice of its Minister of Information, Mr Duff Cooper, was clever enough, and elegant enough, to let me use the BBC microphone for the purpose, however disagreeable for the British the terms of my statement may have been. But it was a terrible blow at our hopes. It showed at once in the recruitment of the volunteers. Many of those, military or civilian, who were preparing to join us, turned on their heels then. In addition, the attitude adopted towards us by the authorities in the French Empire and by the naval and military elements guarding it, changed for the most part from hesitation to opposition. Vichy, of course, did not fail to exploit the event to the utmost. The consequences were destined to be grave as regards the rallying of the African territories.

CHAPTER XI

OPERATIONS AGAINST THE FRENCH, PART 2

Operation Lever: Mers-el-Kébir, 6 July 1940

Many situations arose where, due to vastly superior performance, the enemy could have inflicted casualties, but resisted doing so.

Lt John Christian 803 Squadron

At 05:20 on the morning of 6 July, six Swordfish of 820 Squadron arrived up sun at the height of 60 feet over the bay of Mers-el-Kébir. Led by Capt Alan Newson RM (with Lt-Cdr Guy Hodgkinson as observer), they commenced a shallow dive in line ahead down the path of the sun. Aircraft attacked in succession, coming in low over the breakwater. Complete surprise was achieved and no opposition was encountered except that one of the six aircraft was fired on by a machine-gun during the getaway. According to the CO, five out of the six torpedoes hit the target. One of these five, however, failed on impact and after running up the ship's side eventually struck a jetty and exploded. The sixth torpedo missed and exploded on the beach at St Andre. All Swordfish safely returned to the *Ark* over a calm sea from which the haze had already begun to lift. In fact, only one hit was obtained and this on the patrol ship *Terre Neuve*, anchored on the starboard side of *Dunkerque*.

This first attack had been unescorted but the next was escorted by six Skuas from 803 Squadron. Mid(A) Griffith recorded:

Was awakened at 05:00, and at 06:00 Blue and Red Sections took off on fighter patrol over Oran, to protect the three waves of Swordfish while they torpedoed *Dunkerque*. We reached the Algerian coast at about 06:45 at 10,000 feet and at once saw large numbers of French fighters, mostly Morane-Saulniers [*sic*], a few American Curtiss Hawks and a few Dewoitines.

Their charges were six Swordfish from 810 Squadron that attacked in two sections of three. The first section attacked at 07:00. This time AA fire was heavy and the first attacker failed to release its torpedo while two other hits were claimed on *Dunkerque*. In fact, only one torpedo struck home, again hitting the unlucky *Terre Neuve* where all the 42 depth charges on board exploded, cutting the patrol ship in two and opening a 120 feet long hole in the side of *Dunkerque*:

Three more torpedo-carrying Swordfish from 810 Squadron made a further attack under the command of Capt Alan Newson RM. This half squadron had taken off an hour previously in 7/10th low cloud lying at 500 to 1,000 feet and at the same time six Skuas were flown off as fighter protection. They were to be needed. Unfortunately, the low protective cloud ceased about six miles from the objective. The sub-flight formed up in line astern at 2,000 feet close to the shore coast of Oran in order to come on the target from up sun. They turned to attack at 06:47 and from then on came under heavy anti-aircraft fire. Violent avoiding action was taken during the approach. The attack was delivered over the shattered breakwater and they thus had an ideal, stationary target beam on to their approach.

Captain Newson in A2A attacked first:

> As he passed over the breakwater, his air gunner saw some men running to man a gun, gave them a burst of fire with his rear gun and dispersed them. The pilot, alas, had omitted to turn on his master switch and thus failed to drop his torpedo. The second aircraft, A2G, attacked next. That torpedo was seen to hit by the pilot of the third and last aircraft, A4F, whose torpedo also struck home. As the sub-flight was making its getaway, a large explosion was observed in the direction of the *Dunkerque* which by this time was out of sight behind the headland of Fort Santon. The 6-inch and 4-inch batteries from the east of Oran to Mers-el-Kébir point kept up a continuous and accurate anti-aircraft fire until the sub-flight had reformed well out to sea. All bursts were black and many burst within 20 yards of the aircraft. The sound of the burst could be distinctly heard and the concussion felt by the aircraft. No casualties were sustained but a bullet passed through the main spar of the port lower main plane of A4F, the last aircraft to attack. This, however, did not affect the airworthiness of the aircraft.[1]

At 07:10, the second section under Lt David Godfroy-Faussett attacked. This time two torpedoes hit. One (failing to explode) was the only effective hit on *Dunkerque*, The other sunk the tug *Esterel*.

By the time the second sub-flight of 810 Squadron flew off from *Ark Royal* to make the final torpedo attack, the French were fully alert and able to mount considerable opposition. This group of three Swordfish, under the command of Lt Godfrey-Faussett, had by far the toughest time. This final attack was made from the opposite direction to the others. The visibility was still hazy and there were patches of low cloud at 1,500 feet. Landfall was made ten minutes before seven, and they passed over Cap Falcon at 4,000 feet. But there was no protective cloud over the headland. Immediately they came within range, the *Provence* with her quarterdeck awash, the *Mogador* and the shore batteries opened up a heavy barrage of anti-aircraft fire. Weaving violently to avoid this peppering, they made their final approach low over St Andre town. The first aircraft, piloted by Lt Godfrey-Faussett, dropped its torpedo at short range. This torpedo struck the *Dunkerque* amidships on the port side. A large swirl was observed but no one could be certain whether the torpedo exploded. The second aircraft, piloted by Sub-Lt Pearson dropped its torpedo at a longer range. Unfortunately a tug about a hundred yards from the *Dunkerque* was in the direct line of fire. The tug, as the pilot curtly observed, disintegrated. The third aircraft dropped its torpedo at short range. This hit the *Dunkerque* but failed to explode.

Of his experience Sub-Lt Randy Pearson in Swordfish L2760/A2C, reported:

Whilst making a getaway from a torpedo attack on the French battle cruiser and at a height of about 100 feet some small splashes were seen on the port bow. Although no fighters were seen, it was realised that the splashes were caused by machine-gun fire from above. The observer reported that he saw a fighter turning away. A few seconds later the observer reported that there was a fighter approaching from the direction of the sun on the starboard quarter.

The pilot immediately turned steeply to starboard and noticed a large burst of machine-gun fire in the water on the port bow. A third attack was made exactly the same as the others and the rounds missed to port as before. It was not until the fighter broke away after this attack that the pilot of A2C saw him for the first time. The fighter turned back and attacked from astern. The pilot of A2C turned 180° and dived beneath the fighter. It was in this attack that the pilot of A2C thinks that most of the hits on his aircraft occurred. The fighter gave up the attack, but was followed by another of the same type. The same tactics were employed as before and the pilot was able to turn beneath him and fire about 50 rounds with his front gun. The fighter made off at great speed and A2C was unable to follow. The rear-gunner managed to fire a few bursts at the first fighter but the violent manoeuvring and damage to his scarf-ring made it impossible to fire accurately.

The attacker was Sgt-chef Jean Gisclon in one of three Hawks led by Cne Portalis from GCII/5, which were patrolling over the harbour. Portalis together Gisclon engaged Pearson's aircraft, which they reported disappeared into clouds when the Skuas counter-attacked. Mid(A) Stephen Griffith, flying as Blue 3 with N/Air Fred Dooley in L2961/A7G in Lt Christian's section, continued:

My section broke up and attacked a flight of three Moranes [sic] about to attack one of the Swordfish and succeeded in attracting their attention. Fired two short bursts at one from about 200 yards and it left the fight. The other two were joined by four more fighters and as things were then so hopeless, I had to dive into a layer of thin cloud at 1,500 feet and escape seawards. Four aircraft pursued me for 40 minutes, three above the clouds and one fellow below so that at the end of that time my position was uncertain and, after endeavouring to find the carrier by square-search, Dooley obtained a D/F bearing and we were able to reach the ship with 30 gallons of petrol in our tanks after being in the air for five hours.

Before leaving Oran I witnessed the amazing sight of a torpedo striking a tug [the *Esterel*] instead of the *Dunkerque*. There was nothing left at all when the water subsided. Altogether, six hits were scored on the battleship and although it is aground and cannot sink, there must be little left of its starboard side. Considerable AA fire was encountered but all our Swordfish returned safely. One Skua of 803 Squadron – PO(A) Peacock with N/A Dearnley – was lost in the sea but the crew are safe. My squadron have now lost three aircraft altogether, leaving us with nine.

Of the action, his TAG Dooley simply noted in his logbook: 'Chased by Moranes.' Blue Leader, Lt John Christian (with Sub-Lt Alric Gore-Langton in L2953/A7F) also engaged the Hawks:

The Dewoitine [*sic*] retired losing height with smoke coming from engine after a dogfight lasting about 30 minutes. Own aircraft spun three times. The French did not appear to put their heart into the fight. If they had done so, their superior performance would have told on the Skuas. Enemy did not fire or fired very wide. He was always in position after avoiding action and could not be got in sights. If enemy had been trying, he could not have helped shooting Skua down. Rear-gunner unable to fire owing to avoiding action. Enemy stall-turned and dived steeply seawards through cloud. Attacked one of the flights of three Moranes [*sic*]. They were joined by a further four aircraft and we fought rear-guard action until reaching safety of layer of clouds. No hits were observed. The French fighters appeared to be holding their fire. Enemy in every case appeared to be unwilling to engage our aircraft closely. Many situations arose where, due to vastly superior performance, the enemy could have inflicted casualties, but resisted doing so.

Red Section Leader Lt Donald Gibson (L2953/A7P) was tasked with taking photographs of the situation at Mers-el-Kébir, with PO(A) Jimmy Gardner DSM (L2874/A7Q) and PO(A) Geoff Peacock (L2956/A7R) as cover. Gibson wrote:

My section got involved in a fight with several Dewoitine 520s flown by very angry Frenchmen, and the matter was complicated by our instructions that we were not to fire at them unless they fired at us (rules of engagement so loved by politicians). On one occasion, anxious to rid myself of an infuriated Frenchman on my tail, I pulled hard back on the stick and the aircraft went into a spin at once, when I took a normal recovery action she came out almost immediately. My gallant observer, still Pat Gordon-Smith, had his own pet K gun in the back and the Lewis gun, provided by the government, was stowed loose, but during the spin the Lewis gun had an argument with Pat, and on landing I was asked not to do it again.

PO(A) Peacock and N/Air Brian Dearnley failed to return. It transpired that they had been shot down.

> The Hawks appeared to be working in pairs. Lower one providing sitting target until attacked, when it quickly outmanoeuvred Skua, one in rear and above diving down on to Skua's tail. Own port guns put out of action. Holes in tail plane and holes and large rent in starboard main plane, large rent in fuselage, but attacking aircraft broke off into cloud.

Peacock was obliged to ditch the damaged aircraft. The destroyer HMS *Vidette* was quickly on the scene, picked up Peacock and Dearnley and they were soon back aboard the *Ark*, none the worse for their enforced dip in the sea. It would seem that the Skua had been attacked by Cne Portalis and Sgt-chef Gisclon, who reported:

> ... three seconds later I was on his tail as he levelled out.. I gave him a long burst from fifty metres, which struck home. My incendiaries danced across his wings, setting them alight, while his gunner peppered my starboard wing. I gave him a second burst and he tipped over into a downwards spiral and disappeared into the cloud deck over the sea ...

Cne Portalis claimed another – or the same Skua – as probably destroyed. He reported engaging three Skuas in a dogfight, and as they broke away, fired at the last one at very close range. The Skua pulled up to the vertical, stalled to starboard and fell away vertically. At 1,800 feet he entered cloud and lost sight of the Skua. At the end of the day Lt Christian reflected:

> Although vastly outmanoeuvred by the French aircraft, the French pilots did not seem to care to press home their attacks and in many cases our pilots found themselves in such positions that would certainly have resulted in damage had the French pilots fired seriously. Dogfights lasted for over half an hour, during which time all the Swordfish escaped. Blue Leader remained for a further forty minutes on patrol, but beyond AA fire was not attacked again. All our aircraft returned independently, Blue 3 [Griffith] having been literally escorted out to sea for half an hour by seven French fighters.

The action at Mers-el-Kébir was over. French casualties had increased to 1,297 sailors killed and 351 wounded. The *Dunkerque* was effectively out of the war. She did however reach Toulon in February 1942 but was still under repair when the Vichy government collapsed at the end of that year.

The Vichy Government of Pétain broke off diplomatic relations with Britain because of the attack on Mers-el-Kébir and urged a declaration of war against Britain. It was rumoured that the French World War I air ace, Colonel René Fonck, had organized some two hundred Vichy-French pilots who were prepared to join Germany in the fight against Britain. Eventually the idea of war with Britain was rejected by Foreign Minister Paul Baudouin who said 'War with Britain would worsen France's already pitiful condition.'

The German propaganda machine relished the situation. The *Berliner Beersen Zeitung* reported:

Germany had given a binding undertaking that the Reich had no intention of seizing the French naval fleet. Churchill ignores this incontestable act and summoning every element of brutality at his disposal, orders an attack on French ships. With unique but pitiable notoriety, this hero of unparalleled ignominy, Churchill, achieves the distinction of being the greatest criminal in the world. We are anxious to see whether there is still enough sense of honour left in the British people to make them separate themselves now from a Prime Minister who stands in the pillory of world condemnation. Have the British people not courage enough to free themselves from this crime and from the one who is responsible for it? If not the English people will themselves be treated as criminals.

While Dr Goebbels declared:

The British Navy's attack on the French Fleet at Oran is to be used for a detailed exposition of how Britain first dragged France into the war, how she then let France make the main preparations, how France was required to supply most of the materials, how the struggle was fought on French soil, how French divisions bled themselves white while the British carried out a 'withdrawal without losses' policy, how Britain eventually tried to force France to continue the struggle, how the British abused them after the collapse and blamed them for the defeat, how they then set up a French pseudo-government on British soil and how, to top it all, they were now attacking the French ships – all 'in France's interest.' Here Britain has really revealed herself without her mask.

CHAPTER XII

OPERATIONS AGAINST THE FRENCH, PART 3

Operation Black: Dakar, 7-8 July 1940

Five were back! And finally half-an-hour later the sixth came home.
All our little steam pigeons safely home. Their reports were not
particularly encouraging.

Revd Alan Leeke, HMS *Hermes*

While the French warships at Mers-el-Kébir had been effectively put out of commission, the British still had battlecruiser *Richelieu* to contend with at Dakar. In an attempt to eradicate this major problem, an attack was planned with immediate action. The carrier HMS *Hermes* had sailed from Freetown together with a small task force and, on the afternoon of 7 July, an ultimatum was given to the French authorities in line with that presented to Admiral Gensoul at Mers-el-Kébir. The offer to join the British was refused.

To defend the harbour, the French had a mediocre air force comprising Escadrille 6 with three antiquated D.500 and three D.501 fighters under the command of Cne Labit based at Dakar-Ouakam, while 20 miles away at Thiés was the 43rd Autonomous Group equipped with an assortment of three Potez 542s, three Farman 222s and three Potez 25TOEs, which hardly posed a threat to the British force, although *Hermes* did not possess any fighters with which to defend herself or her escort. In harbour, the Aéronavale had two escadrilles, E4 with three Late 302 seaplanes, and 8S3 with three Loire 130 seaplanes.

Hermes had embarked a half-squadron of Swordfish, six aircraft of 814 Squadron although it was considered by senior officers that these were unlikely to cause havoc against the *Richelieu,* even if they were able to penetrate the expected hail of AA fire that would undoubtedly greet them. The carrier's Chaplin, the Rev Alan Leeke,[1] fortunately left a record of what transpired:

It was doubtful whether six torpedoes would make any impression on *Richelieu*. So heads were put together and one of the boldest, maddest plans in the history of the sea was devised. Bobby Bristowe [Lt-Cdr R. H. Bristowe] volunteered to take our crash boat, an ordinary 25-foot motor boat, and four depth charges into harbour in the middle of the night and drop the depth charges under *Richelieu's* stern. It seemed possible that he might reach his objective but impossible, if he did not blow himself up, that the French would either kill him or capture him, and the crew of nine. This attack was to be followed by a torpedo attack three-quarters of an hour before dawn. I don't know if you can imagine what flying off a small carrier like *Hermes* is like in the dark carrying a 1,500lb torpedo. It is enough to give the most experienced pilot the jitters but when you have to, and launch it at a ship, you can hardly fail to see it becomes no mean feat. Well, that was our plan and we reckoned that it was the best we could do though we weren't very sure of our explosives making any impression on a ship of the *Richelieu's* strength.

The C-in-C Dakar had been given until 20:00 to respond. No response was forthcoming but *Hermes* did incept a radio signal from the Governor-General of Dakar ordering the French to "Resist our English enemies with all our might." Rev Leeke's account continued:

No answer came and so at 08:50 pm Bobby and his party started to climb into the crash boat. It had been painted black all over, they were dressed in dark clothes and had blacked their faces with burnt cork. At 09:30 they went away amid vociferous remarks and cheers. I watched them vanish into the darkness and thought we should never see them again.

The arrival of dawn on 8 July witnessed the departure of the six Swordfish, the sub-flights led by Lt-Cdr Norman Luard (the CO, affectionately known as 'Loopy') and Senior Pilot Lt-Cdr Trevenen Coode respectively, tasked to carry out a torpedo strike on the *Richelieu*. Rev Leeke:

I was sitting in the After Medical Station when I heard the arrester gear go 'Boomph'. One aircraft on again at any rate, then another and another and another and another. Five were back! And finally half-an-hour later the sixth came home. All our little steam pigeons safely home. Their reports were not particularly encouraging. They had carried out a copybook attack under intense AA fire from *Richelieu*, destroyers, armed merchant cruisers and merchant men armed with machine-guns, together with shore batteries. Torpedo tracks had been seen running straight but there had been so much row that they hadn't heard any explosions. They were rather depressed about this, and most of them were sick after passing through the inferno of AA fire.

One torpedo did however find its target and the battlecruiser suffered a strike on the starboard side that caused a serious leak. Also damaged was a shaft line that put the main tiller motors out of action. Five loud explosions were then heard between 05:00 and 05:15 and shortly thereafter *Hermes* received wireless message from Lt-Cdr Bristowe (he had taken with him a small portable transmitter), "Exploded four depth charges under *Richelieu's* stern one hour ago."

At the start of the torpedo attack, Late E4-1 managed to take-off in poor conditions and become disorientated. Instead of flying out to sea, the pilot flew towards Tiaroye where a submarine was sighted. Assuming this to be British, he released his bombs albeit without success. This was fortunate – the submarine was the French *Glorieux*. Later, the British fleet was located as was a patrolling Swordfish, which hurriedly entered cloud to avoid interception. A second Late 302 (E4-3) followed on the tail of E4-1, Lt.deV Hacard also locating the fleet, being greeted by a heavy AA concentration. The seaplane was not hit and returned safely to Dakar. An hour before midday, the fleet came under aerial attack from two lumbering Farman 222s and two Potez 25TOEs, which jointly dropped about sixty small bombs with scoring a hit. *Hermes'* air staff must have been furious for not having at least one Sea Gladiator on board for defence. During the afternoon, two Potez 542s set out to repeat the attack but failed to find the ships. Rev Leeke:

Then the French bombers arrived and our little party started, little McLochlan more Scotch [*sic*] than ever, pumping shells into the gun he was in charge of: it was so exciting, we were at action stations from 13:30 on Sunday until 06:30 Tuesday morning. Meanwhile more of our planes went off to take photographs of *Riehelieu* and report what they'd seen. Then we picked up the crash boat about mid-day. I've never seen a tougher looking lot.

Hermes returned to Freetown. Meanwhile, having returned to Gibraltar following Operation Lever, *Ark Royal* joined forces with Force H and briefly forayed back into the Mediterranean on 8 July and saw further action. The Fleet was back at Gibraltar by 11 July.

Dakar would be back in the news a few weeks later.

APPENDICES

I. Continuation of Sgt Ginger Lacey's Adventures (see page 25)

Having been hit in a skirmish with Bf109s on 9 June, Sgt Lacey attempted to carry out an emergency landing. Flung forward into his straps so that his head hit the instrument panel, then thrust against the back rest of his seat so that all the air was driven from his lungs, and finally left suspended upside down with his head in a whirl and his stomach churning, Lacey cursed the treachery of the smooth, boggy field that had beckoned him so alluringly. His ears smarted in the heavy silence after the loud throb of his engine.

For several seconds he hung motionless, gathering his senses. First of all he became aware that water was seeping through the cockpit canopy as the aircraft sunk slowly into the soggy earth. He had a vision of drowning, trapped in the inverted cockpit. Next, a loud hissing came to his ears. That, he recognised: petrol dripping from his carburettors, over the hot engine. This galvanized him. Struggling furiously with his harness straps, he struggled around so that he was no longer upside down although he now had his feet on the roof of his cockpit hood and his head a few inches from the floor, near the rudder bar. Easing his way forward he found that he was in about 18 inches of water and cold panic gripped him with the certainty that he was trapped here do drown.

A nauseating wave of claustrophobia washed through him and he flung himself against the side of the perspex, trying to batter a way out with his fists and feet. His head throbbing from the crisp blow it had received as his Hurricane tumbled on to its back, his mind confused with anger and fear of a vile death, he flung himself again and again at the perspex through which he could tantalizingly see the bright sunlight shining on the world outside. He kicked at the transparent panes, but his soft flying boots were of no avail; and he could never have made a hole big enough to crawl through. And all the while the water was rising. And as it rose, reducing the air space, more petrol fumes were swirling into the cockpit. With his mind a confusion of thoughts about drowning, being burned to death when the petrol vapour exploded, or dying of asphyxiation, he lost consciousness.

> The next thing I knew was that I was lying flat on my back, in water, looking up into the face of a delightful French girl. The only thing that crossed my mind was, 'where on earth did I find her?' I struggled up unto a sitting position, but she hurled herself at me and pushed me flat again.

Lacey ventured a few slow words of French, trying to convince her that he was unhurt; but she kept telling him to lie still. He passed his hands over his body, moved his legs cautiously, and he could find no sign of damage. His head ached a bit, but that was all. Yet the pretty French girl would not allow him to sit up.[1]

*****

He had been rescued by French farmer workers who had cut him free using hacksaws and wire cutters – and nursed and comforted by the French girl – and before long British troops arrived on the scene. He was carefully placed in an ambulance that had also arrived. After treatment for a gash on the head that looked worse than it really was, having oozed blood that had covered his face, he was despatched to a hospital for further care and treatment but on the way passed Le Mans airfield, where he saw 501 Squadron's Hurricanes assembled. Thanking his driver, he exited the ambulance and rejoined his colleagues. From Le Mans Sgt Lacey flew to Dinard but missed the air evacuation to Jersey, instead reaching the island aboard a potato boat from St-Malo, and from there flew back to England. Having been credited with five victories during the earlier fighting in France, the announcement of a DFM was shortly forthcoming.

II. Continuation of Sgt Eric Jones' Adventures (see page 77)

Having been shot down on 10 June, Sgt Jones had jumped from his force-landed Hurricane and ran for it, finding himself in the middle of the advancing German spearhead. He got hold of some civilian clothes and a tattered old French smock from a farmhouse and joined a party of refugees trudging along the road for Arras. He plodded along with them for several days, begging food in a variety of villages passed on the way, met three Tommies, also trying to get back, and with them reached the Somme River.

They hid up in a deserted village for three days waiting for a chance to cross the river and penetrate the German lines, and eventually purloined a German officer's motor launch and reached the other bank. As they were scrambling out of the launch, German soldiers opened fire on them from a nearby road and almost the first shot neatly severed the heel of one of Eric's shoes. They got away, crawling through long grass, but shortly after that Eric became separated from the three Tommies and continued on alone, making now for Cherbourg, where British troops were still holding out, according to a farmer, who directed him.

From another farmhouse Eric bought a bicycle for 370 Francs, rode it for about one kilometre and then it collapsed under him. He disgustedly threw it into a ditch and walked on. At a village near Lisieux, a German guard suddenly confronted him and asked for his papers. Eric told him in schoolboy French he lived in a nearby house and the guard let him walk into the house to get his papers. Eric walked straight out of the back and away again.

He went through Lisieux and Caen, and at Bayeux went into a small café for a meal. A minute later a motor-cycle pulled up outside and a German *Obergefreiter* (lance-corporal) entered. He was a friendly, voluble soul and sat down beside Eric while waiting for his meal. Eric pretended he was French, and got away with it, though the German spoke better French than his schoolboy version. They chatted uncomfortably for a few minutes and the German pulled out photographs of his wife and children, which Eric tactfully admired. On the subject of politics, the German soldier said what a brute 'Chamberlain' (the German, it appeared, was unaware that Churchill was now Prime Minister) was and wanted to know why he should have to fight because of 'Chamberlain's' warmongering. Eric discreetly agreed again. He was posing as a demobilised French soldier returning to his home in Cherbourg.

After his meal the German soldier went back to his motorcycle to resume his journey. He kicked the self-starter and nothing happened. Again he kicked, and again and again, and still nothing happened. Eric, who was somewhat of an authority on motorcycles, wandered out and told the German he was probably having carburettor trouble. Between then they soon had it fixed and the engine chortled away happily. The grateful *Obergefreiter* beamed warmly at Eric: 'I, too, to Cherbourg am going,' he said. 'On the back jump, and I the lift to Cherbourg will give you.' So Eric nipped on the pillion and eventually the German dropped him on the outskirts of Cherbourg, by which time Eric realised that there were no free British soldiers left in the city.

He branched off down the west coast of the Cherbourg Peninsula, his plan then to 'win' a boat from somewhere and cross to Alderney, in the Channel Islands. He was nearly caught trying to purloin, single-handed, a large coastal barge at St-Valéry, and then scuttled off down the coast to Cartaret, where he succeeded in commandeering a small fishing-smack, rowed it outside the harbour, raised the sail and set course for Alderney. It took him 14 hours, and his twenty-second birthday dawned while he was in the boat.

At sunrise there was an enormous number of aircraft flying overhead out to sea, and Eric wondered vaguely what it was all about. He found out when he arrived at the islands. He had seen the airborne invasion of the Channel Group and found himself in enemy-held territory once more. Again he was lucky, received help from the inhabitants and hid up in a barn for a week, but on 7 July, twenty-eight days after he had been shot down, the Germans suddenly entered the barn and the game was up, Eric was captured and went into kriegydom.

Sgt Eric Jones ended up at Stalag Luft III, scant reward for his perseverance.[1]

III. Continuation of Sgt Alex McNay's Adventures (see page 37)

Sgt McNay of 73 Squadron was forced to carry out an emergency landing on 15 June, following combat. His subsequent report reveals many adventures before his eventual escape from France:

I was bundled into an ambulance and commenced a circular tour of French hospitals before he returned, so I was left to assume the squadron would salvage the machine. We visited three hospitals before we got to one which was not evacuated. They took me in and cleaned and dressed my wound properly. I spent about three or four hours there, before they took me to a hospital at Laval. It was about half an hour's journey by ambulance. We reached Laval at 21:00 hours and were just in time to meet the patients walking out of the hospital – evacuating! I was getting used to evacuation by this time. We went up to the station, and having all boarded the train, we were told to hop out again as the train was not moving off until next morning.

Next morning, after a breakfast of a mouthful of black coffee and a piece of bread, an English Tank Corps chap and myself decided to go and hunt up a supply of food. We wandered back armed with long loaves and other odds and ends only to find that the ambulance train had gone! When we were about to see about commandeering a car, we spotted a train which turned out to be ours in another siding. Once we were aboard, it took off but, instead of going direct to Nantes, it went via Rennes, taking two days as it took three or four hours rest for every half hour's run.

We at last arrived at Nantes, and I was sent to Broussais Hospital, as I was still waiting to have the bullet extracted. My shoulder was X-rayed on the morning of my arrival which was Sunday. By Monday dinnertime I was nearly crazy with trying to speak French all the time and watching Hurricanes sailing over the town. I went to the Commandant and asked to be sent to the English hospital at La Boule. He willingly gave me permission to go but had no transport. When outside, I decided to try and see my squadron MO. I made my way out towards the Nantes aerodrome at Château-Bougon. When about halfway there, I was told that all the English squadrons had gone that morning! I jumped on to the tail-board of a lorry which was going back to Nantes and from there I managed to hitch-hike to La Boule.

Before I entered St-Nazaire, I saw at least a thousand motor vehicles, including Ford V-8s, Bren-gun carriers, and heavy lorries. French people were bringing up petrol, filling the tanks, and driving them off. I myself was given a lift from the dump to La Boule in one of our own lorries. Having reached La Boule, I found the hospital had packed up and gone back to England two days before. I then considered picking up a motor launch and sailing to England if I could get enough petrol. I decided first of all to try La Boule-les-Pins aerodrome to see if I could get a lift to Britain in a French bomber. While wandering along the promenade, I was stopped by a Special Constable. I had no papers except my Broussais discharge paper and he was all for running me in, but a French boy who could speak a little English helped me to explain what I was doing there and what my intentions were. Another French lad, who was a member of the 'defence passive', told me to wait, and he dashed off to return a few minutes later with a car. He insisted on running me up to the aerodrome, and he dashed around trying to help.

I was soon the centre of a gaping crowd of Armée de l'Air pilots and ground staff. They were all asking questions and I was tied in a knot trying to answer them. I met a Yankee at the drome and I was never more pleased to hear an English voice. He was an employee of the Lockheed Company and was assembling the civil version of our Hudsons so that the civilian ground staff could clear out to Toulouse. He told me about some Harvards which were to be burned, so that Jerry would not get them and he suggested that the owner would be only too glad if I would fly one away.

I next saw the CO of the French squadron who said that his machines were fighters. He couldn't help me but said that it would be a good idea to fly a Harvard if possible. I returned to the civilian hangars and after a grand meal I had a sleep in the Lockheed's cabin. I was wakened at about one o'clock, in time to watch a raid on St-Nazaire. Whoever the raiders were, they were unchallenged as not a shot was fired at them. I returned to the machine and slept again until about five o'clock. The owner of the Harvards turned up shortly afterwards and he willingly gave me a machine.

My first intention was to go north to Brest, refuel there, and then cross the Channel. I was very strongly advised not to risk it as this was Tuesday morning and by that time the Boche were probably there. One of the ground staff wanted to go to Bordeaux to join his father, who was a major in the French army so I decided to go south to Bordeaux. As I had not flown a Harvard before, I had to do some lightning calculations to make sure of my airspeed in miles per hour, particularly on coming in to land as they were supposed to be vicious at lowish speeds. I had to land at a drome near the mouth of the Garonne to check my course but I could hardly get her down as she preferred to float along.

When I reached Bordeaux, I found, after two ineffectual attempts at landing, that the rule of the road there was just barge in and let the other fellow clear out of the way. This time I closed my throttle completely and, gliding in at about 90 mph, found the Harvard handling like a Tiger Moth. I arrived there at about 11:00 hours, and the manager of the Potez hangar very kindly put a car at my disposal to go down to the town to have my shoulder dressed. While I was in hospital the driver went to the docks and made enquiries about a boat for England. There was no boat so I returned to the aerodrome. I had spotted a Rapide sitting on the drome. Apparently the pilots, who were English, had left two four-engined 'buses' and two twin-engined while they cleared off to England by boat. I thought of trying to fly the four-engined machine to Britain, but four engines rather scared me as I had never even flown a twin-engined machine. The machine I chose was an eight-seater, or nine including the pilot. It hadn't the range to reach home but I thought of going to Marseilles and from there to Morocco if I couldn't get a boat.

While sitting there, I saw a Potez bomber take off in a stalled condition and as soon as the pilot tried to turn he half-rolled into the deck from about 100 feet. The full petrol tanks simply blew up and this didn't cheer me any as I was about to do my first trip in a twin, and with umpteen passengers. I heard later that there was a boat going from Bayonne, which is 20 or 30 km from the Spanish frontier so I changed my plan and had as a result only one passenger.

I took off about 7:15 on Tuesday evening and decided to follow the shore, because my map was about 50 miles to the inch and showed no landmarks, only Imperial Airways European routes. After about an hour's flying, I ran into violent rain, and I was scared stiff because my port engine wasn't running too well, and I did not fancy spinning-in from a low altitude. I ran out of it, and reached Biarritz, but saw no aerodrome. I kept on as the aerodrome was supposed to be practically on the shore. I reached St-Jean de-Luz and was sure I had crossed the frontier, as the coast was running east to west, which on my map was wrong. Turning back, I was forced down by low cloud, and I saw lightning flashes, which I didn't like because I had a large aerial out. When I was ready to force-land, I saw a largish field, which on inspection proved to be Biarritz aerodrome. I attempted to land as though I was flying a Hurricane. I shot across the fields at about 90 miles per hour, drifting like the deuce because the landing T was dead across a fairly stiff breeze. I repeated my attempt, but this time at about 70 miles per hour and got in with no bother. I had hardly got in when a Potez came along to land. It was quite dark by this time and he hit a ridge in the field, collapsed his undercart, and practically stood on his nose. The crew were alright and no damage was done.

I reported to the Consul in Bayonne whom I reached in the only available transport - an ambulance. He told me to come back the following morning so I and my ex-passenger searched around for a bed. The place was choked with refugees but finally we bedded down in an ambulance in the garage. Next morning, when I turned up, I met an RAF officer who took me into the Consul and I found myself helping on the Consular staff. There was no need for panic but the way in which a number of middle-aged Britishers fought to get to the door was sickening. However, it was interesting work, and I managed to get a bed with the F/O driver in Biarritz. He got away on the first boat but I was remaining as I was going to fly my machine to Toulouse, destroy it there, and pick up a decent French military machine which I would take on to Morocco. How I would get home from there I had not thought about, or the fact that I was still the unwilling host of a bullet.

The day I was going to leave for Toulouse, my machine's battery was u/s, so we arranged with the French to charge it and we would call for it after lunch. Even if it hadn't been serviceable I would have taken a new Stinson Reliant which was on the drome instead. However, we had a puncture, and by the time we had it mended and reached the Consul's office, we found a bit of a panic on. We were rushed to the boat and there we sat for two days in the harbour, doing nothing. It was decided to mount guards on the ship, as we had a number of known and suspected 'fifth column' on board. All arms were collected, including those of the Polish officers.

The voyage home was uneventful. I had to stay an extra night on board on arriving at Plymouth because of the guard business. Exactly 14 days from the time of being wounded, I got to a decent hospital. I was X-rayed on Thursday evening, and on Friday morning they decided to operate. In the hospital I met one of the squadron, who had been on the *Lancastria* when it was bombed and sunk by the Germans, and from him I gathered that the squadron didn't know what had happened to me. I got definite news of the report when my telegrams home were answered. As I could not write for a day or two after the operation. I asked the authorities to notify the Air Ministry and my squadron. I spent a week in Stoke Military Hospital, and I was then sent up to Victoria Hospital. Glasgow, as an out-patient until my shoulder had progressed sufficiently to allow me to return to my squadron, on July 21st.[1]

IV. Plt Off Frank Carey's Adventures in France

Plt Off Frank Carey DFM of 3 Squadron, who had been wounded on 14 May and hospitalised, searched for a way back to England following his discharge. He related his adventures:

I was attacking a Dornier 17 [on 14 May] and it did a snap half-roll – which was an extraordinary thing for a kite of that size to do. I did the same and followed it closely down. It was nearly vertical; in fact, the pilot was dead, I think, because it just went straight on in. But before I'd realised that, the rear-gunner fired and hit me well and truly. Stupidly, perhaps, I'd been following it rather close – because it was such a fast aircraft and I knew it could get away from me. If I'd known the pilot was dead, of course, I wouldn't have bothered. Then I was busy getting down myself. First of all, I was on fire. So I thought, right, I must get out. I thought what I had to do in my mind, pulled the thing up into nearly a stall, and stood up. Of course with a 100 mph draught over me I got thrown back, and my parachute pack got caught up in the hood. Well, of course the aircraft slowly got itself into a dive, and the faster it went, the harder it was for me to get out. Eventually, I climbed up on to my own legs to get back into the cockpit. Then of course my ticker was going at a fairly fast rate; but at least the fire seemed to have gone out and I was able to select a big ploughed field and had no difficulty in getting it down. When I stood up in the cockpit I heard a little clink – it was the core of an armour-piercing bullet which had come straight through the engine and finished up in my parachute! I knew I'd been hit in the leg, but didn't know how lucky I'd been till I examined the bullet holes in my trousers: I could have finished up with a very different category of voice! I was very lucky because I was in what they would have called, in the First World War No-Man's-Land. The British ground forces had retired to a river a few miles back just the night before. Being ignorant of the changed circumstances on the ground I started walking due east, which was quite the wrong way. I'd gone quite a distance when I heard two motorcycles coming. I pulled out my revolver to sell myself dearly and greeted these two chaps by shouting at them to halt. I didn't know who they were. When they started to talk it was even more confusing because they were Belgian motorcyclists who had been on a morning patrol and had met some German tanks up the road. They'd seen me come down and they jolly bravely went across a lot of ploughed fields to where I was – and they were greeted by a revolver! I got on the back of one of these motorbikes and they rushed me back. But all the time, of course, they were pretty worried about being caught themselves. They left me with four or five British sappers who were blowing up a bridge we had just come over, which saved me a swim across the river.

I then took up walking with the refugees along the roads; we were regularly strafed by Heinkels. Then a British army truck came along and took me to a village somewhere south of Brussels. I had a slight leg wound, and they said there was an army medical officer in one of the houses. I went along to see him, and he gave me some brandy and cleaned up my leg quite painlessly. Then I was put on another truck for a while and joined up with a bloke [Plt Off W. G. Spencer of 57 Squadron] who had the best part of a Blenheim front end in his eyes, and his bomb-aimer [Sgt R. Pike], who had only one hand. They'd been shot down a few miles from where I was. They were strafing one of the German columns and ran into a solid block of anti-aircraft guns, which threw an awful lot of stuff at them. It blew the nose off the long-nosed Blenheim straight into his face and took a hand off the front bomb-aimer. Of course, the pilot only had very imperfect sight through all the bits of Perspex in his face and eyes; he crash-landed it with what little he could see plus the directions of the one-armed bomb-aimer. They'd done their best to bury the rear-gunner [AC2 Owen Beaumont] who had been killed outright, and collected the contents of his pockets for his next of kin. They not only brought back their parachutes, they'd disconnected the gun and brought it with them, too. And they'd crossed a river with that lot! I thought they were fantastic. It sort of pulls you back and makes you think how proud you are of them. There was I, limping along, thinking I was badly wounded! It took all the limp away from me, I can tell you.

We then got into a 1914 Crossley ambulance, where they asked us if we would hold down a poor chap who was badly shattered in the pelvis with a bit of shrapnel. We were taken to a casualty clearance station which was just over the French border. That took an hour or two and it was a very bumpy trip; the poor devil was screaming his head off. On arrival, I sat on a bench in a tented camp with a lot of other people, delighted to sit down stationary at last. Then I don't remember any more, and they said that, by the time it was my turn to be dealt with, I was fast asleep. Well, I'd had four nights with almost no sleep and no clean clothes – I must have smelt to high heaven. They dressed my wounds – they didn't bother about any anaesthetic, put me into a bed, and I woke up late the following day.

I was taken out of this casualty clearing station to a Dieppe hospital; I finished up in a ward where there were only four of us. There was the Blenheim pilot [Spencer], a chap with meningitis, me and the Duke of Norfolk – a very nice fellow, very shamefaced because he was in with gout! We played Rummy for two or three days. But the Hun was moving along fast and getting closer, and eventually the commander of the hospital decided to evacuate everybody. He arranged for a hospital train, and we had just settled into our seats when a couple of dozen Heinkels came and unloaded everything they had on us. They hit the train.

That was when the boat *Maid of Kent* was sunk in Dieppe Harbour: it was alongside the train. The interesting thing was that, when the bombing started, there was I with the leg, limping again, and his Grace with gout, and it was touch and go who was beating whom! We did about a hundred yards in four seconds! Then we felt rather sheepish because we could see all the fire and damage behind us, so we sort of tottered back and did what we could to save the seriously wounded and move them into the part of the train that wasn't burning. The walking wounded then disconnected the burning part of the train. The French driver had already unhooked his engine and disappeared.

Then we pushed the train out. It was very flat there, and once we got it moving it was all right to keep it going. We pushed it out of the danger area – probably about a mile or so. Those that were able to just leaned against it. It staggered me that we were able to do it, but we did. We were left with a very limited number of medical supplies and no medical officer that I could remember seeing; but several medical orderlies did a wonderful job. We also got our driver and engine back once the bombs had stopped. After two or three days we finished up in La Baule, a well-known resort town right on the Atlantic coast. There the *Hermitage*, an immensely posh hotel, was the officers' hospital

Suddenly it was impossible to believe that there was any war going on at all. All lights were on, we had strawberries and cream – we were in totally new surroundings! And very thankful we were for it, too. The next thing was that they were going to evacuate that hospital back to England. Much to our disgust, the chap with the damaged eyes [Spencer] and I were discharged back to the nearest Royal Air Force unit, which was an aircraft stores depot not too far away from Nantes. I was still in the same uniform; it was full of bullet holes, but at least the shirt had been washed. There we joined up with two similar RAF derelicts. None of us knew where our units were, so we were stuck.

In the second week of June we got a message that there was a British aircraft on an adjacent airfield that somebody had left several days previously. It was a Bristol Bombay – a bright yellow transport plane. We checked it over and filled it up with some petrol we got from a small French Air Force contingent there. The next morning at dawn we left, all four of us. They put me in the back at the rear-gun, as I was the only one who had fired a gun. All the way back I was trying to find out how to work the thing! We felt very naked, I can tell you – a bright yellow plane, clear blue sky and doing about 120 mph! We were not sure where the front line was: the whole place was a mass of rumours. Even the Forces broadcasts didn't seem to know where anybody was. We had to take our chance. We didn't see a thing until we got just off the English coast, where the British fighters intercepted us. There were all sorts of funny looking aircraft coming from the Continent over those days; nobody took a pot at us. Everybody knew what we were – bright yellow, 120 mph – complete lunatics! They could have hit us with rocks. We landed at Hendon, and then I had to find out where my unit was.

It turned out that my squadron [3] had left France only two days after I was shot down! They had nothing much left, so they were sent up to Wick to relieve 43 Squadron, who came back to Tangmere. Well, 43 was my old squadron, and I wanted to get back into action. I asked Air Ministry if I might rejoin them. They said they'd have a word with the CO, Sqn Ldr George Lott. Two days before, he had taken twelve aircraft on a Dunkirk patrol, and arrived back with just two. One flight commander and himself. They didn't all get killed – some of them were shot down over the water and were picked up by boat. Others fell on land the other side and scrambled out; they were coming back in broken condition for quite a few weeks. So I was very lucky because the CO was dying to get some pilots, and I started flying again with 43 in late June.

V. Disastrous Reinforcement Flight to Malta (see page 82)

Day One
Orders were given for the aircraft to be ready to start at 04:30 on 18 June, and the majority were ready at this time. However, some of the Hurricanes had not arrived

until late the previous evening and refuelling had not been completed, while further delay had been ocassioned by the changes in route. As a result, take-off commenced at 06:30. The orders called for the aircraft to take off in flights, but this was not complied with since no attempt had been made to form up correctly on the ground. In the case of D Flight, the Blenheim leader, Sqn Ldr Dicky Pryde DFC, found that his R/T was u/s and ordered the other two Blenheims to take off with the rest of the formation, and for his three Hurricanes to remain behind with him. The three Hurricanes of C Flight were also delayed, partly because they were not refuelled in time, and partly because they had formed up behind the D Flight leader and could not get past. The result was that 11 Blenheims and six Hurricanes (A and B Flights) left at 06:45.

The Hurricanes were flown by:

A   Flight: Plt Off R. H. Barber (P2653); Plt Off A. G. Maycock (P2584); Plt Off C. R. Glen (P2651)
B   Flight: Plt Off R. W. H. Carter (P2544); Plt Off M. A. Sims (P2642); Plt Off J. Mansel-Lewis (P2648)
C   Flight: Plt Off W. P. Collins (P2623); Plt Off W. R. C. Sugden (P2629); Flg Off J. C. Smyth (P2626)
D   Flight: Plt Off C. Haddon-Hall (P2625); Plt Off G. D. H. Beardon (P2650); Plt Off A. G. McAdam (P2641)

The aircraft endeavoured to get into formation before the left Tangmere's airspace, but owing to the absence of those left on the ground, the formation was irregular and all aircraft flew in one big gaggle although spread out fairly widely; generally, the Blenheims led and the Hurricanes followed. The weather was excellent as far as the French coast and for some 50 miles onward. Then it began to get hazy and visibility deteriorated. Some 70 miles south of the Loire, when beginning to approach the Monts d'Auvergne, they encountered heavy and continuous cloud reaching from ground level up to 16,000 feet. Soon the cloud became so thick that it became impossible for the pilots to see their own wingtips, and broke formation to avoid collisions.

Four Blenheims and two Hurricanes (Glen and Carter) eventually arrived at Marignane. Of the missing aircraft, two Blenheims had returned to Tangmere, but disaster had overtaken the remaining five Blenheims. All had crashed at different locations in France, with the loss of all members of the crews. Of the four missing Hurricanes the news was somewhat better. Barber had returned to Tangmere in company with one of the Blenheims, and Mansel-Lewis and Sims had landed at Angouleme, where they would spend the night. The fourth Hurricane pilot, George Maycock, was not so fortunate. Having lost sight of the others in the appalling weather conditions, he found himself alone:

My aircraft then flew into a clearing in the clouds and I flew in a complete circle so as to give the other aircraft time to reappear. Almost immediately a Blenheim appeared and I, now having no idea as to my exact position, altered course and flew towards him. I tried to contact him but was unable to do so owing to the electrical interference, and I took a quick look at my compass and realised that he was flying on an easterly course, which was in the direction of enemy-held territory. Increasing my speed I flew alongside him in order to point out his error. Unfortunately, he was unable to understand my signals, and I broke formation with him.

Maycock eventually found himself over the village of Loudon. He was about to land nearby when he noticed, to his consternation, that the village was being bombed. Next moment he spotted an aircraft closing on his tail. He tried to take evasive action, but the fighter opened fire, a short burst hitting the tail of the Hurricane and damaging its controls. His assailant may have been a French fighter pilot since no German claim has been found. Maycock attempted to land but hit a hedge and the aircraft flipped over on to its back. Shaken but unhurt, he made his way to the local French army command post, where he learned that the Germans were only about ten miles away. After setting fire to his wrecked aircraft, he managed to reach Bordeaux from where he boarded a RN cruiser (probably HMS *Galatea*) and arrived back in England three days later.

Meanwhile, at 17:45, Sqn Ldr Pryde decided that his group of four Blenheims and two Hurricanes should fly to Calvi on the island of Corsica, before heading for Tunisia. However, his aircraft suffered a loss of power on take-off and hit the bounday fence, although no one was hurt. The five remaining aircraft reached Calvi at 19:00, where they stopped for the night.

While this disastrous progression was underway, the remaining Blenheim and six Hurricanes which had been left behind at Tangmere had followed at 09:30. Initially these too had found the weather very good over France, but on approaching Monts d'Auverge they encountered the same bad conditions as had the earlier flight. Dick Sugden recalled the treacherous conditions:

The cloud base was down to 2,000 feet, which we found by cautious exploring. All the time we were dodging those damn clouds, keeping the Blenheim and each other in sight. After about three hours flying it became obvious that we should not get through to Marseille. The mountains were hidden in dirty grey fog, getting worse. I kept peering down at what land I could see, wondering what were the chances of a forced-landing. My petrol gauge had ceased to function so every half hour I switched on my overload pump and trusted to luck. It was now raining all the time and visibility was wretched. Suddenly, we made a turn to port and there in front of us lay an aerodrome. Not a pukka thing with runways and rows of hangars hut a large, wet-looking field on top of a hill, with one miserable-looking shed. Still, any port in a storm . . .

The airfield was near the village of Ussel, situated about halfway between Clermont-Ferrand and Brive. The field, although on high ground, was found to be boggy and the second Hurricane to put down, flown by Smyth, tipped up on its nose: the other five landed safely. After a brief conference with the French authorities, it was discovered that there was no food available, so, after a collection among the pilots, bread, ham and cheese were purchased from the nearby village. An inspection of Smyth's Hurricane revealed that it was only slightly damaged and was deemed to be flyable. Following their meal the pilots sought to refuel their machines, as Sugden recalled:

All this time various French aircraft were taking-off and landing, some of them unbelievably ancient looking Blochs. the most ramshackle machines I have ever seen. Of course, all the French pilots were very impressed with the Hurricanes and Blenheims, and I shot the best line that my French was capable of. When we had eaten our lunch we started on the business of refuelling. It was a business too, as each machine had to be taxied to a pump through what resembled a bog. As all the French machines were nosing in front of us, it was each man for himself. And, bless me, it started to rain in torrents. It was like a nightmare, pushing aircraft through mud nearly a foot deep, arguing in French and then having to unscrew the fairings off those infernal overload tanks. Just when my machine was being filled there was a cloudburst: everybody huddled together under the mainplanes, while I tried to shield the petrol tank with my body, whilst rain was pouring in cascades down the mainplanes. I don't know how much water got into the tanks, but it must have been a hell of a lot. I had long ceased to care; everything seemed so bloody awful. We knew that if the rain kept on. then we should never get those Hurricanes off the ground, let alone move them. At about 17:00 the rain stopped. Everybody's machine had been more or less refuelled.

It was now too late to continue, and accommodation was found for the night. Meanwhile, Plt Off Jock Barber, having returned to Tangmere at noon in company with a Blenheim, was ordered to take off again:

We landed back at Tangmere after being airborne for five hours. We had a bite to eat in the Mess and then reported to the briefing officer, and told him we couldn't get through, particularly with no oxygen to overfly. He didn't think much of this and implied we were pretty useless, and that we were to get airborne. So we took off at 15:00, having decided to try to fly underneath the cloud. When we got over France we again found the weather bad although there was a slight improvement. My problem was that after about four and a quarter hours flying I was unable to use the fuel in my long-range tanks and that my wing tanks were reading practically zero. We were by then threading our way through the Alps and I looked around for somewhere to land.

Finally Barber spotted a small field on a mountainside and, after a couple of approaches, dropped the Hurricane onto the ground. Unfortunately, the force of the landing broke off the tail wheel assembly, thereby causing damage to the underside of the rudder and rear fuselage. He had landed close to the village of Monde, and was able to reach habitation on foot with ease. A curious crowd formed, none of whom were English-speaking. Fortunately, there were a number of Belgian refugees present and Barber, a South African, was able to understand the Flemish speech due to its similarity to Afrikaans:

> I introduced myself to a young boy, Jan, and we were able to strike up a means of communication. As it was getting late, Jan took me to meet his friends who lived in some barrack huts, where I met old grandma and an exceedingly attractive young girl who could speak a little English and provided the romance. I shared their meagre food – some good bread and home-made jam – and fiery brandy, and they gave me a straw mattress on which to sleep. I might add that by this time I had stuck up a very reasonable acquaintance with this very good-looking young lady, who wanted to accompany me out of France. I was sorely tempted but it wasn't really on.

Day 2

Early in the morning Barber set out for Monde with his new-found friends and 'borrowed' a 12-volt car battery. With power provided by the battery, fuel from the long-range tanks was pumped up into the wing tanks. The Hurricane was then turned in the direction of proposed take-off. and was started by hand cranking – no mean feat. Revving the engine hard against the brakes to raise the broken tail quickly, he got off safely and flew to Marseilles, landing at the civil airport which caused further damage to the tail. No fuel was available there and he was advised to fly to the military base at Marignane, where he landed at 11:20.

At Ussel meanwhile, due to the previous day's torrential rain, all aircraft were found to be bogged down. However, the six Hurricanes were manhandled to firmer ground but, as the Blenheim taxied out, it stuck fast and all efforts to free it were to no avail. Resolved to go on alone, the Hurricane pilots taxied into wind but Smyth again stood his aircraft on its nose, this time causing serious damage to the propeller. Collins and McAdam got off safely, followed by Sugden but, in taking off, the latter lost his maps from the cockpit. He circled the airfield waiting for the others to join him but, realising what had happened. Haddon-Hall called him over the R/T to land again. Meanwhile, Collins and McAdam flew on to Marignane, arriving at 12:10.

Leaving Smyth and the Blenheim crew to make their way back to England, and Barber to sort out his damaged aircraft, Haddon-Hall, Sugden and Beardon eventually took off for Marignane, but en route ran into heavy rainstorms and were unable to find their destination. While circling in an effort to find the airfield, Beardon became separated. Subsequently, Haddon-Hall and Sugden landed at

Toulon – the first sizeable airfield they could find. After lunch they were shown around the base, seeing in one hangar an Italian CR42 biplane fighter, which had recently been brought down during a raid on the airfield. Meanwhile, Beardon had found Marignane alone, and landed there shortly before the two Hurricanes of Mansel-Lewis and Sims arrived from Angouleme, where they had spent the night.

At about 17:30, Sqn Ldr Pryde, who had commandeered another Blenheim having detailed its crew to make its way back to England, set out again from Marignane and was accompanied by five Hurricanes (Collins, McAdam, Mansel-Lewis, Sims and Beardon). Under normal circumstances Pryde would probably have waited until the next morning. However, the French feared an air attack on Marignane if the Germans became aware of the presence of British aircraft, and he had been pressurised by the authorities into leaving at the earliest possible opportunity. Collins and McAdam turned back after about an hour owing to problems with the feed pumps on the under wing tanks – similar trouble to that experienced by the earlier reinforcement flight. The remaining three Hurricanes followed Pryde's Blenheim south-eastwards. Bad weather was encountered soon after leaving Marignane. The formation passed over Corsica and kept to the east of Sardinia. Dusk approached about half way across and it was quite dark before the African coast was reached, where they were greeted by thunderstorms.

Approaching the coast, Sqn Ldr Pryde's aircraft fired a Very light, presumably as a signal to the French, but shortly afterwards it crashed into the sea and turned over onto its back. Pryde and his gunner were killed instantly, and the navigator died two days later. Mansel-Lewis tried to pancake his Hurricane near the Blenheim but his aircraft turned on its nose and sank at once. His parachute, which was still in its pack, kept him afloat until he could inflate his life-jacket. He swam in the direction of the Blenheim, where he found one body, and then set out for the coast which he reached three hours later. In the morning he was found by Arabs and taken to Bizerta. Meanwhile, Sims had reached the coast, only to be fired on by machine-guns. Completely lost in the darkness, he baled out; he too was picked up by Arabs and joined Mansel-Lewis in Bizerta. The third Hurricane crashed on the beach nearby and Derek Beardon was killed. Both Mansel-Lewis and Sims were taken to Casablanca by the French, where they met some Fleet Air Arm officers from *Ark Royal*. They were flown out to the carrier, which took them to Gibraltar that same night. From there they were shipped back to England. (see page 195)

While this drama was unfolding, back at Marignane Barber had set out for the nearby village of Estres to recruit the aid of the local blacksmith. A tail skid was swiftly fabricated from an old car spring, taken back to the airfield and bolted to the damaged Hurricane's rudder sternpost. A test flight resulted in the collapse of this lash-up on landing, but a new skid using double the number of spring leaves was made and fitted. Rather than risk a further collapse, Barber decided to await his next destination – Tunis – to make the test. He was joined by the returning Hurricanes of McAdam and Collins and, later still, by Haddon-Hall and Sugden from Toulon. They decided to continue next day.

Day 3

The five Hurricanes left Marignane at 14:00 and set course for Tunis. After half an hour they ran into a heavy rainstorm and became somewhat disorientated. Landfall was however made after about three hours, but Haddon-Hall, leading the flight, turned east along the coast instead of west. Realising that he was wrong, Barber flew ahead, waggled his wings, and turned westwards. The others followed and all soon landed safely at El Aouina at about 17:30. There they were shocked to learn that Sqn Ldr Pryde's flight had not arrived.

Day 4

Following a good night's sleep, the five pilots prepared to fly to Medjez-el-Bab, from where they would embark on the final leg to Malta. First off was Haddon-Hall but his engine cut and his aircraft crashed through the airfield boundary fence. He was unhurt apart from minor cuts and abrasions to his face, but he now had to be left behind. On landing at the dusty Medjez airstrip, the remaining four were delighted to find two more Hurricanes – those of Glen and Carter – and three Blenheims. Refuelling was very slow, taking about three hours due to inadequate equipment. Four tankers were used in succession but each either broke down or ran dry. Furthermore, Carter's Hurricane refused to start until a magneto adjustment had been made. By then it was too late to set out for Malta. No accommodation was available at Medjez, so the airmen were driven into Tunis for the night.

Day 5

Next morning, at 10:50, the Blenheims and two Hurricanes (Carter and Glen) finally took off for Malta, where they arrived safely at 13:00. Two more Hurricanes (Collins and McAdam) followed at 12:30, but they turned back when Collins' aircraft again developed fuel problems. They took off again at 14:45, landing safely at Luqa two and a quarter hours later. This left two Hurricanes at Medjez, where Sugden could not get the engine of his aircraft to start, as he recalled:

> The batteries of course were flat and Jock [Barber] and I took turns in cranking it with the starting handle. For about an hour and a half we cranked my wretched engine – starting a hot engine is always a bit tricky – and at last it started. We were both absolutely dripping, and I felt very sick. The sun was blazing down out of a cloudless sky. And so we set off on the last lap, across the bluest sea I had ever seen. Jock had the only map – a chart of the Mediterranean – and I flew in line astern, trying to crouch down out of the sun's rays. We flew over the tiny islands of Linosa and Lampedusa and then, like a white biscuit in the sea, appeared Malta.

They landed at Luqa in darkness. All the stranded Hurricane pilots and Blenheim crews, who had fallen along the way, eventually returned to England by one means or another, but it had been a disastrous operation. Following a Court of Inquiry, Air Chief Marshal Sir Robert Brooke-Popham reported:

> Apart from the weather, the chief causes of the failure of the Flight were:
> (a) The great importance of the time factor which necessitated all preparations having to be made at high pressure;
> (b) The daily, if not hourly, change in the situation in France, causing changes of instructions up to a few hours before the departure of the Flight;
> (c) The inadequate attention paid during the preparations to the operational side, as distinct from the administrative side;
> (d) The issue of meteorological route forecast so incomplete as to be misleading;
> (e) The amount of work that fell upon the shoulders of S/Ldr Pryde before the start;
> (f) Unwise airmanship on the part of the commander.

Extracted from *Hurricanes over Malta* by Brian Cull and Frederick Galea.

VI. Luftwaffe fighter aircrew released from French captivity at the end of June 1940

From research undertaken by Laurent Rizzotti

The release of all POWs was one of the armistice terms imposed by the Germans (Article XIX of the armistice):

> All German war and civil prisoners in French custody, including those under arrest and convicted who were seized and sentenced because of acts in favour of the German Reich, shall be surrendered immediately to German troops.
> The French Government is obliged to surrender upon demand all Germans named by the German Government in France as well as in French possessions, colonies, protectorate territories, and mandates.
> The French Government binds itself to prevent removal of German war and civil prisoners from France into French possessions or into foreign countries. Regarding prisoners already taken outside of France, as well as sick and wounded German prisoners who cannot be transported, exact lists with the places of residence are to be produced. The German High Command assumes care of sick and wounded German war prisoners.

Some 400 Luftwaffe aircrew were thus released from French captivity. The following is a list of known fighter aircrew only. Not included were those shot down over the surrounded Allied armies in Northern France, who were probably liberated at the end of the Dunkirk fighting, and those that are known to have been liberated before the end of the campaign, either in hospitals overrun by the Wehrmacht, or who were evaders:

Bf110 aircrew

Auinger, Ltn Friedrich 1./ZG26 (no known victory claim)

d'Elsa, Hptm Eberhard Staka 5./ZG 26 (no known victory claim)

Eckert, Gfr Paul 9./ZG 26 (AG)

Gaffal, Ltn Hans 13.(Z)/LG1 (no known victory claim)

Grabmann, Major Walter Kommodore ZG76 (no known victory claim)

Knop, Oblt Hans-Jochen (and AG Uffz Jakob Neumayer) 6./ZG76 (two victory claims on 13/05/40)

Landgraf, Uffz Erwin 4./ZG26 (no known victory claim)

Maurer, Ltn Walter (and AG Uffz Stefan Makera) 3./ZG2 (one victory claim in Poland)

Mentzel, Ltn Franz (and AG Gfr Wilhelm Oechsle) 3./ZG2 (possibly one victory claim in 1941)

Nülle, Ltn Dieter (and AG Ogfr Georg Rothenberger) Stab II/ZG1 (no known victory claim)

Oertel, Ofw Johannes 3./ZG52 (no known victory claim)

Radzko, Uffz Fritz 4./ZG76 (AG)

Schultze, Ltn Helmut 13.(Z)/LG1 (no known victory claim)

Welzel, Gfr Alfred 9./ZG 26 (AG)

Ziebarth, Oblt Herwarth Stab I/ZG52 (no known victory claim)

Bf 109 pilots:

Beese, Uffz Artur 9./JG26 (KiA 6/2/44, 22 victory claims, all after 1940)

Böhner, Oblt Otto Stab II./JG53 (9 victory claims, all after his release)

Borth, Oblt JGr.152 (heavily wounded, probably never flew again)

Bosch, Ltn Hans Stab II./JG27 (first victory claim in Battle of Britain, another later)

Burkhardt, Fw Alfred 3./JG26 (2 victory claims in May 1940 before his capture)

Carnier, Ltn Gerhard 2./JG53 (first victory claim in Battle of Britain)

Deinzer, Gfr Georg 8./JG52 (KiFA 16/3/42, 2 victories both in 1941)

Falkensamer, Ltn Anton 2./JG51 (3 victory claims in May 1940 before his capture, 4-8 in 1941 or later, KiA 22/12/43)

Galubinski, Fw Hans 7./JG53 (9 victory claims in May 1940 before his capture; KiA 13/1/44 with 28 victory claims)

Grond, Uffz Paul 1./JG53 (no known victory claim, KiA 22/8/44)

Hager, Uffz Rudolf 1./JG76 (1 victory claim in May 1940 before his capture, 4 in BoB, 5+ on Eastern Front. MiA 19/7/42)

Hesselbach, Gfr JGr.152 (no known victory claim)

Hier, Fw Karl 1./JG76 (1 victory claim before, 1 at unknown date, 13 during BoB, KiA 15/11/40)

Hotzelmann, Uffz Fritz 1./JG54 (no known victory claim, POW 5/9/40)

Jaczak, Ltn Max 1./JG 2 (1st victory claim in 1941 with JG3)

Keil Uffz Josef 8./JG3 (4 victory claims in May 1940 before his capture, 3 in BoB, survived the war with 16 victory claims)

Kirchner, Ltn Kurt Stab I/JG52 (1 victory claim before his capture, 2 in BoB, POW 30/9/40)

Kloimüller, Ofw Herfried 2./JG51 (no known victory claim)

Kröschel, Uffz Josef 8./JG53 (KiA 30/4/42, 1 victory claim)

Madler, Gfr Adalbert 6./JG51 (no known victory claim)

Mannske, Uffz Albert 2./JG76 (no known victory claim)

Mielke, Hptm Bernhard 3./LG2 (3 victory claims in May 1940 before his capture, 1 in BoB, KiA 30/8/40)

Mietusch, Ltn Klaus 7./JG26 (1 victory claim in May 1940 before his capture, 1 in BoB, KiA 17/9/44, 76 victories.

Mölders, Hptm Werner Kdr III./JG53 (25 victory claims in 1939-40 before his capture; KiFA 17/11/41, 101 victory claims (+14 in Spain)

Pavenzinger, Uffz Georg 2./JG51 (4 victory claims in BoB, 5th victory claim on unknown date)

Reibel, Uffz Ludwig 1./JG53 (1 victory claim in May 1940 before his capture, KiA 20/12/42, 38 victory claims)

Roth, Fw Willi 4./JG26 (4 victory claims in May 1940 before his capture, 20 victory claims including 5 in BoB)

Rozenkranz, Ltn Kurt JGr.152 (no known victory claim)

Saborowski Uffz Rudlof 8./JG3 (3 victory claims in May 1940 before his capture, 3 in BoB, KiA 8/7/42, 39 victory claims)

Schäfer, Oblt Hans-Christian Staka 5./JG27 (2 victory claims in May 1940 before his capture, 2/3 in 1941 with JG77)

Schröder, Fw Erich 2./JG27 (no known victory claim, POW 26/5/41)

Schultz, Ltn Heinz 1./JG76 (no known victory claim)

Stephan, Uffz Hubert 9./JG3 (no known victory claim)

Stolte, Ltn Paul Stab I./JG54 (KiA 18/10/43, 43 victory claims, all after his release)

Strakeljahn, Ltn Friedrich 2./LG2 (2 victory claims in May 1940 before his capture, 3 in BoB, 4 on Eastern Front. KiA 6/7/44)

Tismer, Uffz Artur 1./JG1 (no known victory claim)

Unterberger, Ltn Josef 2./JG27 (survived the war, 4 victory claims, all after his release (1st in 1941)

Voigt, Ltn Günther Stab/JGr.102 (no known victory claim)

von Balka, Ofw Wilfried 1./JG51 (no known victory claim)

von Massow, Oberst Gerd Jafü 3 (no known victory claim)

Wagner, Uffz Wolfgang 2./JG54 (left foot amputated, probably never flew again)

Walter, Ltn Albert 1./JG54 (a pilot with the same name scored 37 victory claims with JG51)

Wilcke, Oblt Wolf-Dietrich Staka 7./JG 53 (3 before his capture by the French; KiA 23/3/44, 162 victory claims

Total: 43 pilots, who claimed at least 549 victories after their release.

When Prime Minister Churchill learned of the facts he was naturally very angry, and told the House of Commons:

> They would be used to bomb this country and thus force our airmen
> to shoot them down for the second time over!

Which, in many cases, they did.

VII. A German POW's Account of a Supposed Heinkel Raid on a Target South of London on 1 July 1940

Today's objective is a town somewhat south of London, where important factories are hidden among woods. We have looked at the photos until our eyes popped out. When we get there, we'll know just where to drop our sticks. Something vital is made in those factories. We weren't told anything more, but Putzke, who knows a lot about engineering, thinks they assemble the Vickers-Wellingtons there. We are approaching the area. Oberleutnant Friemel says so. He laughs softly, I can hear it through the intercom. And then he says, "Better keep your eyes open! Gentlemen of the flak!"

It's funny how things stick in your memory. Maybe it's a little exaggerated to talk of memory; after all, the whole thing happened just about twenty-four hours ago. But what happened after he spoke could easily have made you forget anything that had been said before. The gentlemen of the flak weren't there, but all of a sudden Spitfires and Hurricanes zoomed up, a little too suddenly for my taste. Out of the nowhere they came at us. It seemed as though they had been lurking in the clouds. Probably they had been. I don't know how many there were. I was too busy to count them, and the others couldn't count them either. But I think there were a lot more of them than of our Messerschmitts.

Our Messerschmitts formed a box around us and then hell broke loose. From all sides they came, dived, swooped up. You felt as though you were in a cage with birds that had suddenly gone crazy. I take it all in, and then again I don't see because I'm looking straight ahead. We must go on. We must get through to the target. That's the idea; that's why we have Messerschmitts around us to tie up the enemy while we get through.

Naturally, Oberleutnant Friemel has already put the steel helmet on my head and ordered the others to put on theirs. Now he tells Putzke to open the hatch. Putzke stretches out on the bottom so he can watch the sticks when they fall. Lederer and Zoellner are behind the machine-guns, just in case. I don't see any of this, yet I know just what's going on. I have so clear a picture of it I could paint it. Beside me Oberleutnant Friemel is bent over the bombsight, all concentration. Now we are there. He directs me until we are exactly where he wants us to be. Then he drops the first stick. Then another. Bank and turn. We take a second run and drop the other sticks. Each time the ship [aircraft] takes a little jump, as though she were relieved, which she really is. But in a moment I level her out again. I don't know whether the bombs have made a hit or not, but Putzke has been watching everything. He lies on the bottom and tallies them, and then reports.

We've done a good job. Direct hits. Putzke says it looked as though a tremendous explosion blew up everything at once. All the factory sheds, everything. Then he couldn't see much more because a great cloud of dust and smoke spread out over the whole town. He could only see indistinctly that fires had broken out, and every few seconds or so there was another explosion. Good work. They won't make any more ships [aircraft] there.

All of a sudden we're surrounded by Hurricanes again. The enemy has sent up reinforcements. Too late, though. Our mission is fulfilled. But now they are out to get us. Naturally, our Messerschmitts are there, too, and doing wonders. But they are outnumbered. It looks as though we have lost a lot of them. We get hit a few times, too. Twice the ship [aircraft] jerks and bucks, but it doesn't seem to be anything serious. I pull her up. My hands are sweaty and I wipe them on my breeches. The motors are running smoothly and we push upward for altitude and get away. Then we are on our way back to base. The Messerschmitts have to get away now, too. They can't have very much fuel left. That's a hard job because more and more enemy planes keep coming. We fly on. We have to get back. We cross the Channel without any interference and I set her down smoothly.

The above is an extract from *I Was a Nazi Flier,* published in America in 1941 and edited by Curt Riess. The presumed compiler of this piece was supposedly the pilot of the Heinkel, one Obfw Gottfried Leske, a fictitious name, as are those of the other members of his crew. The account was allegedly written when he was in a Canadian POW camp after being shot down in late 1940, using a pseudonym to cover his real identity. On the other hand, this may be a fictional account concocted for the American market and therefore it may have been purely for propaganda purposes. It is included here since it provides a taste of reality of an actual event. On 1 July there was a raid in the Bristol area.

VIII. Obfw Leske provides another account (diary entry dated 8 July) relating to night attack on a British mainland target on the night of 7/8 July

Oberleutnant Friemel said we were there. Here, right here, we had to dive. So I pushed her lower and lower. The searchlights stabbed upward, very white. They formed a kind of second layer of clouds upon the clouds. Now we are through the clouds. Putzke has opened the hatch. He's already lying on the bottom of the ship. The Oberleutnant has his hand on the release. Then I hear Putzke counting through the intercom. Then he reports that our sticks landed right on the target.

The flak is coming closer and closer. The Oberleutnant tells me to pull her up and get out of reach of the flak as fast as I can. At first I don't know what's changed. I look at my instruments. Everything is all right. But I know something has happened. Then I realize that the sound of the motors is different. At the same time I feel that the ship is pulling slightly to starboard. Something is wrong. Yes, there it is. The port motor – something's wrong with it. And then the port motor cuts out completely.

Well, it could be worse. I can still pull out of this with one motor. If only we had more speed. We are still within range of the flak. The Oberleutnant is also staring at the gauge. However, he avoids looking at me. I know what he's thinking and he knows what I'm thinking. If we had more altitude we could probably glide back over the damned Channel easily enough. But will we be able to get enough altitude before the flak gets us? And if we don't – shall we jump? Bale out over enemy territory? Not what you'd call a pleasant thought.

We glide. But it's so terribly slow. And it seems even slower to all of us than it is. And during all these minutes, which seems like years to us, we are still within the cone of the searchlights and around us the flak is concentrated. I look at the altimeter. 4,200 metres. I ought to feel relieved, but somehow I don't. Somehow I feel that the danger isn't over yet. I look at the Oberleutnant out of the corner of my eye. His face, too, is still grave and tense. And yet we are already away from the searchlights and the flak can't reach us anymore. Still, we both have the feeling that this business isn't finished yet. And then it comes. The starboard motor begins to cough. What the hell's wrong with that damn motor? I throttle … ease up… throttle again. I try that a few times. Sometimes it works, and the motors pick up again. We'll have to let our good old Heinkel crack up somewhere in this Goddamned England. I keep trying.

We are dropping. We are dropping very fast. We drop to 2,300 meters. Oberleutnant Friemel snaps out commands. The crew must get ready to jump. He's right, of course. There's nothing else for us to do. It's kind of automatic. I throttle … ease up … throttle again. My mind is racing trying to figure out what to do. It's automatic, really, because all the time I know that there's nothing else I can do.

We keep dropping. Fortunately, we're in the middle of a thick fog now.

Otherwise the Tommies would have seen us long ago, and this time we would have been an easy target. I feel Oberleutnant Friemel's hand on my arm. He doesn't say anything, but I know that is the signal. And at that moment, just at that moment, I hear a kind of roaring. I glance at the gauge. It's the starboard motor, cutting in again. Later on we talked about it for a long time trying to figure out why. Probably it was because we dropped into a warmer layer of air. But of course that's just a guess.

Well, very slowly the numbers on the gauge rose. And very slowly we climbed again. Soon we were up to 3,800 meters. That would be enough to get us across the Channel. Once we were on the other side we could make a forced-landing almost anywhere. There would be nothing to it. I hear whistling through the intercom. It's the Oberleutnant. He whistles only when he's feeling particularly good.

And from then on everything ran like clockwork. Halfway across the Channel – it's hard to believe – the port motor suddenly cut in again, just like that. We got back as though nothing had happened. And to think that the whole thing was a matter of seconds. I mean, if the starboard motor had stayed out a few seconds longer, we would have baled out over England and would probably be sitting in a prison camp by now.

IX. An Airman's Letter to his Mother

On 30 May 1940, a force of seventeen Wellingtons from RAF Marham took off to provide close ground support to troops as they withdrew from the beaches of Dunkirk. R3162 from 38 Squadron was shot down near the town of Veurve in Belgium and the crew was killed including 23-year-old co-pilot Flg Off Vivian Rosewarne from Brentwood, Essex. A letter written by Flg Off Rosewarne was found among his personal possessions. It had been left open, so that it could be passed by the censor. The station CO was so moved by the letter that, with permission of the dead man's mother, it was published anonymously in *The Times* on 18 June 1940.

Dearest Mother:

Though I feel no premonition at all, events are moving rapidly and I have instructed that this letter be forwarded to you should I fail to return from one of the raids that we shall shortly be called upon to undertake. You must hope on for a month, but at the end of that time you must accept the fact that I have handed my task over to the extremely capable hands of my comrades of the Royal Air Force, as so many splendid fellows have already done.

First, it will comfort you to know that my role in this war has been of the greatest importance. Our patrols far out over the North Sea have helped to keep the trade routes clear for our convoys and supply ships, and on one occasion our information was instrumental in saving the lives of the men in a crippled lighthouse relief ship. Though it will be difficult for you, you will disappoint me if you do not at least try to accept the facts dispassionately, for I shall have done my duty to the utmost of my ability. No man can do more, and no one calling himself a man could do less.

I have always admired your amazing courage in the face of continual setbacks; in the way you have given me as good an education and background as anyone in the country: and always kept up appearances without ever losing faith in the future. My death would not mean that your struggle has been in vain. Far from it. It means that your sacrifice is as great as mine. Those who serve England must expect nothing from her; we debase ourselves if we regard our country as merely a place in which to eat and sleep.

History resounds with illustrious names who have given all; yet their sacrifice has resulted in the British Empire where there is a measure of peace, justice and freedom for all, and where a higher standard of civilization has evolved, and is still evolving, than anywhere else. But this is not only concerning our own land. Today we are faced with the greatest organized challenge to Christianity and civilization that the world has ever seen, and I count myself lucky and honoured to be the right age and fully trained to throw my full weight into the scale. For this I have to thank you. Yet there is more work for you to do. The home front will still have to stand united for years after the war is won. For all that can be said against it, I still maintain that this war is a very good thing: every individual is having the chance to give and dare all for his principle like the martyrs of old. However long the time may be, one thing can never be altered – I shall have lived and died an Englishman. Nothing else matters one jot nor can anything ever change it.

You must not grieve for me, for if you really believe in religion and all that it entails that would be hypocrisy. I have no fear of death; only a queer elation ... I would have it no other way. The universe is so vast and so ageless that the life of one man can only be justified by the measure of his sacrifice. We are sent to this world to acquire a personality and a character to take with us that can never be taken from us. Those who just eat and sleep, prosper and procreate, are no better than animals if all their lives they are at peace.

I firmly believe that evil things are sent into the world to try us; they are sent deliberately by our Creator to test our mettle because He knows what is good for us. The Bible is full of cases where the easy way out has been discarded for moral principles.

I count myself fortunate in that I have seen the whole country and known men of every calling. But with the final test of war I consider my character fully developed. Thus at my early age my earthly mission is already fulfilled and I am prepared to die with just one regret: that I could not devote myself to making your declining years more happy by being with you; but you will live in peace and freedom and I shall have directly contributed to that, so here again my life will not have been in vain.

Your loving son

ENDNOTES

1. By the beginning of June the Germans were at the front door of Britain. Newly installed Prime Minister Churchill asked America for help – "Give us the tools and we will finish the job" – thereby hoping to ensure the safety of what was left of the free world. But America would not 'give' anything without payment.

   Consequently, after two years of war, Roosevelt had drained Britain dry, stripping her of all her assets in the USA, including real estate and property. The British-owned *Visco* Company worth £125 million was liquidated, Britain receiving only £87 million. Britain's £1,924 million investments in Canada were sold off to pay for raw materials bought in by the United States. To make sure that Roosevelt got his money, he dispatched the American cruiser *Louisville* to the South African naval base of Simonstown to pick up £42 million worth of British gold, Britain's last negotiable asset, to help pay for American guns and ammunition. Not content with stripping Britain of her gold and assets in return for 50 old destroyers, he demanded that Britain transfer all her scientific and technological secrets to the USA. Also, he demanded leases on the islands of Newfoundland, Jamaica, Trinidad and Bermuda for the setting up of American military and naval bases in case Britain should fall. Lord Beaverbrook was later to exclaim: "The Japanese are our relentless enemies, the Americans our unrelenting creditors."

Chapter I

1. Believed to have been/included N3116, P9313, P9331, P9385, P9396 and P9453 (armed). The PDU lost four Spitfires during sorties from Heston: N3069 shot down by I/JG20 on 22/3/40; N3071 lost to II/JG51 on 21/4/40; P9308 on 19/5/40, and P9392 on 19/6/40.
2. Extracted from *One of the Few* by John Kent.
3. See *History of 73 Squadron* by Don Minterne.
4. See *The Merchant Airman*. G-ADSX *Ettrick* was later captured by the Germans, fitted with Daimler-Benz engines and flew again.

Chapter II

1. *The War in France and Flanders 1939-1940* Major L. F. Ellis.
2. See 67 Wing War Diary.
3. Conversation with author.

4. Account provided by the late Rudi Hengst to his Irish friend Justin Horgan.

5. Extracted from *One of the Few*.

6. Flg Off Count Manfred Czernin was born in Berlin, son of an Austrian diplomat Count Otto von Czernin and Lucy, daughter of 2nd Baron Grimthorpe. He was educated in England and joined the RAF in 1935. Having fought in the May battles, he already had 5 victories to his credit.

7. Sgt Lewis' loss is recorded in David Watkins' *Fear Nothing* but has not been substantiated in official records.

8. Extracted from *One of the Few*.

9. See *Canadians in the Royal Air Force* by Les Allison.

10. An urgently required replacement Hurricane (P3051) crashed on take-off from Bricy, its ATA pilot 1st Off P. J. Grenside being killed.

11. See *Hurricane and Spitfire Pilots at War* by Terence Kelly.

12. See *The Sinking of the Lancastria* by Jonathan Fenby.

13. Extracted from *Eagle's Wings* by Hajo Herrmann.

14. Reference Wayne Ralph *Aces, Warriors & Wingmen*.

15. On reaching England Lt Moses Demozay underwent a refresher course and qualified as a fighter pilot on Hurricanes. When the war ended he held the rank of LtCol (Wg Cdr) with the DSO DFC & Bar and was credited with 18 air victories.

16. See *The Merchant Airman*.

17. See *Hurricane: The Last Witnesses* by Brian Milton.

18. Reference Wayne Ralph *Aces, Warriors & Wingmen*.

Chapter IV

1. This chapter is extracted from *Blue on Blue Volume I* by Brian Cull.

Chapter V

1. The 53rd RICMS (*Régiment d'infanterie coloniale mixte sénégalais* – mixed Senegalese colonial infantry regiment) comprised mainly of black West Africans with a white commanding officer supported by a black deputy, Capitaine Charles N'Tchoréré. Following the surrender at Airaines, Capt N'Tchoréré and about 50 black soldiers were massacred by the Germans. Sadly, this was one of many massacres committed against the black colonial troops during June 1940 (see *Hitler's African Victims* by Raffael Schenck).

2. See *Valiant Wings* by Norman Franks.

3. Extracted from *Combat Report* by Hector Bolitho.

4. Although most burned airmen were treated by the celebrated plastic surgeon Archie McIndoe and his team at the Queen Victoria Hospital, East Grinstead – thereby earning membership of the Guinea Pig Club – Sgt Ottewill was treated elsewhere. He was, however, fortunate in that his case was supervised by Sir Harold Gillies; he was the First World War father of plastic surgery who had trained McIndoe, a fellow New Zealander and distant cousin.

   On 6 June 1943, then a squadron leader, Peter Ottewill rescued the two crewmen from Beaufighter X7947 of 488 Squadron which had crashed into an ammunition store at RAF Kirknewton, Scotland during take-off, and was awarded the George Medal: The citation read:

   One day in June, 1943, a Beaufighter aircraft crashed into an ammunition store when taking off and immediately caught fire. Both occupants [Flt Sgt C. W. Collins and Plt Off H. J. Evans] of the aircraft were stunned and unable to get out unaided. Despite the bursting of the aircraft's war load of ammunition (which included cannon shells), the

30,000 rounds of ammunition which were exploding in the store and the grave danger of the petrol tanks exploding, Sqn Ldr Ottewill, accompanied by 2 others, went to the scene of the accident in an endeavour to rescue the crew. Sqn Ldr Ottewill, ignoring a burning petrol tank, jumped on to the wing and after opening the front hatch, he succeeded in releasing the pilot and dragged him clear. Sqn Ldr Ottewill then returned and rescued the observer who was in happened. Shortly afterwards a petrol tank exploded. Sqn Ldr Ottewill, who had been severely burned on a previous occasion when his own aircraft was shot down by the enemy, accepted the risk of further severe burns, and injury in going to the assistance of his comrades and effecting their rescue. Fortunately he sustained only slight burns during this rescue.

5. See *43 Squadron* by J. Beedle.
6. Extracted from *The Vivid Air* by Alex Revell.
7. See *Their Finest Hour* by Winston S. Churchill.
8. *Ibid*
9. Flg Off Leonid Ereminsky was born in London of White Russian parentage. A naturalised Briton, he represented England at rugby.
10. Extracted from *Nine Lives* by Al Deere.
11. Whilst a Lufthansa Ju52 was lost on this date, some sources suggest it was involved in a collision at Brussels/Evere, a completely separate incident. However, GenMaj Löb was killed together with eight of the occupants of the aircraft.
12. See *Coastal Dawn* by Andy Bird.
13. Other sources suggest that the Blenheims were shot down by four pilots of I/JG76: Ltn Joachim Schypek of 2 Staffel, Oblt Roloff von Aspern also 2 Staffel, Obfw Franz Eckerle of 3 Staffel, and Obfw Max Stotz of 1 Staffel. However, it seems likely that their victims were two Blenheims of 40 Squadron and one of 82 Squadron.

Chapter VI

1. See *RAF in the World War Volume II* by Captain Norman MacMillan.
2. See *Operation Sea Lion* by Egbert Kieser.
3. *Ibid*.

Chapter VII

1. Extracted from *Flying Sailors at War Volume II* (forthcoming).

Chapter VIII

1. See *So Few* by David Masters. Sqn Ldr Allen was awarded the DFC and Sgt Williams the DFM for this performance.
2. The 2./KGr.126 crew were all badly wounded: Ltn Günther Schulz, Ltn zur See Hans Müller, Uffz Karl-Wilhelm Schlegel, and Uffz Helmut Müller were admitted to various hospitals, as was Obfw Helmut Kaselitz (of 1./KG4) who was admitted to hospital in Ypres.
3. The following month the Met Office was given a card that contained the code used to transmit weather reports. Until that moment it had not been possible to decypher the transmitted weather reports so the find was of considerable importance. Written at the bottom of the code card was the name of the met observer, Hermann Freudenberg, who drowned before he could be rescued. The card showed hardly any damage, suggesting it had not been exposed to the water. A member of the fishing boat crew, Ben Richards, apparently told a friend that the body of Freudenberg had been recovered and was handed over to the Navy on returning to the harbour. However, there is no official record

of the body being recovered or subsequently buried.

4. See *Battle over Essex* by R. J. Thompson.

5. One of the searchlights was probably manned by Gunner Harry Cull, 429th Searchlight Battery, 9/Middlesex, the author's late father.

6. See *Soldier, Sailor & Airman Too* by Martin Woodhall.

7. Much of the information regarding Operation *Banquet* has been culled from Wikipedia.

Chapter IX

1. Extracted from *The Luftwaffe Bombers' Battle of Britain* by Chris Goss.

2. *Ibid.*

3. See *Lions Rampant* by Douglas McRoberts.

4. Extracted from *Flying Start* by Hugh Dundas.

5· Plt Off Tommy Burne later retrained on Hudsons. He was at Singapore in 1942 and lost a leg when a bomb landed close to his aircraft on the ground. Fitted with an artificial leg he retrained on fighters and flew with 41 Squadron later in the war. He was seriously wounded again but survived.

6. A time bomb was planted in the British Pavilion at the New York World's Fair of 1939-40. After it was carried to a remote area, two bomb squad detectives, Joe Lynch and Freddy Socha, tried to defuse it. The bomb went off in their faces, killing them instantly. It was a tragedy, but it could have been worse. Police Commissioner Lewis Valentine noted that it was only a miracle that hundreds of fairgoers were not killed.

7. Extracted from *The Luftwaffe Bombers' Battle of Britain*.

8. Extacted from *The Other Few* by Larry Donnelly.

9. There is no official confirmation of this incident.

10. Extracted from *The Luftwaffe Fighters' Battle of Britain* by Chris Goss.

11. Extracted from Jean Dillen's *Fliegerhorst*.

12. Extracted from *No. 43 'Fighting Cocks' Squadron* by Andy Saunders.

13. Regarding the Heinkel's crew, Plt Off Dimsie Stones of 79 Squadron noted in his account that there was one survivor, and that he took guard of him when taken to his airfield. The name of the German airman was given as Ernst Fischmutt, a purported 1936 Olympics Gold Medallist. There was no survivor of the Heinkel and no German Olympian of that name. Obviously facts had become distorted with the passing of time (see *Operation Bograt*).

14. Extracted from *Nine Lives*.

15. Extracted from *Spitfire Pilot* by D. M. Crook.

16. Plt Off John Rodger survived flying Blenheims and by 1944 was one of the first Meteor jet pilots flying with 616 Squadron; he accounted for one V-1 flying bomb.

17. Extracted from *The Other Few*.

Chapter X

1. Extracted from *Mach One*.

2. Plt Off John Mansel-Lewis (see Appendix V) received no recognition for his performance; he later fought in the Battle of Britain with 92 Squadron, before being posted to Singapore as a flight commander with 243 Squadron; he was killed in a flying accident.

3. Three M167Fs (Nos.167, 171 and 224) escaped from Ecole de Metines on 30 June; one was shot down by Spanish AA (Sous-Lt Weil, Sous-Lt Duplessis, Cne De Vendeuve and Lt Berger killed); one overturned on landing at Gibraltar; and one arrived safely. On this date Simoun No. 374 also reached Gibraltar but Simoun No. 297 failed to escape and its pilot was sent to jail; sadly Potez 540 (No. 47) crashed five minutes after take-off and all eight on board were killed.

The first escapee to arrive at Gibraltar was Simoun (No. 344) on 26 June, followed by MS315 (No. 107) and M167F (No. 62) two days later, when an attempted escapee Bloch 174 crashed on take-off. C.510 (F-AOFN), MS230 (No. 925), MS315 (No. 4), Simoun (No. 299) and MB175 (No. 117), arrived on 29 June. During the first few days of July, M167Fs (Nos.82 and 102), Potez 650 (No. 14), Simoun (No294) and Goeland (No. 92) also reached Gibraltar. Towards the end of the year two escapees 'borrowed' a Goeland belonging to the Italian Armistice Commission at Oran, and flew to Gibraltar (Information from Bertrand Hugot).

4. Captain Holland, a fluent French speaker, had formerly been Naval Attaché at the British Embassy in Paris and subsequently Liaison Officer to Admiral Darlan, and had also been acquainted with Admiral Gensoul.

5. These included including Cne Marie Monraisse (6 shared victories); Cne Gérard Portalis (with 1 victory and 3 shared); Lt René Trémolet (1+4 shared); Sous-Lt Paul Boudier (4 shared); Adjt-chef Jean Dugoujon (1+6 shared); Sgt-chef André Legrand (2+4 shared); and Sgt-chef Jean Gisclon (2 shared).

6. See *Mach One* by Mike Lithgow.

7. Quoted in Warren Tute's *The Deadly Stroke*.

8. Seventy-two survivors were rescued and taken to Algiers.

Chapter XI

1. Extracted from *The Deadly Stroke*.

Chapter XII

1. The Revd Alan Leeke was lost when *Hermes* was sunk by Japanese bombers off Ceylon in April 1942. See *The Hermes Adventure* by Rex Morgan.

Appendix I

1. See *Ginger Lacey – Fighter Pilot* by Richard Townshend Bickers.

Appendix II

1. See *Escape to Danger* by Paul Brickhill and Conrad Norton.

Appendix III

1. Extracted from *The Battle of France Then & Now*.

ACKNOWLEDGEMENTS

As ever, my wife Val tops the list of acknowledgements. Nothing in my life is possible without her never-failing support. Alan Sutton, Jay Slater, and Jasper Hadman of *Fonthill Media* are thanked for their encouragement and expertise in the production of this book.

The efforts of my faithful lieutenant Bruce Lander, and that of Matti Salonen, Mark Sheridan, Col Bruggy; Justin Horgan, Ross McNeil, author Chris Goss, Bertrand Hugot, Laurent Rizzotti (re Appendix VI), Alex Smart, author Andy Thomas (photographs), Martin Goodman (photographs), author David Watkins (*Fear Nothing*), author Chris Ehrengardt (for permission to use extracts from *L'Aviation de Vichy au Combat*), Gaël Elégoët (for translations), and Ronnie Olsthoorn, are acknowledged with gratitude, as are the staff at The National Archives, who are thanked for their efficiency. Thanks are due to Ruy at *TOCH* and Ross at *RAF Commands* for their generosity in allowing me access to their respective websites. I apologise to those formulites whom I may have failed to acknowledge.

Sadly, in 2010, Francis K. Mason passed away. He was the author of the mighty tome *Battle for Britain*, published in 1969, which turned out to be an inspiration to a generation of Battle of Britain enthusiasts, both professional and amateur. Although Frank's research was found to be at fault on occasion he was, nonetheless, a pioneer in amassing relevant data, both British and German. However, Peter Cornwell's masterly trilogy – *The Battle of France Then & Now*, *The Battle of Britain Then & Now*, and *The Blitz Then & Now* – that has superseded Francis Mason's work may never be matched.

SELECT BIBLIOGRAPHY

Arthur, Max: *There Shall be Wings* (Hodder & Stoughton)
Bickers, Richard Townshend: *Ginger Lacey – Fighter Pilot* (Consul)
Bickers, Richard Townshend: *The Battle of Britain* (Salamander)
Bird, Andy: *Coastal Dawn* (Grub Street)
Bolitho, Hector: *Combat Report* (Batsford)
Brickhill, Paul & Norton, Conrad: *Escape to Danger* (Faber & Faber)
Clayton, Tim & Craig, Phil: *Finest Hour* (Simon & Schuster)
Cornwell, Peter: *The Battle of France Then & Now* (After the Battle)
Crook, David: *Spitfire Pilot* (Faber & Faber 1942)
Cull, Brian: *Blue on Blue Volume I* (Tally Ho! Publications)
Cull, Brian: *Flying Sailors at War Volume I* (D&V Publications)
Cull, Brian: *Flying Sailors at War Volume II* (forthcoming)
Cull, Brian & Lander, Bruce with Weiss, Heinrich: *Twelve Days in May* (Grub Street)
Deere, Alan: *Nine Lives* (Hodder)
Donnelly, Larry: *The Other Few* (Red Kite)
Dundas, Hugh: *Flying Start* (Penguin)
Ehrengardt, Chris: *L'Aviation de Vichy au Combat* (Lavauzelle)
Franks, Norman: *Frank 'Chota' Carey* (Grub Street)
Franks, Norman: *Valiant Wings* (Crécy)
Goss, Chris: *Luftwaffe Bombers' Battle of Britain* (Crécy)
Halliday, Hugh: *242 Squadron: The Canadian Years* (Canada's Wings)
Herrmann, Hajo: *Eagle's Wings* (Guild)
Kent, John: *One of the Few* (The History Press)
Kieser, Egbert: *Operation Sea Lion* (Weidenfeld & Nicolson)
Leske, Gottfried: *I Was a Nazi Flier* (Dial Press)
Lithgow, Mike: *Mach One* (Wingate)
MacMillan, Captain Norman: *RAF in the World War Volume II* (Bexley)
Mason, Frank: *The Battle for Britain* (McWhirter Twins)
Minterne, Don: *History of 73 Squadron Volume I* (Tutor)
Morgan, Rex: *The Hermes Adventure* (Robert Hale)
Ralph, Wayne: *Aces, Warriors & Wingmen* (Wiley)
Revell, Alex: *The Vivid Air* (William Kimber)
Saunders, Andy: *No. 43 'Fighting Cocks' Squadron* (Osprey)

Stones, Donald: *Operation Bograt* (Spellmount)
Tute, Warren: *The Deadly Stroke* (Collins)
Vasco, John & Cornwell, Peter: *Zerstörer* (JAC)
Watkins, David: *Fear Nothing* (Newton)
Woodhall, Martin: *Soldier, Sailor & Airman Too* (Grub Street)

WWW
Much of the detail in Chapter III came from Louis Capdeboscq's website
Wikipedia: regarding Operation *Banquet*

TNA
Air 35/252 & 253 (67 Wing War Diary)
Air 27/ various (Squadron ORBs)
Air 50/ various (Squadron Combat Reports)

FLYING PERSONNEL INDEX